Pelican Books
Churchill: A Study in Failure 1900–1939

Robert Rhodes James, a former fellow of All Souls College,
Oxford, has served as an Assistant Clerk and a Senior
Clerk in the House of Commons. He is Director of the new
Institute for the Study of International Organization at
Sussex University. His other publications are: *Lord
Randolph Churchill*, *Rosebery*, *An Introduction to the House
of Commons*, *Gallipoli*, and *Memoirs of a Conservative:
The Papers of J. C. C. Davidson*, and *Ambitions and Realities:
British Politics 1964–1970*. He was a contributor
to *Churchill: Four Faces and the Man*, and edited *Chips:
The Diaries of Sir Henry Channon* (both published by
Penguins, and has also edited a study of the
Czechoslovak crisis of 1968.

Churchill: A Study in Failure 1900–1939

Robert Rhodes James

> *But the case has proved that to be true which Appius says in his songs, that each man is the maker of his own fate.*
>
> SALLUST: Ad Caesarem

Penguin Books

Penguin Books Ltd, Harmondsworth,
Middlesex, England
Penguin Books Australia Ltd, Ringwood,
Victoria, Australia

First published by Weidenfeld & Nicolson 1970
Published in Pelican Books 1973

Copyright © Robert Rhodes James, 1970

Made and printed in Great Britain by
Richard Clay (The Chaucer Press) Ltd,
Bungay, Suffolk
Set in Monotype Modern Extended

THIS BOOK IS DEDICATED TO THE HONOURED
MEMORY OF MY COUSIN AND FRIEND

Flight-Lieutenant Timothy Mermagen

ROYAL AIR FORCE 1938–65

> *Still are thy pleasant voices,*
> *Thy nightingales, awake;*
> *For Death, he taketh all away,*
> *But these he cannot take.*

William Johnson Cory: Heraclitus

Contents

Maps

Preface

It is evident that the time has not yet come for a complete and measured estimate of Sir Winston Churchill's exceptionally long, complex and controversial life. No career of modern British political history save that of Gladstone can compare with it in length, drama and incident. None since that of Chatham has enjoyed so splendid a climax. His father, Lord Randolph Churchill, once described Disraeli's career as 'Failure, failure failure, partial success, renewed failure, ultimate and complete triumph'. The same description is not exactly apposite to Lord Randolph's son, but the parallel is close enough to justify remark, and the very completeness of this triumphant conclusion has tended to obscure the vicissitudes and controversies of the forty years of intense political activity that preceded Churchill's accession to the premiership in May 1940.

It is inevitable that a serious and fundamental revaluation of such a remarkable personality so shortly after his death invites the risk of the accusation of deliberate perversity, or even that of calculated sensationalism. The purpose of this study is, however, a serious and an important one, for my object has been to endeavour to answer the questions which particularly puzzled my generation, namely, why did Churchill's career, after so successful a beginning, lapse so drastically; and why did it require a desperate national crisis to restore his fortunes? Long before I embarked upon this study of Churchill's career up to September 1939 I had become somewhat sceptical of what had become the orthodox explanation for his failure in the 1930s, of which the most common and the most hallowed was that expounded by Lloyd George to the effect that it was the consequence of 'the distrust and trepidation with which mediocrity views genius at close quarters'. While conceding that such emotions undoubtedly played their part – and an important part – I found it difficult to accept that the whole truth could be summarized with such satisfying succinctness, nor that any politician could arouse mistrust and dislike on such a scale and for so long without substantial causes. This study accordingly began as a relatively brief examination of Churchill's part in the politics of the 1930s. But, as I proceeded, I found myself drawn back to the events of the previous decade, and, finally, realized that I was embarked upon a critical examination of the whole of Churchill's career before 1939. I have endeavoured to keep the study in the original form, as an extended essay rather than a biography, and although it incorporates new information and documents that have only recently become available – notably the Cabinet Papers up to the close of 1938 – it will be seen that it is essentially an attempt to study the public man through his public life and its public impact. This approach to the study of political biography has tended to be somewhat neglected in recent years, and the public lives of politicians – on which, after all, contemporary judgements have to depend – have often taken an excessively subordinate place. Letters and diaries have great value in a political study, but so also do speeches and newspaper articles. The principal difficulty in presenting an extended essay on Churchill's career lies in the fact that he wrote so much and said so much that the usual problems of selection and emphasis are considerably compounded.

It may well be asked why such a study should be attempted at all, while the official biography, with its mass of unpublished material, is in course of preparation. I should emphasize that this study was virtually completed before the death of Mr Randolph Churchill in June 1968 and the subsequent decision of the Churchill Trustees to entrust the completion of the biography to Mr Martin Gilbert. Although I greatly admired the thoroughness and determination with which Randolph Churchill addressed himself to his formidable task, which was for him a labour of love, I was not convinced that his techniques in preparing and writing the biography were the most suitable. Furthermore, his devotion to his father's memory was intense, but what was so admirable in the son, was, I felt, less desirable in the biographer. In any event, there is an important difference of approach between an official biography and an independent assessment, and there is – and should be – a place for each. In addition, no single biography, however excellent and conscientious, can properly be described as definitive. It is rather by means of a number of portraits that a reasonably accurate presentment can be created. My purpose has been to provide an assessment which is of reasonable length and which, while it cannot pretend to furnish a complete account of Churchill's personality and career, may serve as a useful link between those studies which have already appeared and the official biography.

*

I have attempted to limit the number of footnotes, and I have followed my practice of eschewing the lamentable modern habit of placing references at the end of the book. For the benefit of those readers who are unfamiliar with many of the leading personalities referred to in the narrative, I have incorporated brief biographical notes in the Index.

I am most grateful to the owners of copyright material for their kind permission to make quotations. A list of the principal works consulted will be found in the Select Bibliography.

I am particularly indebted to Mr David Astor for having first suggested the project to me. I also wish to thank the following for much kind assistance and advice: the late Lady Asquith, Lord and Lady Avon, Lord Baldwin, Lord Boothby, Lord Butler, Lord and Lady Davidson, Mr F. W. Deakin, Mr Martin Gilbert, Mr Alan Hodge, Mr Harold Macmillan, Mr Keith Middlemas, Sir Desmond Morton, Mr Duncan Sandys, Lord Salter and Lord Swinton. Many others have been most generous with their time and assistance, and I hope that they will be content with a general expression of my gratitude. Neither they nor any of the individuals I have mentioned are in any way responsible for any of my opinions or my conclusions.

I also wish to thank my publishers, Mr Nicolas Thompson of Weidenfeld & Nicolson and Mr Peter Ritner of the World Publishing Company, who are also my friends and advisers on a wide variety of matters unconnected with the mechanics of publishing.

Only those ladies who have the misfortune to be married to students of political history can have any conception of the patience, understanding and fortitude of my wife.

My debt to All Souls College is so great that I cannot adequately give expression of my gratitude to its Warden and Fellows for their manifold kindnesses to me when I was a Junior Research Fellow from 1965 to 1968.

I should like to include the name of Randolph Churchill in this list of acknowledgements. I had given him some assistance in Volume One of his biography of his father, and he had given me most valuable and stimulating reminiscence and help in my project, which, initially, he warmly encouraged. Unhappily, our respective attitudes and judgements began to vary so fundamentally that these pleasant relations were abruptly interrupted, and on the occasion of our last meeting he made it plain that he did not wish to have the fact of his assistance publicly acknowledged. But I consider that our last unhappy compact may be abrogated, and I accordingly desire to record the very considerable debt I owe him for his assistance and advice, and, above all else, for the warm friendship and kindness he gave me before our sincere differences led to high words and an estrangement that was destined never to be repaired.

All Souls College, Oxford, 1966–8

Summary of Churchill's Career, 1874–1939

30 November 1874	Born, prematurely, at Blenheim Palace, Oxfordshire, elder son of Lord Randolph Spencer-Churchill (1849–95) Conservative MP for Woodstock (subsequently Secretary of State for India, June 1885–January 1886 and Chancellor of the Exchequer and Leader of the House of Commons August–December 1886) and Lady Randolph Spencer-Churchill, *née* Jeanette Jerome (1854–1921), who had married at the British Embassy, Paris, on 15 April 1874.
November 1882–December 1892	Educated at St George's School, Ascot (1882–4), private school in Brighton (1884–8), and Harrow School (1888–92).
September 1893–December 1894	Cadet at Royal Military Academy, Sandhurst.
February 1895	Commissioned in the Fourth Hussars.
November–December 1895	Observer in Cuban civil war.
September 1896	Goes to India with Fourth Hussars.
26 July 1897	First political speech at Claverton Manor, Bath.
August–September 1897	With Malakand Field Force, North-West Frontier, India. (Subsequently publishes, March 1898, *The Story of the Malakand Field Force*.)
August–October 1898	Attached 21st Lancers in Sudan campaign; takes part in Battle of Omdurman, 2 September. (Campaign described in his book, *The River War*, published in December 1899.)
July 1899	Unsuccessfully contests Oldham by-election as Unionist (Conservative) candidate.
October 1899	Goes to South Africa as War Correspondent of *Morning Post*.

November– *December 1899*	Captured by Boers and subsequently escapes from prisoner-of-war camp at Pretoria. Resumes activities as War Correspondent.
1 October 1900	Elected Unionist MP for Oldham in General Election. Goes on lecture tour in United States before meeting of Parliament.
18 February 1901	Maiden speech in House of Commons.
13 May 1901	First attack on 'Brodrick Scheme' in House of Commons.
May– *December 1903*	Attacks Tariff Reform proposals of Joseph Chamberlain.
23 December 1903	Disowned by General Purposes Committee of Oldham Unionist Registration Association for attacks on Balfour Government. (Decision ratified by full Association on 8 January 1904.)
31 May 1904	Takes seat on Liberal benches.
13 December 1905	Appointed Parliamentary Under-Secretary of State, Colonial Office, on formation of Liberal Government by Sir Henry Campbell-Bannerman.
13 January 1906	Elected Liberal MP for North-West Manchester.
8 April 1908	On reorganization of Government following Asquith's succession as Prime Minister, appointed President of the Board of Trade, with seat in the Cabinet.
23 April 1908	Defeated at by-election at North-West Manchester; elected for Dundee, 9 May.
12 September 1908	Married, at St Margaret's Church, Westminster, to Miss Clementine Hozier (b. 1885).
February 1910– *September 1911*	Home Secretary.
October 1911– *May 1915*	First Lord of the Admiralty.
May 1915	On formation of first Coalition Ministry, appointed Chancellor of the Duchy of Lancaster.
November 1915	Resigns from Government.
November 1915– *June 1916*	On active service on Western Front.
June 1917– *December 1918*	Minister of Munitions, in Lloyd George Coalition Government.

January 1919– *February 1921*	Secretary of State for War and Air. Involved in demobilization of Army (1919), Intervention in Russia (1919), and Irish crisis (1919–21).
February 1921– *October 1922*	Secretary of State for the Colonies.
November 1922	Defeated at Dundee as Coalition candidate in General Election.
December 1923	Defeated at West Leicester in General Election as Liberal Free Trader.
March 1924	Defeated in by-election at Abbey Division, Westminster, as 'Independent and Anti-Socialist' candidate.
November 1924	Elected as 'Constitutionalist' candidate for Epping. Appointed Chancellor of the Exchequer in second Baldwin Government. (Rejoins Conservative Party, 1925.)
1925	Involved in return to the Gold Standard and 'cruiser crisis'.
May 1926	General Strike; responsible for publication of *British Gazette*. Involved in unsuccessful attempts after Strike to improve terms for miners.
June 1929	Defeat of Baldwin Government in General Election.
October 1929	'Irwin Declaration' relating to granting of Dominion Status to India published, and attacked by Churchill.
28 January 1931	Resigns from Conservative Business Committee over India. (Campaigns against Government of India Act, 1935, 1931–5.)
August 1931	Not included in National Government.
23 November 1932	First major speech in House of Commons on German ambitions, following visit to Austria.
12 August 1933	Warns that Germany is actively re-arming.
7 February 1934	First major speech in House of Commons on Britain's unpreparedness in the air.
June 1935	Appointed to Air Defence Research Committee.
March 1936	German remilitarization of Rhineland; Churchill not appointed Minister for Co-ordination of Defence.

December 1936	First meeting of 'Arms and the Covenant' movement at Albert Hall. Churchill involved in Abdication Crisis.
September 1938	Attacks Munich Agreement in House of Commons as 'an unmitigated defeat'. (Narrowly avoids censure by Epping Conservative Association for opposition to foreign policy of Chamberlain Government in January 1939.)
March– *August 1939*	Following German occupation of Czechoslovakia and British guarantee to Poland, publication of articles and letters in some newspapers urging Churchill's appointment to Government.
1 September 1939	German invasion of Poland.
3 September 1939	Declaration of war with Germany. Churchill makes last speech from back benches. Appointed First Lord of the Admiralty.

Part One YOUNG
TRIBUNE
1900–1914

Down the centuries, in spite of vast differences in its composition, the personality of the House of Commons has remained essentially and remarkably unchanged. 'Reading the reports of debates two hundred years ago,' it has been written, 'it is possible to recapture exactly the mood of the House on that particular day. The forms of speech, the interruptions, the procedure, the very characters of individual Members, are as authentically reproduced in our own times as the chimes of an eighteenth-century clock.'[1] Yet an observer, contemplating this perplexing maelstrom in any of its variable moods, may justifiably ponder on the factors that brought together such an apparently disparate collection of individuals. The conventional descriptions – ambition, public service, chance, social ardour, eagerness for power – rarely seem satisfactorily applicable. What brought these men here? And – perhaps an even more intriguing question – what holds them here?

Many men have drifted into the House of Commons as of right, having made no particular move of any consequence in its direction. Of this category Gladstone, Peel and Balfour afford good examples. Others – and Disraeli, Joseph Chamberlain, Lloyd George and Ramsay MacDonald spring quickly to mind – have had a less smooth path. Although Winston Churchill, the junior Conservative Member for Oldham in the Parliament elected in November 1900, had not enjoyed the assured ease of entry to the House of Commons of a Gladstone or a Balfour, neither had he experienced the lengthy struggles, difficulties and humiliations of a Disraeli or a MacDonald.

Only twenty-six when he was first elected, Churchill had been obliged to make his way by his own abilities and enterprise, but the advantages of birth and connection had been substantial. In his biography of his father he compared Lord Randolph's difficulties with those of the young Disraeli, and his own son has depicted him in similar terms. Of his father Churchill wrote

1. Nigel Nicolson: *People and Parliament*, p. 62.

in 1905: 'No smooth path of patronage was opened to him. No glittering wheels of royal favour aided and accelerated his journey. Whatever power he acquired was grudgingly conceded and hastily snatched away. Like Disraeli, he had to fight every mile in all his marches.'[2] Mr Randolph Churchill has used very similar phrases to describe his father's early difficulties: 'He had to fight every inch of his road through life; nothing came easily to him, not even oratory and writing, in which he was later to excel.'[3]

Although these claims are not wholly unjustified, in each case the initial obstacles had been relatively small. Lord Randolph Churchill had inherited a family constituency that was virtually in the possession of his father, the seventh Duke of Marlborough. His subsequent difficulties and successes had been entirely of his own making. Winston Churchill had inherited much less than his father; he had no financial backing at all, and no convenient constituency available to him such as the dutiful – and formerly venal – Borough of Woodstock, which had been extinguished by the 1885 Reform Act. But he was in no sense a social or a political outsider. Born with considerable advantages of family and position, he used them well and augmented them by his own ambition, ability and determination. He demonstrated these qualities and exploited his assets as a young officer, war correspondent, author and political candidate. If Fortune smiled on him in his early adventures, he toiled hard and risked much to earn that vital benediction.

Behind him, at the age of twenty-six, was a childhood devoid of parental love, though love had been partially supplied by his nurse, Mrs Everest, about whom Churchill was to write so movingly in *My Early Life*. It is difficult to assess the full effects upon his character of this experience. He was clearly a sensitive child, as his letters and the recollections of his family and friends emphasize, and capable of deep loyalties. In appearance he was somewhat unprepossessing as a boy and a young man, and was described by Wilfrid Scawen Blunt when he first met him in 1903 as 'a little, square-headed fellow of no

2. Churchill: *Lord Randolph Churchill* (1951 one-volume edition), p. 11.
3. Randolph S. Churchill: *Winston S. Churchill*, Volume 1, p. 185.

very striking appearance'. A contemporary commentator in 1901 described him as 'a medium-sized, undistinguished young man, with an unfortunate lisp in his voice'. The sturdy consti-tution that was to serve him so well in later years was not apparent in his boyhood. He very nearly died of pneumonia while at school in Brighton, and was fortunate to survive an accident at the age of eighteen when he jumped from a bridge to avoid capture in a family chase and ruptured a kidney. His head was large, and his skin remarkably clear and soft. He spoke with a decided lisp. His hands were striking in their revelation of an essentially artistic and sensitive character.[4]

This aspect of his personality was usually well concealed, yet already there had been public indications of it. The depiction of Mrs Everest in his novel *Savrola* was a case in point:

> She had nursed him from his birth with a devotion and care which knew no break. It is a strange thing, the love of these women. Perhaps it is the only disinterested affection in the world. The mother loves her child; that is maternal nature. The youth loves his sweetheart; that too may be explained. The dog loves his master; he feeds him. A man loves his friend; he has stood by him perhaps at doubtful moments. In all there are reasons, but the love of a foster-mother for her charge appears absolutely irrational. It is one of the few proofs, not to be explained even by the association of ideas, that the nature of mankind is superior to mere utilitarianism, and that his destinies are high.

Of the fact that his parents were neglectful of him and not greatly concerned in his doings there can be no doubt. His idealization of both, and particularly of his remote, aloof father, was natural in itself, but exceptional in its intensity. We find him, in his early twenties, learning Lord Randolph Churchill's speeches by heart, and then engaging in a long search of dis-covery of his father through Lord Randolph's friends. Until Lord Rosebery's death in 1929, Churchill came to his house

4. 'Mr Churchill's carefully composed attitudes as he sits at the corner of the gangway and makes beautiful inflections with his hands when talking to his neighbour tell of the dramatic artist who has nearly ruined a statesman,' the perceptive Harry Boardman wrote in the *Manchester Guardian* in May 1937.

principally to hear him reminisce of Lord Randolph, and Lord Justice FitzGibbon had fulfilled much the same role. There is more in this than ordinary filial piety. In his father's lifetime he had struggled without success to establish with him the kind of informal relationship built of love and comprehension that he had seen elsewhere. Thereafter, he continued the endeavour. To the end of his life one was conscious that this quest for his father's recognition had not ceased.

It is to this deprivation of parental love for a sensitive child that we may look for the explanation of his career in his early twenties rather than to the fact that he had suddenly found himself head of a family that was largely dependent upon him. The latter surely played its part, but it cannot so adequately explain the compulsive fervour of his early ambition and energies. The point has been well made by Mr Anthony Storr: 'Ambition, when, as in Churchill's case, it is a compulsive drive, is the direct result of early deprivation. For if a child has but little inner conviction of his own value, he will be drawn to seek the recognition and acclaim which accrue from external achievement.'[5] Certainly, these had been turbulent years of adventure and achievement, of which perhaps the most remarkable aspect of all was Churchill's laborious self-education as a young officer in the 4th Hussars at Bangalore; 'All through the long glistening middle hours of the Indian day, from when we quitted stables till the evening shadows proclaimed the hour of Polo, I devoured Gibbon,' as he has related. '. . . It was a curious education.'[6] In fact, it was a very wide and remarkable one; Churchill's reading was eclectic and random and there were many gaps, but the purpose was serious; what he read he remembered, and he questioned what he read. This self-education was the first real indication of his ability, his determination and his independence. It may also be seen as the first clear sign of a personal ambition to succeed in life.

Behind him also at the age of twenty-six were considerable financial problems that had been temporarily overcome entirely

5. Anthony Storr: 'Winston Churchill; The Man' (*Churchill: Four Faces and the Man*, p. 224).

6. *My Early Life*, pp. 109–10.

by his own efforts. He had already secured a substantial literary reputation. His first venture, *The Story of the Malakand Field Force*, published in 1898, had attracted favourable attention and interest, and had been followed by *The River War*, a lengthy history of the campaign of 1897–8 to recapture the Sudan, and in which he had actively participated. *The River War* was at once recognized as a classic of contemporary history, in which the young author had not omitted to bestow praise, censure and comment with generosity, while he had shed the more excessive floridities of his early style.[7] *Ian Hamilton's March*, although of interest and quality, was, in contrast, less impressive, and gave evidence of hasty preparation. *Savrola*, Churchill's only venture into fiction, published in 1900, had been a financial if not a literary success; it is a work in which somewhat characterless individuals strike melodramatic poses, deliver melodramatic utterances, and undergo even more melodramatic adventures in the Republic of Laurania. Nevertheless, it remains a work of very considerable interest in the self-portrait of the author and hero.[8]

But even at this early stage, one fact about Churchill was already apparent. No observer could remain long in doubt about what had brought him to the House of Commons. He was already manifestly a career politician, a man clearly who was to devote himself for his entire adult life to the profession of politics. His other interests and attainments were so extensive that it is not difficult to lose sight of this essential and fundamental fact; but these other achievements – notably his writing – were vital adjuncts to the central career and not in serious competition with it. He had started young. He had made his

7. The first edition should be studied, not the latter ones, for by then Churchill had had second thoughts on many of his most vigorous comments, particularly those on the British Commander-in-Chief, Sir Herbert Kitchener, which were omitted.

8. Among other felicities, this one may be noted: ' "You would rise in the world?" said Savrola. "You must work while others amuse themselves. Are you desirous of a reputation of courage? You must risk your life. Would you be strong morally or physically? You must resist temptations. All this is paying in advance; that is prospective finance. Observe the other side of the picture; the bad things are paid for afterwards!" '

first political speech at Bath in July 1897 at the age of twenty-two and fought his first election two years later in the summer of 1899, when he failed to win a by-election at Oldham as a Conservative candidate. 'He was,' as Lord Beaverbrook later wrote, 'in every sense a professional politician, having trained himself for his vocation.'[9]

Indeed, politics had been his life almost from the very beginning. G. W. Steevens, in a famous portrait published in the *Daily Mail* on 2 December 1898, wrote that 'Churchill can hardly have seen much of Government of Parliament and forensic politics at twenty-four, but he moves in and out among their deviations with the ease, if not with the knowledge, of a veteran statesman.' He had been twelve years of age when Lord Randolph Churchill's career had crashed to irretrievable disaster in December 1886. He was not twenty-one when his father, after a poignant struggle against denigration and disease, died at the age of forty-five in January 1895. All attempts made by the son for a close relationship had been brusquely rejected by the father. Nevertheless, the influence and example of the neurotic, wayward, doomed Lord Randolph must be accounted the most significant of those that impelled Churchill towards a political career and dominated his early attitudes.

The outlines of Lord Randolph Churchill's career can be swiftly described. He was born in February 1849, the younger son of the Marquess of Blandford, subsequently the seventh Duke of Marlborough. In April 1874, after strong parental resistance had been overcome, he married Miss Jeanette Jerome, the daughter of a celebrated New York entrepreneur, Leonard Jerome. Shortly beforehand he had become Conservative MP for Woodstock, but in 1876 a lamentably maladroit intervention in the marital affairs of his elder brother brought him into a violent personal dispute with the then Prince of Wales (subsequently King Edward VII).[10] Lord and

9. Beaverbrook: *Men and Power*, p. xiv.
10. The complete story is to be found in P. Magnus: *King Edward VII*; further papers are published in Randolph S. Churchill: *Winston S. Churchill*, Companion Volume I, pp. 26–77. Certain papers were not discovered in the

Lady Randolph, with the infant Winston, went into virtual
exile in Dublin, where the Duke of Marlborough had been sent
as Viceroy by the understanding Prime Minister, Disraeli. In
1880, after the fall of the Conservative Government, Lord
Randolph returned, to fling himself into politics with unexpected ardour and skill. It was the estimate of all who knew
him well that it had been the bitter experiences of 1876 that
had accentuated already strong anti-authoritarian attitudes.
'That he felt this ostracism deeply, cannot be doubted,' his
friend Rosebery had written. '. . . This, however, was the
turning-point of his life. The "saeva indignatio", excited in
him by this social conflict, turned to politics. That was the vent
for his suppressed wrath.'[11]

His political rise was indeed remarkable. Within five years
he had established himself – at the age of thirty-six – as the
outstanding new figure in the Conservative ranks. Virtually
unknown in 1880, he was a major national political figure by
1885. In 1886 he was one of the principal architects of the
alliance against Home Rule for Ireland between the Conservatives and those Liberals – led by Joseph Chamberlain and
Lord Hartington – who separated from Gladstone and the bulk
of the party on the issue. After the Liberal Government was
defeated in the General Election of July 1886 Lord Randolph
became Chancellor of the Exchequer and Leader of the House
of Commons. His hour of triumph was a brief one. In December,
as a result of disagreements over the size of the Army Estimates,
he resigned his offices. This was to be the effective end of his
career, and he died virtually insane in January 1895.

If the outlines of this career can be delineated briefly, the
substance is more complex. It is not possible to categorize with
any precision the factors that drove Lord Randolph along his
brief, spectacular and eventually tragic career. It is equally
difficult to explain or define the intensity of the impact of his
personality on his contemporaries. His public speeches, vivid

Royal Archives until after the present author's biography of Lord Randolph
was published in 1959, and the account of the Aylesford Scandal in it is not
complete.

11. Lord Rosebery: *Lord Randolph Churchill* (1906), pp. 37–8.

10 *Churchill: A Study in Failure, 1900–1939*

and exciting though they were, do not supply the answer; nor do his private letters. He has been the subject of two full-length biographies and a memorable personal memoir by his friend Lord Rosebery. We know more about Lord Randolph than we do about most leading politicians; yet he eludes us still.

He once described Gladstone as 'an old man in a hurry', and he himself was a young man in a hurry, driven fiercely onwards by some devouring inner daemon. To his contemporaries he was a phenomenon. One moment he was unknown; then, he was almost at the summit; and then, in a twinkling, he was gone. The adjective 'meteoric', so often applied to political irridescence, was for once wholly apposite. For a brief period, from 1880 to 1886, Lord Randolph dazzled and fascinated his contemporaries to an extent that prompted Rosebery to write of his career without exaggeration that 'while it lasted it eclipsed the fame of almost all who were then engaged in politics,' while Max Beerbohm considered that Lord Randolph was, 'despite his halting speech, foppish mien, and rather coarse fibre of mind . . . the greatest Parliamentarian of his day'.

This was perhaps an exaggeration. Lord Randolph Churchill never possessed the controlled passion of Gladstone, nor the steely resolve of Joseph Chamberlain, nor the awesome dominance of Parnell. But, both on the platform and in the House of Commons, he stood in the front rank. 'It was as a popular orator that Randolph's aptitude came nearest genius,' Almeric Fitzroy wrote; '– the imaginative instinct that controls and dominates circumstance, and in addressing a great meeting he had the faculty, almost alone among his contemporaries, of drawing inspiration from a vast auditory and transmuting it into golden sentences of impassioned logic.'[12] He played the party game with vigour, and without excessive concern for scruple; yet he was capable of longer and wiser views; on the big issues he usually took his own course.

But even before the cataclysm of December 1886 it was apparent that there were many flaws in his character and constitution. He was impetuous and impatient and his moods were exceptionally variable. He would veer from tearing high spirits

12. Sir Almeric Fitzroy: *Memoirs*, Vol. I, p. 290.

to utter depression, and from mocking irresponsibility to
funereal gravity, with bewildering speed and unpredictability.
Even those who knew him best could not foresee these sudden,
violent and apparently inexplicable shifts of mood. He often
sought advice; he very seldom took it. 'No man,' he once
remarked, 'is so entirely alone and solitary as I am.' It was a
revealing comment, and a true one. His marriage did not give
him private companionship or solace. It was a strange, complex
relationship. An intense infatuation was soon followed by a
subtle but definite estrangement. Behind Lady Randolph's
vivid beauty and warming vivacity there lay an essentially
selfish and frivolous character. It is improbable that she ever
understood her brooding, mercurial, sensitive but essentially
serious husband. The marriage held, but it would be wholly
wrong to say that the bonds between Lord Randolph and his
wife were of the kind that might have given that restless
personality the complete companionship that his sons were to
have and which he needed.[13]

Furthermore, Lord Randolph had friends, but no confidants,
and he recklessly squandered his capital of personal and
political friendship. At times almost neurotically obsessed by
his own difficulties, he was usually less sensitive to those of
others. His dedication to politics was fatally total. Into that
profession he invested all his energies, all his intellect, all his
ambitions. His very existence came to depend upon politics,
and the satisfaction and enjoyment that they afforded his
complex, uneven personality.

His originality and independence were of incomparable

13. In a recent biography of Lady Randolph Churchill by Mr Ralph G.
Martin (Prentice-Hall, 1969), the allegation by Frank Harris that Lord
Randolph had contracted syphilis while an undergraduate at Oxford forms
the essential foundation for an analysis of the marriage. The unreliability of
Harris as an authority need hardly be emphasized, and most of Mr Martin's
evidence is highly circumstantial. The suggestion, for example, that Lord
Randolph became homosexual may be regarded with very considerable
scepticism. Lord Randolph did die of General Paralysis of the Insane, and
this is the only solid fact which gives some credence to the Harris story. To
put the matter at its mildest, Mr Martin's book should be approached with
very considerable caution.

value in his rise; after he had arrived they were contemplated
with apprehension by his colleagues and with cool suspicion by
Lord Salisbury, who had appointed him to the Exchequer
without enthusiasm. 'He feared Lord Randolph Churchill must
be Chancellor of the Exchequer and Leader, which I did not
like,' the Queen had noted on 25 July. 'He is so mad and odd,
and has also bad health.' The apprehensions of the Queen and
her Prime Minister were fulfilled, for, although Lord Randolph
was a more effective and patient leader of the House of Commons than had been expected, he had soon taken up independent
positions on many crucial matters of policy within the Cabinet.
'His character,' Salisbury subsequently wrote, 'is quite un-
tamed. Both in impulsiveness and variability, and in a tendency
which can be described by the scholastic word "vulgaris", he
presents the characteristics of extreme youth.'[14] And it was not
only Salisbury who had become alienated. When compromise,
patience and diplomacy would have secured most of Churchill's
objectives, he chose to be dictatorial and hectoring. Colleagues
who had admired him in August 1886 were disenchanted by
December. This was the essential background to the startling
events of that month.

In Salisbury, Churchill met a superior will. Looking back, we
can see that a confrontation between the two was hardly a fair
contest; Lord Randolph ensured that he had no chance at all.
Salisbury patiently awaited the moment when Lord Randolph's
impetuosity would place him in an impossible position. He did
not have to wait long. In December 1886, faced with opposition
to his projected Budget, Lord Randolph recklessly called to
hand the perilous weapon of resignation. Salisbury accepted
battle.[15] Behind the actual issue of War Office economies – in
itself a trumpery affair – there lay other matters of contention.
In which direction was the Conservative Party to go, and who
was to lead it? Over a wide range of subjects, from British
policy in the Middle East to the relationship of the Conservative

14. Salisbury to Fitzjames Stephen, 30 December 1886.

15. Or, as Lord Randolph subsequently put it, 'he jumped at my
resignation like a dog at a bone'. (*The Autobiography of Margot Asquith*, p.
48).

party with Chamberlainite Liberal Unionism, Lord Randolph
had stumbled into serious conflict with the Prime Minister, to
the point where the latter would be pressed no more.

The Ministerial Crisis of December 1886 was fierce but very
brief. Lord Randolph had made no preparation; the issue itself
was unlikely to stir much activity – particularly in the Conservative Party – on his behalf; the timing – a few days before
Christmas – could hardly have been worse. Such was Lord
Randolph's prestige that the Government tottered, but it did
not fall. Lord Randolph found himself out of office, without a
following, and utterly isolated. He remained in public life. He
was still under forty years of age, and still greatly respected and
feared. Yet something in that delicately balanced and febrile
personality had been irretrievably destroyed by the brutality,
suddenness and completeness of his fall. All that remained was
what Rosebery has called 'a public pageant of gloomy years',
in which hope flickered occasionally and then slowly disappeared.

To live in close proximity with such a downfall and such a
personal tragedy had a profound effect on Winston Churchill.
He has written simply and movingly of his relationship with his
father in *My Early Life* and of the impact of his death: 'All my
dreams of comradeship with him, of entering Parliament at his
side and in his support, were ended. There remained for me
only to pursue his aims and vindicate his memory.'[16]

*

It would not have been easy for contemporaries to specify Lord
Randolph's aims, save personal ambition, with any exactness.
It had been difficult to detect in him any really profound beliefs
or political faith beyond the creed of 'Tory Democracy' which
was, perhaps wisely, somewhat vaguely defined. Behind Lord
Randolph's most arresting phrases and lengthy speeches there
lay a certain emptiness of philosophy and a considerable
imprecision on essentials. Supremely successful on the attack,
particularly in Opposition between 1880 and 1885, he was
noticeably less convincing when proposing alternatives. He had

16. *My Early Life*, p. 62.

a series of attitudes – which tended to change without warning – rather than any policies or real political principles. In answer to the question of what did Lord Randolph 'stand for', it would have been possible to give an answer at any given moment; it was far from certain that the same answer would have been appropriate a month or so later. John Morley was struck on one occasion by a critical statement of Lord Randolph to the effect that 'Balfour and you are men who believe in the solution of political questions.' Morley's comment was to the point: 'This belief may or may not be a weakness, yet the alternative, that the statesman is a man who does not believe in the solution of political questions, was startling.'

Politics provide so many changes of fortune and opportunity that a fixed stance invites ridicule and disaster; but day-to-day opportunism contains comparable perils if it becomes apparent that there is no dominant theme and resolve in a man's endeavours. Lord Randolph's career, although brief, had many changes of attitude and emphasis. Thus, in the early 1880s he took the side of the Irish Nationalists protesting against the coercive policies of the Gladstone Government, and earned the respect and trust of many of the Irish Members;[17] in the summer of 1885 he gave assurances to Parnell concerning future Conservative policy towards Ireland that materially affected Irish attitudes towards the Conservatives in the 1885 elections; within months, after Gladstone had manifestly resolved on Home Rule, Churchill was 'playing the Orange card' and declaring that 'Ulster will fight, Ulster will be right'; he was one of the principal architects of the 'Unionist' alliance of the Conservatives and Liberals that defeated the Home Rule Bill in the Commons in June 1886 and which maintained a common front against the Gladstonian Liberals in the election that immediately followed.

His attitudes to other subjects showed comparable inconsistencies. He opposed, almost alone in his party, the bombardment of Alexandria and the occupation of Egypt in 1882, categorizing it, in the best Radical traditions, as a 'bondholders' war'; as Secretary of State for India, he was responsible

17. See Conor Cruise O'Brien: *Parnell and His Party*, pp. 117–18.

for the successful invasion and annexation of Upper Burma in December 1885. For a time he flirted with 'Fair Trade' in a series of speeches that perilously approached the borders of advocating a Protectionist policy; he then veered back without warning to the orthodox Free Trade position.

In this rampaging, extraordinary career, it was not altogether surprising that, as Roseberry has commented, 'to many persons, both Tory and Liberal, Randolph was little less than an incarnation of evil, a reckless and insolent iconoclast . . . He was, in their judgement, scrupulous, violent, unprincipled; an intriguing schemer, a ruthless plotter; one who, to serve the personal ambition which was his sole motive, would stick at nothing.' These were severe judgements whose validity could be challenged; but their existence could not be challenged. Salisbury's comments on his young lieutenant were sceptical and critical. Friends and supporters of Sir Stafford Northcote, whom Lord Randolph had persistently attacked and derided and in effect driven from the leadership of the Conservative Party in the House of Commons, could not easily forget his jibes. One opponent, Lord Ripon, described him as a 'reckless and unprincipled mountebank'. He had friends – few but true – and hardly one who could deny that there had been periods of estrangement in their relationship. Politically, he had many followers and large audiences at public meetings; in the Cabinet and in the Parliamentary Party he was a solitary figure. In the years of his advance these weaknesses had not been apparent; but when he made his first serious error they ensured not merely his downfall but the impossibility of a complete revival.

No satisfying brief estimate can be made of Lord Randolph's career and personality. One of the most shrewd was given by the then Warden of Merton College, Oxford, the Hon. G. C. Brodrick, in a memoir published in the *Oxford Magazine* in 1895. Brodrick had known Lord Randolph both as an undergraduate and as a political opponent at Woodstock, and his estimate may be resurrected from its forgotten obscurity:

His audacity was perfectly natural; it showed itself in season and out of season, both at school and at College; it was restrained by few scruples, and by little respect for others . . . But he added to his

audacity and independence a truly admirable industry, little sus-
pected in the early stages of his career. . . . In fact, his strength as
well as his weakness largely consisted in his combinations of two
natures, both equally genuine – the one prompting to an almost
shameless and aggressive self-assertion, the other tempered by kind-
liness, public spirit and patriotism . . . Few have ever enjoyed 'one
crowded hour of glorious life' more fully than he did; fewer still have
atoned for a too reckless enjoyment of it by a swifter Nemesis of
political failure and premature decay.

Although Lord Randolph's life has a singular dramatic completeness, it is as well to remember how young he was and that
he never reached political fulfilment in terms of office, power or
influence. If he conspicuously lacked most of the heavy political
virtues, he possessed many others. His very unpredictability
had an excitement and attractiveness, and his approach to all
matters was fresh and original. His son subsequently presented
a somewhat idealized filial portrait, but, as Rosebery's essay on
Lord Randolph and the estimates of others have demonstrated,
the impact of his personality was intense, and had a particular
appeal to those who chafed at the restrictions of conventional
party strife and dialogue. His life had, above all, a dramatic and
romantic quality to which men could respond. And none
responded more ardently than the son whom Lord Randolph
had hardly known and for whom he had not had much regard.

*

When Lord Randolph's son was first elected to the House of
Commons in the General Election of 1900 he was already a
controversial national figure, and the memory of his father was
still vivid. And recollections of Lord Randolph were not always
agreeable. Around Lord Randolph and his brother, the equally
ill-fated eighth Duke of Marlborough, there had hung a faint
but tangible air of disreputableness that had been engaging and
attractive to some but rather less to the majority. And it may
have been that a generation heavily influenced by Macaulay
had drawn some comparisons between the cavalier methods of
John, the first Duke of Marlborough and Lord Randolph.

The young Winston Churchill himself was manifestly an

adventurer and an opportunist. As such, and with only his own
enterprise, courage and ability to rely upon to make his
fortunes, it had been sometimes necessary to cut corners with a
sharpness that did not endear him universally. Unlike many
soldiers of fortune he had been prepared to put his own life to
the hazard,[18] but the accusations – far from unmerited – that
he was an adventurer and a medal-hunter dimmed the very real
and substantial military, literary and political achievements
that stood to his credit.[19] As his career advanced, he could have
complained, in Disraeli's words, that 'when I was a young and
struggling man they taunted me with being an adventurer. Now
that I have succeeded they still bring the same reproach against
me.' But, as with Disraeli, the reproach was not without
foundation. It was to be a very long time indeed before he shook
off these early prejudices. And it may be noted that the young
Churchill made no attempt to conceal his ambition. He possessed Lord Randolph's lack of interest, amounting almost to
carelessness and which some attributed to patrician arrogance,
about his reputation among the majority of mankind. As A. G.
Gardiner, the editor of the Liberal *Daily News*, commented in
1908: 'To the insatiable curiosity and the enthusiasm of the
child he joins the frankness of the child. He has no reserves and
no shams. You are welcome to anything he has, and may pry
into any corner you like. He has that scorn of concealment that
belongs to a caste which never doubts itself.'[20]

There is a common misconception to the effect that, in
England, Youth and Ambition are regarded with approval. In
reality, Youth is deemed a regrettable interlude, to be borne
with appropriate patience and modesty; Ambition is tolerable
only if it is decently concealed. Churchill was brash, assertive,
egocentric, wholly absorbed in himself and in his own career,

18. 'I rode on my grey pony all along the skirmish line where everyone
else was lying down in cover. Foolish perhaps, but I play for high stakes and
given an audience there is no act too daring or too noble. Without the
gallery, things are different' (Churchill to his mother, 19 September 1897,
quoted in Randolph S. Churchill, op. cit., Companion Volume I, p. 793).

19. For the controversy over the circumstances of his escape from a Boer
prisoner-of-war camp, see p. 304.

20. A. G. Gardiner: *Prophets, Priests and Kings*, p. 108.

and unashamedly on the make. A colleague in the 1901–5 Parliament has written that 'Churchill made no attempt to dispel the suspicion and dislike with which he was regarded by the majority of the House of Commons. He seemed to enjoy causing resentment. He appeared to have, in modern parlance, a "chip on his shoulder" when in the Chamber itself or in the Lobbies.'[21]

What was difficult to see in the young Churchill was, as in the case of Lord Randolph, any specific objective in his life save that of an intense and somewhat alarming personal ambition. 'He is ambitious and he is calculating,' Steevens had written in 1899; 'yet he is not cold – and that saves him. His ambition is sanguine, runs in a torrent, and the calculation is hardly more than the rocks or the stump which the torrent strikes for a second, yet which suffices to direct its course.' Sir Charles Dilke, who in 1880 had described Rosebery in his diary as 'about the most ambitious man I had ever met', subsequently added 'I have since known Winston Churchill.'[22] Beatrice Webb's impression was that he was 'restless, egotistical, bumptious, shallow-minded and reactionary, but with a certain personal magnetism, great pluck and some originality not of intellect, but of character'. Rosebery was not the only one of Lord Randolph's friends who initially found the son's manifest personal ambition thoroughly unattractive.

In *Savrola* there had been an interesting passage which justifies quotation:

His nervous temperament could not fail to be excited by the vivid scenes through which he had lately passed, and the repression of his emotion only heated the inward fire. Was it worth it? The struggle, the labour, the constant rush of affairs, the sacrifice of so many things that make life easy or pleasant – for what? A people's good! That, he could not disguise from himself, was rather the direction than the cause of his efforts. Ambition was the motive force, and he was powerless to resist it . . . 'Vehement, high and daring' was his cast of mind. The life he lived was the only one he could ever live; he must go on to the end.

21. Lord Winterton: 'Churchill the Parliamentarian' (*Churchill by His Contemporaries*, edited by Charles Eade, pp. 86–7).

22. Dilke Papers (British Museum Addition Manuscripts 43,934/195–7).

His dedication to his profession was complete, 'living with Blue Books and sleeping with encyclopedias' as Hugh Massingham wrote of him during this period. Another observer wrote of him at this time that

Mr Churchill's head is carried with a droop which comes to those who read and study hard. When he is thinking he drops his head forward as if it were heavy. That is how you see him at one moment – a pose prophetic of what is likely to fasten itself upon him before he reaches middle age. But it requires two plates to take a fair photograph of him, for the next time you look at him he has sprung to his feet with the eagerness of a boy, his pale blue eyes are sparkling, his lips parted, he is talking a vocal torrent, and his head and arms are driving home his words.[23]

One of his friends of the time has related:

He gave himself to work. When he was not busy with politics, he was reading or writing. He did not lead the life of other young men in London. He may have visited political clubs, but I never met him walking in Pall Mall or Hyde Park where sooner or later one used to meet most friends. I never met him at a dinner-party that had not some public or private purpose.[24]

It was not surprising that many estimates were hostile. Beatrice Webb commented in 1903 that he was 'bound to be unpopular – too unpleasant a flavour with his restless, self-regarding personality and lack of moral or intellectual refinement'. But she – unlike many others – also saw the qualities: 'But his pluck, courage, resourcefulness, and great tradition may carry him far unless he knocks himself to pieces like his father.'[25]

This last qualification was significant. At this stage it seemed that Churchill was intent upon re-creating his father's career, in fighting his enemies, battling for his policies, and repeating his errors. He took at once an individualistic stance; he launched a crusade for economy; he adopted what seemed to be deliberate 'Little England' attitudes; by his membership of a group of

23. *Daily Mail*, 2 October 1901.
24. J. B. Atkins: *Incidents and Reflections*, p. 135.
25. Beatrice Webb: *Our Partnership*, pp. 269–70.

Conservative free-lances who called themselves the 'Hugh-ligans' in honour of Lord Hugh Cecil, one of their members, he seemed to be reviving Lord Randolph's famous 'Fourth Party' of 1880–3; he even emulated his father's dress and mannerisms, and in his attitude towards the Conservative hierarchy there were strong echoes of Lord Randolph's iconoclasticism. The fact that he was, throughout this period, writing Lord Randolph's biography was not without its significance. Wilfred Blunt wrote of him in 1903 that 'In mind and manner he is a strange replica of his father, with all his father's suddenness and awareness, and I should say more than his father's ability. There is just the same gaminerie and contempt of the conventional and the same engaging plain spokenness and readiness to understand.'[26]

It is difficult to over-emphasize the extent to which Churchill at this time leaned upon his father's career and experiences. The biography of Lord Randolph Churchill was his principal pre-occupation, apart from his own career, between 1902 and 1905, and the two had so many common themes that it is unwise to treat them separately. Certainly the contemplation of the events of the 1880s was not likely to heighten Churchill's estimation of the Conservative Party in general and certain individuals in particular. His subsequent statement that the study of his father's life had played a major part in his disenchantment with the Conservative Party may be regarded with some scepticism, but it would be unwise to assume that it played no part. It was Churchill's opinion before he embarked on the book that the party had treated his father badly; he emerged with the conviction that it had treated him scurvily, and Rosebery was not the only commentator who saw the significance of a quotation from a letter written by Lord Randolph to his wife in November 1891:

So Arthur Balfour is really leader [of the House of Commons] – and Tory Democracy, the genuine article, at an end . . . No power will make me lift a hand or foot or voice for the Tories, just as no power would make me join the other side . . . I expect I have made great mistakes; but there has been no consideration, no indulgence,

26. W. S. Blunt: *My Diaries*, Vol. II. pp. 488–9.

no memory or gratitude – nothing but spite, malice and abuse. I am quite tired and dead-sick of it all, and will not continue political life any longer . . .

And there was another significant quotation, from a letter written by Lord Randolph in 1892 to the Liberal-Unionist candidate for Tyneside upon the emergence of 'Labour' as a separate force in British politics:

If under the Constitution as it now exists, and as we wish to see it preserved, the Labour interest finds that it can obtain its objects and secure its own advantage, then that interest will be reconciled to the Constitution, will find its faith in it, and will maintain it. But if it should unfortunately occur that the Constitutional Party, to which you and I belong, are deaf to hear and slow to meet the demands of Labour, are stubborn in opposition to those demands, and are persistent in the habit of ranging themselves in unreasoning and short-sighted support of all the present rights of property and capital, the result may be that the Labour interest may identify what it will take to be defects in the Constitutional Party with the Constitution itself, and in a moment of indiscriminating impulse may use its power to sweep both away.

The portrait of Lord Randolph that emerged was a very formal one, and *Lord Randolph Churchill*'s outstanding quality lies in its depiction of the politics of the 1880s rather than in that of the subject's character. Nevertheless, there could be no doubt of the concept of his father that Churchill had conceived, and which he portrayed with such emphasis and vigour. The concluding passage is as revealing as any:

There is an England which stretches far beyond the well-drilled masses who are assembled by party machinery to salute with appropriate acclamation the utterances of their recognized fuglemen; an England of wise men who gaze without self-deception at the failings and follies of both political parties; of brave and earnest men who find in neither faction fair scope for the effort that is in them; of 'poor men' who increasingly doubt the sincerity of party philanthropy. It was to that England that Lord Randolph Churchill appealed; it was that England he so nearly won; it is by that England he will be justly judged.[27]

27. *Lord Randolph Churchill* (1951 one-volume edition), p. 764.

There were many who, in 1905, found difficulty in recognizing
the Lord Randolph they had known in this portrait, and the
passage, like many others in the biography, throws more light
on the author than on the subject. The significance, for a
biographer of the son, lies in the portrait of the father that he
had created, not in its fidelity to the original. Time and again
one is struck by the emphasis placed by the son on the factors
that had made his father famous, and those that, in his judgement, had caused his downfall. Thus would he do, thus would
he not do. One example more may be taken from this brilliant
and self-revealing work:

> No one could guess beforehand what he was going to say nor how
> he would say it. No one said the same kind of things, or said them in
> the same kind of way. He possessed the strange quality, uncon-
> sciously exerted and not by any means to be simulated, of compelling
> attention, and of getting himself talked about. Every word he spoke
> was studied with interest and apprehension. Each step he took was
> greeted with a gathering chorus of astonished cries. As Tacitus said
> of Mucianus: *Omnium quae dixerat, feceratque, arte gradam ostentator*
> (He had the showman's knack of drawing public attention to every-
> thing he said or did).[28]

It is not fanciful to draw reasonably close parallels between
Lord Randolph's attitudes and tactics and Churchill's career at
this time. There was a very conscious and deliberate emulation
by the son of the father's example, and by his interpretations of
the strengths and weaknesses of the father. Nor is this to be
wondered at. A young man entering politics, or, indeed, any
other calling, is very exceptional if he does not lean upon some
example that is close to him. Both Peel and Gladstone were very
much their father's sons in their early years in public life, and
it was only gradually that their own political personalities began
to develop, and the assumptions on which they had been
brought up were one by one subjected to the challenge of new
circumstances and personal experiences. What was out of the
ordinary was the intensity of Churchill's emphasis upon his
father's experiences and his deliberate framing of his actions
upon his father's example. And in this we can clearly see some-

28. ibid, p. 217.

thing more profound and significant in Churchill's own personality and the experience of his childhood than normal fidelity to
a deeply admired father who had fought the same battles two
decades before.

*

From the very beginning, Churchill's approach was deliberately
aggressive, and he fully appreciated the importance of gaining a
name by assailing the biggest men. He was not prepared to
undergo the normal period of quiet apprenticeship enjoined on
new Members of the House of Commons by those with greater
experience of the perils of starting too swiftly and too dramatically. But it is doubtful if calculation lay behind this crucial
decision – a decision that many politicians have made and
virtually all have regretted.

It is a common error in the study of politics to ascribe
rational thinking to emotional and intuitive causes. Churchill's
sense of the dramatic, even at this early stage of his life, was
absolutely natural. It was said of Disraeli that he was an actor –
but that the actor was the real man. This could not be applied
with strict accuracy to Churchill, but he saw himself always in
an essentially dramatic light.[29] When drama did not exist, he
created it. 'The applause of the House,' Lloyd George wrote of
him in 1907, 'is the breath of his nostrils. He is just like an
actor. He likes the limelight and the approbation of the pit.'[30]
As A. G. Gardiner was to write in 1912, 'he is always unconsciously playing a part – an heroic part. And he is himself his
most astonished spectator.'

In these processes, calculation played a small part. In the
essay to which reference has already been made,[31] Mr Storr has
drawn attention to Jung's delineation of the 'extroverted

29. After he had been defeated at the Oldham by-election in July 1899,
Sir Edward Hamilton who had known and worked for Lord Randolph,
recorded that he 'showed any amount of pluck and self-assurance, but I am
told he was always thinking of the impression which his speeches would
make, not on his immediate audience, but on London (as if London were
hanging on his lips)' (Brit. Mus. Add. MSS 48,674).

30. William George: *My Brother and I*, p. 211.

31. 'Winston Churchill; The Man', op. cit., p. 213.

intuitive', and to the following remarkable passage which has such relevance to Churchill's complex personality:

> Wherever intuition predominates, a particular and unmistakable psychology presents itself . . . The intuitive is never to be found among the generally recognized reality values, but is always present where possibilities exist. He has a keen nose for things in the bud pregnant with future promise . . . Thinking and feeling, the indispensable components of conviction, are, with him, inferior functions, possessing no decisive weight: hence they lack the power to offer any lasting resistance to the force of intuition.

Jung goes on to ascribe this to the intuitive's lack of judgement, and his 'weak consideration for the welfare of his neighbours'. At first sight, this last comment may be challenged. Churchill's loyalty to his close friends, and above all his family, was already a very strong feature of his personality. But what was also evident was his remarkable egocentricity and lack of interest in the thoughts and sayings of others. His son has written that he had no small talk and preferred to talk about himself.[32] (It may be emphasized that Jung refers to the intuitive's 'weak consideration'; he does not say that the intuitive has *no* consideration.) And Jung concludes with the comment that the extroverted intuitive's 'capacity to inspire his fellow-men with courage, or to kindle enthusiasm for something new, is unrivalled'. It is perilous for the amateur, or perhaps even the professional, to embark upon the murky and treacherous waters of psychological analysis. But in this case the essential similarities between Jung's portrait of the extroverted intuitive and Winston Churchill are so striking that they merit at least a digression, and not least because Jung points out that an individual of this type is 'not infrequently put down as a ruthless and immoral adventurer'.

Certainly, such terms had often been applied to Lord Randolph, and were now to be applied to his son. The fact that the most swift and the most dangerous path to the political limelight is to challenge the supremacy of an established figure had often been demonstrated, and not least by Lord Randolph.

32. Randolph S. Churchill, op. cit., Vol. II, p. 249.

Churchill began by assailing St John Brodrick, Secretary of
State for War, in much the same way that Lord Randolph had
sharpened his dialectical teeth on the hapless Mr Sclater-
Booth.[33] Then he became one of the most vigorous critics of
Joseph Chamberlain after the latter had thrown contemporary
politics into utter confusion by his dramatic espousal of Tariff
Reform in May 1903 and resignation from the Unionist Government[34] of which he had been, although not Prime Minister, the
dominant figure.

The sincerity of Churchill's opposition to Chamberlain and
his espousal of the cause of Free Trade was questioned at the
time, and subsequently. His friend J. E. B. Seely later remarked
that 'Winston was not really moved by the sanctity of the
principle of Free Trade. He rather dragged along on the
economic argument, but thought it good troubled water to fish
in.'[35] This is unquestionably too severe a judgement. Churchill
launched his first attack on Chamberlain in the Commons on
28 May, at a time when it appeared that Conservative solidarity
was going to be preserved; although he was supported by Hugh

33. Mr Sclater-Booth had been President of the Local Government
Board, and was the author of a County Government Bill, designed to effect
some modest changes in local administration. Lord Randolph, whose
impatience with the Beaconsfield Government was becoming very marked,
assailed the Bill and its sponsor in a devastating speech in the Commons on
7 March 1878. He described it as 'just the sort of little dodge and contrivance
that would be proposed by a President of the Local Government Board
who finds himself called upon to legislate on a great question', and, among
other jibes, he remarked that 'it is remarkable how often we find mediocrity
dowered with a double-barrelled name'. The Bill was quietly abandoned by
the Government after this unexpected onslaught, and Henry Lucy commented that 'it is a dangerous thing when a reckless youth comes by, and,
with audacious hands, thrusts pins into the stuffed figure'.

34. After the split in the Liberal ranks over Home Rule for Ireland in
1886 the dissident Liberals, led by Lord Hartington and Chamberlain, had
gradually been drawn into alliance with the Conservatives. The phrase 'the
Unionist Alliance' was Lord Randolph's, but it was not really until 1895,
when the last Salisbury Government contained the leading Liberal Unionists, that the alliance was formalized. But although this party was called
'The Unionist Party' until 1922, I have used the word 'Conservative'
throughout this book.

35. Quoted in Julian Amery: *Joseph Chamberlain and the Tariff Reform
Campaign*, Vol. V, p. 263.

Cecil, this was a brave and politically perilous stand. As he wrote to Chamberlain in August, 'You know yourself something of "bitter pilgrimages" and of the difficulties of those who are out of sympathy with one party without belonging to the other.'[36] The passions that Churchill's speeches on Tariff Reform aroused in the Conservative Party, and the doubts cast upon his sincerity, demonstrated the amount of mistrust that he had already evoked within three years of entering Parliament. It is important to emphasize that long before the tariff issue arose, Churchill had achieved much prominence as a persistent and even violent critic of the government he had been elected to support.

The vigour of Churchill's early political utterances was in itself remarkable, and played a significant part in the dislike he aroused. In the 1900 election campaign he had described the Liberals as 'prigs, prudes and faddists'; he had also declared that the Liberal Party was 'hiding from the public view like a toad in a hole, but when it stands forth in all its hideousness the Tories will have to hew the filthy object limb from limb'. By 1903 a different picture had emerged. His assaults on the Balfour Government became characterized by increasingly vivid phraseology. He accused Balfour of 'gross, unpardonable ignorance'; he attacked him for his 'slipshod, slapdash, haphazard manner of doing business'; he declared that 'the dignity of a Prime Minister, like a lady's virtue, is not susceptible of partial diminution'. And then: 'To keep in office for a few more weeks and months there is no principle which the Government are not prepared to betray, and no quantity of dust and filth they are not prepared to eat.'

In these circumstances it was not surprising that his constituency association disowned him, the Conservatives regarded him with the antipathy reserved for the renegade, nor that the Liberals eyed their new recruit with some reservation. Austen Chamberlain[37] icily remarked that 'his conversion to Radicalism coincided with his personal interests'; Alfred Lyttleton

36. ibid.
37. The elder son of Joseph Chamberlain, he had remained in the Government after his father's resignation, as Chancellor of the Exchequer.

said that 'he trims his sails to every passing wind'; Bonar Law
– who had entered Parliament in 1900 and who had made his
maiden speech on the same evening as Churchill, and whose
antipathy to Churchill developed from an early stage – described
him bluntly as a turn-coat; Leo Maxse wrote that he was 'half
alien and wholly undesirable'. There was much more in the
same vein.

One of the most effective counter-attacks came from
Chamberlain in the House of Commons on 29 July 1903:

> I remember my hon. friend at the time he came into Parliament,
> and I did the best I could then. I remember how, in the heyday of his
> enthusiasm, he was going to give his ready and cordial support to his
> own party – and to his own Government . . . but it is clear that all
> those expectations of my hon. friend have been disappointed. One
> by one his fond delusions have vanished. First he discovered that the
> Prime Minister was unworthy of his confidence. Then came the
> Secretary for War, who was also found unworthy. Next it was the
> Foreign Secretary; then it was the President of the Board of Trade;
> and then, after all that – it is with deep regret I have to say it – he
> came to the Colonial Secretary. But my hon. friend still has one hope,
> he clings to the Chancellor of the Exchequer.[38] Well, I hope that the
> confidence of my hon. friend will not be again misplaced; but I
> warn my right hon. friend not to place too much faith in the valued
> and continued confidence of my hon. friend.

Churchill responded with vigour, and raised the temperature
even higher. After he joined the Liberals in 1904, a detached
observer, the experienced parliamentary commentator H. W.
Lucy, wrote at the time: 'Winston Churchill may be safely
counted upon to make himself quite as disagreeable on the
Liberal side as he did on the Unionist. But he will always be
handicapped by the aversion that always pertains to a man
who, in whatsoever honourable circumstances, has turned his
coat.'[39]

38. C. T. Ritchie, Chamberlain's principal adversary in the Cabinet, and
public champion of Free Trade in the Government.
39. H. W. Lucy: *The Balfourian Parliament*, p. 322. For Campbell-
Bannerman's lack of excitement over Churchill's defection, see Spender:
Campbell-Bannerman, Vol. II, p. 131.

As his biographer has emphasized,[40] Churchill's disenchantment with the Conservatives had many causes, and it is not
possible to identify the decisive factor. But it seems probable
that he might have been retained had he been given office when
the Government was reconstructed in July 1902, when Balfour
succeeded Salisbury. In this context, there was a significant
passage in his biography of Lord Randolph:

> Even in a period of political activity there is small scope for the
> supporter of a Government. The Whips do not want speeches, but
> votes. The Ministers regard an oration in their praise or defence as
> only one degree less tiresome than an attack. The earnest party man
> becomes a silent drudge, tramping at intervals through lobbies to
> record his vote and wondering why he came to Westminster at all.
> Ambitious youth diverges into criticism and even hostility, or seeks
> an outlet for its energies elsewhere.[41]

As always in these matters, motives were probably mixed,
and there was no single cause of Churchill's swift alienation
from the Conservatives. His comment in October 1903 that 'I
am an English Liberal. I hate the Tory party, their men, their
words and their methods'[42] was, no doubt, sincere. So also was
his opposition to Protection. But it would be disingenuous to
believe – and would be to underestimate Churchill's ability –
that no considerations of personal advantage played a part. He
wanted to get on. He thought himself held back and frustrated
in the Conservative ranks. He was, like his father, in a hurry.

Churchill was not driven out of the Conservative Party, but
his actions and speeches in 1901–2 had made him so uncongenial to his colleagues that the mood of personal hostility
against him, which became very manifest in the Tariff Reform
debates, played an important part in his movement towards the
Liberals. As usually happens in such circumstances, the lowest
of motives were ascribed to his actions. While such insinuations
did Churchill less than justice, there seems little doubt that he
could have been retained – at least temporarily – in the
Conservative Party had he been given promotion to the

40. Randolph S. Churchill, op. cit., Vol. II, Chapter 2.
41. *Lord Randolph Churchill*, p. 66.
42. Randolph S. Churchill, op. cit., Vol. II, p. 71.

Ministry. But young men who lustily throw stones at their elders are not usually rewarded for their activity. The mutual lack of esteem between Churchill and the Conservative leaders that developed in 1901–2 effectively precluded him from office, and that exclusion certainly played a part in his decision to leave the Conservative Party.

Churchill's shift of party allegiance won him substantial advantages. From the fall of the Balfour Government in December 1905 until May 1915 Britain was ruled by Liberal governments. Throughout this period Churchill was in office and, after the middle of 1908, in high office. These were years of high attainment and success. But the personal and political animosities that he had aroused during his brief and spectacular advance in 1900–1905 were to stalk him relentlessly, were to temporarily destroy him in 1915, and were never to be wholly eradicated. In politics, both individuals and parties have long memories. Churchill, within five years of active politics, had arrived – but at a price.

*

It was already apparent by the end of 1905, when he first received office as Parliamentary Under-Secretary at the Colonial Office, that Churchill was not merely an attractive speaker but was showing signs of becoming a very formidable one.

The spoken word is the politician's essential public weapon, and it is one of the curiosities of modern British politics that there is such a conspicuous failure to comprehend this elementary fact and to develop this weapon. It is true that the modern House of Commons style is, as Churchill himself remarked, 'conversational', and that thundering oratory is regarded with scepticism. It is also true that Grand Oratory, like Grand Opera, is rarely suited to the English temperament. It is also perhaps the case that the pace of modern political life militates against the careful and lengthy apprenticeship in public oratory to which Gladstone had applied himself, or the detailed preparation that men like Lord Randolph, Rosebery, Asquith and Churchill devoted to their major pronouncements. But it is strange and melancholy that so little care and attention is now given to the professional art of public speaking. In this, Churchill may be said to have been behind his time. Yet, when one compares the impact of his personality upon his contemporaries with that of a man of the high ability of Leo Amery – whose speeches were usually excellent in content but dull both in form and delivery and almost invariably too long – the crucial importance of his oratorical powers for his political fortunes can be best appreciated.

Churchill was not a natural impromptu speaker. In addition to his voice impediment, which made him unattractive to listen to,[43] he experienced considerable difficulty in thinking when on his feet in the Commons and even on the public platform. 'I had never the practice which comes to young men at the University of speaking in small debating societies impromptu on all sorts of subjects,' he has written, adding that for many years he was unable to say anything in public that he had not written out beforehand and learnt by heart. Fortunately, learning by heart was an attribute at which he had always excelled, even as a schoolboy. It was an inherited aptitude, as Lord Randolph's memory was exceptionally acute. In his early years he committed his speeches to memory, but on 22 April 1904 he lost the thread of his argument towards the end of a long speech in the House of Commons and had to sit down. Afterwards, although he still prepared his speeches and learned them by heart, he came fully furnished with copious notes which could extricate him from a comparable misfortune.

Thus, from the outset he had to attempt to anticipate the mood of the House of Commons or a public meeting and to impose his prepared views and arguments upon his audience. To do this in the Commons presented difficulties of such magnitude that it would ordinarily have proved fatal to parliamentary ambitions. But the fact – and, above all, the frank recognition of the fact – gave Churchill's speeches their careful and well-planned character. It would be foolish to claim

43. 'Churchill was no natural orator. He had in his youth an imperfection of speech which often made it painful to listen to him. It was only by an extraordinary self-discipline that he made himself fit for what he was to achieve at the climax of his life' (Lord Salter: *Slave of the Lamp*, pp. 53–4).

that Churchill never made a bad speech; it would be equally foolish to claim that he never made an unwise one; but it is valid to assert that he rarely, if ever, made a slovenly one. It is indeed strange that this most articulate of men – of whose private conversation it has been written that 'It can be said of Churchill, as it was of Burns, that his conversation is better than anything he has ever written; and those who have not had the opportunity of listening to it can hardly appreciate the full quality of the man'[44] – should have been in public so completely dependent upon preparation. It was all the more remarkable when it is realized that all his books and articles after *The River War* were, in whole or in substantial part, dictated; and that, in his own words, 'I lived from mouth to hand.' In a sense, he wrote his speeches and spoke his books.

This curious feature of Churchill's political personality was to remain with him throughout his life. 'Discussion, as understood by the Under-Secretary for the Colonies,' Almeric Fitzroy recorded in January 1908, 'is an uninterrupted monologue, and certainly he sustained the part assigned to himself with extraordinary vigour, verve, and resource'; and he wrote three years later: 'Certainly he is a wonderful talker, daring, not to say reckless, but always with a subcurrent of method, striking in phrase, vivid in colour, elegant to the verge of romance, picturesquely vehement, and at the same time persuasive.'[45] We have, accordingly, a strange paradox. In private, a voluble and articulate talker – and a somewhat less satisfactory listener – and yet in public almost wholly dependent upon careful preparation and rehearsal.

Gladstone once wrote that 'I wish you knew the state of total impotence to which I should be reduced if there were no echo to the accents of my own voice.' For Churchill, the task was always to provide the echo – or at least to provide *for* it. This caused some famous disasters, but on the whole it became a powerful advantage. It has been rightly said of Lloyd George that 'his real fault was his desire to please his audience – his weakness was an extreme responsiveness to atmosphere and,

44. R. Boothby: *I Fight to Live*, p. 45.
45. Fitzroy, op. cit., Vol. I, p. 339 and Vol. II, p. 436.

in place of an immovable candour, a too adroit opportunism.'[46] This criticism could not be directed against Churchill. As Balfour once remarked (House of Commons, 7 March 1916), 'Anybody who knows my Right Honourable Friend is aware that when he makes one of these great speeches they are not the unpremeditated effusions of a hasty moment.'

In his portrait of the young Churchill, G. W. Steevens wrote that 'He has not studied to make himself a demagogue. He was born a demagogue, and he happens to know it. The master strain in his character is the rhetorician.' In one respect this was not correct; Churchill had written in 1897 an essay entitled 'The Scaffolding of Rhetoric' in which he put forward views on the power wielded by the orator and his techniques which merit reading.[47] His views anticipated what he wrote in *Savrola* in 1900: 'He . . . knew that nothing good can be obtained without effort. These impromptu feats of oratory existed only in the minds of the listeners; the flowers of rhetoric were hothouse plants.'

It may be argued whether this dominant characteristic of Churchill's speaking was in the long run a disadvantage or an asset; what cannot be controverted is the fact that he faced and overcame a temperamental feature of his personality and indeed turned it to advantage. This required courage and application, and to the end he was dependent upon careful preparation for any major speech. What Sir Harold Nicolson has called 'the combination of great flights of oratory with sudden swoops into the intimate and conversational', which eventually became the outstanding feature of Churchill's speaking technique, had to be worked for.

His first major speech in the Commons, a devastating attack on Brodrick on 12 May 1901, took six weeks to prepare; in his own words, 'I learnt it so thoroughly off by heart that it hardly mattered where I began it or how I turned it.'[48] It was

46. T. Jones: *Lloyd George*, p. 91.

47. Randolph S. Churchill, op. cit., Companion Volume I, Part 2, pp. 816–21.

48. Curiously enough, H. W. Lucy described this as Churchill's maiden speech, which had in fact been delivered some three months before. But

a considerable success, and an examination of Churchill's style reveals the careful preparation. Of Brodrick's plan to create six Army Corps, of whom three were to be held ready for dispatch abroad, Churchill said:

The Secretary of State for War knows – none better than he – that it will not make us secure, and that if we went to war with any great Power his three Army Corps would scarcely serve as a vanguard. If we are hated, they will not make us loved. If we are in danger, they will not make us safe. They are enough to irritate; they are not enough to overawe. Yet, while they cannot make us invulnerable, they may very likely make us venturesome.

As this particular campaign developed it was marked by a number of remarkably mature and powerful speeches by Churchill. One extract may be taken to demonstrate this:

Europe is now groaning beneath the weight of armies. There is scarcely a single important Government whose finances are not embarrassed; there is not a Parliament or a people from whom the cry of weariness has not been wrung . . . What a pity it would be if, just at the moment when there is good hope of a change, our statesmen were to commit us to the old and vicious policy! Is it not a much more splendid dream that this realm of England . . . should be found bold enough and strong enough to send forth for the wings of honest purpose the message which the Russian Emperor tried vainly to proclaim: that the cruel and clanking struggle of armaments is drawing to a close, and that with the New Century has come a clearer and calmer sky?

Churchill was still under thirty years of age when he delivered this judgement.

Already, both in his writings and in his speeches, the rhetorician that Steevens had discerned in 1898 was becoming evident. Charles Masterman wrote a few years later:

In nearly every case an *idea* enters his head from outside. It then rolls round the hollow of his brain, collecting strength like a snowball. Then, after whirling winds of *rhetoric*, he becomes convinced that it

---

although Lucy considered that 'Winston Churchill is not likely to eclipse the fame of Randolph', he was struck by the fact that in an hour-long speech Churchill never looked at his notes (*The Balfourian Parliament*, pp. 62–4).

is *right*; and denounces everyone who criticizes it. He is in the Greek
sense a Rhetorician, the slave of the words which his mind forms
about ideas. He sets ideas to Rhetoric as musicians set theirs to music.
And he can convince himself of almost every truth if it is once allowed
thus to start on its wild career through his rhetorical machinery.

The campaign against Brodrick can be cited in support of this
contention. His argument that 'a European War can only end
in the ruin of the vanquished and the scarcely less fatal com-
mercial dislocation and exhaustion of the conquerors' was a
justified foundation for his attack on the Brodrick Scheme,
whose conspicuous weakness was, as he remarked, that three
Army Corps were insufficient 'to begin to fight Europeans'.
But this was developed into the contention that 'the honour
and security of the British Empire did not depend, and could
never depend, on the British Army', and that 'the only weapon
with which we can expect to cope with great nations is the
Navy'.

It would be possible to argue that Churchill's lack of formal
scholastic education was at least partly responsible for a certain
crudity of thought and expression in many of his early speeches
and writings. It was perhaps unfortunate for him that his early
experiments with words had had to be conducted, in the main,
in public; there are passages in *The Story of the Malakand
Field Force* in particular which are almost comic in their uncontrolled lushness of adjectives and similes. But in this, as in
so many other things, he learned rapidly. Although, to the end,
he loved words as an artist loves colour, he learned how to
control and exploit them. *The River War* revealed this growing
power; *Lord Randolph Churchill* confirmed it. In his public
speeches, however, this control was less evident. Eager to make
an impression, and always conscious of the importance to the
Press of dramatic phrases, his choice of words was often unhappy in this early period and was not calculated to win the
respect of more sophisticated politicians. But there was a strong
credit side to this, as Lady Asquith has pointed out:

My father and his friends were mostly scholars, steeped in the
classical tradition, deeply imbued with academic knowledge, erudi-

tion and experience. Their intellectual granaries held the harvests of the past. On many themes they knew most of the arguments and all the answers to them. In certain fields of thought there was to them nothing new under the sun. But to Winston Churchill everything under the sun was new – seen and appraised as on the first day of creation. His approach to life was full of ardour and surprise. Even the eternal verities appeared to him to be an exciting personal discovery . . . he was intellectually quite uninhibited and unselfconscious. Nothing to him was trite. The whole world of thought was virgin soil. He did not seem to be the least ashamed of uttering truths so simple and eternal than on another's lips they would be truisms. This was a precious gift he never lost. Nor was he afraid of using splendid language . . . There was nothing false, inflated, artificial in his eloquence. It was his natural idiom. His world was built and fashioned in heroic lines. He spoke its language.[49]

Although Churchill was not bombastic, nor thoughtlessly demagogic, the rhetorician – in private as well as in public – was never far absent. It is not difficult to detect the authentic note in his early letters; we find him, for example, writing in February 1897: 'That British warships should lead the way in protecting the blood-bespattered Turkish soldiery from the struggles of their victims is horrible to contemplate.'[50] He accordingly, even as a young man, tended to be carried away into distant personal realms of thought and attitude. As Isaiah Berlin has commented: 'Churchill is preoccupied by his own vivid world, and it is doubtful how far he has ever been aware of what actually goes on in the heads or hearts of others. He does not react, he acts; he does not mirror, he affects others and alters them to his own powerful measure.'[51]

But there were great and unique advantages in Churchill's approach to words and their employment. His early style owed much to Gibbon, Macaulay and Lord Randolph Churchill, but it was, even at this early stage, peculiarly his own. Even then, at its best it soared to considerable heights of imagery and feeling, then swooping dramatically to detail, humour or the deliberate commonplace. The narrative, whether in speech or in

49. Violet Bonham Carter: *Winston Churchill As I Knew Him*, pp. 17–18.
50. Randolph S. Churchill, op. cit., Companion Volume I, Part 2, p. 734.
51. Isaiah Berlin: *Mr Churchill in 1940*.

writing, was never permitted to be checked by digression. Churchill's almost sensuous feeling for words, his joy in alliteration and his relish for majestic phrases, gave to his private conversation a quality and a power which were quite exceptional. When these were transferred to his public speaking the effect was enthralling. But the problem lay in this very fact of transference, and it was with this problem that Churchill was struggling in these early years, and which was to remain a problem throughout his life.

But there are many perils in the rhetorical approach, of which the principal one is that it can in time lose its impact. Gardiner wrote sharply, but again with some justification, in 1921 of Churchill: 'He does not want to hear your views. He does not want to disturb the beautiful clarity of his thought by the tiresome reminders of the other side. What has he to do with the other side when his side is the right side? He is not arguing with you; he is telling you.' It is possible to discern some impatience with Churchill's rhetoric before 1914; but it was to be in the inter-war years that this became something more than impatience. This voice had been exhorting, cajoling, ordering, thundering, for nearly forty years; it was not surprising that men turned with relief to other voices and other styles.

The world 'style' requires emphasis. Churchill was brought up at the close of the Antonine Age of British parliamentary oratory, 'before the liquefaction of the British political system', as he subsequently wrote. The changes in the structure of British politics after the First World War, and particularly the universal suffrage which Churchill so much deplored and disliked,[52] resulted in a subtle but important alteration to the plane on which political controversy was conducted. There was, furthermore, a new medium of public communication, the radio, which required entirely different techniques from the formal mass-meetings of late Victorian and Edwardian politics.

All this lay far in the future when the young Churchill was struggling against a serious voice impediment and a natural inability to speak in public without copious and lengthy

52. See pp. 381–2.

preparation. Yet these eventual consequences can be traced back to these early problems of technique and temperament. He tended, as Lady Asquith has rightly commented, 'to ignore the need to feel his way about other minds'. There was from the outset an insensitiveness to other opinions which was in one respect a source of strength; he had a mind of his own. But, in the politician as well as in the man, it was a deficiency which was reflected – and was given emphasis – in his oratory. Further-more, there was not yet in his speaking any substantial difference in his techniques for the platform and the House of Commons. He had not yet developed – nor was he ever fully to develop – that change in style and language between Parliament and the platform that characterized Lloyd George, or which had also been a conspicuous feature of Lord Randolph's success. In essence, Churchill had only one style, and it had to be developed for use on all occasions and in all contexts.

But although Churchill's capacities as a public speaker were developing in these years, they were already formidable for so young a man. In invective and raillery he was particularly effective. By 1905 he had stung the Conservatives on several occasions; between 1905 and 1914 he was to do so again and again. He had his father's remarkable capacity for phrases which men remembered when the speech and the context had been forgotten; 'terminological inexactitude' was one example, and another was when he denounced the House of Lords as a 'one-sided, hereditary, unpurged, unrepresentative, irrespon-sible, absentee'. Except on isolated occasions, his early invective lacked the essential ingredient of cruelty, and he was at his most effective when he made deliberate use of humour and sarcasm. In the early years it was perhaps too deliberate, and was usually lacking in subtlety.

One example of this may be seen in an attack on the House of Lords in 1908 as 'filled with old doddering peers, cute financial magnates, clever wirepullers, big brewers with bulbous noses. All the enemies of progress are there – weaklings, sleek, smug, comfortable, self-important individuals.' It was this sort of thing that merited Balfour's sharp comment in 1905 that 'if there is preparation, there should be more finish; and if there

is so much violence there should certainly be more obvious
veracity of feeling'. But the touch became gradually more sure
and effective. Humour, when applied at the correct moment, in
the correct context, and forming part of the argument, is a
valuable weapon; it is also a dangerous one. As Churchill's
style matured, his use of humour became more frequent and
more effective, and constituted an important part of his
oratorical equipment. It was seen to excellent effect in *The
People's Rights*, issued at the end of 1909, of which one example
may suffice:

> 'All civilization,' said Lord Curzon, quoting Renan, 'all civilization
> has been the work of aristocracies.' They liked that in Oldham. There
> was not a duke, not an earl, not a marquis, not a viscount in Oldham
> who did not feel that a compliment had been paid to him. 'All
> civilization has been the work of aristocracies.' It would be much
> more true to say: 'The upkeep of aristocracies has been the hard
> work of all civilizations.'

Another good example may be taken from a speech in the
Commons on 7 August 1911:

> All forms of courage are praiseworthy. But there are two features
> of the courage of the Right Hon. Gentlemen which deserve the
> momentary passing notice of this House. First, it is that kind of
> courage which enables men to stand up unflinchingly and do a foolish
> thing, although they know it is unpopular. Second, it is that kind of
> courage which cannot only be maintained in the face of danger, but
> can even shine brightly in its total absence.

Churchill's application to every major speech was such that
he came armed with facts and with his arguments carefully
developed. In the early years they were often too obviously
carefully developed, and his first major speech as a minister
early in 1906 was a famous disaster.[53] The occasion was a
motion moved by a Liberal back-bencher censuring the conduct
of Lord Milner, the former High Commissioner in South Africa,
with relation to the punishment of Chinese labourers in South
Africa. This was almost the final episode in the unhappy story
of the Chinese labourers introduced into South Africa, in 1903,

53. Although the fact is not evident from Mr Randolph Churchill's
account (op. cit., Vol. II, pp. 181–6).

and which had bulked large in Liberal speeches in the general election campaign. Churchill responded to the motion by proposing an amendment which declared that the House 'while recording its condemnation of the flogging of Chinese coolies in breach of the law, desires, in the interests of peace and conciliation in South Africa, to refrain from passing censure upon individuals'. Churchill's attempt to defend Milner while at the same time criticizing his policies was not successful. Significantly, even when he realized that he was marching towards a fiasco, there could be no departure from the set speech. Read today, it is a good speech; it certainly seemed so when rehearsed to his new secretary, Edward Marsh; but it was fatally ill-tuned to the mood of the House. 'Something went wrong with the delivery,' Marsh has related. 'The harshness of utterance, which in its proper place is one of Winston's assets as a speaker, asserted itself out of season.'[54] Margot Asquith described the speech as 'ungenerous, patronising, and tactless'. 'There is no doubt,' Winterton wrote, 'that this first ministerial speech of Mr Churchill's was a complete failure. His many enemies in the Conservative Party exultantly claimed that he was finished.'[55] Chamberlain was not unjustified in writing on 4 April 1906 that 'Winston Churchill has done very badly as a speaker since he has been in office'.[56] He was much more successful on later occasions, and quickly overcame the bad effects of this initial set-back to his ministerial career. But the peril of a repetition always remained.

Oratory is not merely a matter of technique, and it is impossible to divorce what Rosebery once called 'the character breathing through the sentences' from the impact of a speech. Nevertheless, the technique itself is of supreme importance, and, in Churchill's case, it also revealed much of the character of the man. In the early essay on rhetoric to which reference has already been made, he wrote: 'Abandoned by his party,

54. Edward Marsh: *A Number of People*, pp. 151–2. For Marsh's introduction to Churchill, and the beginning of a lifelong friendship, see Christopher Hassall: *Edward Marsh*.

55. Winterton, op. cit., p. 19.

56. Julian Amery, op. cit., Vol. VI, p. 876.

betrayed by his friends, stripped of his offices, whoever can command this power is still formidable.' The truth of this was to be seen throughout Churchill's career, and never more vividly than in the 1930s. And, when his opportunity finally came, he was in this respect exceptionally well equipped to seize it.

*

This digression has taken us well beyond the point of Churchill's entry into ministerial office for the first time in December 1905. But there was another feature of his personality which, even at that early stage, was plain to see, and which was to remain consistent throughout his career.

Already he had changed parties once, and had incurred deep dislike on this account. To a very exceptional and remarkable extent, Churchill stood apart from Party in the sense that he had no permanent commitment to any. Few men could indulge in the exchange of party acerbities with greater vigour, yet he always regarded Party as essential in the sense that the horse is essential to the rider. Perhaps unhappily, modern political confederations resent such attitudes, particularly as Churchill's shifts of allegiance were never unconnected with his personal interests. Parties like to use men; they intensely dislike being used. 'To his imperious spirit,' as Gardiner commented in 1911, 'a party is only an instrument.' The lines of Pope that he had applied to his father were equally applicable to him:

> Sworn to no master, of no sect am I;
> As drives the storm, at any door I knock.

This lack of total commitment to any party, manifested by his perennial interest in what Asquith once called 'coalitions and odd regroupings', goes far to explain many of the vicissitudes of his career. His dream of the great Centre Party, in perpetual office (a vital factor in the equation), was always present. Yet, whenever Coalitions were formed – as in 1915 and 1931 – Churchill's fortunes were not improved. The advocate of the Centre Party was the principal sufferer whenever it manifested itself in practical terms. Indeed, it was in such circum-

stances that his political rootlessness was most clearly demonstrated, for these were Coalitions of *parties,* and Churchill's
tenuous links with his Party of the time were insufficient to
protect him from his former political opponents who were now
uneasy allies.

Churchill's relationship with the Conservative Party was
destined to be stormy throughout his career. Between 1901 and
1904 he was a turbulent rebel within its ranks; for the next
decade he was among its most vigorous opponents; in the Lloyd
George Coalition between 1917 and 1922 he was a colleague, but
never viewed with enthusiasm by the Conservatives; in 1924 he
rejoined the Conservative Party, but broke with the leadership
in 1931 and henceforward, until war broke out in 1939, was
once again a rebel. It was not altogether to be wondered at
that, as Churchill wrote in the late 1920s, 'the Conservatives
have never liked nor trusted me'. The feeling was reciprocated.
In 1940 their mutual interests brought them together in what
was something considerably less than a love-match and, to the
end, the Conservative Party and Churchill viewed each other
with wariness.

The irony of the situation lay in the fact that Churchill was
fundamentally a very conservative man, a fact that gradually
became more evident in the years 1909–14. 'Lloyd George was
saturated with class consciousness,' Lady Asquith has written.
'Winston accepted class distinction without thought.' This was
one aspect of Churchill's attitudes, but it was an important one.
Although he made vehement common cause with Lloyd George
against the Naval Estimates for 1909–10, this was an episode
which was politically out of character. It may be at least partly
ascribed to Lloyd George's personal influence over him, which
was strong at this time, and also to recollections of Lord
Randolph's battles in the cause of economy. 'I hope you will
not expect me to advocate a braggart and sensational policy of
expenditure on armaments,' he said in a speech at Manchester
in May 1909. 'I have always been against that as my father was
before. In my judgement a Liberal is a man who ought to stand
as a restraining force against an extravagant policy.' The dispute was for a time a very fierce one, and one of its many

oddities was an open letter by Churchill to his constituents – a
form of public address that had been used by Lord Randolph on
many occasions, and to which Churchill frequently made
recourse – that claimed to expose 'four cardinal errors' in
government policy. But after this episode, Churchill's attitudes
towards foreign affairs and naval matters were in principle very
close to those of the Conservatives. And it was during this
period that the gap opened between himself and the bulk of the
Liberal Party. But, even in the immediately preceding period,
Churchill's basic conservatism was a conspicuous feature of his
political attitudes.

When Asquith succeeded the dying Campbell-Bannerman in
1908 he promoted Churchill to the Cabinet as President of the
Board of Trade. The promotion was well merited. As Under-
Secretary of State for the Colonies Churchill had taken a leading
part in the establishment of independent constitutions for the
Boer Republics. His contribution to this success has been
rightly emphasized by his biographer and by Mr Ronald Hyam,
who have told the story in its full detail. The speech in which he
appealed – in vain – to the Opposition to support the Government was perhaps the most formidable he had yet delivered,
and substantially added to this growing reputation:

There is a higher authority which we should earnestly desire to
obtain. I make no appeal, but I address myself particularly to the Rt
Hon. gentlemen who sit opposite, who are long versed in public
affairs, and who will not be able all their lives to escape from a heavy
South African responsibility. They are the accepted guides of a
Party which, though a minority in this House, nevertheless embodies
nearly half the nation. I will ask them seriously whether they will
not pause before they commit themselves to violent or rash denunciation of this great arrangement . . . with all our majority we can only
make it the gift of a Party; they can make it the gift of England.

He had done very well in his first ministerial post, although it
would be unwise to accept his son's estimate that 'it may be
concluded that already at the age of thirty-two he was a fully
equipped statesman'.[57]

57. Randolph S. Churchill, op. cit., Vol. II, p. 193; Ronald Hyam: *Elgin
and Churchill at the Colonial Office, 1905–8.*

Other posts had been considered for him by Asquith, including the Local Government Board, which Churchill had rejected, among other reasons, because of his ignorance of social legislation and domestic politics. At the Board of Trade he was to be deeply involved in both. Indeed, Churchill flung himself into the cause of social reform with characteristic ardour and determination, and his achievements were considerable. The establishment of labour exchanges in 1909; the measures to curb the excesses of 'sweated' labour; the Miners Accidents Act, 1910, and the Coal Mines Act of 1911, owed much to his direct intervention and energy, and constituted, as the author of the labour exchange project, William Beveridge, has written, 'a striking illustration of how much the personality of the Minister in a few critical months may change the course of social legislation'.[58] Perhaps most important of all was his part in the passage of the National Insurance Act of 1911, of which his responsibility was the unemployment insurance section. As a minister he had three outstanding qualities. He worked hard; he put his proposals efficiently through the Cabinet and Parliament; he carried his Department with him. These ministerial merits are not as common as might be thought.

Churchill could never do his abilities justice unless he was excited about a matter, and he quickly invested his work at the Board of Trade with a dramatic and romantic quality. It was indeed this very vitality and air of drama that alarmed even those who liked and admired him, and which aroused a certain scepticism about his motives among men who had been long concerned with the social problems that Churchill now so fervently espoused. As Gardiner commented – part in admiration, part in alarm – in 1908: 'More than any man of his time, he approaches an issue without mental reserves and obscure motives and restraints. You see all the processes of his mind. He does not "hum and ha". He is not paralysed by the fear of consequences, nor afraid to contemplate great changes. He is out for adventure. He follows politics as he would follow the hounds.'

Charles Masterman, perhaps the most acute and sensitive of

58. Beveridge: *Power and Influence*, p. 87.

the young Liberal social reformers, wrote to his future wife in
February 1908:

Winston swept me off to his cousin's house and I lay on his bed
while he dressed and marched about the room, gesticulating and
impetuous, pouring out all his hopes and plans and ambitions. He is
full of the poor whom he has just discovered. He thinks he is called
by Providence – to do something for them. 'Why have I always been
kept safe within a hair's breadth of death,' he asked, 'except to do
something like this? I'm not going to live long,' was also his refrain.
He is getting impatient, although he says he can wait. I challenged
him once on his exposition of his desire to do something for the
people. 'You can't deny you enjoy it all immensely – the speeches,
and crowds, the sense of increasing power.' 'Of course I do,' he said.
'Thou shalt not muzzle the ox when he treadeth out the corn. That
shall be my plea at the day of judgement.' I always feel of immense
age when I am with him – though he's only a year younger than I
am. 'Sometimes I feel as if I could lift the whole world on my
shoulders,' he said last night.[59]

It is in no sense to denigrate Churchill's considerable achievements at the Board of Trade and subsequently at the Home
Office in 1910–11 to question his son's reiterated claim that he
was one of 'the architects of the modern Welfare State'. A
definition of this phrase would furnish a complicated digression,
but the definition of the word architect is less difficult. In none
of Churchill's speeches, save in the most florid and generalized
terms, is there any serious attempt to challenge the essential
foundations of the existing structure nor to depict another one
to replace it. Improvement and reform were desirable and
necessary in Churchill's eyes not to transform society but to
preserve it more effectively. It would have been strange had it
been otherwise, and it would be foolish to judge Churchill's
views on social reform in the years 1908–10 by standards of a
later age. But there was a very substantial difference in approach between Churchill and Lloyd George. As Lady Asquith
has observed:

59. Lucy Masterman: *C. F. G. Masterman*, pp. 97–8. References to
Masterman's comments on Churchill at this time are conspicuous by their
absence in Randolph S. Churchill, op. cit., Volume II. Gardiner, also, is
wholly omitted.

From Lloyd George he was to learn the language of Radicalism. It was Lloyd George's native tongue, but it was not his own, and despite his efforts he spoke it 'with a difference'. This difference may not have been detected by his audiences but it was recognized by those who knew both the teacher and his pupil.[60]

'He desired in England,' as Masterman wrote, 'a state of things where a benign upper class dispensed benefits to an industrious, *bien pensant*, and grateful working class.'

It was not surprising that there were many Liberals who wondered how deep Churchill's radicalism went, and who doubted the consistency and sincerity of Churchill's social reform period.[61] This concern was fairly expressed when Beatrice Webb remarked on his 'capacity for quick appreciation and rapid execution of new ideas, whilst hardly comprehending the philosophy beneath them'.[62] In 1908 A. G. Gardiner was not alone when he pondered on the questions of whether the young man possessed staying power and whether he had any driving motivation save ambition:

Can one who has devoured life with such feverish haste retain his zest to the end of the feast? How will forty find him? – that fatal forty when the youth of roselight and romance has faded into the light of common day and the horizon of life has shrunk incalculably, and when the flagging spirit no longer answers to the spur of external things but must find its motive and energy from within, or find them not at all . . . The sense of high purpose is not yet apparent through the fierce joy of battle that posesses him. The passion for humanity, the resolve to see justice done though the heavens fall and he be buried in the ruins – these things have yet to come. His eye is less on the fixed stars than on the wayward meteors of the night. And when the exhilaration of youth is gone, and the gallop of high spirits has run its course, it may be that this deficiency of abiding and high-compelling purpose will be a heavy handicap. Then it will be seen how far courage and intellectual address, a mind acutely responsive

60. Lady Asquith, op. cit., p. 161.

61. One reason is suggested by Lady Asquith (op. cit., p. 135): 'It was not in principle or theory that he differed from the rank and file of his party. It was the soil from which he had sprung, his personal background, context and experience which made him seem a foreign body among them, and as such, at times (unjustly) suspect.'

62. Beatrice Webb: *Our Partnership*, p. 404.

to noble impulses, and a quick and apprehensive political instinct will carry him in the leadership of men.

*

Churchill's Liberalism may be examined in his speeches, and particularly those which he published in *Liberalism and the Social Problem* in 1909. Churchill, in company with all Liberals, had the problem of retaining in a single political structure what might be loosely called the 'old' Liberal Party and the new Labour Party, which was not yet – and was not to be until 1918 – a separate party with a separate programme, but nevertheless carrying with it individuals and ideologies that were not accommodated in the traditional Liberal philosophies and attitudes.

In October 1906, at Glasgow, he declared that 'the fortunes and the interests of Liberalism and Labour are inseparably interwoven. They rise by the same forces, they face the same enemies, they are affected by the same dangers.' The theme that he expounded in this speech, and in many later ones, was that the moderateness of Liberal reforms would ensure success, whereas extremism would imperil it: 'By gradual steps, by steady effort from day to day, from year to year, Liberalism enlists hundreds of thousands upon the side of progress and popular democratic reform whom militant Socialism would drive into violent Tory reaction. That is why the Tory Party hate us . . . The cause of the Liberal Party is the cause of the left-out millions.' The State, he argued, had real responsibilities – up to a point. Thus, competition and free enterprise should not be impaired, but 'the consequences of failure' could be mitigated: 'We do not want to pull down the structure of science and civilization, but to spread a net over the abyss.' There was then a sentence of considerable significance: 'I am sure that if the vision of a fair Utopia which cheers and lights the imagination of the roving multitudes should ever break into reality, it will be by developments through, modifications in, and by improvements of, the existing competitive organization of society.'

The principal interest of these speeches lies in their increasing insistence upon the maintenance of the structure of society and the importance of 'gradualness'. The 1905–14 Liberal Government was far removed from any revolutionary instincts, and, for all its achievements, it tinkered in a conspicuously *ad hoc* manner with the great social and economic problems. An Administration headed by Asquith, and in which Sir Edward Grey, Haldane, Augustine Birrell, Lord Crewe and John Morley held prominent positions, was unlikely to adopt sweeping and dramatic novelties unless – as in the case of the House of Lords' wanton provocation between 1906 and 1909, culminating in the rejection of the 1909 Finance Bill – such acts were forced upon it. Particularly in industrial and economic matters, this was a very conservative government, deeply committed to the economic *status quo*, and, in fact, elected to defend it. It was natural and proper for Churchill to denounce Protection as 'a mere grimace of cynical mockery' and an 'impudent irrelevance'. Churchill, although among the most vigorous and energetic of ministers, did not inject a revolutionary spirit into the Administration. Churchill's radical attitudes began to harden into something close to conservatism as early as 1909, when serious industrial unrest began to cause real concern, but even in 1908, in the course of the by-election at Dundee occasioned by his defeat in Manchester,[63] he delivered an assault on Socialism which merits quotation:

Liberalism is not Socialism, and never will be. There is a great gulf fixed. It is not a gulf of method, it is a gulf of principle . . . Socialism seeks to pull down wealth, Liberalism seeks to raise up poverty. Socialism would destroy private interests; Liberalism would preserve private interests in the only way in which they can be safely and justly preserved, namely by reconciling them with public right. Socialism would kill enterprise; Liberalism would rescue enterprise from the trammels of privilege and preference . . . Socialism exalts the rule; Liberalism exalts the man. Socialism attacks capital; Liberalism attacks monopoly.

63. Under the electoral law that existed until 1918, all ministers on taking office had to vacate their seats and seek re-election. On his promotion to the Cabinet as President of the Board of Trade Churchill was obliged to seek re-election. He was defeated at North-West Manchester, but found succour at Dundee.

Disillusionment with Churchill in the Labour Party and in
parts of the Liberal Party was not based on his attacks upon
Socialism – which were echoed by Lloyd George and other
Liberal ministers – so much as on his conduct of the railway
strike of 1911. Before this there had been a potentially dangerous situation in the South Wales coalfields, in which Churchill,
as Home Secretary, had acted with restraint and skill; in May
1910 he had been rightly very reluctant to consider the dispatch
of troops to cope with violence in Newport, and in the event the
situation had been taken under control before the necessity
arose. In November an even more serious strike began in the
Rhondda Valley, and the local authorities appealed for troops
to put down the disorder; troops were made available, but their
employment was strictly controlled at Churchill's insistence.
Throughout, Churchill insisted that neither the police nor the
military were to be used as strike breakers, nor were they to be
regarded as being at the disposal of the mine-owners. 'Looking
back now,' George Isaacs wrote in 1953, 'it is difficult to see
what else a resolute Home Secretary could have done, given the
situation in which such bitter industrial relations were allowed
to develop.' [64] Nor were these isolated incidents. In the London
Dock Strike of 1911 Churchill's influence was described by the
dockers' leader, Ben Tillett, as a moderating and responsible
one [65] as, indeed, it was. In Churchill's defence it must be further
recalled that the wave of industrial unrest in 1910–11 was
characterized by exceptional violence and disturbance, which
no government could tolerate. Churchill's responsibility as
Home Secretary was for the preservation of law and order, and
this had been most successfully achieved until the rail strike of
1911. In this crisis his conduct was less easy to explain or
defend, and it was the kind of action that merited Lloyd
George's comparison of him to 'a chauffeur who apparently is
perfectly sane and drives with great skill for months, then
suddenly takes you over a precipice'. [66] Without waiting for

64. George Isaacs: 'Churchill and the Trade Unions' (*Churchill by His
Contemporaries*, p. 369).
    65. Ben Tillett: *History of the London Transport Workers' Strike, 1911.*
    66. Diary of Thomas Jones, 8 June 1922.

requests from the local authorities, Churchill mobilized fifty
thousand troops supplied with twenty rounds of ammunition
each, and dispatched them to all strategic points.

These actions aroused a storm of criticism, some of which was
echoed in ministerial circles. Mr Randolph Churchill has
hastened so swiftly past this crucial episode that only the most
attentive reader will be aware of its significance. The important
point was Churchill's instruction that the military commanders
were to ignore the regulation that forbade the use of the military
unless it was specifically requested by the civil authority. This
was a very serious abrogation of control by the Home Secretary,
whose consequences could have been alarming.

The most violent hostility came from the normally placid
Labour Party. 'This is not a medieval state,' Ramsay Mac-
Donald declared, 'and it is not Russia; it is not even Germany.
. . . If the Home Secretary had just a little bit more knowledge
of how to handle masses of men in these critical times, if he had
a somewhat better instinct of what civil liberty does mean . . .
we should have had much less difficulty during the last four or
five days in facing and finally settling the problem.' Masterman
criticized Churchill for his 'whiff-of-grapeshot attitude' and
even of 'longing for blood', which was somewhat excessive
criticism. The concern of the Liberal press at Churchill's
attitudes was well demonstrated in a memorable attack by
Gardiner in the *Daily News*:

He is always unconsciously playing a part – an heroic part. And
he is himself his most astonished spectator. He sees himself moving
through the smoke of battle – triumphant, terrible, his brow clothed
with thunder, his legions looking to him for victory, and not looking
in vain. He thinks of Napoleon;[67] he thinks of his great ancestor.
Thus did they bear themselves; thus in this awful and rugged crisis
will he bear himself. It is not make-believe, it is not insincerity; it
is that in this fervid and picturesque imagination there are always
great deeds afoot, with himself cast by destiny in the Agamemnon

67. The point was a good one. Napoleon fascinated Churchill, and Margot
Asquith records that in 1906 John Morley remarked that 'he would do better
to study the drab heroes of life. Framing oneself upon Napoleon has proved
a danger to many a man before him' (M. Bonham Carter: *The Autobiography of Margot Asquith*, p. 251).

role. Hence that portentous gravity that sits on his youthful
shoulders so oddly, those impressive postures and tremendous
silences, the body flung wearily in the chair, the head resting gloomily
in the hand, the abstracted look, the knitted brow. Hence that
tendency to exaggerate a situation which is so characteristic of
him – the tendency that sent artillery down to Sidney Street during
the railway strike, dispatched the military hither and thither as
though Armageddon was upon us.

This was an important incident, as it demonstrated one
aspect of Churchill's personality that had already occasioned
some disquiet in a party dedicated to 'Peace, Retrenchment,
and Reform'. Immediately before the strike there had occurred
the tragi-comic episode known as 'the siege of Sidney Street',
in which Churchill had personally superintended military operations against a gang of desperadoes taking refuge in a house in
the East End of London.[68] It was all very colourful and melodramatic, but it seemed to many commentators to be excessively
so and to reveal indications not merely of a delight in dramatic
situations, but also a lack of a sense of proportion.

The railway strike intervention seemed to emphasize this
latter feature. It was described by MacDonald as 'diabolical',
and the general reaction of Labour was vehement. In George
Isaacs's words, 'his reputation with organized labour suffered a
severe blow', and it was significant that the Conservative press
applauded his actions, whereas it had attacked his policy of
restraint in South Wales. The railway strike was settled almost
immediately after Lloyd George intervened to restore the situation, but this was a real turning-point in Churchill's relations
with Labour. In Labour mythology, indeed, Churchill became
held responsible – wholly unjustly – for the deaths of two miners
at Tonypandy, and his actions in the railway strike were transferred to the South Wales situation. 'Once more,' Keir Hardie
declared, 'the Liberals are in office and Asquith is Prime
Minister, and troops are let loose upon the people to shoot
down if need be whilst they are fighting for their legitimate
rights.' Despite numerous and unanswerable accounts of what

68. By far the best account is by Churchill himself in *Thoughts and
Adventures*.

actually occurred, the canard of 'Tonypandy' has proved enduring.

*

Churchill's early attitudes to expenditure on the Army have
been referred to; in 1908 he was Lloyd George's most vigorous
ally in his battle against increased Navy expenditure. But these
attitudes were changing before the Agadir Crisis of 1911.
Characteristically he then became totally absorbed in the
potential dangers. As he has written:

> Once I got drawn in, it dominated all other interests in my mind.
> For seven years I was to think of little else. Liberal politics, the
> People's Budget, Free Trade, Peace, Retrenchment and Reform – all
> the war cries of our election struggles began to seem unreal in the
> presence of this new preoccupation. Only Ireland held her place
> among the grim realities which came one after another into view.[69]

Churchill's move from the Home Office to the Admiralty in
August 1911 marked the decisive end of the 'social reform'
period. Before this moment he had acquired a reputation for
interesting himself in activities beyond his own departmental
sphere, that had prompted Grey to remark that 'Winston, very
soon, will become incapable from sheer activity of mind of being
anything in a Cabinet but Prime Minister.' This intellectual
activity was responsible for a memorandum written in August
1911 on 'Military Aspects of the Continental Problem', described subsequently by the author as 'an attempt to pierce the
veil of the future; to conjure up in the mind a vast imaginary
situation; to balance the incalculable; to weigh the imponder-
able'.[70] This remarkable document preceded the celebrated
meeting of the Committee of Imperial Defence on 23 August,
when the performance of the War Office was so superior to that
of the Admiralty that Haldane informed Asquith that he 'could
not continue to be responsible for military affairs unless he made
a sweeping reform at the Admiralty'.[71] Haldane wanted the

69. *The World Crisis*, Vol. I, p. 52.
70. *The World Crisis*, Vol. I, p. 60. The text is on pp. 60–64.
71. Haldane: *Autobiography*, p. 228.

Admiralty; so did Churchill, and he secured it. Henceforth, until May 1915, the Navy was his whole life. 'I could not think of anything else but the peril of war,' he wrote. 'I did my other work as it came along, but there was only one field of interest fiercely illuminated in my mind.'[72] 'His high-mettled spirit,' Grey subsequently wrote, 'was exhilarated by the air of crisis and high events.'[73]

The break was so complete, and his absorption with his new task so total, that it inevitably revived the suspicions that his commitment to the cause of social reform had been shallow, and even opportunist. Even if this charge was unfair, his transfer to the Admiralty did emphasize one important aspect of Churchill's character which has tended to receive inadequate attention, and which was well expressed by Lord Esher in 1917: 'He handles great subjects in rhythmical language, and becomes quickly enslaved by his own phrases. He deceives himself into the belief that he takes broad views, when his mind is fixed upon one comparatively small aspect of the question.'

His period at the Admiralty was far from uncontroversial, but although a close analysis of his work will find much to criticize, there was far more to praise.[74] He had foresight, he worked indefatigably, and his dedication to the Navy was complete. Mistakes were made, and his flamboyance was on occasions regarded as disagreeable, but the credit side was very substantial. This was perhaps the happiest period of Churchill's life. He was at the height of his abilities and energies, in charge of a department which he administered with dash and zeal. It is impossible to think of any of his colleagues in the pre-war Liberal Government accomplishing so much – or half as much – in so short a time. This is a point which many of his critics have failed to take into account. This was a predominantly pacifist Government, notably deficient in men with any practical experience of – and even interest in – naval and military affairs. This applied with far greater strength to the Parliamentary

72. *The World Crisis*, Vol. I, p. 65.

73. Grey: *Twenty-Five Years*, Vol. I, p. 238.

74. Professor Marder's *From the Dreadnought to Scapa Flow* is the most objective and comprehensive account that has yet appeared.

Liberal Party and to its Labour wing. Many of Churchill's contemporary critics denigrated him at least partly because he was not a Conservative, and was accordingly reckless, ignorant, and unprincipled, a political upstart with no understanding of the glorious traditions and methods of work of the Royal Navy. Some of his subsequent detractors have censured him for not being a military and political paragon. Within the limits in which he had to work, Churchill did a great deal, for which he did not at the time receive adequate credit, and which has been denied to him by some subsequent commentators.

It has already been remarked that Youth and Ambition are regarded with suspicion in England. Activity and Energy are hardly less suspect. Young men who tackle problems with ardour, unafraid of committing errors and prepared to accept these as the necessary price for great advances, tend to be regarded with much concern. As the young man strides on his way, eager and impetuous, fascinated admiration quickly changes to alarm and criticism, and ugly mutterings are to be heard. When the young man is flamboyant, conscious of the value of personal publicity, and evidently relishing his situation, the ill-will increases further. It is always safest in England, and particularly for young men, to do nothing save by stealth and guile; the safest course of all is to do nothing whatever, and thereby acquire a reputation for shrewdness and soundness. For Churchill, stealth and guile were unfathomable and un-worthy methods and, above all, too slow. And so he charged on, making some mistakes and doing much that was excellent, and leaving in his path an ever-growing multitude of critics who were repelled less by the actions themselves than by their originator and his methods, and who formed a hostile element to the activity and energy which Churchill so completely exemplified.

It was not possible for him to hold himself apart from domestic politics, now entering a particularly harsh and difficult period. Some at least of this intervention must have been prompted by the realization that his policies and attitudes at the Admiralty were looked at askance by his colleagues and in the Liberal Party at large. But his interventions did little to arrest the decline in his position in the Liberal Party, and it resulted in a further heightening of the mistrust felt towards him in the Conservative ranks. The immediate cause was the Irish Question, which at the beginning of 1912 had entered a new and violent phase with the introduction of the third Home Rule Bill.

*

The division between the main parties – and it was a deep and wide one indeed – concerned the future of the nine counties of Ulster. In 1886 Lord Randolph had coined the ringing phrase 'Ulster will fight: Ulster will be right'. This was once more the cry of Ulster in 1912 when again threatened with subordination to Southern Ireland in an Irish Parliament. The Ulstermen had a new leader at Westminster, Sir Edward Carson. The new Conservative leader – who had succeeded Balfour in November 1911 – was Andrew Bonar Law, who was deeply committed, personally and politically, to the maintenance of Ulster's ties with Britain. It was, from the onset, a bitter, exhausting, and dangerous dispute; it was to get progressively more bitter, exhausting, and dangerous. It was to bring the United Kingdom to the edge of civil war in the summer of 1914. It was to poison further the already dark relations between the main political parties. As had happened so often in the past, it was to cast down reputations, raise others up, and warp and distort the course of British political history.

As Lord Randolph Churchill's son, Churchill's position was a difficult one. In a particularly striking passage in the biography of his father he had compared the study of the 1886 Home Rule crisis to a visit to a deserted battlefield, long abandoned by the armies that had contested those few acres 'of rank grass and scattered stone'. The impression given by that passage is that the author regarded the Irish Question as belonging to the realm of far-off things. Yet there was one significant passage:

A proposal to establish by statute, subject to guarantees of Imperial supremacy, a colonial Parliament in Ireland for the trans-action of Irish business may indeed be unwise, but is not, and ought not to be, outside the limits of calm and patient consideration. Such a proposal is not necessarily fraught with the immense and terrific consequences which were so generally associated with it.[75]

Between the downfall of Parnell in 1891 and the fall of the Balfour Government the Irish Question had passed through a period of relative quiescence. The hideous divisions in the Irish Nationalist Party that had followed Parnell's crash had temporarily paralysed the movement that had, throughout the 1880s, in one manner or another dominated the British political scene. Gladstone's second Home Rule Bill had been rejected by the House of Lords in 1893 without any demonstration of surprise or even regret in England and with relatively few indications of bitterness in Ireland. After the turmoil of the previous twenty years, the issue seemed to have relapsed in exhaustion on both sides. Following the policy of 'killing Home Rule by kindness' on the one hand and maintaining order under the inspiration of Salisbury's dictum of 'Twenty years of resolute government', many of the old sources of Irish grievance were removed.[76] The settlement of the land question in 1902 seemed to mark the effective close of a particularly tragic period in the dismal story of the Anglo-Irish relationship. The emergence of an entirely new and more profound form of nationalism was undetected. The creation of Sinn Fein by Arthur Griffith in 1906 was not regarded as significant. It was only much later that it was realized that the elimination of the disparate courses of former grievances – and particularly that of the land – had resulted in a coalescing of the various movements into one movement. But this was wisdom long after the event. To all appearances, Ireland remained peaceful.

Thus, compared with the other issues of contemporary British politics, the Irish Question seemed to have faded away into insignificance. John Redmond had patiently re-created the shattered Parnellite party, but he was no Parnell. Churchill, who had described an Irish Parliament in 1904 as 'dangerous and impracticable', wrote in his biography of his father of 'some unthinkable coincidence' which would re-create the

75. *Lord Randolph Churchill*, p. 439.
76. See L. P. Curtis: *Concession and Conciliation in Ireland, 1880–92.*

circumstances of 1886. Liberal references to Home Rule in the 1905 General Election were positive enough to alarm Lord Rosebery,[77] yet were in fact deliberately evasive. Home Rule, it was seen on close inspection, remained in the Liberal programme, yet so far down as to be virtually invisible. For his part, Churchill in his campaign in North-West Manchester in the 1905 election attacked 'the harsh and senseless reiteration of the cry of Home Rule'. Between 1906 and the first General Election of 1910, the Liberals made no move towards Home Rule. But the removal of their independent majority immediately transformed their attitude. In the constitutional struggles against the entrenched Conservative majority in the House of Lords, the Liberals and the Irish had a common interest. But Irish support, essential to the survival of the Government, had its price. Without either enthusiasm or illusions the Liberal Party turned back to the issue that had wrecked them in 1886 and which had done much to keep them in sterile Opposition for most of the succeeding two decades.

Home Rule was not a cause to which Churchill warmed. (Nor, it may be remarked, was it one that greatly stirred the passions either of Asquith or Lloyd George.) 'A settlement of the Irish difficulties on broad and generous lines,' Churchill had said in April 1908, would be 'indispensable to any harmonious conception of Liberalism.' There were many other statements of a similar nature. Put together they might at first sight constitute the basis for an argument that Churchill had retained an active interest in the Irish Question for some time. In fact, in relation to his manifold other interests, Ireland counted for very little. His refusal to contemplate the post of Chief Secretary for Ireland in 1910 was understandable; with the notable exception of Arthur Balfour, the post had been disastrous for aspiring politicians. Ireland had, however, now become a major political issue again, and isolation from it was impossible.

By April 1912, when the Government brought forward the third Home Rule Bill, the chances of 'a settlement of the Irish difficulties on broad and generous lines' had already almost vanished. In Ulster the old alarms and antagonisms had been

77. See the author's biography of Rosebery, pp. 454–7.

fiercely revived, and in Carson the Ulster Unionists had found a leader whose determined mien and belligerent statements faithfully reflected their harsh intransigence. It was not possible for Redmond or his followers to accept the demands of Ulster for separate treatment and exclusion from an Irish Parliament. In England, old passions – religious, social, political and national – were re-awakened. The events of 1905–11 and the resultant bitter feelings between the two major parties ensured that the battle would be fought with intensity and ardour in the House of Commons.

In private, Churchill accepted the strength of the Ulster case, and his actions throughout 1912 and 1913 were designed to secure a compromise, however remote the possibility might be. 'My general view is just what I told you earlier in the year,' he wrote to Redmond on 31 August 1912, ' – namely, that something should be done to afford the characteristically Protestant and Orange counties the option of a moratorium of several years before acceding to the Irish Parliament.'[78] Introducing the second reading of the Home Rule Bill in the Commons on 30 April he had said that 'I admit that the perfectly genuine apprehensions of the majority of the people of North-East Ulster constitute the most serious obstacle to a thoroughly satisfactory settlement . . . But whatever Ulster's rights may be, she cannot stand in the way of the whole of the rest of Ireland.'

Private moderation was not always reflected in Churchill's public attitudes. In this he was not alone. At Blenheim Palace, in June 1912, Law, Carson and F. E. Smith addressed a Unionist rally in terms which invited extreme measures and attitudes in Ulster. Bonar Law described the Government as

a revolutionary committee which has seized upon despotic power by fraud. In our opposition to them we shall not be guided by the restraints which would influence us in an ordinary constitutional struggle . . . I said the other day in the House of Commons and I repeat here that there are things stronger than Parliamentary majorities . . . I can imagine no length of resistance to which Ulster can go in which I should not be prepared to support them, and in

78. Dennis Gwynn: *Life of John Redmond*, p. 214.

which, in my belief, they would not be supported by the over-whelming majority of the British people.

The full implications of these attitudes did not escape Churchill. In an open letter to the Chairman of the Dundee Liberal Party he declared that:

There are many millions of very poor people in this island, divorced from the land, crowded into the back streets of cities, forced to toil for a scanty reward through their whole span of existence, who suffer the cruel sting and pressure of circumstances and have little else, except their lives, to whom these counsels of violence and mutiny may not be unattractive and who may be lured to their own and public disaster by hearkening to them. The doctrines of Mr Bonar Law at Blenheim are the doctrines of Mr Ben Tillett on Tower Hill. But Tillett's men were starving.

A visit by Churchill to Belfast in February 1912 was charac-teristically courageous, but was hardly calculated to calm passions in that divided and fevered city. 'The flame of Irish nationality is inextinguishable,' he declared on that occasion; and then, with defiance, he said: 'If Ulster would fight for the honour of Ireland, for reconciliation of races, and for forgiveness of ancient wrongs, for the consolidation of the Empire, then indeed "Ulster will fight and Ulster will be right."'

By the end of 1913 the situation had deteriorated grievously. The Ulster volunteers were arming and training, urged on by Carson, Bonar Law, and F. E. Smith. The relations between the two British parties were as bad as they could have been, short of actual physical combat. There was every indication that the Government was rapidly losing – if it had not lost it already – any measure of control over the situation. The Lords had rejected the Home Rule Bill twice; under the terms of the Parliament Act of 1911 Home Rule would come into force in the autumn of 1914 notwithstanding the House of Lords – and what then?

It was at this moment that Churchill, endeavouring – as he has frankly admitted – to strengthen himself with the Liberal Party, 'mingled actively in the Irish controversy'.[79]

79. *The World Crisis*, Vol. I, p. 178.

In *The World Crisis* Churchill sought to explain his intervention by weighing sombrely on the pressures to which a
politician is exposed because of the violence of the feelings of his
supporters:

It is greatly to be hoped that British political leaders will never
again allow themselves to be goaded and spurred and driven by each
other or by their followers into the excesses of partisanship which on
both sides disgraced the year 1914 . . . To fall behind is to be a
laggard or a weakling, not sincere, not courageous; to get in front of
the crowd, if only to command them and to deflect them, prompts
often very violent action.[80]

The pressures to which politicians are subjected are often very
formidable, and were very heavy indeed in 1914, but there were
other factors involved. The remarkably well publicized disputes
in the Cabinet over the Naval Estimates necessitated the
restoration of Churchill's *bona fides* with his party. Furthermore,
a policy of drift and indecision was alien to his own temper, and
also to that of the Liberal rank and file. These were factors
enough, but it was characteristic of Churchill that, once he had
resolved to intervene, he went in whole-heartedly to the point
of folly. It was exactly this kind of thing that had made Haldane
write of him in 1911 that 'he is too apt to act first and think
afterwards, though of his energy and courage one cannot speak
too highly'. It was all very well to have been in private, as
Austen Chamberlain acknowledged, 'the prime mover' in
proposing compromises and working for a settlement; what the
public saw was the manifestation of a devout party firebrand,
heedless of the damage he might cause by violent and aggressive
action. Such contrast in political stances is not uncommon. It is
frequently necessary to raise the party banner in public while
planning compromise in private. But such manœuvres require
finesse and caution, and neither adjective can reasonably be
applied to Churchill's actions in the spring of 1914.

A student of Churchill's attitudes to Ireland has commented
with justice that 'Churchill's policy was, in essence, an English
policy and not an Irish policy, either Unionist or Nationalist.

80. *The World Crisis*, Vol. I, p. 183.

In his childhood he had grown up on the assumption that the
independence of a hostile Ireland menaced Britain . . . By
means of compromise he hoped for a friendly Ireland.'[81] The
loss of control of the situation by the Government – the first
example of Asquith's deficiencies as a Prime Minister in a
crisis, that were to be more clearly demonstrated in the war –
irked Churchill, and justifiably. As always, he wanted to have
a policy, and a clear and simple one. Furthermore, the threat
posed by the Ulster Volunteers was not one which he was
prepared to tolerate.

We are here seeing another crucially important aspect of
Churchill's character, and one that can hardly be over-
emphasized. He was prepared to negotiate – but not under
duress. Whenever confronted by an adversary in serious mood,
he stood his ground. When the adversary was crushed, he would
offer the hand of conciliation and friendship. It was an essential
part of Churchill's philosophy that capitulation had to precede
negotiation.[82]

The circumstances under which, with the apparent approval
and certainly the knowledge of the Cabinet, Churchill ordered
units of the Home Fleet to Lamlash, have often been described.
On 11 March Asquith appointed a Cabinet Committee consisting
of Lord Crewe (Chairman), Birrell, Churchill, Seely (Secretary

---

81. Mary C. Bromage: *Churchill and Ireland*, p. 51.

82. He himself emphasized this point repeatedly during his career, and
perhaps the most striking example is to be found in *My Early Life* (pp.
327–8):

> I have always urged fighting wars and other contentions with might
> and main till overwhelming victory, and then offering the hand of
> friendship to the vanquished. Thus, I have always been against the
> Pacifists during the quarrel, and against the Jingoes at its close . . . I
> thought we ought to have conquered the Irish and then given them
> Home Rule: that we ought to have starved out the Germans, and then
> revictualled their country: and that after smashing the General Strike,
> we should have met the grievances of the miners.

Another example may be found in a note by Duff Cooper of a conversation
with Churchill in 1920: 'His great line was that you could only make concessions to people you had beaten. He instanced the success of this in South
Africa' (Duff Cooper: *Old Men Forget*, p. 103).

of State for War) and Sir John Simon (Attorney General), to consider the danger posed to British depots by the Ulster Volunteers. Lord Crewe was taken ill on the following day, and took no part in the proceedings of this body. On 14 March Lt.-Gen. Sir Arthur Paget, Commander-in-Chief of the Forces in Ireland, was warned by the War Office that attempts might be made 'by evil-disposed persons' to raid ammunition stores and that he should take 'special precautions'. Paget reported that he had issued instructions but (17 March) telegraphed that he did not propose to send troops north to Armagh, Omagh, Carrickfergus and Enniskillen, which had been specifically mentioned in the original communication from the War Office. Paget was summoned to London for consultations.

The Cabinet Committee reported on 17 March that the guards on the depots were to be reinforced, and Churchill announced that the forthcoming practice of the Third Battle Squadron – which consisted of eight battleships and which was lying in Arosa Bay in north-west Spain – would take place off the Isle of Arran. The Cabinet was informed of these actions on 17 March, as Asquith reported to the King on the following day.[83] The allegation that Asquith first heard of the dispatch of the Third Battle Squadron to Lamlash on 21 March is incorrect,[84] but there is some justification for the suspicion that Churchill and Seely were going further than their Cabinet colleagues appreciated. Mr Churchill's defence of his father[85] is somewhat weakened by his failure to mention the fact that no date was given to the Cabinet of the forthcoming practice of the Third Battle Squadron; the orders were given by Churchill on his own responsibility on 19 March. H. A. Gwynne has recorded that Churchill told the Chief of the Imperial General Staff (Sir John French) on the next day 'that if Belfast showed fight his fleet would have the town in ruins in twenty-four hours'.[86]

83 Public Record Office (hereafter referred to as PRO) CAB 42/35/8.

84. See, for example, A. T. Q. Stewart: *The Ulster Crisis*, p. 163. It should be emphasized that the allegation originated with Asquith himself, in the Commons, on 23 March.

85. Randolph S. Churchill, op. cit., Vol. II, p. 491.

86. Robert Blake: *The Unknown Prime Minister*, p. 189.

Acting in close conjunction with his close friend Jack Seely, Churchill forced the pace for applying direct pressure on Ulster.

On 14 March, at Bradford, he flung down the gauntlet in a speech of considerable truculence. He struck a partisan note from the outset, accusing Bonar Law – whom he described as 'a public danger seeking to terrorize the Government and to force his way into the Councils of his Sovereign' – of using the Ulster question purely as a matter of party politics: 'Behind every strident sentence which he rasps out you can always hear the whisper . . . Ulster is our best card: it is our only card.' But this thrust – severe and, it so happened, unfair – was obscured by the declaration that 'there are things worse than bloodshed, even on an extended scale', and by the final threat:

> This is the issue – whether civil and Parliamentary government in these realms is to be beaten down by the menace of armed force . . . If the civil and Parliamentary systems under which we have dwelt so long, and our fathers before us, are to be brought to the crude challenge of force, if the Government and the Parliament of this great country and greater Empire are to be exposed to menace and brutality; if all the loose, wanton and reckless chatter we have been forced to listen to, these many months, is in the end to disclose a sinister and revolutionary purpose, then I can only say to you: 'Let us go forward together and put these grave matters to the proof!'[87]

The Bradford speech, followed by the movement of warships to Lamlash, and the actions of Seely with regard to the officers of the British Army stationed in Ireland, brought the issue to its moment of greatest tension. Carson, after a fierce attack on Churchill on 16 March, made a dramatic departure to Ulster from the House of Commons. In a debate in the Commons on 30 March, F. E. Smith accused Churchill of 'finessing for the firing of the first shot'.[88] Churchill's repudiation of the attacks made

87. This latter phrase was repeated by Churchill in a speech made at Manchester on 29 January 1940. Mr Churchill (op. cit., Vol. II, p. 488) states that the Bradford speech was approved in advance by Asquith, but cites no authority for this statement.

88. This was a particularly interesting comment, in view of the fact that Austen Chamberlain recorded in his diary the previous November that

on him as 'a vote of censure by the criminal classes upon the police' was very much to the point, but hardly calculated to lower the temperature, and invited Balfour's scathing riposte that 'there is one character disgusting to every policeman and which even the meanest criminal thinks inferior to himself in point of morals, and that character is the *agent provocateur.*'

The circumstances under which Seely's political career crashed have been well described in two recent accounts.[89] The Curragh 'mutiny' ended, as a result of Seely's inexperience and folly, in a dire humiliation for the Government. Seely resigned and Asquith took over the War Office himself. The movement of the warships to Lamlash was cancelled on 21 March by Asquith. There was not very much chance of the Ulster Question being discussed calmly and rationally by the opposing sides before March 1914, but what chances there had been were destroyed by the dramatic and extraordinary events of that month. The full story is not yet clear, and Mr Randolph Churchill's account adds nothing to our previous knowledge. As Sir James Fergusson has written of the allegation that a plot was conceived by Churchill and Seely to provoke the Ulster Volunteers into a foolhardy act, 'No categorical answer can be given until the relevant files of the War Office and the Admiralty are laid open to the historian, and even then it may not be complete.'[90] Mr Stewart writes that: 'Whatever may be said about provocation, there can no longer be any doubt that an operation was planned for the coercion of Ulster, and that it was badly planned.'[91] Even if there was no 'plot' as such, and the Conservatives' allegations of an 'Ulster Pogrom' were wildly excessive, the significance of the incident lies in the fact that such charges were generally believed, and it must be conceded

---

Churchill had said to him that 'a little red blood had got to flow before agreement would be reached . . . We shall give no provocation. The Ulstermen will have no excuse, and we think that public opinion will not support them if they wantonly attack' (Petrie: *Chamberlain*, p. 572).

89. A. P. Ryan: *Mutiny at the Curragh*, and Sir James Fergusson: *The Curragh Incident.*

90. Fergusson, op. cit., p. 204.

91. Stewart, op. cit., p. 175.

that the actions and statements of Churchill and Seely had given substantial *prima facie* justification for them.

This episode must be regarded as one of Churchill's least fortunate ventures. To the rank and file Conservatives his actions seemed provocative and belligerent; the failure of the Government to intimidate Ulster removed the last vestiges of confidence in southern Ireland as to the capacity of the Government to control the situation; the Larne gun-running in July was the logical response to the Government's constant timidity towards the Ulstermen in 1912 and 1913; the existence of the Ulster Volunteers was eloquent enough commentary on the extent to which the Liberal Government had failed to take Carson's threats with adequate seriousness until too late.

The events of March 1914 made Churchill an object of peculiar hatred to the Conservatives. Throughout the summer their attacks on him, both inside and outside Parliament, were violent and persistent, and Bonar Law in particular did not forget or forgive what he regarded as Churchill's gross and un-forgivable irresponsibility. Mr Randolph Churchill has written in some mystification that 'no documentary evidence can be found to justify the extraordinary personal malevolence of which he was made the victim.'[92] The justification lay in Churchill's speeches and known actions, and perhaps even more in suspicions that much had been suppressed by the Government. It was indeed the marked reluctance of the Government to reveal any information except after intense parliamentary pressure that furthered this conviction in the Opposition.[93]

Churchill's defence is clear. Throughout, he had attempted to

92. Randolph S. Churchill, op. cit., Vol. II, p. 500.
93. See Blake, op. cit., pp. 205–6: 'Every time Asquith misled the House of Commons, Bonar Law and his colleagues felt a mounting suspicion that there was some dark secret which the Government had been trying to conceal. As the facts were elicited – and the process was as slow and painful as drawing teeth – the Unionists, who were by now in a state of feverish and frenzied rage with the Government, became more and more convinced that Gough's actions alone had frustrated a sinister conspiracy on the part of Seely and Churchill.'

introduce reason into a dispute which, largely because of the
lack of proportion and public responsibility shown by the
Unionist leaders, had degenerated into bitterness and semi-
hysteria, and which threatened the nation with civil war. He
claimed – as has his biographer – that his was a moderating and
sane voice in the dispute until the beginning of 1914, when,
faced with a potentially critical situation in Ulster and a decline
in his standing in the party, he resolved to force the issue
towards a conclusion. Certainly some positive leadership was
required early in 1914 with regard to Ireland, and it is a severe
indictment of Asquith's leadership that matters had drifted
into this crisis situation. But it can also be said that if Churchill's
strategy was justifiable, the manner in which it was conducted
was inept. The Belfast speech of February 1912 had been
virtually the first shot in the controversy, and the Bradford
speech of 14 March 1914 – whether or not it had been approved
by Asquith – had marked a crucial moment in the degeneration
of the dispute. The serious doubts that were cast upon his
judgement in a dangerous and complex situation do not appear
unmerited. And even his 'moderate' attitude between 1912 and
March 1914 must be qualified. Lansdowne was justified in
commenting that Churchill's tactics were 'to make speeches
full of party claptrap and No Surrender with a few sentences
on the end for wise and discerning people to see and ponder'.

The eruption of the European crisis at the end of July pushed
the Irish Question into temporary abeyance. But political
memories are long, and although Churchill – obsessed by the
new and infinitely more serious menace – quickly forgot the
events of March 1914, others did not. When the war opened,
no Act of Oblivion could be passed to obliterate men's memories
of what had occurred so recently. Churchill thus joined the long
list of English politicians whose fortunes were deeply harmed by
intervention in the Irish Question.

*

Churchill has dramatically described the scene in the Cabinet on
24 July when, at the end of a wearying discussion on Ireland,
Grey informed his colleagues of the Austrian ultimatum to

Serbia.[94] Morley's account, although less vivid, is no less dramatic:

> Then Grey in his own quiet way, which is none the less impressive
> for being so simple, and so free from the *cassant* and over-emphatic
> tone that is Asquith's vice on such occasions, made a memorable
> pronouncement. The time had come, he said, when the Cabinet was
> bound to make up its mind plainly whether we were to take an active
> part with the two other Powers of the Entente, or to stand aside in
> the general European question, and preserve an absolute neutrality.
> . . . The Cabinet seemed to heave a sort of sigh, and a moment or
> two of breathless silence fell upon us.[95]

When the European crisis burst open the Government the Cabinet was acutely divided. Of all the ministers, Churchill – 'with his best dæmonic energy', in Morley's words – was the one with the least doubts, going further even than Asquith or Grey in his insistence upon the inevitability and necessity of intervention.

His position was clear from the outset, and his principal contribution was to put pressure on Lloyd George, who was at first opposed to intervention, became hesitant, and finally cast his vote emphatically for war. Morley detected in his conversion the arguments of 'the splendid *condottiere* at the Admiralty' and Lloyd George's calculations of personal advantage. No doubt these played their part, but the most significant role of all was that of the swirling pace of events in Europe. Given time, the Cabinet might well have determined to remain aloof from the conflict, despite the arguments of Grey and Churchill; but time was not vouchsafed to it. So quickly did the crisis develop that Liberal opposition to intervention outside the Cabinet scarcely had time to make itself heard before Belgium's neutrality was violated and the bulk of the Cabinet swung over in favour of intervention. In the Intervention Crisis Churchill's was not the decisive voice. The calm management of the Cabinet by Asquith – whose principal purpose seems to have been the preservation of Cabinet unity *per se*, but whose

94. *The World Crisis*, Vol. I, pp. 192–3.
95. Morley: *Memorandum on Resignation, August 1914*.

personal conviction that intervention was inescapable steadily grew – and the sheer pace of events brought Ministers together. At one point it seemed as though ten Ministers would resign; in the event only Morley and John Burns went. Neither they, nor the former dissidents, misrepresented the Liberal Party. Such evidence as exists[96] points to the dismay of the Liberal rank and file at the prospect of the war, followed by uneasy acceptance. Enthusiasm for the war in the Liberal Party followed, and did not precede, the declaration. Beaverbrook has given a vivid portrait of Churchill – then not forty years of age – on the evening of 1 August:

> For my own part, I simply saw a man who was receiving long-expected news. He was not depressed; he was not elated; he was not surprised. He did not put his head between his hands, as many another eminent man might have done, and exclaim to high heaven that his world was coming to an end. Certainly he exhibited no fear or uneasiness; neither did he show any signs of joy. He went straight out like a man going to a well-accustomed job. We have suffered at times from Mr Churchill's bellicosity. But what profit the nation derived at that critical moment from the capacity of the First Lord of the Admiralty for grasping and dealing with the war situation![97]

But perhaps the best portrait of all is given by Churchill himself in a letter to his wife, written at midnight on 28 July:

> Everything tends towards catastrophe and collapse. I am interested, geared up and happy. Is it not horrible to be built like this? The preparations have a hideous fascination for me. I pray to God to forgive me for such fearful moods of levity. Yet I wd do my best for peace, & nothing wd induce me wrongfully to strike the blow. I cannot feel that we in this island are to any serious degree responsible for the wave of madness wh has swept the mind of Christendom. No one can measure the consequences. I wondered whether those stupid Kings & Emperors cd not assemble together & revivify Kingship by saving the nations from hell but we all drift on in a kind of dull cataleptic trance. As if it was somebody else's operation!

96. There is a particularly interesting collection of letters and resolutions passed by local Liberal Associations in the papers of Lewis Harcourt, then Secretary of State for the Colonies and – until the invasion of Belgium – an opponent of intervention (*Harcourt Papers*).

97. Beaverbrook: *Politicians and the War*, p. 30.

The two black swans on St James's Park lake have a darling cygnet – grey, fluffy, precious & unique. I watched them this evening for some time as a relief from all the plans & schemes . . .[98]

*

In the speed of his elevation and the solid achievements of office Churchill had already outstripped his father by the beginning of August 1914. But he had not succeeded where his father had also failed, for in the eyes of many he had not yet made the crucial development from politician into statesman. Of all the political qualities, that of stature is the most difficult to describe and recapture. The most that can be said is that some men have it, and others do not. Churchill, like his father, was not, politically, a man of stature by August 1914. It was not merely the fact that he had not succeeded in avoiding the same kind of resentment, distrust, and dislike that Lord Randolph had aroused. He had good friends and allies, and those who knew him best liked him best. Although he was a career politician, profoundly ambitious and eager for prominence, he lacked any capacity for intrigue and was refreshingly innocent and straightforward. 'His conversation was pleasing, his companionship was exciting,' as Beaverbrook has remarked. 'He had no rancours and few hatreds.' His vigorous defence of Lloyd George and Rufus Isaacs in the Marconi Affair[99] had demonstrated that he possessed the rare political quality of personal loyalty. Mrs Masterman has written: 'He is an extraordinarily transparent eccentric. Many of his friends have complained of his intriguing in his early days. I never heard or saw any attempt by him that could have taken in a kitten; and

98. Randolph S. Churchill, op. cit., Vol. II, pp. 710–11.

99. This was a strangely-lighted episode, which may be studied in Frances Donaldson: *The Marconi Scandal* (1962). Many commentators have emphasized the fact that neither Lloyd George nor Isaacs made any profit out of their dealings in shares of the American Marconi Company, but it can hardly be assumed that the desire to make a profit was absent from their minds. In fact, they did very well out of the transaction, and it was only when they purchased more shares subsequently that they incurred losses. Looked at in the most favourable light it was an act of astonishing imprudence, and the two Ministers owed everything to the support they received from Asquith and Churchill.

his very vanity is somehow childish and disarming.' His marriage, in 1908, had brought him deep contentment and an ever-loyal – although by no means uncritical – ally. 'There is no more fortunate man than Winston at home or in his political prosperity,' Blunt had noted in 1909.[100] But despite domestic happiness, personal affection and political success, his political character evoked controversy and criticism.

Churchill, both at this stage and for much of his career, followed his own star, and his impetuosity and belligerence not infrequently brought himself – and the Government of which he was a member – into unnecessary difficulties. His enjoyment of adventure and his restless physical and mental energy led him into unfortunate political by-ways, and inevitably raised the question of whether he possessed a sense of political proportion. One such foray in 1909 had resulted in a protest – by no means the first – from the King, and a formal rebuke by Asquith before the Cabinet for 'purporting to speak on behalf of the Government.' in a manner 'quite indefensible and altogether inconsistent with Cabinet responsibility and Ministerial cohesion'.[101]

The young Churchill was a political prodigy, but even his friends wondered whether he had not, after all, inherited some of his father's variability and lack of steadiness. It seemed to many contemporaries that his character, like that of his father, still retained 'the characteristics of extreme youth'. 'It is no disparagement to Winston's extraordinary qualities,' Almeric Fitzroy wrote in March 1914, 'to say that his judgement is not quite equal to his abilities, nor his abilities quite equal to his ambitions. His defect is that he sees everything through the magnifying-glass of his self-confidence.'[102] In the Liberal hierarchy he was well-liked, and comments by John Morley and Asquith are of relevance, if only because they demonstrate the paternal note that is appropriate when dealing with the follies of a gay, reckless, warm-hearted and impulsive boy in whom

100. Lytton: *Wilfred Scawen Blunt*, p. 115.

101. P R O C A B 41/32/26. The episode is not mentioned in Mr Churchill's biography.

102. Fitzroy, op. cit., p. 544.

there is so much potential good. Contemplating this remarkable phenomenon, Morley comments:

> I have a great liking for Winston for his vitality, his indefatigable curiosity and attention to business, his remarkable gift of language and skill in argument and his curious flair for all sorts of political causes as they arise, though even he now and then mistakes a pretty bubble for a great wave. All the same, as I so often tell him in a paternal way, a successful politician in this country *needs* a good deal more computation of other people's opinions without anxiety about his own.

Asquith's comment was written in March 1915:

> It is a pity that Winston hasn't a better sense of proportion. I am really fond of him, but I regard his future with many misgivings. . . . He will never get to the top in English politics, with all his wonderful gifts; to speak with the tongue of men and angels, and to spend laborious days and nights in administration, is no good if a man does not inspire trust.

These apprehensions and concerns had become more insistent and significant between 1911 and 1914. Churchill's career had continued to prosper, but it is not fanciful to detect the shadows that were now falling over it. He was profoundly disliked and mistrusted by his opponents. Moreover, despite all his achievements, the doubts and apprehensions of even those close to him could not be allayed. 'I think his future one of the most puzzling enigmas in politics,' Asquith noted on 9 February 1915. And the persistent Gardiner had commented in 1912:

> You may cast the horoscope of anyone else; his you cannot cast. You cannot cast it because his orbit is not governed by any known laws, but by attractions that deflect his path hither and thither. It may be the attraction of war and peace, of social reform or of a social order – whatever it is he will plunge into it with all the schoolboy intensity of his nature. His loves may be many, but they will always have the passion of a first love. Whatever shrine he worships at, he will be the most fervid in his prayers . . . 'Keep your eye on Churchill' should be the watchword of these days. Remember, he is a soldier first, last, and always. He will write his name big on our future. Let us take care he does not write it in blood.[103]

103. Gardiner: *Pillars of Society*, pp. 61–3.

Part Two THE HAZARDS
OF WAR
1914–1918

In his *Memorandum on Resignation* Morley wrote that 'if there is a war, Winston will beat Lloyd George hollow, in spite of ingenious computation.' In the Intervention Crisis Churchill had never doubted what decision should be taken, and his actions in sending the Fleet to its war stations and the mobilization of the reserves without Cabinet authority had demonstrated that there was at least one minister who was seized of the urgent necessity to ensure that the nation would not be caught unprepared. Asquith subsequently wrote that Churchill during the last days of peace was 'very bellicose' and was in 'tearing spirits' at the prospect of war, and Margot Asquith's somewhat over-coloured account of the events of 4 August describes 'Winston Churchill with a happy face striding towards the double doors of the Cabinet Room'. These accounts should be set against others, and the portrait which emerges is that of a man who had no doubts that the right decision had been taken and who possessed full confidence in his own abilities and the nation's capacity to ensure success. This confidence was not really misplaced, but the course of events in the first year of the war was to render invalid Morley's estimate of its consequences upon the careers of Churchill and Lloyd George.

At that time it seemed as though the war would provide Churchill with the opportunity that he craved. In a sense, it did. As Hankey has written:

Winston Churchill was a man of a totally different type from all his colleagues. He had a real zest for war. If war there must needs be, he at least could enjoy it . . . Churchill's courage was an invaluable asset to the Cabinet, to Parliament, and to the nation in these early days. When all looked black and spirits were inclined to droop, he could not only see, but could compel others to see, the brighter side of the picture . . . He brought an element of youth, energy, vitality, and confidence that was a tower of strength to Asquith's Cabinet in those difficult days.[1]

1. Hankey: *The Supreme Command*, Vol. 1, pp. 185–6.

The naval war, initially, did not appear to prosper for the British. The nation, eager for resounding victories at sea, was at first disconcerted and then angered by a series of reverses. The *Goeben* and the *Breslau* escaped to Constantinople, and they arrived at a time when Turkish feelings were bitter as a result of the British decision to commandeer two Turkish warships being completed in British dockyards;[2] the combination of events propelled Turkey sharply towards intervention on the side of the Central Powers. For a time the cruiser *Emden* paralysed the movement of British transports in the Indian Ocean. A squadron under the command of Admiral von Spee eliminated an inferior British force commanded by Admiral Cradock off Coronel. Three British cruisers were sunk in the North Sea in broad daylight by a single German submarine, with great loss of life. For this last disaster Churchill did not bear any responsibility whatsoever, and he had already drawn the attention of Prince Louis of Battenberg, the First Sea Lord, to the danger to which these ships were exposed. He was, however, severely criticized, and Mr Thomas Gibson Bowles wrote and circulated what Churchill has justly described as 'a small but venomous brochure' in which Churchill was directly charged with the responsibility for ignoring the warnings 'of admirals, commodores and captains'. Much more serious was the persistence, and malignity, of the criticisms of the Admiralty in general and the First Lord in particular, by the Conservative press. Churchill's unfortunate capacity to draw fire upon himself unnecessarily was exemplified in a most injudicious speech delivered at Liverpool on 21 September, in which he declared that if the German Navy did not come out to fight 'it would be dug out like rats from a hole'. On the following day the three cruisers were sunk, an event that occasioned the King to remark to Asquith that 'the rats came out of their own accord and to our cost'.

None of these set-backs amounted to anything more than embarrassments. But at the time, the check to public confidence by these reverses was considerable, to the point that the

2. The decision itself was probably right, but the manner in which it was done was maladroit, for which Grey must share responsibility with Churchill.

Cabinet resolved – on Churchill's advice – to suppress all news of the sinking of the battleship *Audacious* and on 4 November Asquith reported to the King: 'The Cabinet were of opinion that this incident [Coronel] like the escape of the *Goeben*, the loss of the *Cressy* and her two sister-cruisers, and that of the *Hermes* last week, is not creditable to the officers of the Navy.'[3]

From criticism of the Navy it was a short step to criticism of Churchill. In addition to all this there was the unhappy episode of the removal of Prince Louis of Battenberg as First Sea Lord,[4] which did not reflect great credit on anyone concerned – neither the Press who hounded the First Sea Lord for his alleged 'Germanism' nor the Government that apparently gave way before this vicious campaign. Battenberg's defenders have claimed that it was he who, on 26 July, had stopped the demobilization of the Fleet on his own initiative, and that although Churchill had promptly endorsed this crucial and courageous decision, the main credit should have gone to Battenberg.[5] In fact he had done so on Churchill's orders. There were, however, other factors in Battenberg's removal than scurrilous Press clamour. For all his many qualities, he did not possess the dynamism and strength of character that Churchill considered was required. Battenberg himself has testified to Churchill's loyalty and support, but Churchill himself was well

3. PRO CAB 41–35–37.

4. See Marder, *From Dreadnought to Scapa Flow*, Vol. II, pp. 82–8, for a detailed account of this episode. The removal of Admiral Sir George Callaghan from command of the Home Fleet on 30 July and his replacement by Sir John Jellicoe had caused a very heated controversy within the Navy, whose reverberations lasted for some time. The manner of Prince Louis's retirement did not improve matters.

5. 'Ministers with their weekend holidays are incorrigible,' he subsequently wrote. 'Things looked pretty bad on Saturday [25 July] . . . but Asquith, Grey, Churchill and all the rest left London. I sat here [at the Admiralty] all Sunday, reading all the telegrams from embassies as they arrived. On Monday morning the big fleet at Portland had orders to disperse, demobilise, and give leave. I took it upon myself to countermand everything by telegraph on Sunday afternoon. When the Ministers hurried back late that evening they cordially approved my action, and we had the drawn sword in our hands to back up our urgent advice' (E. H. Cookridge: *From Battenberg to Mountbatten*, p. 142).

aware of Battenberg's deficiencies. As Esher wrote at the time:
'It has been felt for some time that the Board of Admiralty
requires renovating . . . More driving power is required.' It
can now be seen that the failures of the Navy were principally
the result of poor staff work, but it is also evident that Battenberg was a tired man. The change in the holder of the post of
First Sea Lord was accordingly desirable in itself, whatever the
immediate causes of his resignation. But the really significant
event was not Battenberg's retirement but Churchill's selection
of the aged Lord Fisher, then seventy-four, as his successor. It
was in some respects an inspired choice, for it brought back
from retirement one of the most dynamic and determined men
in British naval history; in others, it was an invitation to disaster, for Fisher came on his own terms, and with his own ideas.
For some time the arrangement seemed to be working admir-
ably, but Churchill was heedless of the many signs that Fisher
was intent upon supremacy. As Admiral Wemyss wrote on 3
October 1914: 'They will be as thick as thieves at first until
they differ on some subject, probably as to who is to be Number
1, when they will begin to intrigue against each other.' [6] 'The
situation is curious,' Beatty wrote to his wife on 4 December;
' – two very strong and clever men, one old, wily and of vast
experience, one young, self-assertive, with great self-satisfac-
tion but unstable. They cannot work together, they cannot
both run the show.' [7] The final and fatal clash came over the
Dardanelles, but it was only a *casus belli*. The division between
the old Admiral and the young First Lord was fundamental.
'Churchill co-opted Fisher to relieve the pressure against himself, but he had no intention of letting anyone else rule the
roost,' Beaverbrook has commented. 'Here, then, were two
strong men of incompatible tempers both bent on an auto-
cracy.' [8]

Churchill's absorption in the war was total. 'His mouth
waters at the sight & thought of K[itchener]'s new armies,'
Asquith wrote on 7 October 1914:

6. Lady Wester Wemyss: *Admiral Sir Wester Wemyss*, p. 186.
7. Chalmers: *Beatty*, p. 179.
8. Beaverbrook: *Politicians and the War*, p. 98.

Are these 'glittering commands' to be entrusted to 'dug-out trash', bred on the obsolete tactics of 25 years ago – 'mediocrities who have led a sheltered life mouldering in military routine' etc., etc. For about ¼ of an hour he poured forth a ceaseless cataract of invective and appeal, & I much regretted that there was no shorthand writer within hearing – as some of his unpremeditated phrases were quite priceless. He was however, quite three parts serious, and declared that a political career was nothing to him in comparison with military glory. . . . He is a wonderful creature, with a curious dash of schoolboy simplicity (quite unlike Edward Grey's), and what someone said of genius – 'a zigzag streak of lightning in the brain'.[9]

The Assistant Director of Naval Operations, Richmond, found him in a very different mood on 24 October.

He was in low spirits . . . and oppressed with the impossibility of *doing* anything. The attitude of waiting . . . and the inability of the Staff to make any suggestions seem to bother him. I have not seen him so despondent before . . . He wanted to send battleships – old ones – up the Elbe, but for what purpose except to be sunk I did not understand.[10]

Churchill's self-confidence and impatience with slower minds – or what appeared to be slower minds – was understandable. He had, as Asquith has written, 'a pictorial mind brimming with ideas'; he had, furthermore, at his disposal the mightiest weapon of war, apart from the German Army, in the world. The prospect of this weapon being inadequately employed was indeed one to fill someone of his restless and eager temperament with impatience. Professor Marder has written:

The First Lord had too inflated a conception of his functions. 'I accepted,' he writes, 'full responsibility for bringing about successful results, and in that spirit I exercised a close general supervision over everything that was done or proposed. Further, I claimed and exercised an unlimited power of suggestion and initiative over the whole field, subject only to the approval and agreement of the First Sea Lord on all operative orders.' Churchill's large view of his office – 'his business everything and his intent everywhere' – worked badly,

9. Roy Jenkins: *Asquith*, p. 340.
10. Marder: *Portrait of an Admiral*, p. 121.

and it tended to diminish the authority of the First Sea Lord and the Chief of the War Staff, and to cramp their freedom of action.[11]

There is, of course, much substance in this criticism. Fisher wrote on 20 December that 'the Sea Lords are atrophied and their departments run really by the Private Office, and I find it a Herculean task to get back to the right procedure, and quite possibly I may have to clear out, and I've warned Winston of this'.[12] But in time of war it is necessary for a War Minister to dominate his Department, particularly if – as in Churchill's case – he has a high position in the Cabinet and strong views on the prosecution of the war. The trouble was that a minister, and particularly a young minister, must recognize (or appear to recognize) the experience and position of his Service colleagues. In war, as in peace, it is of supreme importance for a minister not to become embroiled in wearying details; but the latter cannot, and must not, be ignored if they have a crucial bearing on the successful execution of policy. It was already apparent, even at this relatively early stage, that administration was not to be numbered among Churchill's ministerial qualities. Although it would be unreasonable to blame him personally for the many failures – some of them very serious indeed – made by the fledgling Naval War Staff, he must carry some responsibility. This was not an area of political activity in which he excelled or, indeed, took much interest. Even in 1940, when he had so much ministerial experience, this deficiency was still most apparent.[13]

Churchill saw himself in the role of a Commander cast in the Napoleon mould. 'The fundamental fault of his system,' Lord Selborne subsequently wrote, 'is his restlessness.'[14] Restlessness in a war leader is no deficiency in itself and, if properly harnessed, may be regarded as an outstanding quality. But the crucial qualification is that it must be harnessed, and the fundamentally obsolete and inefficient Admiralty machine, now combined with the violent and unpredictable personality

11. Marder: *From the Dreadnought to Scapa Flow*, Vol. II, p. 40.
12. Marder: *Fear God and Dread Nought*, Vol. III, pp. 99–100.
13. *Action This Day*, pp. 51–2.
14. *National Review*, August 1923.

of Fisher, did not furnish this essential discipline. Fisher was in many respects an impossible colleague, but Churchill's conception of his position was somewhat imperious, and the insensitiveness in his character did not alert him to the resentment and suspicion with which his actions and attitudes were viewed both in the Admiralty and outside it. Consultation with his Service advisers, notably with Fisher, indeed took place, but it tended to take the form of seeking approval for actions that had already been taken. Churchill's restlessness and eagerness for action swiftly brought him into controversial adventures which eventually destroyed his position at the Admiralty.

*

Now almost entirely forgotten, the 'Dunkirk Circus' was an important contributory factor. In September 1914 Joffre suggested that a British force should land at Dunkirk to make a demonstration of force to alarm the Germans on their right flank. Churchill, at Kitchener's request, took over the operation. A mixed force of marines and yeomanry carried out an elaborate charade; Churchill relished the operation, and took a close personal interest in it. Others – including Asquith – grew progressively less amused, and the 'Circus' was wound up.

This was, however, a minor episode in the decline of Churchill's reputation at the Admiralty when compared with the ill-fated attempts to save Antwerp in October 1914 and to force the Dardanelles in the spring of 1915.

The Antwerp episode can now be seen to have been substantially to Churchill's credit. Churchill went to Antwerp – which the Belgian Government was proposing to evacuate – on 3 October in order to keep the Government abreast of developments, arriving, in the account of one observer, in 'undress Trinity House uniform' making an entrance that 'reminded me for all the world of a scene in a melodrama where the hero dashes up bare-headed on a foam-flecked horse, and saves the heroine, or the old homestead, or the family fortune, as the case may be'. The Government had decided to send the Royal Marine Brigade (which arrived on 4 October), and then, on

Churchill's urgent request, the 1st and 2nd Naval Brigades, which were mainly composed of untrained naval reservists. The Royal Naval Division had been established by Churchill, and its existence was a source of constant friction between the Admiralty and the War Office. There were also elements in the Navy who did not approve of this venture.

Churchill took command of events and on 4 October even offered to resign his position at the Admiralty to take executive command of the British forces. His offer, when read out to the Cabinet, only provoked 'roars of incredulous laughter', and he was recalled to London. Only Kitchener saw nothing absurd in the request. All observers have paid tribute to the energy and skill with which Churchill handled the crisis before he was recalled; and the episode rekindled all his military enthusiasm. But when Antwerp fell and over 2,500 men of the newly formed and largely untrained Naval Division were interned or lost as battle casualties the brunt of popular disillusion fell on Churchill. Churchill's defence of his actions in *The World Crisis* was that the British Naval detachments prolonged the defence of Antwerp for several crucial days. In fact, it had prolonged it for a week. The Belgians would have surrendered on 3 October, and the seven days' respite almost certainly enabled Dunkirk and Calais to be secured. Churchill had behaved impulsively and swiftly, and his enterprise deserved better than the storm of criticism and ridicule that descended upon his head. But he himself subsequently acknowledged the strength of his critics: 'Those who are charged with the direction of supreme affairs must sit on the mountain-tops of control; they must never descend into the valleys of direct physical and personal action.'

The historian must always remember the significance of what people thought at the time, however unfair these views might have been. Subsequent revelations and explanations enable a more just estimate to be formed of a man's actions. Churchill brought to the war an imagination allied with a practical eye which placed him in a unique position among his contemporary politicians. His role in the development of the tank is perhaps over-stressed in his account in *The World Crisis*, but his enthusiasm for the project and the energy he put into the early experiments were invaluable, and played a crucial part in the gradual development of what could – if properly employed – have been the war-winning machine. Nothing of this was known at the time, and because a man's political and personal fortunes essentially depend upon contemporary judgements, opinion was extremely critical of his action, and not least Antwerp.[15] Indeed, it was perhaps the most significant of the succession of events which, by the end of 1915, imperilled his position as First Lord.

*

The long-term effects of Antwerp upon Churchill's career – important though they were – were of lesser significance than those of the Dardanelles Campaign.

It is doubtful whether any campaign of either of the two World Wars has aroused more attention and controversy than this tragic venture. 'Nothing so distorted perspective, disturbed impartial judgement, and impaired the sense of strategic values as the operations on Gallipoli,' Edward Grey subsequently wrote. Much the same comment could be applied to the political, military, and historical controversies that followed the campaign, and which still rumble sulphurously over fifty years afterwards.

By the end of 1914, the character of the fighting on the Western Front had already become grimly apparent, and ministers other than Churchill were thinking in general terms of using British strength – and particularly sea power – in another, and more effective and rewarding, manner than, in Churchill's phrase, 'to chew barbed wire in Flanders'. He wrote to Asquith on 29 December:

We ought not to drift. We ought now to consider while time remains the scope and character we wish to impart to the war in the early summer. We ought to concert our action with our allies, and particularly with Russia. We ought to form a scheme for a continuous and progressive offensive, and be ready with this new alternative when and if the direct frontal attacks in France on the German lines and

15. See Marder: *From the Dreadnought to Scapa Flow*, Vol. II, pp. 83–5, for some of the views of Churchill's responsibility.

Belgium have failed, as fail I fear they will. Without your direct
guidance and initiation, none of these things will be done; and a
succession of bloody checks in the West and in the East will leave the
Allies dashed in spirit and bankrupt in policy.

Lloyd George's argument ran on very similar lines:

If our army on the Continent was to be thrown away and shattered
in an operation which appeared to him impossible, the war might
continue indefinitely, or at any rate for two or three years more. Was
it impossible, he asked, to get at the enemy from some other direction, and to strike a blow that would end the war once and for all?[16]

Fisher, Lloyd George, Hankey and Churchill were the most
prominent exponents of attack elsewhere than in France or
Flanders, and this movement of opinion in the War Council
coincided with an appeal for assistance by the Russians, hard
pressed by Turkish forces in the Caucasus, at the beginning of
January 1915.[17]

It was Churchill who emerged with the most attractive proposal. Naval and military opinion had for some years been
opposed to the project of forcing the Dardanelles by ships
alone, and Churchill himself had written in 1911 that 'it
should be remembered that it is no longer possible to force the
Dardanelles, and nobody would expose a modern fleet to such
peril.' But he, as had so many others, had been deeply impressed by the effect of modern artillery bombardment on the
Belgian forts – a fact to which he gave considerable emphasis in
his evidence to the Dardanelles Commission, but which he
played down very heavily in *The World Crisis*[18] – and he had
been anxious to eliminate the *Goeben* and *Breslau* from an early
stage.

16. Minutes of the War Council, 7 January 1915 (PRO CAB 42/1/11).
17. In fact, the Turkish threat to the Caucasus almost immediately
disappeared, as the Turks were defeated at Sarikamish on 4 January; the
British were not informed of this fact.
18. In his evidence Churchill said that 'the war had brought many sur-
prises. We had seen fortresses reported throughout Europe to be impreg-
nable collapsing after a few days' attack by field armies without a regular
siege.' The matter is discussed in the author's *Gallipoli*, pp. 11–12. To be
absolutely fair to Churchill, Admiral Oliver – who had witnessed the effects
of the German shelling on the Belgian forts – was equally impressed.

It is important to emphasize this point. The idea of forcing the Dardanelles was raised by Churchill at the end of August 1914, and on 1 September he had requested the General Staff, in conjunction with two officers from the Admiralty, to propose a 'plan for the seizure of the Gallipoli Peninsula, by means of a Greek army of adequate strength, with a view to admitting a British fleet to the sea of Marmara'. The report of the Director of Military Operations, Callwell, was not sanguine, but Churchill eagerly pursued the project. 'Mr Churchill was very keen on attacking the Dardanelles from a very early stage,' Callwell later told the Dardanelles Commission. '. . . He was very keen to get to Constantinople somehow.'[19]

On his orders, the British squadron off the Dardanelles shelled the Outer Forts of Sedd-el-Bahr and Kum Kale on 3 November, following the bombardment of Odessa and Sebastopol by *Goeben* and *Breslau* under the Turkish flag on 28 October and the opening of hostilities between Turkey and Russia. On 30 October the Cabinet had decided 'to wait for the developments of the next few days before taking ourselves, or suggesting to other Powers, a new departure'.[20] On 4 November the Prime Minister reported to the King, 'the Cabinet came to the conclusion that a formal declaration of war against Turkey could no longer be postponed'.[21] Indeed not! This action was subsequently severely criticized, and Professor Marder has written that 'The cost of this premature attack far outweighed the slight advantages, since it put the Turks and their German military advisers on the alert. From that moment there was no possibility of surprise, and the Turks began to pay special attention to the defences of the Straits.' In fact, the attention paid was not very considerable, and what action was taken was characteristically lethargic.

At the first meeting of the newly constituted War Council on 25 November Churchill had proposed a naval attack on the Dardanelles; 'Mr Churchill suggested that the ideal method of defending Egypt was by an attack on the Gallipoli Peninsula.

19. Dardanelles Commission: Evidence, Q.3665.
20. PRO CAB 41/35/315.
21. PRO CAB 41/35/37 (Asquith to the King, 4 November 1914).

This, if successful, would give us control of the Dardanelles, and we could dictate terms at Constantinople. This, however, was a very difficult operation requiring a large force.'[22] The idea was not accepted, but Churchill had taken certain preparatory steps to enable an operation to be mounted if it were sanctioned.[23] Hankey had stressed the significance of this first airing of a project which Churchill now, in January 1915, urged upon his colleagues in the War Council.[24] As Lloyd George has written, when Churchill 'has a scheme agitating in his powerful mind . . . he is indefatigable in pressing it upon the acceptance of every one who matters in the decision'.[25]

Churchill first secured the agreement of Admiral Carden,[26] commanding the Allied force in the Aegean, that the attack was practicable. The telegrams that passed between Churchill and Carden were highly significant. On 3 January Churchill asked Carden for his views on the possibility of forcing the Dardanelles by warships alone; Carden replied on the 5th that 'I do not think that the Dardanelles can be rushed, but they might be forced by extended operations with a large number of ships.' As Carden subsequently emphasized in his evidence to the Dardenelles Commission, the operative word was 'might'.[27]

22. War Council Minutes, 25 November 1914.

23. He instructed that ships at Suez which had been used to convey Australian and New Zealand troops should not disperse.

24. Hankey, op. cit., Vol. I, p. 243.

25. Lloyd George: *War Memoirs*, Vol. I, p. 395.

26. Carden had been Superintendent of the Malta Dockyard before his promotion in September 1914 to command the Allied squadron in the Aegean. His career had been undistinguished, and he had never commanded a force of this size. Churchill and Fisher were under no illusions about him, and one of the puzzles of the operation is why Carden was not replaced when the importance of the naval attack was recognized. Other senior naval officers of greater distinction had been unceremoniously removed from less important posts.

27. In his evidence Churchill agreed that his telegram was framed to provide a favourable answer. 'Frequently we asked, could this or that be done . . . and in the overwhelming majority of cases the answer was: No, it cannot be done' (Dardanelles Commission: Evidence, Q.1264). Carden said in his reply that 'I did not mean distinctly that they [the Dardanelles] could be forced . . . I thought it might be done' (ibid., Q.2332-3). Fisher had not

Churchill replied: 'High authorities here concur in your opinion. Forward detailed particulars showing what force would be
required for extended operations . . .' The 'high authorities'
subsequently turned out to be Admiral Oliver, the Chief of
Staff, and Admiral Sir Henry Jackson, with whom Churchill
had discussed the matter briefly and orally. Oliver was extremely cautious – he has recorded that his opinion was that 'we
should push on slowly until we overcome the enemy's defence,
or till the enemy's defence brought us to a standstill' – and
Jackson's views – as can be seen from an appreciation that he
wrote on 5 January – were even more guarded. Neither Fisher
nor the War Staff Group at the Admiralty were consulted.
Carden assumed that the words 'high authorities' meant something a good deal more than this.[28]

This beginning was to characterize the relationships between
Churchill and his Service advisers throughout the inception of
the Dardanelles campaign. As Churchill went to great pains to
emphasize in *The World Crisis*, Fisher and his colleagues were
involved in the planning, and were responsible for what was
done. The operation, indeed, could never have started without
the approval and support of the First Sea Lord. Nevertheless,
there was a substantial and crucial difference of attitude towards the operation between the First Lord and his advisers.
Fisher had many causes for disliking the Dardanelles plan, of
which perhaps the single most important one was his preoccupation with his own scheme for a major landing in the Baltic.
Churchill was enthusiastic for the Dardanelles assault, believed
that it had great potentialities and an acceptable element of
risk, and pressed it forward as a matter of priority. Fisher and
the Service advisers did not regard it in this light. At best, they
accepted that the operation might succeed. When Carden's
detailed plans were received at the Admiralty on 11 January
Churchill circulated them, and he has written:

Both the First Sea Lord and the Chief of Staff seemed favourable
to it. No one at any time threw the slightest doubt upon its technical

seen Churchill's telegram, but said that he was 'quite conversant with it'
(Q.3115).

28. Dardanelles Commission: Evidence, Q.2338.

soundness. No one, for instance, of the four or five great naval authorities each with his technical staff who were privy said, 'This is absurd. Ships cannot fight forts,' or criticized its details. On the contrary, they all treated it as an extremely interesting and hopeful proposal . . .

It will be seen that the genesis of this plan and its elaboration were entirely naval and professional in their character. It was Admiral Carden and his staff gunnery officers who proposed the gradual method of piece-meal reduction by long-range bombardment. It was Sir Henry Jackson and the Admiralty staff who embraced this idea and studied and approved its detail. Right or wrong, it was a Service plan. Similarly the Admiralty orders were prepared exclusively by the Chief of Staff and his assistants. . . . At no point did lay or civilian interference mingle with or mar the integrity of a professional conception.

I write this not in the slightest degree to minimize or shift my own responsibility. But this is not where it lay. I did not and I could not make the plan. But when it had been made by the naval authorities, and fashioned and endorsed by high technical authorities and approved by the First Sea Lord, I seized upon it and set it upon the path of action; and thereafter espoused it with all my resources.[29]

This passage contains the kernel of Churchill's defence. It can be challenged on many points. In actual fact, the reaction of Fisher and his colleagues to the Carden proposals had been one of surprise. The comments of Jackson, far from 'embracing' and 'approving' the plans, were critical and even sceptical. When the Third Sea Lord attempted to discuss the subject with Churchill his viewpoint 'was not welcomed and had no effect'. Admiral Sir Percy Scott, the foremost gunnery expert in the Navy, considered it 'an impossible task'. The Naval Air Staff did not formally meet to discuss the proposed operations at all. Fisher, as he frankly admitted, found it impossible to controvert Churchill's arguments when they met – 'He always outargues me,' Fisher repeatedly declared – but, when he reflected on the matter, his doubts and apprehensions returned. At the War Council he was silent, a silence that was assumed to be acquiescence, when in fact it was loyalty, and a misunderstanding of the role of the Service members of the Council. 'I

29. *The World Crisis*, Vol. II, pp. 102, 121–2.

made it a rule that I would not at the War Council kick
Winston Churchill's shins,' he subsequently said. 'He was my
chief, and it was silence or resignation.'[30] All the evidence now
available demonstrates the fact that Churchill initiated the
Dardanelles project, and pushed it forward with vigour, over-
ruling or ignoring the doubts and criticisms of his Service
advisers. This course of action may have been justified, but it
was a very different course to that described in *The World
Crisis*.

On 13 January, at the end of a long and trying meeting of the
War Council, Churchill produced his plan, with an exposition
that was cogent and highly attractive. As Hankey has recorded:

> The idea caught on at once. The whole atmosphere changed.
> Fatigue was forgotten. The War Council turned eagerly from the
> dreary vista of a 'slogging match' on the Western Front to brighter
> prospects, as they seemed, in the Mediterranean . . . Churchill
> unfolded his plans with the skill that might be expected of him,
> lucidly but quietly and without exaggerated optimism.[31]

The prospects presented by Churchill were alluring indeed.
The forts, he said, would be systematically reduced 'within a
few weeks. Once the forts were reduced the minefields could be
cleared and the Fleet would proceed up to Constantinople and
destroy the *Goeben*. They would have nothing to fear from field
guns or rifles, which would be merely an inconvenience.'[32]
The Council caught his enthusiasm,[33] and resolved that 'the
Admiralty should also prepare for a naval expedition in
February to bombard and take the Gallipoli Peninsula with
Constantinople as its objective.'

Reactions to this resolution were illuminating. Churchill took
it as a definite decision. Asquith, however, considered it to be
'merely provisional, to prepare, but nothing more'. Admiral

30. Dardanelles Commission: Evidence, Q.3122.
31. Hankey, op. cit., Vol. I, p. 265.
32. Minutes of the War Council, 13 January 1915.
33. Fisher was the exception. As he subsequently told the Dardanelles
Commission: 'He was beautiful! He has got the brain of Moses and the voice
of Aaron. He would talk a bird out of a tree, and they were all carried away
with him. I was not, myself' (Dardanelles Commission: Evidence, Q.3112).

Sir Arthur Wilson, a member of the War Council, told the Dardanelles Commission that 'it was not my business, I was not in any way connected with the question, and it had never in any way officially been put before me.' Commodore de Bartolomé, Churchill's naval secretary, subsequently said that the naval members 'only agreed to a purely naval operation on the understanding that we could always draw back – *that there should be no question of what is known as forcing the Dardanelles*'.[34]

Whatever else may be said about the Dardanelles Campaign, it cannot be seriously maintained that 'the genesis of this plan' was 'entirely naval and professional in their character'. This was Churchill's plan, which he persuaded the War Council and his Service advisers to accept. The latter did so, but with manifest reluctance, and with the feeling that Churchill had acted to a large extent independently of the normal policy-making procedures in the Navy. As Professor Marder has emphasized, they had solid justification for resentment at being in a major operation which most of them regarded with alarm. This resentment was to be increased when Churchill – with Asquith's support – withheld from the War Council an Admiralty memorandum strongly critical of the whole operation.

It was established naval and military opinion – fortified by a joint appreciation ordered by the Committee of Imperial Defence in 1906 – that a joint operation was essential for a successful attack upon the Dardanelles. The study had concluded that although a squadron of 'His Majesty's least valuable ships might force the Dardanelles, the attempt was much to be deprecated'. On 8 January 1915 Kitchener had reported the conclusions of a new War Office study at a meeting of the War Council:

> The Dardanelles appeared to be the most suitable objective, as an attack here could be made in cooperation with the fleet . . . Lord Kitchener thought that 150,000 men would be sufficient for the capture of the Dardanelles, but he reserved his final opinion until a closer study had been made.

34. Author's italics.

Mr Lloyd George expressed surprise at the lowness of this figure . . .[35]

By the end of January the possibility of using troops was being discussed, and throughout February was to be a major topic. It was pressed particularly vigorously by Jackson and Fisher,[36] and Kitchener sent Lt.-Gen. W. R. Birdwood, the commander of the Australian and New Zealand Army Corps then training in Egypt, to the Dardanelles to report back privately on the prospects. On 16 February the War Council decided to authorize the despatch of the 29th Division – the last remaining Regular Division – to the island of Lemnos, whither Admiral Wemyss had been sent to set up an advanced base with no facilities whatever to do it with, and other troops in the area to 'be available in case of necessity to support the naval attack on the Dardanelles'. Churchill states that 'The decision of February 16 is the foundation of the military attack upon the Dardanelles.'

Four days later Kitchener announced that he had changed his mind about the 29th Division. Churchill urged him to review this decision, and on 25 February he circulated a memorandum that argued that 'The Anglo-French lines in the West are very strong, and cannot be turned . . . With proper military and naval co-operation, and with forces which are available, we can make certain of taking Constantinople by the end of March, and capturing or destroying all Turkish forces in Europe (except those in Adrianople). This blow can be struck before the fate of Serbia is decided. The effect on the whole of the Balkans will be decisive. It will eliminate Turkey as a military factor.' Churchill went on to state that 115,000 troops '(at least) are available immediately', and 'are capable of being concentrated within striking distance of the Bulair Isthmus by March 21 if orders are given now. If the naval operations have not succeeded by then, they can be used to

35. PRO CAB 41/1/12.
36. Fisher wrote to Jellicoe on 21 January: 'I just abominate the Dardanelles operation, unless a great change is made and it is settled to be made a military operation, with 200,000 men in conjunction with the Fleet.'

attack the Gallipoli Peninsula and make sure the fleet gets through . . .'

At the War Council meeting on 26 February, however, Churchill specifically denied any intention of using troops to force the Dardanelles and he emphasized that they 'were required to occupy Constantinople and to compel a surrender of all Turkish forces remaining in Europe after the fleet had obtained command of the Sea of Marmara . . . *The actual and definite object of the army would be to reap the fruits of the naval success.*'[37] He informed the Council that Carden had been told not to land troops in Gallipoli, and that 'the military forces were not intended to participate in the immediate operations, but to enable him to reap the fruits of those operations when successfully accomplished.'[38] 'I wish to make it clear,' he wrote to Kitchener on 4 March, 'that the naval operations in the Dardanelles cannot be delayed for troop movements, as we must get into the Marmara as soon as possible in the normal course.' Not surprisingly, Kitchener did not consider these to be overwhelmingly persuasive arguments to make him release his last available Regular Division. In the course of his interesting evidence to the Dardanelles Commission, Admiral Wilson gave his opinion that Churchill had not represented the difficulties of the operation to the War Council; 'he kept on saying he could do it without the army; he only wanted the army to come in and reap the fruits, I think, was his expression; and I think he generally minimised the risks from mobile guns.'

But on 10 March, having received from Birdwood a bleak and realistic estimate of the chances of the Navy getting through, Kitchener changed his mind. Churchill, both in his evidence to the Dardanelles Commission and in his account in *The World Crisis*, has laid great stress upon the importance of this delay. No reference is made in these accounts to the actual arguments that Churchill brought forward in the War Council. In one account,[39] indeed, he said that he ought to have broken off the naval attack 'when Lord Kitchener went back upon his under-

37. Author's italics.
38. PRO CAB 42/1/47.
39. *Thoughts and Adventures*, p. 17.

taking to send the 29th Division to reinforce the army gathering
in Egypt for the Dardanelles expedition and delayed it for
nearly three weeks'. As many historians of the campaign have
echoed Churchill's comments on this point, it is important to
emphasize that the criticism of Kitchener is ill-founded, and
Churchill conceded this in his evidence to the Dardanelles
Commission.

I had no right at this stage to complain if Lord Kitchener had said
'I am not going to land on the Peninsula.' I could not have said,
'Oh! you have broken faith with the Admiralty.' On the contrary,
we had said we would try it without committing him to that, and he
would have had a right to complain if we had turned round and
immediately demanded that he should undertake this very serious
military operation.[40]

It may also be remarked that no account was taken of the
weather in the Aegean at that time of year. Even if the 29th
Division had been available for a landing on the Dardanelles
shores, it is very doubtful whether this could have been satisfactorily accomplished before the end of April. Churchill's
claim is quite unrealistic: 'Had the 29th Division been sent as
originally decided from February 22 onward, it would have
reached the scene by the middle of March instead of three
weeks later. Had it been packed on the transports in order of
battle, it would have gone into action within a few days of its
arrival.'[41] The problems of an amphibious landing are severe;
there are no indications at the time or subsequently that
Churchill appreciated their scale and complexity, even in good
weather. And the spring weather in the Aegean is not good.[42]

40. Dardanelles Commission: Evidence, Q.1251.

41. *The World Crisis*, Vol. II, p. 214.

42. On this point, for the reasons I have given, I am not in agreement with
Professor Marder's statement that 'Had Kitchener acted boldly at the end
of February and bent every effort towards preparing a large and well-
organized amphibious operation, the Peninsula probably could have been
taken. There was only one Turkish division there at the time. It could have
been quickly polished off, had an adequate military force been available
quickly, before the Turks could reinforce their troops substantially (*From
the Dreadnought to Scapa Flow*, Vol. II, p. 237).

It can be argued that modern military commentators tend to be over-obsessed by problems of logistics and *matériel*, but the opposite extreme is even more disastrous. But it is only fair to emphasize that today, with the advantage of the bitter experience gained at the Dardanelles and Dieppe (not to mention Anzio), we are much wiser on these matters. In 1915 the hazards of amphibious operations were not so familiar. As Sir Ian Hamilton subsequently pointed out: 'The landing of an army upon the theatre of operations I have described . . . involved difficulties for which no precedent was forthcoming in military history, except possibly in the sinister legends of Xerxes.' It is necessary to record, however, that there were those who foresaw – however dimly – the enormous problems involved; Churchill was not among their number. Grand strategic concepts are fine things; but it is of value to have the wherewithal to accomplish them. It is also desirable to have a clear conception of the advantages that will accrue from success and some thoughts on the price that would have to be paid for failure.

In pressing for military support, Churchill's position was a difficult one. In order to secure agreement to the naval attack, at a time when it was quite clear that no troops were available, it had been necessary to emphasize the gleaming prospects of the purely naval assault. Richmond wrote on 9 February that 'Winston, very, very ignorant, believes he can capture the Dardanelles without troops.' This was certainly the impression he gave. When troops were to be possibly available, any arguments to the effect that their presence in the attack was vital to its success could hardly have been convincing. Churchill accordingly rested his case on the argument that they were essential, in his own words at the meeting of 26 February, 'to fortify our diplomacy' and to be employed only *after* the successful forcing of the Dardanelles. These examples may serve to demonstrate why Churchill's defence of his actions in *The World Crisis* should be approached with very considerable caution.

*

The naval bombardment of the Outer Defences opened on 19 February.[43] At first progress was made, and the Outer Forts quickly subdued. But as the warships penetrated into the Straits, their difficulties mounted. The minesweeping force consisted of east coast fishing trawlers manned by civilian crews and commanded by a naval officer with absolutely no experience of sweeping. Struggling against the fierce Dardanelles current, and under constant fire, the sweepers consistently failed to eliminate the minefields.[44] These were the key to the battle. Carden resolved to reverse his strategy; the suppression of the guns would precede the sweeping of the minefields. On the eve of the attack, Carden collapsed, and was replaced by Rear-Admiral de Robeck.

The famous naval attack of 18 March 1915 has been often described. It opened propitiously for the Allies, but shortly before 2 p.m. the French battleship *Bouvet* sank with heavy loss of life. The sweepers, advancing with difficulty, hardly touched the main Turkish minefields. Shortly after 4 p.m. *Inflexible* and *Irresistible* reported that they had struck mines. At 5 p.m. orders were given for a general retirement. The battleship *Ocean* then struck another mine. She and *Irresistible* sank, and although *Inflexible* and the French battleship *Gaulois* – badly damaged by gunfire – reached safety, de Robeck was faced with the sombre fact that, out of nine battleships engaged in the attack, six had been sunk or crippled.[45]

The real significance of the attack of 18 March was that it emphasized the fact that the true defences of the Dardanelles were the minefields, still protected by the mobile howitzers and intermediate batteries. Churchill has written that:

If the Navy had tried again they would have found that the door was open. Their improved sweeping forces could have concentrated

43. See map on p. 95.
44. They were subsequently blamed very severely – particularly by Roger Keyes – for their failure. The folly lay in their presence at the Dardanelles at all in this impossible role.
45. It is probable that *Bouvet* was hit in the magazine by a plunging shell; *Inflexible*, *Irresistible*, and *Ocean* struck a row of mines laid in Eren Keui Bay only a few days previously, and whose existence was unsuspected.

upon clearing the few remaining mines out of the Eren Keui Bay. The battle of March 18 could have been resumed a month later in overwhelmingly favourable conditions; and had it been resumed it would, in a few hours, have become apparent that it could have only one ending.[46]

The confidence of the final statement is open to much challenge,[47] but it was certainly the case that the new sweeping force of converted destroyers proposed by Roger Keyes – de Robeck's Chief of Staff – had the best chance of success; indeed, it was the only chance of success. But Keyes did not anticipate that the new force could be ready before 10 April. The events of 18 March had been a severe check to the British, and it marked the end of the attempt to force the Dardanelles by the Navy.

On 22 March de Robeck and General Sir Ian Hamilton – appointed by Kitchener on 12 March to command the Mediterranean Expeditionary Force[48] – conferred on the battleship *Queen Elizabeth*. They were in full agreement that a joint attack was essential, and Hamilton returned to Alexandria to regroup his forces that were now scattered around the Eastern Mediterranean in some disarray. Churchill was dumbfounded, and was eager for urging de Robeck to persevere. Fisher, supported by Wilson and Jackson, refused adamantly. 'For the first time

46. See *The World Crisis*, Vol. I, pp. 254–76 for Churchill's case.

47. This point has been made by the author in his *Gallipoli*, pp. 64–6. The evidence on the matter is conflicting, but that taken by the secret Admiralty inquiry in 1919 – in which the other Services were represented – makes a very strong case against the arguments of Churchill and Roger Keyes which is, in my opinion, very difficult to controvert. In particular, the statement by Churchill that the Navy 'would have found that the door was open' cannot be substantiated. The key to the door was the clearing of the mine-fields, not the amount of heavy ammunition available in the Dardanelles forts.

Much has been made of the fact that the equipment of the 29th Division was so badly loaded on the transports that it was necessary entirely to reorganize matters at Alexandria. Professor Marder makes the point that the Director of Transports at the Admiralty was a Churchill appointment, and one strongly criticized by some of the Sea Lords (*From the Dreadnought to Scapa Flow*, Vol. II, p. 238).

48. Churchill had pressed for the appointment of Hamilton, a close friend, but it is not clear whether this had a decisive effect (Kitchener Papers).

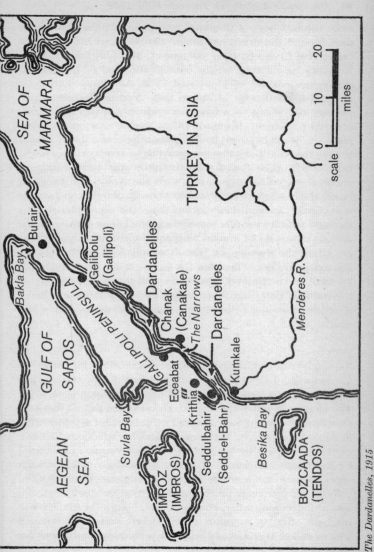

The Dardanelles, 1915

since the war began,' Churchill has related, 'high words were used around the octagonal table.' Churchill, with deep reluctance, had to accept their judgement. The allegation that de Robeck's action was wholly outside the area of his responsibility cannot be substantiated. The Admiralty had telegraphed to Carden on 14 March that 'You must concert any military operations on a large scale which you consider necessary with General Hamilton when he arrives on Tuesday night . . . it might [then] be found that decisive military action to take the Kilid Bahr Plateau would be less costly than a naval task.' De Robeck found that Hamilton was very willing to undertake a military operation with the Navy, and thus, on board the battleship *Queen Elizabeth* on 22 March, the decision was taken. Churchill has written that 'the silent plunge into this vast military venture must be regarded as an extraordinary episode'. It could be argued with equal vigour that the events preceding the decision of Hamilton and de Robeck were no less extraordinary. Thus was the scene set for the landings of 25 April on the Gallipoli Peninsula, and for the long agony of the Gallipoli Campaign, that was to cost the allies a quarter of a million casualties before it was abandoned at the end of the year.

*

No single man can, or should, bear responsibility for the series of decisions, half-decisions and evasions of decisions that marked the story of the initiation of the Gallipoli Campaign. The manner in which the Asquith Government drifted into this vast commitment of men and resources – neither of which were in adequate supply for even one campaign – condemns not any individual but rather the system of war government practised by the Administration. As Hankey has written: 'Behind each episode there lay a whole history of rumour, contradiction, conjecture, planning, preliminary movement, discussion, decision, indecision, order, counter-order, before the climax was reached, often in a welter of bloodshed and destruction.'[49] The so-called War Council was not a suitable instrument for

49. Hankey, op. cit., Vol. I, p. 182.

the conduct of the war; indeed, it in no sense operated in the manner its title would imply. Admiral Oliver has written of Asquith's handling of the Council that 'When he thought there had been talk enough he would look up and say, "So-and-so is decided." There was never anything said after that and nothing was put to the vote.' The failure of the War Council was that it was an extension of the Cabinet, and operated on Cabinet lines, and it lacked strong leadership. Nevertheless, when all this has been fairly taken into account, it cannot be seriously denied that there was justification for identifying Churchill personally for the project and for the manner in which it progressed. If ministerial responsibility means anything, Churchill was to a very real extent deeply responsible. He had at no stage conducted anything approaching a really thorough examination of the manifold problems involved in such an operation; he had been personally responsible for launching a massive enterprise on the most flimsy evidence; he had grossly over-estimated the effect of naval guns with flat trajectory against land defences; he had entered the naval operation without adequate realization of the very serious problems involved, and with insufficient contact with his Service advisers; the War Council had not been adequately informed of the doubts that existed in the Admiralty about the operation; and Churchill had consistently underrated the capacity of the Turks. In this he was not alone, but his summary dismissal of Hankey's concern at the beginning of April is significant.[50]

Churchill is entitled to disclaim responsibility for the subsequent failures by the Allied commanders on Gallipoli that destroyed the chances of victory. Nevertheless, the initiator of an enterprise on this scale cannot be completely absolved even from the failures of men on the spot. Men who initiate major policies cannot evade responsibility if they turn out ill. At no time did the War Council assess the operation in the

50. '... Lieutenant Colonel Hankey said that the difficulty would be to land the troops at all ...

'Mr Churchill did not agree. He anticipated no difficulty in effecting a landing' (Minutes of a Meeting of Ministers, 6 April 1915 (PRO CAB 42/2/17)).

context of the national resources or national objectives. The entire business had, from the outset, an infuriating amateurishness that was well demonstrated by Wemyss's experience of being sent to the Aegean to set up an advanced base with the assurance from Churchill that he would receive detailed instructions from Carden when he arrived, only to discover that Carden was astonished to see him and had no idea of the role he was to play.[51] Throughout the Eastern Mediterranean, there were countless similar instances of baffled and eventually angry senior officers. The plaint of one – 'Who is coordinating and directing this great combine?' – could have been echoed by many others. Wemyss wrote: 'Never has a big campaign been so hastily organized and got together, and never has such an undertaking had so little consideration given it from home.' The comment of Hankey on 12 April was just: 'The military operation appears, therefore, to be to a certain extent a gamble upon the supposed shortage of supplies and inferior fighting qualities of the Turkish armies.'[52] This is exactly what it was. Churchill and others have argued that the gamble was justified, and that it nearly came off. They have particularly cited the situation with regard to the Turkish supplies of heavy ammunition on the evening of 18 March and the absence of substantial and well-organized troops in the area before the middle of April. The first point is not valid, and on the second it must be remarked that Ian Hamilton and his staff were impressed by the Turks' preparations on the Peninsula when they sailed up the coast on 18 March;[53] the subsequent claim of the German commander, Liman von Sanders, that the Turkish forces were poorly positioned before he was appointed to the area on 24 March has been effectively challenged by Turkish historians and other students of the campaign. There is, indeed, considerable justification for the Turkish claim – made, among others, by Mustapha Kemal, then an unknown colonel – that von Sanders's policy of dispersal and withdrawal from the coast made the initial task of the British much easier

51. Robert Rhodes James: *Gallipoli*, pp. 40–1.

52. Hankey, op. cit., Vol. I. p. 302.

53. Hamilton: *Gallipoli Diary*, pp. 22, 29–30.

than it should have been. The margin between limited success and catastrophe was very small on 25 April. On the five beaches at the southern point of the Gallipoli Peninsula, where the 29th Division landed, resistance was only met at two; yet, out of some nine thousand men landed, over three thousand were killed or wounded. This in spite of a numerical superiority of over ten to one, and the full force of a massive naval bombardment.

Churchill described the operation in November 1915 as 'a legitimate war gamble'. In war, nothing can ever be certain, and most military enterprises are to some extent a gamble. But the crucial element is the degree of that gamble – the extent to which the operation is a matter of hazard. The dictum that in war one cannot guarantee success, one can only deserve it, may be recalled. It is difficult to avoid judgement that the Dardanelles venture did not deserve to succeed.

This assessment is put forward in defiance of many distinguished military authorities, including Sir Basil Liddell Hart, who has described the project as a 'sound and far-sighted conception, marred by a chain of errors in execution almost unrivalled even in British history'. It is here argued that the errors in execution stemmed directly from the fundamental fallacies in the original conception; that this conception was not, in itself, 'sound'; and that it was, in short, a wholly illegitimate war gamble, which demonstrated a fundamental deficiency in Churchill's equipment as a military strategist, subsequently described by the Australian, Sir John Monash, as 'the Churchill way of rushing in before we are ready, and hardly knowing what you are going to do next'. The Gallipoli catastrophe cannot be better described.

It was swiftly seen that the gamble had comprehensively failed. By 9 May the shocked and exhausted British and Dominion troops were definitely checked on the rugged cliffs of Anzac and the bald slopes of Achi Baba.[54] The Allies had

54. In *The World Crisis* Churchill refers to 'the vital observation-point of Achi Baba', whose capture 'would have enabled the indirect naval fire to be directed with the utmost accuracy upon the forts at the Narrows'. This was a misconception, and one that has been often repeated. The forts at the

suffered over twenty thousand casualties in the field, and three
more battleships sunk. On the Western Front, the three
battles of Aubers Ridge (March), Second Ypres (April) and
Festubert (May) had resulted in heavy casualties and no gains.
By the middle of May the Asquith Government's position had
become precarious in the extreme.

*

The combination of the Dardanelles reverse, the looming crisis
in Parliament over the alleged shortage of shells, and – on 15
May – the dramatic resignation of Fisher,[55] brought the Government down. The actual circumstances of Fisher's resignation
were of less relevance than the disclosure of the rift between
the young First Lord and the aged First Sea Lord. Churchill
always believed that the challenge to the Ministry could – and
should – have been met and defeated in public debate. 'I am
sure,' he has written, 'I could have vindicated the Admiralty
policy.' This was not the opinion of others, then or later.
Churchill was completely unprepared for the hostility with
which he personally was regarded, although a reading of the
Press – particularly *The Times* and the *Morning Post* – should
have given him ample warning. 'Mr Churchill's characteristics,' the *Morning Post* declared, 'make him in his present
position a danger and an anxiety to the nation'; and, at the
end of April, 'Mr Churchill's instinct for the melodramatic has
blossomed into megalomania.' What was far more significant,
and far more deadly, was the fact that Churchill had so little
support within the Cabinet, the Admiralty, or the Liberal
Party. The episodes in which he had been involved since the
outbreak of war had illuminated Churchill's eagerness – which,
in the opinion of some, amounted to a mania – to establish a
military reputation. His excitement and ardour for action,
and his fascination for bold and dramatic enterprises had made
many men regard him with increasing alarm. His feverish

Narrows are not visible from the Achi Baba summit; it is necessary to move
about a mile to the East across difficult country, before a somewhat
unsatisfactory view of the forts can be obtained.

55. For the circumstances, see Marder, op. cit., Vol. II, pp. 266–93.

activity, often high-handed conduct, and manifest enjoyment of drama evoked admiration in a few, apprehension in many, and genuine and profound fear in others. Confidence in his judgement and stability had been grievously undermined in the Admiralty, the Navy, the Cabinet and – above all – in the Conservative Opposition. When the crash came, he found himself – like Lord Randolph in December 1886 – completely isolated. Absorbed in his great work, dominated by the war and his part in it, he was wholly unaware of the abrupt fall of his reputation, and impatient of any attempt to warn him of the true situation. A clear warning was delivered in private by Bonar Law, and was strongly resented. Beaverbrook has written:

His attitude from August 1914 was a noble one, too noble to be wise. He cared for the success of the British aims, especially in so far as they could be achieved by the Admiralty, and for nothing else. His passion for this aim was pure, self-devoted, and all-devouring. He failed to remember that he was a politician and as such treading a slippery path; he forgot his political tactics . . . As he worked devotedly at his own job, the currents of political opinion slipped by him unnoticed.[56]

As soon as he received warning of Fisher's resignation, Law saw Lloyd George, and they agreed that the situation was impossible. If Churchill came to the House of Commons and said that Fisher had resigned but that he remained, and proposed to re-cast the Board of Admiralty, there would have been a major parliamentary ·explosion. Asquith quickly appreciated the situation. He had no wish to have a Coalition, but he acted with decision and celerity to retain the reality of power while conceding a nominal partnership to the Conservative leaders.

It was ironical that Churchill, who had consistently been an advocate of Coalition, should have initiated it under circumstances so disastrous to his own fortunes. When he awoke to the tides sweeping inexorably against him, he desperately attempted to save himself. Messages were dispatched to

56. Beaverbrook: *Politicians and the War*, p. 125.

Asquith, to Bonar Law and even to Fisher, to whom he
offered (on 17 May) a seat in the Cabinet if he would remain,
with himself as First Lord. The episode is not related in *The
World Crisis*. On 17 May he was putting suggestions to Asquith
for the new Cabinet; by 21 May he was appealing for 'any
office – the lowest if it is to be of use in this time of war'.[57]
In those four days he had at last appreciated the peril of his
position. Fisher destroyed himself on 19 May when he sent
in a preposterous series of demands to Asquith; by this point,
he had effectively destroyed Churchill as well. The Ministerial
Crisis of May 1915 is still characterized by some mystery, and
on several important points there is considerable controversy.
But it is clear that the removal of Churchill from the Admiralty
was virtually a *sine qua non* for Conservative participation. In
later years Churchill persuaded himself that he had been
destroyed by blind Tory hostility and by lack of loyalty on
Asquith's part. According to Lord Riddell, Churchill described
Asquith at the time as 'Terribly weak – supinely weak. His
weakness will be the death of him.' The events of May 1915
opened up a gulf between Churchill and Asquith that was
never to be bridged. Churchill was preserved, with the sinecure
post of Chancellor of the Duchy of Lancaster and membership
of the new Dardanelles Committee. He subsequently wrote
with asperity:

When Lord Fisher resigned in May and the Opposition threatened
controversial debate, Asquith did not hesitate to break his Cabinet
up, demand the resignations of all Ministers, end the political lives
of half his colleagues, throw Haldane to the wolves, leave me to
bear the burden of the Dardanelles, and sail on victoriously at the
head of a Coalition Government. Not 'all done by kindness'! Not
all by rosewater! These were the convulsive struggles of a man of
action and of ambition at death-grips with events.[58]

57. Asquith Papers. Mrs Churchill wrote to Asquith: 'Winston may in
your eyes and in those with whom he has to work have faults, but he has the
supreme quality which I venture to say very few of your present or future
Cabinet possess – the power, the imagination, the deadliness, to fight
Germany' (Jenkins, op. cit., p. 361).

58. *Great Contemporaries*, p. 122.

In fact, in very difficult circumstances, Asquith had done reasonably well for Churchill and very well for the Liberals. In the new Government all the key posts remained in Liberal hands, and only one – the Admiralty, under Balfour – was held by a Conservative. It was a remarkable exercise in political legerdemain. It was, however, just a bit too clever. The Asquith Coalition was, from its inception, an uneasy, suspicious, divided confederation. 'You cannot imagine,' Birrell wrote to Redmond, 'how I loathe the idea of sitting cheek by jowl with these fellows.' And Walter Long wrote to Carson: 'I loathe the very idea of our good fellows sitting with these double-dyed traitors.'

This had been the first reverse Churchill had suffered in his political career, and it was a severe one indeed. For a time, as Lloyd George has related, 'the brutality of the fall stunned Mr Churchill'. Churchill himself subsequently related that 'Like a sea-beast fished up from the depths, or a diver too suddenly hoisted, my veins threatened to burst from the fall in pressure. . . . At a moment when every fibre of my being was inflamed to action, I was forced to remain a spectator of the tragedy, placed cruelly in a front seat.' [59]

He had fallen virtually unmourned. In the hour of disaster his considerable achievements at the Admiralty in the three years before the war were forgotten, his deficiencies magnified out of true proportion. The public could not know, nor was it to know for many years, the extent of his contribution to the expansion of the Navy in 1911–14, nor of his actions in the first vital weeks of the war; nor, above all, of his initiation of the tank in the teeth of official scepticism, the weapon that held the secret of the breakthrough on the Western Front. His errors, real and imagined, of his administration of the Admiralty were all that men saw. Richmond described him as 'a shouting amateur', and commented that Churchill's 'personal vanity occupies so large a place in the arrangements that the operation is either a fiasco or is most wasteful in lives or material – or both'. Beatty wrote that 'the Navy breathes freer now it is rid of the succubus Churchill'. Jellicoe described

59. *Thoughts and Adventures.*

him as 'a public danger to the Empire'. The King curtly commented that Churchill was 'impossible'. Many Liberals,
chagrined by their downfall, saw him as the author of all their
woes. Mrs Asquith wrote with bitterness that the Cabinet had
been 'smashed', 'by the man whom I always said *would* smash
it – Winston'.[60] He had his defenders. J. L. Garvin wrote in
the *Observer* (23 May): 'He is young. He has lion-hearted
courage. No number of enemies can fight down his ability and
force. His hour of triumph will come.' From the Conservative
side, F. S. Oliver wrote to his brother that 'the only two men
who really seem to understand that we are at war are Winston
and Lloyd George. Both have faults which disgust one peculiarly at the present time, but there is a reality about them, and
they are in earnest, which the others aren't.'[61] But such supporters were few as Churchill surveyed the desolation of his
hopes and ambitions. But, as he once wrote in another context:
'Thus the beaver builds his dam, and thus when his fishing is
about to begin, comes the flood and sweeps his work and luck
and fish away together. So he has to begin again.'[62]

*

Churchill, although a member of the Dardanelles Committee,
was in the main a frustrated spectator of the events of June–
November 1915. On 28 May Kitchener circulated a memoran-

60. In an interesting article in *The Journal of Modern History* (Vol. 40,
No. 2, June 1968, pp. 257–77) Mr Stephen Koss argues that Churchill had
played a substantial part in engineering the crisis that led to the fall of the
Asquith Government, and had been part of a conspiracy that included Lloyd
George and Balfour. Mr Koss states that Churchill, while on a visit to
French's headquarters on 8–9 May, had arranged with Colonel Repington,
the military correspondent of *The Times*, for the publication of the sensational article describing the acute shortage of shells in France, which appeared on 14 May. 'As was so often the case,' Mr Koss writes, 'his impatient
pursuit of his goals, however laudable, rebounded to his disadvantage as a
politician.' This new interpretation of the events of May 1915 is stimulating,
but in my judgement Mr Koss's evidence does not substantiate his claims
to a degree that would make me seriously re-evaluate the crisis. Other
historians may of course find Mr Koss's evidence more convincing than I do.

61. F. S. Oliver: *The Anvil of War*, p. 92.

62. *My Early Life*, p. 159.

dum on the military situation that stated that 'it will be seen that nearly all the arguments on which the decision to attack the Dardanelles was based still apply with undiminished force. The difficulties of the enterprise, on the other hand, have proved more formidable than was at first anticipated, and a much greater effort than was originally budgeted for is now required.'[63] Churchill followed this with 'A Note on the General Situation' on 1 June that argued on the same lines:

. . . We should be ill-advised to squander our new armies in frantic and sterile efforts to pierce the German lines. To do so is to play the German game . . .

The position at the Dardanelles is at once hopeful and dangerous. The longer it lasts the more dangerous it will become. The sooner it is settled the sooner everything can again, if desired, be concentrated on the French and Flemish front . . . It seems most urgent to try to obtain a decision here and wind up the enterprise in a satisfactory manner as soon as possible.[64]

Churchill expressed these views publicly in a speech at Dundee on 5 June when he declared that 'there never was a great subsidiary operation of war in which a more complete harmony of strategic, political and economic advantages has combined, or which stood in truer relation to the main decision which is the central theatre. Through the Narrows of the Dardanelles and across the ridges of the Gallipoli Peninsula lie some of the shortest paths to a triumphant peace.'

The Dardanelles Committee[65] was impressed by these arguments, and authorized the dispatch of three Divisions of Kitchener's New Army to the Eastern Mediterranean and a substantial reinforcement of the naval forces. Although the Cabinet sanctioned these movements with some reluctance the Committee authorized the dispatch of two more Divisions at

63. P R O CAB 37/128/27.

64. ibid., 37/129/1.

65. Its membership was: Asquith, Grey (Foreign Office), Lloyd George (Munitions), Balfour (Admiralty), Bonar Law (Colonies), McKenna (Exchequer), Churchill, Kitchener, Lansdowne (Minister without Portfolio), Crewe (Lord President of the Council), Selborne (Agriculture) and Curzon (Lord Privy Seal). Carson (Attorney-General) joined in August.

the beginning of July. 'There was at first evidence of considerable divergence of opinion,' Asquith reported to the King on 19 June, 'some members of the Cabinet thinking that the steps proposed committed us to an offensive strategy on a large & increasing scale. It was pointed out, however, that both the Committee, and the General & Admiral on the spot, were agreed that we should aim at a "starving" rather than a "storming" operation . . . In the end the steps proposed were unanimously approved.'[66]

The division of opinion within the Cabinet reflected the developing contest between the 'Western' and 'Eastern' concepts of fighting the war. On 18 June Churchill pointed out in another memorandum that Joffre's May offensive had cost 220,000 casualties, and that the British had suffered some 100,000 casualties since 22 April on the Western Front: 'Out of approximately 19,500 square miles of France and Belgium in German hands we have recovered about 8.' He went on to emphasize that Constantinople was 'the prize, and the only prize, which lies within reach this year. It can certainly be won, without unreasonable expense, and within a comparatively short time. But we must act now, and on a scale which makes speedy success certain.'[67] Nevertheless, although Kitchener urged on 26 June that 'the right attitude for the Allied forces to adopt in the West is that of active defence',[68] the Cabinet agreed on 3 July that 'we regard the Western Theatre as, for the time being, the dominant one'. French was urged to defer any major offensive, but if the French 'think it necessary to undertake such an operation, Sir John French will lend such co-operation with his existing force as, in his judgement, will be useful for the purpose, and not unduly costly to his army'.[69] These weak compromises prompted Churchill to write in July a memorandum that was not circulated until 6 October, but which may be quoted at this point:

66. PRO CAB 37/130/14.
67. ibid., 37/130/16.
68. ibid., 37/139/27.
69. ibid., 37/131/3.

. . . The governing instrument here has been unable to make up its mind except by very lengthy processes of argument and exhaustion, and the divisions of opinion to be overcome, and the number of persons of consequence to be convinced, caused delays and compromises. We have always sent two-thirds of what was necessary a month too late . . . Opportunity after opportunity, military and diplomatic, has been lost in the south-east of Europe. Risks have been taken in the name of prudence before which foolhardihood itself would pale . . .[70]

The Gallipoli Campaign reached its climax at the beginning of August, when Hamilton launched a highly ambitious night attack from the Anzac position to capture the crucial heights of the Sari Bair Ridge. Simultaneously, a holding attack was delivered at Helles and a New Army Corps was landed on the virtually undefended beaches at Suvla, to the north of Anzac.[71] Although daring in conception, the offensive was over-ambitious, inadequately planned and wretchedly bungled. All the mistakes of the original landings of 25 April were faithfully repeated. Several new ones were added for good measure. The British and Dominion troops on the Peninsula were exhausted by three months of almost incessant fighting and strain, and most of the army was ravaged with dysentery. In contrast, the fresh troops of the New Army were painfully inexperienced. Neither the veterans nor the newcomers were given a fair chance.

It is always easy to bestow judgements upon military commanders in safety and comfort long after the event. But the events of 6–10 August on Gallipoli, and the planning that preceded them, may be fairly cited as a classic example of how not to conduct an operation of such crucial importance. The errors of GHQ and the Corps Commanders were nearly redeemed by the errors of the Turks, by the numerical preponderance Hamilton enjoyed, and by the prodigious valour of the troops. But by noon on 10 August it was evident that the offensive had failed terribly. On 21 August Hamilton made

70. ibid., 37/135/9.

71. The details of Hamilton's plans are described in the author's *Gallipoli*, Chapter 10.

a last vain attempt to break through at Suvla. He had lost over forty thousand men in less than three weeks. When his request for further reinforcements reached the Dardanelles Committee despair and disillusionment gripped the British Government.

Churchill's isolation became very marked after the disastrous failure of the August offensive. The acrimony that now characterized the exchanges of the Dardanelles Committee may be demonstrated by two extracts from its Minutes:

19 August

MR BONAR LAW said that though Sir Ian Hamilton stated what he wanted, he was much less hopeful than he had been. He was always *nearly* winning. . . . Mr Bonar Law considered that a further attack would be a useless sacrifice of life.

SIR E. CARSON agreed . . .

MR CHURCHILL inquired why the losses incurred in Gallipoli were felt so much more, apparently, than the losses incurred in France.

SIR E. CARSON suggested that the reason was that in France the losses are incurred in killing Germans.[72]

27 August

SIR E. CARSON said that the public was kept in ignorance, and would be very much surprised when they heard of the losses . . .

MR CHURCHILL asked if it was suggested that the hoardings should be placarded with 'Great Disaster'! . . .

SIR E. CARSON said that the slaughter which had gone on was no success, and inquired if it were to be continued.

MR BONAR LAW asked if Sir Ian Hamilton was supposed to be acting on the defensive, or if he was going to continue on his course of sacrificing men without a chance of success.[73]

From the end of August the voices of those ministers who began to favour withdrawal from Gallipoli became more insistent. Confidence in Hamilton had, not surprisingly, almost vanished, and ugly reports were drifting back to London of the manner in which the August offensive had been conducted.[74] Churchill fought against the campaign's critics, but

72. PRO CAB 42/3/15.
73. PRO CAB 42/3/17.
74. See the author's *Gallipoli*, pp. 312–16.

with diminishing effect. On 11 October Hamilton's estimate of the possibilities of a successful evacuation were sought, and he replied that approximately half his men and all their major equipment would be lost. By this time Lloyd George had joined Bonar Law in his determination to press for the evacuation of the Peninsula. On 14 October the Committee decided to recall Hamilton; General Sir Charles Monro was appointed in his stead. On the following day Churchill circulated another memorandum:

Nothing leads more surely to disaster than that a military plan should be pursued with crippled steps and in a lukewarm spirit in the face of continual nagging within the executive circle. Unity ought not to mean that a number of gentlemen are willing to sit together on condition either that the evil day of decision is postponed, or that not more than a half-decision should be provisionally adopted. Even in politics such methods are unhealthy. In war they are a crime . . . The soldiers who are ordered to their deaths have a right to a plan, as well as a cause.

He went on to accept Hamilton's estimate of the cost of leaving Gallipoli, and described the decision as the most terrible since the loss of the American Colonies; 'to re-embark and row out of range under the full pressure of a victorious and exulting army must be one of the most shocking tragedies of war . . . The whole episode will stand as an example of superior will power over superior resources.'[75]

It is difficult to accept Churchill's proposition that the movement towards evacuation was misjudged. The advocates of this policy in the Government were enormously fortified by Monro's firm recommendation for withdrawal. Churchill's anger at this advice was intense, and his harsh condemnation of Monro in *The World Crisis* must not be permitted to stand uncontroverted. Monro's decision was courageous, and it was right.[76] Nevertheless , the bluntness of his advice and the pro-

75. PRO CAB 37/136/12. The memorandum was in response to one by Law recommending evacuation.

76. See *The World Crisis*, Vol. II, p. 489; Lady Asquith: *Winston Churchill As I Knew Him*, p. 424; and the author's *Gallipoli*, pp. 323–5. On the publication of this book he received a letter from Lady Monro that movingly described the wound inflicted by Churchill's assault on her husband.

spect of evacuation made several ministers have second thoughts. Kitchener went out to the Dardanelles. Curzon circulated horrific forecasts of the probable slaughter on the beaches. Keyes produced a dramatic scheme for the Navy to smash through the Dardanelles defences. These plans were met with obdurate opposition by Bonar Law and those ministers who now agreed that Gallipoli had been an unmitigated disaster. By November the die was almost cast, but it was not until 8 December that the decision to evacuate Suvla and Anzac was taken. By this stage Churchill had left the Government.

By the autumn of 1915 the Government was beset on all sides. On every front the war was going dismally badly. The central dilemma of whether the war was to be run on the lines of the 'nation in arms', and whether military compulsion would be needed, had been continuously postponed. Criticism of the Government in general, and of Asquith, Kitchener and Churchill in particular, was becoming very vehement. The House of Commons was in a difficult temper. The Government itself was acutely divided. On 12 October Kitchener put his manpower requirements at 35,000 men a week. McKenna and Runciman led a group of ministers who questioned this figure. Lansdowne, Curzon, Lloyd George, Walter Long and Churchill not only accepted them but 'urged that our voluntary system of recruiting . . . could not be made to fill the gap'. Asquith, Balfour and Grey considered that 'it was by no means clear that any form of compulsion yet suggested . . . would be found capable of producing a better result'.[77] Lord Derby, the new Director of Recruiting, was entrusted with producing a scheme that would harmonize these divergent views. On 22 October, when Crewe was presiding in Asquith's absence, there was in effect a spontaneous Cabinet revolt. 'It was the unanimous view of the Cabinet,' Crewe reported to the King, 'that the present system is the opposite of effective. . . . Lord Crewe . . . was instructed to convey to him [Asquith] the unanimous conviction of the Cabinet that a drastic change is imperatively necessary.'[78]

77. P R O C A B 37/135/23.   78. ibid., 37/136/26.

On 11 November the Dardanelles Committee formally wound up, and was replaced by a War Committee; Curzon and Churchill were excluded. On the 15th Churchill resigned (for the first and last time in his career) and announced his determination to serve with the Army in France. He made a defiant resignation speech in the Commons before he left for the trenches. It was listened to with sympathy, but it was unfortunate that he referred to Gallipoli as 'a legitimate war gamble', a phrase that left an impression of lack of remorse or sense of personal responsibility for the emphatic reverse that had been suffered at the Dardanelles.

I have devoted such lengthy attention to Churchill's part in the Dardanelles Campaign because it was one of the most crucial episodes in his career. Up to this point, his career had been one of great success both in terms of office and power (and the two are far from synonymous). Now, at a single blow, the advance had been shatteringly checked. It was to be many years before the Gallipoli campaign was regarded in a less censorious light. At the time, and for many years afterwards, Churchill's critics were in the ascendant. Wemyss wrote that his name would be handed down to posterity 'as that of a man who undertook an operation of whose requirements he was entirely ignorant'. The Dardanelles Commission – appointed in 1916 to investigate the campaign – commented on his evidence that he had 'assigned to himself a more unobtrusive part than that which he actually played'. *The Times*, commenting in 1917 on the publication of the first part of the Report, conceded that Churchill had been consistent, but commented that it was 'the consistency of a dangerous enthusiast, who sought expert advice only when he could be sure of moulding it to his own opinion'. The Australian official historian, C. E. W. Bean, wrote that 'through a Churchill's excess of imagination, a layman's ignorance of artillery, and the fatal power of young enthusiasm to convince older and slower brains, the tragedy of Gallipoli was born'. An American commentator wrote in 1925 that 'it is doubtful if even Great Britain could survive another world war and another Churchill'. A hostile biographer wrote in 1931: 'The ghosts of the Gallipoli dead will always rise up to damn him anew in time of national emergency. Neither official historians, nor military hack writers, will explain away or wipe out the memories of the Dardanelles.'

This final forecast was not accurate. Churchill's measured defence of his actions in *The World Crisis* was profoundly impressive. Ian Hamilton and Keyes came to his defence, and the British official history – published in 1932–3 – marked the decisive moment in the rehabilitation not only of Churchill but of the Gallipoli campaign itself. And, with the knowledge of what subsequently happened in France and Russia, the Dardanelles venture seemed to make considerably more sense than had appeared to be the case in 1915. In particular, the sheer imaginativeness of the concept invested it with an attraction that was in sharp contrast with the dreary and bloody slogging-match on the Western Front. Perhaps this rehabilitation went too far, and both the campaign itself and the possibilities of victory have tended to become exaggerated and over-romanticized. As one commentator of the campaign has remarked, 'no campaign so easily lends itself to retrospective sentimentality'.[79]

But this rehabilitation was far distant in 1915, and, as late as 1923, Churchill was still being shouted down at election meetings with cries of 'What about the Dardanelles?'

Even if an overwhelming case could be made to support the thesis that Churchill was 'right' over Antwerp and the Dardanelles, it would still not meet the question of why Churchill's major enterprises had ended in virtual disaster. While emphasizing again the point that Churchill cannot bear full responsibility for these failures, it also requires emphasis that he cannot be fully exonerated for his part in them. These points may be fairly made: he over-estimated his own knowledge and capacities; once enamoured by an idea and a plan, his total concentration on it and devotion to it hindered him from a cooler appreciation of the facilities available for its execution and the probable hazards that it would face; he

79. John North: *Gallipoli, The Fading Vision*, p. 20.

made insufficient use of the professional advice and experience
that was available to him, and too often beat down criticism
by argument rather than heeding it and utilizing it. The
epitaph on the Dardanelles campaign had in effect been written
by Lloyd George before it had begun: 'Expeditions which are
decided upon and organised with insufficient care generally end
disastrously.' [80]

Not the least of the misfortunes of this disastrous campaign
was that it removed from the Government a man at the height
of his energies and abilities with real ardour for the cause in
hand. Of all the members of the Asquith governments – even
Lloyd George [81] – Churchill was by far the most original and
capable War Minister – as Fisher said admiringly, 'He was a
War man!' – but his approach was too personalized, too
dramatic and too imperious. The observer is struck, once
again, by Churchill's impulsiveness and even impetuosity in a
crisis situation. There is a real difference between energy and
impetuosity. It is not necessary, when great matters are in the
balance, to clothe every episode and fact with drama; nor is it
necessary to take personal charge of operations in order to
ensure that they are being conducted with vigour. Churchill's
aggressiveness has been considered by some commentators as
his most valuable characteristic at the Admiralty. This may be
accepted, while making the qualification that his definition of
military aggressiveness had a tendency to the simplistic, in
which his appetite for operations such as the storming of Zee-
brugge or the Dardanelles was not matched by an adequate
appreciation of other methods by which the initiative could be
seized and maintained. One is reminded again of Churchill's
excitability, an important part of his character, and one that
is well illuminated by his tenure of the Admiralty from August
1914 to May 1915. There are great dangers in war of being too

80. Memorandum to the War Council, December 1914.
81. It is to be hoped that a critical examination of Lloyd George as a War
Minister will shortly be attempted. As the evidence remorselessly accumu-
lates, it does not appear probable that the first glowing estimates will be
confirmed.

calm; but the other extreme is no less perilous. As F. E. Smith subsequently wrote of Churchill: 'His able, restless, ambitious temperament was hardly content with its own legitimate ambit. He saw too much, and he tried to do too much. No one department, hardly one war, was enough for him in that sublime and meteoric moment.' And, over thirty years later, with this experience and other subsequent ones assimilated, Churchill wrote: 'I was ruined for the time being over the Dardanelles, and a supreme enterprise was cast away, through my trying to carry out a major and combined operation of war from a subordinate position. Men are ill-advised to try such ventures.'

*

'Nobody imagines that his disappearance from the political arena will be more than temporary,' *The Times* commented on Churchill's resignation. ' . . . Those who know the man best think he will come again. No man of his calibre can be content for long with a minor part.' This expectation was correct. Churchill's period at the Front with 'those magnificent Fusiliers' lasted for six months.[82] In March 1916 he returned to the House of Commons to deliver an attack on the Government that included the extraordinary proposal that Lord Fisher should be recalled to the Admiralty. Much of the good impression created by his departure to the war was destroyed by this hapless intervention, which gave the strong impression of a deeply resentful and ambitious man capable of using any opportunity or argument to effect his return to office. It was with difficulty that he was persuaded to return to France, and it was not surprising that many of his political friends viewed his conduct with despair. The episode also occasioned an exceptionally fierce assault upon him by the *Spectator*, in which it was charged that 'he has a restlessness of mind and an instability of purpose, joined with the restless egotism of the political

82. For a delightful account of this period see *With Winston Churchill at the Front*, by 'Captain X' (Captain A. D. Gibb, who was Churchill's adjutant and was subsequently Regius Professor of Law at the University of Glasgow).

gambler, which would make him a most dangerous element '.[83]

Sir Max Aitken – better known as Lord Beaverbrook, the title he took in December 1916 when, to his surprise, he found himself propelled into the House of Lords [84] – had been behind Churchill's return, and he tried to persuade Churchill to stay in the country. Aitken had played a leading part in Bonar Law's accession to the Conservative leadership in 1911; he was now at work in an attempt to reorganize the Government – a reorganization that would involve at least the reduction of the authority of Asquith and the elevation of that of Bonar Law. Churchill's letter to him emphasized his personal dilemma:

. . . the problem wh now faces me is vy difficult; my work out here with all its risk & all its honour wh I greatly value: on the other hand the increasingly grave situation of the war and the feeling of knowledge and of power to help in mending matters wh is strong within me: add to this dilemma the awkwardness of changing and the cause of my I hope unusual hesitations is obvious. In principle I have no doubts; but as to time & occasion I find vy much greater difficulties . . .[85]

Admirable soldier though Churchill may have been, his abilities were inadequately employed in the Army, and he was right to make the decision to return to politics in the summer of 1916. But he remained an outsider. Much of his activity in this period was devoted to his defence of his actions over the Dardanelles before the Dardanelles Commission. His evidence, in its presentation and thoroughness, was a *tour de force*, and contributed substantially to the relative mildness with which

83. In a second article the *Spectator* ended a lengthy assault on Churchill by applying to him the lines of Pope:

> See the same man, in vigour, in the gout
> Alone, in company, in place or out
> Early at business and at hazard late,
> Mad at a fox chase, wise at a debate,
> Drunk at a borough, civil at a ball,
> Friendly at Hackney, faithless at Whitehall.

84. See *Politicians and the War*, p. 533.
85. K. Young: *Churchill and Beaverbrook*, pp. 42–3.

the Commission treated his part. He was also brought in by
Balfour to write an account of the Battle of Jutland, after the
evil effects on public morale of the first communiqué – issued on
2 June – had been realized. The comment of *The Times* (5
June) was tart and to the point: 'This use of Mr Churchill –
who has no association whatever with the Government, who
apparently aspires at this moment to head an Opposition, and
whose strategical utterances during the war have hardly been
models of accuracy – was the most amazing confession of
weakness on the part of the Admiralty.' In this period Churchill
also wrote a series of articles on naval affairs in the *London
Magazine*, whose arguments – veering from approval of British
policy to advocacy of taking the offensive – were strikingly
inconsistent. This was not a happy period of his life. In the
complicated intrigues that resulted in Asquith's downfall and
Lloyd George's accession to the premiership early in December
Churchill played only a very minor role; a sharp clash with
Bonar Law at Aitken's house in November[86] emphasized the
differences between the two men. Churchill was deeply chagrined at his exclusion from the Lloyd George Coalition, and he
did not find the Opposition benches nor the company of the
fallen Asquithians congenial; as Beaverbrook noted, 'there
was a failure of sympathy. They saw him as a useful but
incalculable ally.' The Conservatives regarded him in considerably less favourable terms.

Nevertheless, no Prime Minister – and certainly not one as
acutely conscious of the precariousness of his position as Lloyd
George, who saw conspiracies everywhere – could view with
equanimity the presence in Opposition of this formidable
personality. Lloyd George certainly owed Churchill much, and
not least the spirited and whole-hearted loyalty that Churchill
had shown him in 1913 in the Marconi Scandal.[87] But Lloyd
George was not a man prone to honouring former obligations,
and it was Churchill's potential threat rather than affectionate
memories of joint battles and personal assistance in the past
that made Lloyd George anxious to draw him into the adminis-

86. It is vividly described in *Politicians and the War*, pp. 105–6.
87. See Randolph S. Churchill: *Winston S. Churchill,* Vol. II, pp. 553–8.

tration. Bonar Law always averred that he preferred Churchill against him every time; Lloyd George, fully aware of Churchill's abilities and energies and his position in the divided Liberal Party, took a more realistic view. On 10 May 1917 Churchill eclipsed Lloyd George in debate in secret session, and the Prime Minister resolved to brave the wrath of the Conservatives and secure Churchill.

It is doubtful whether Lloyd George had anticipated the virulence of the storm that his decision to offer Churchill the Ministry of Munitions evoked. Bonar Law, seriously annoyed himself, received angry letters from his colleagues and supporters;[88] over a hundred Conservative members signed a resolution protesting the appointment, and one, describing Churchill as 'a national danger', asked for a debate; the *Sunday Times* considered that his return to the Government constituted 'a grave danger to the Administration and the Empire as a whole'; Northcliffe was vehemently hostile; Lord Charles Beresford[89] organized a committee of protest and delivered a violent philippic against Churchill before a large and appreciative audience in the Queen's Hall. But Lloyd George stood firm, Bonar Law reluctantly accepted the situation, and the passions subsided. It is to Lloyd George himself that we look for the best analysis of the hostility to Churchill at this time:

Here was their explanation. His mind was a powerful machine, but there lay hidden in its material or make-up some obscure defect which prevented it from always running true. They could not tell what it was. When the mechanism went wrong, its very power made the action disastrous, not only to himself but to the causes in which he was engaged and the men with whom he was co-operating . . . He had in their opinion revealed some tragic flaw in the metal.

*

88. See Blake: *The Unknown Prime Minister*, pp. 360–1.

89. Beresford had been the recipient of one of Churchill's best sallies, in 1911, when he had described Beresford as 'one of those orators who, before they get up, do not know what they are going to say; when they are speaking, do not know what they are saying; and, when they have sat down, do not know what they have said'.

Churchill's alignment with Lloyd George was another decisive
moment in his career, which went far beyond his return to
office. The old Liberal Party had been riven by the events of
December 1916, and in the 1918 General Election was to be
destroyed for ever. The wounds of December 1916 were never
to be properly healed. Those Liberals who followed Lloyd
George had to accept the fact that they were dependent upon
Conservative support for their political survival. Lloyd
George's supremacy rested upon Conservative acquiescence and
his personal authority and political adroitness. Bonar Law
stated the situation with truth when he said in 1918 that 'By
our own actions we have made Mr Lloyd George the flag-bearer
of the very principles upon which we shall appeal to the
country. It is not his Liberal friends, it is the Unionist Party
which has made him Prime Minister, and made it possible for
him to do the great work that has been done by this government.'

After an initial period of unease, the nation and the Conservatives were dazzled by Lloyd George. After he had defeated
the last serious threat to his position in the Maurice Debate[90]
in May 1918, and it was seen that the German onslaught of
March was definitely checked, his authority was, for a time,
dominant. It seemed as though the great Centre Party, that
had for so long attracted Lloyd George and Churchill, had at
last materialized.

Churchill was a competent, energetic and efficient Minister of
Munitions, but he inherited a Department that had developed
itself into a going concern, and there was not a great opportunity for the Minister to make a deep impression. It was
noticeable that he was considerably more cautious than before
in his public utterances, and in his ministerial work was
uncharacteristically subdued.[91] He was – and realized himself
to be – a junior member of the Administration, charged with

90 See T. Wilson: *The Downfall of the Liberal Party*, pp. 109–12.

91. For the interesting and revealing episode concerning tank production,
in which he was opposed by Sir Albert Stern, see Lloyd George, *War
Memoirs*, Vol. IV, and Liddell Hart: *The Tanks,* Vol. I. The controversy is
not referred to in *The World Crisis*.

specific duties and an attendant at Cabinet meetings only when called for. Nevertheless, Lloyd George often took his private counsel, and his exclusion from the centre of affairs was less complete than Conservative Ministers appreciated or desired. But the relationship with Lloyd George was not that of pre-war days; it was, as Churchill noted, one of 'master and servant'.

*

When the war ended in November 1918 with what was for many people an unexpected suddenness, Lloyd George immediately called for a General Election, to be fought by the Coalition members. The plan had been maturing for some months past, and political foresight was well rewarded. The General Election of 1918 was the first in British history in which, under the provisions of the Representation of the People Act, 1918, women (over thirty and with a property qualification) could vote, and in which there was full adult male suffrage without any property qualifications. Not only had the electorate been transformed. Liberal fought Liberal; Conservative joined with Liberal and fought Liberal; Labour fought everyone. The only real issue was the continuation of the Lloyd George Coalition. In a somewhat arbitrary manner [92] 159 Liberals were favoured with the Lloyd George–Bonar Law endorsement derided by Asquith as the 'coupon', as compared with 382 Conservatives. The 'coupon' election was not a particularly agreeable contest. Lloyd George's most violent diatribes were directed against the Asquithian Liberals who, he alleged, had tried 'to over-throw a Government that was in the midst of a crisis whilst wrestling for victory' and who now were comparable with Germans who cried 'Kamerad'. When the dust cleared, the consequences of the 'coupon' were evident: 478 of the 541 'couponed' candidates had been returned; only 18 Asquithian Liberals had survived opposition from a sponsored Coalition candidate. [93] The Government had the massive support of 484 (338 Conservatives, 136 Lloyd George Liberals, and 10 other

92. Wilson, op. cit., pp. 144–9.
93. ibid., p. 180.

supporters) as opposed to 59 Labour and 26 Asquithian Liberals. Asquith himself was in the ranks of the defeated. It now remained to be seen whether the mutually profitable wartime alliance could survive the pressures and strains of peace.

*

In 1908, Gardiner had considered that Churchill's future was 'the most interesting problem of personal speculation in English politics'. In 1912 he had described Churchill as 'the unknown factor in politics', and the description still held good in 1918. Although he was once again in office, he was among the least significant and influential members of the Government. Although he had survived the vicissitudes of the war there could be no comparison between his position at the beginning and that which he held at its conclusion. Without a party, a following, or any territorial loyalty, his fortunes rested on far more precarious foundations than they had in 1914.

It is an inescapable feature of political life that it bestows many powerful attractions and rewards but denies security. A position gained by diligence and energy over a relatively long period of time can be lost with shattering suddenness. There are many political careers on which, when matters seem most serene and promising, Fate casts her baleful eye and destroys the agreeable picture. It is in such situations that the calibre of a man is fully tested, and his character exposed to the most cruel and demanding of examinations.

How had Churchill emerged from these tests? The check that he had suffered in May 1915 had been his first, and was in many respects the most serious. Many careers have crashed under far less grievous circumstances, never to recover. It may be argued that his restoration in 1917 was an act of good fortune, but the fact that the opportunity occurred was a tribute to his own persistence and to the recognition by Lloyd George of his strengths and capacities. In politics, as elsewhere, good fortune has to be earned.

By the close of 1918 he was forty-four, having almost reached the age at which Lord Randolph had died. He had started much earlier than his father, and his record in terms both of office and of solid achievement had been immeasurably greater. The advance of 1900–1914 had been prodigious, and although his performance in the war had been controversial and politically of mixed fortune, he could with justice claim achievements greater than any other minister with the exception of Lloyd George. His successes and his failures can be largely ascribed to youth and inexperience, which gave him often an unclouded vision but which often drew him into perilous avenues. He had demonstrated the vigour and dash of youth; also its inexperience, incaution and over-confidence.

He had demonstrated too the strength that he obtained from his exceptional egocentricity, which gave him the persistence and obstinacy which was now evident as one of his most important political attributes. His physical courage had never been in doubt; his moral resilience and determination had been questioned before the war, and now had been demonstrated.

But although it would be possible to assemble a formidable list of achievements at this stage of his career, the most striking feature would be the fact that, politically, it added up to so remarkably little. Egocentricity has its defects as well as its advantages. His shifts of allegiance were not liable to be interpreted favourably by all. If he was courageous, honest and sincere on most issues, he could also be of a blundering disposition, and his political senses too often lacked either subtlety or sensitiveness. There still remained in him much of the ardent pragmatism of youth, and it was still difficult to discern any motive power beyond that of personal ambition and a passionate patriotism. The compelling attraction of office was still manifestly dominant in all his political actions. The shadow of his errors – real and alleged – hung over him, and darkened his successes. His judgement and sense of proportion were still questioned. His stability and political purpose were still seriously doubted.

Let us attempt his portrait in November 1918. Behold him, then, after eighteen years of active politics and over ten years in office. Much of the early aggressiveness has been softened by age and experience. In manner he remains alert, thrusting, eager or, in sharp contrast fitting his mood, sombre, portentous and scowling with leaden responsibility. On the platform or in the House of Commons he is capable of sharp retort and vivid repartee, yet behind all his major speeches there lie hours and even days of meticulous preparation. His dedication to his career is total, even obsessive. Experience has not dimmed the originality of his mind, nor the intensity of his emotions, nor the volubility of his conversation. Partly consciously, but mainly because it is part of his nature, he remains firmly in the public eye, even in his hours of downfall and disgrace.

But his keen and aggressive personality has made enemies and also, by prolonged exposure, evoked a certain indifference in the minds of many. He has not been forgiven for his bold, melodramatic stances and actions that have so often resulted in disaster or humiliation. He has created no bed-rock of support in Parliament, in the Government, or in the country. Behold him, then, in his forty-fifth year, in the front rank of British politics, yet with the dank tides of suspicion and mistrust swirling ominously around him still.

Part Three

THE LLOYD GEORGE
COALITION
1919–1922

Even the most profound of national and international up-heavals seldom provide a satisfying clear and precise break in historical continuity. Severe though the impact of the Great War had been upon British society and institutions, no mortal blows had been delivered to the structure. The full consequences of the Great War were to be long-term, not immediate. The changes that the war had brought were, in the main, disliked and resented. The enormous citizen army was impatient to return to civilian life and pleasures. The Government, with general approval, swiftly dismantled the administrative structures that had been laboriously created as a result of the exigencies of the crisis. The desire to return to 'normalcy' was dominant and all-pervading. In the words of R. H. Tawney, '"Back to 1914" became a common cry.'

Britain had emerged from the war apparently in a far stronger position than she had enjoyed at its outset. The war had ruthlessly swept away all the other familiar European landmarks. Germany and Russia, crushed by military defeat and internal disintegration, had ceased to exist as great powers. The Austro-Hungarian and Ottoman Empires had vanished. France still stood, yet exhausted by her prodigious sacrifices. The German High Seas Fleet rode docilely at anchor in Scapa Flow. The German Colonies had been appropriated; the British stake in the Middle East had been vastly augmented. The war had demonstrated – or had seemed to demonstrate – the absolute unity and solidarity of the Empire. Britain had waged war for four years with no apparent grievous effects on her economy. Indeed, the war had had many beneficial effects upon her industry and commerce, notably in those industries – particularly engineering, chemical and scientific – in which she had lagged far behind her main rivals in 1914. It would be possible to claim that Britain emerged from the war in a con-siderably stronger position, internally and externally, than she had possessed in 1914.

The losses had to be calculated in other terms. The Empire had suffered some 947,000 dead, of which the British loss amounted to some 744,000 in the Army and Navy, to which had to be added 14,661 merchant seamen and more than 1,000 civilians killed as a result of German airship and aeroplane raids, while the terrible influenza epidemic of the dark winter of 1918–19 had killed a further 150,000. One in ten of the generation aged between twenty and forty-five during the war had gone. Some 160,000 wives had been widowed, and over 300,000 children had lost their fathers. Tens of thousands who had returned from the war were to suffer from its physical effects for the remainder of their lives. In 1921, nearly $3\frac{1}{2}$ million persons in Britain were receiving some kind of war pension or allowance.

Yet it did not seem at the close of the war that this sacrifice had been in vain. 'It was with feelings which do not lend themselves to words that I heard the cheers of the brave people who had borne so much and given all,' Churchill has written in *The World Crisis* of the scene on 11 November 1918; 'who had never wavered, who had never lost faith in their country or its destiny, and who could be indulgent to the faults of their servants when the hour of deliverance had come.' There seemed no reason, in November 1918, why Britain should not resume her confident place in the front rank of the Great Powers. Yet, within three years of the Armistice, most of these expectations had been falsified, many hopes had been shattered and the War Leader who was fêted so enthusiastically in November 1918 was to be ejected from office for ever, and to fall almost unlamented. Time was to demonstrate that the disturbance to Britain of the war had been more profound than had appeared at its conclusion, and that the pre-war political attitudes and responses had lost their relevance and attraction. 'Back to 1914' was to prove as inappropriate an attitude as 'Business as usual' had been in 1914.

*

When the new Parliament assembled for the first time in February 1919 a visitor to the House of Commons could swiftly see the political effects of the Great War. The Liberal phalanx of July 1914 had vanished, and its remnants were divided. Asquith and Edward Grey had gone,[1] and Lloyd George reigned at the head of a government that included Bonar Law, F. E. Smith,[2] and Churchill. A hundred and thirty-six Lloyd George Liberals confronted twenty-six supporters of Asquith, grouped disconsolately in Opposition. Politically, the Conservatives – who, having gained over eighty seats on their 1914 total, now thronged the Government benches – had won the war.

Some other changes were not so immediately apparent. In 1914 the Labour Party had been an appendage of the Liberals, thirty-nine strong in Parliament. In the 1910 Election Labour had fielded seventy-eight candidates, fighting on the Liberal programme; now, in February 1919, it had fifty-nine members, having sponsored 363 candidates. Most significantly of all, Labour had fought the election on its own programme, and had won 22·2 per cent of the votes cast as opposed to less than eight per cent in 1910.

The visitor to the Commons would have noticed one startling gap. The Irish Nationalist Party, that had swayed the course of British politics since the 1870s, had vanished and had been replaced by seventy-three Sinn Fein Members, who refused to take their seats at Westminster and proceeded to establish themselves in Dublin as the self-styled Dail Eireann. The absence of the Irish MPs was not, however, an indication of the disappearance of the Irish Question.

This Parliament has been severely criticized. Baldwin's comment that it seemed largely composed of 'hard-faced men who look as though they had done well out of the war' has been echoed by others. Austen Chamberlain described its members as 'a selfish, swollen lot'. Some historians have demonstrated that, statistically, it did not differ greatly from other modern Parliaments. Yet the character of a Parliament cannot be thus gauged with any adequacy, and we may accept

1. Grey had accepted a Viscountcy; Asquith was returned – for Paisley – a year later.

2. Now appointed Lord Chancellor, with the title of Birkenhead.

the overwhelming evidence of contemporaries that this was a hard, selfish, volatile and intolerant Parliament. It is not universally realized that every Parliament has its own character, and its own life. A reputation made in one Parliament may crash to disaster in another. The issues that torment one Parliament weary another. Even the jests that convulse one Parliament can be greeted with incomprehending or contemptuous silence in another. There are tranquil Parliaments; there are stormy Parliaments. All that can be said with any certainty is that no Parliament is like its predecessor or its successor. Even if the main issues remain, the reactions change. For even the most established political personality, every Parliament presents a new beginning and a new challenge.

Thus, on the morrow of his triumph, Lloyd George had to begin again. The Parliament that he had known since 1910 had gone. The House of Commons membership had changed beyond recognition. All the old political landmarks had disappeared. Former colleagues were now bitter opponents; former foes sat beside him on the Treasury Bench. He was surrounded by the Conservative bloc. He was cheered by the Conservative *claque*. He was a Prime Minister with a following that, for the most part, owed him no formal fealty. He reigned because of his great prestige and on account of his political usefulness, now eyed by a Parliament that in the main knew him not and whom he knew not.

But, at least where office was concerned, the immediate political future did not lie with the new men. Virtually all the politicians who were to play dominant roles in the next twenty years had had substantial political experience before 1914. Arthur Balfour had been in the House of Commons since 1874; Lord Curzon had been first elected in 1886; Lord Milner had stood – unsuccessfully – in 1885; Asquith had first entered the Commons in 1886, and Lloyd George had followed four years later; Austen Chamberlain had arrived in 1893, and Churchill and Bonar Law in 1900. Two relative latecomers were Stanley Baldwin and Neville Chamberlain, elected in 1908 and 1918 respectively; yet Baldwin was forty when elected, and Chamberlain was in his fiftieth year in 1918 after a long experience in Midland politics and, in 1917, a short and unhappy period as Director of National Service. Ramsay MacDonald and Philip Snowden had lost their seats in 1918, after being Members since 1906; they were to return to the Commons, and to lead the Labour Party throughout the 1920s.

Of the generation that had fought in the war, several were to make a position before 1939, including Eden, Attlee, Duff Cooper, Harold Macmillan, Edward Wood (subsequently Lord Irwin and then Lord Halifax), Walter Elliot, Hugh Dalton and Leslie Hore-Belisha. But, in the main, British politics between the wars were dominated by men who had been active in public life long before 1914.

Thus, although the visitor to the House of Commons in February 1919 would have been impressed by the many changes, he would also have noticed much that was familiar. The principal domestic political preoccupations of the pre-war years had not been crushed by the war. The manifold problems of Empire and the perennial quandary of handling a Free Trade economy, no less than the spectre of the unsolved Irish Question, came stalking imperiously out of the storm of war. Political memories could not be erased. Indeed, to some observers of Britain in 1919, the remarkable feature was that so little had seemed to have changed. But, as became gradually apparent, everything had changed.

*

It is necessary to move away from the broad picture of the history of the Lloyd George Coalition to contemplate the continuing career of one of its more prominent members.

Churchill was Secretary of State for War and Air between January 1919 and February 1921, but he was not a member of the War Cabinet until November 1919, when Lloyd George wound up the wartime arrangement of a small War Cabinet and reverted to the previous peacetime arrangements. From February 1921 until 19 October 1922 Churchill was Secretary of State for the Colonies.

The double burden of the War Office and the new Air

Ministry was a curiosity, and even in normal circumstances could not have been a very happy arrangement. In the post-war turmoil it was unfortunate that one man should bear the burden of two Service Departments; there was something to be said for having one minister in charge of all the Service Departments, and Churchill tried to persuade Lloyd George to make him in effect the Minister of Defence, but Lloyd George refused to entertain the proposal.[3] Thus, for most of 1919, Churchill found himself in charge of two Departments dominated by exceptionally strong-willed men,[4] coping with a series of major problems at home and abroad, without even being a member of the Cabinet.

As soon as Churchill formally took office in January 1919 he was faced with a major crisis in the Army. The mood of the soldiers had been manifested quickly after the end of the war by the refusal of troops in camps at Dover and Folkestone to embark for France. By January the attitude of substantial numbers of men was ugly. The cause was the decision to grant priority releases to men wanted in certain key industries, and also to men on leave who could produce written offers of employment. This was theoretically a perfectly justifiable action, but it meant in effect that priority for demobilization was being given to men who had been under arms for a short time, and militated against those who had been in the service for longer. Churchill solved what was rapidly becoming a major crisis by scrapping the previous plan and ordering that priority in discharge was to be firmly based on length of service. The disturbances subsided, though there were further isolated episodes in the summer, and demobilization proceeded swiftly and reasonably smoothly.

This was the first major shock that the Government had received. 1919 was to provide many more. Lloyd George and a large part of the Foreign Office moved to Paris, and for the first six months of the year the attention of the Prime Minister was concentrated upon the Peace Conference. Thus the pro-

3. Callwell: *Field-Marshal Sir Henry Wilson*, Vol. II, p. 203.
4. Sir Henry Wilson (Chief of the Imperial General Staff) and Sir Hugh Trenchard (Chief of the Air Staff).

cesses of Cabinet Government were rendered infinitely more complex by the frequent absences not merely of the Prime Minister and the Foreign Secretary but of other senior Ministers as well. This was perhaps inevitable, but the results were unfortunate.

The disturbances in the army – which included the burning of Luton Town Hall – seemed symptomatic of a mood of unrest that swept the country. The miners, the railwaymen and the transport workers formed the 'Triple Industrial Alliance' in February, an event that looked more significant in prospect than it does now in retrospect. In Glasgow there was a general stoppage, and wild scenes that included the flying of the Red Flag from the Town Hall, the hurried dispatch of troops and tanks, and the imprisonment of the alleged ringleaders. The alarm of ministers may seem, in retrospect, somewhat exaggerated. At a Cabinet meeting on 21 July Lloyd George commented on the threatened miners' strike that it was 'practical, and not theoretical Bolshevism, and must be dealt with with a firm hand . . . The whole of the future of this country might be at stake, and if the Government were beaten and the miners won, it would result in a Soviet government. A similar situation might result to that of the first days of the Revolution in Russia, and, although Parliament might remain, the real Parliament would be at the headquarters of the Miners' Federation in Russell Square.'[5] In the discussion that followed, Churchill said that four Divisions of the Rhine Army could be made available in an emergency. This was not an isolated episode; on 7 August he told the Cabinet that 'militarily, we were in a good position to fight the Triple Alliance'.

The Government reacted to each emergency as it arose. The wartime minimum wage was extended until September 1920; the out-of-work donation to ex-servicemen and unemployed civilian workers in firms working for the Ministry of Munitions was extended; a Coal Commission was set up to consider the problem of the coalmines; a grandiloquently titled National Industrial Conference was established. Throughout the year,

5. P R O C A B 23/15 (Minutes of War Cabinet, 21 July 1919).

on every major issue, the Government reacted rather than acted and postponed every issue that could be postponed; it was difficult indeed to detect any coherent policies in the hurried measures that harassed ministers took. Lord Milner told Sir Henry Wilson on 5 February that 'we are in chaos in England as regards these strikes, which under Lloyd George's regime are being dealt with by every sort of man and every sort of department, each acting on a different principle from the other.'[6] These methods did not differ greatly from those employed since December 1916 in the prosecution of the war, and in this both the Prime Minister and the War Cabinet were prisoners of their own former successes.

The new Secretary of State for War and Air was only peripherally involved in many of these matters. He was, however, very deeply involved in what was to develop into one of the major international and domestic issues of the year.

*

The tangled story of the origins of the Allied intervention in Russia may be briefly recounted.[7] The seizure of power by the Bolsheviks on 7 November 1917, and their almost immediate conclusion of an armistice with Germany, had resulted in the landing of small Allied forces at Archangel and Vladivostok in order to protect the substantial war supplies landed at these ports. The signature of the Treaty of Brest-Litovsk in March 1918 made it militarily desirable to give a more active support to those Russian forces prepared to continue the resistance against the Germans. The situation was that, by the end of 1918, there were some 30,000 Allied troops – over half of whom were British – established at Murmansk and Archangel, together with some 600,000 tons of munitions, commanded by General Ironside. In Siberia, there were up to 70,000 Czech troops, stranded by the chance of war, who had risen against the Bolsheviks and were in transit from Vladivostok to Europe; in the summer they had seized the main railway across Siberia. In addition, there were also American, French and

6. Callwell: *Field-Marshal Sir Henry Wilson*, Vol. II, p. 169.
7. See R. H. Ullman: *Intervention and the War*, for an excellent account.

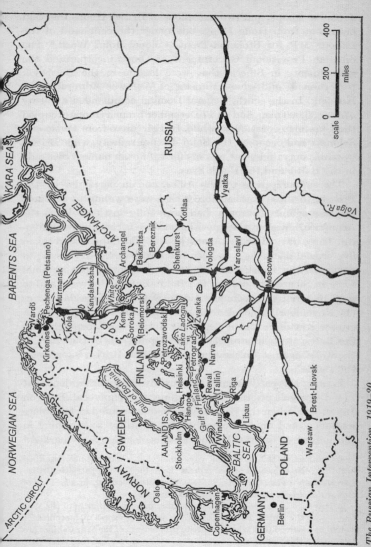

The Russian Intervention, 1919–20

Japanese troops, and two battalions of British troops that had been sent from Hong Kong, one under the command of the Labour MP for Stoke-on-Trent, Colonel John Ward.[8] The Siberian Provisional Government at Omsk incorporated the governments in Siberia that were hostile to the Bolshevik Government, and whose Minister of War was Admiral A. V. Kolchak. In the south, General Denikin commanded an army of over 30,000 men, and on 17 December French troops occupied the Ukrainian coast. Meanwhile, British forces from Persia and Salonika had occupied the Baku–Batum railway, while British warships operated what was in effect if not in name a blockade in the Baltic and the Black Seas.

The support given by the Allies, and in particular by the British, to those Russian forces that were willing to continue the war against Germany had been fully justified. With the Armistice, however, their position at once became more equivocal. Three days after the Armistice the War Cabinet had taken five crucial decisions – to keep the forces in North Russia; to recognize the Omsk Government; to maintain the nominal force in Siberia; to occupy the Baku–Batum Railway; and to send material and technical aid to Denikin. Three days later (17 November) Kolchak took over the Omsk Government. A cruiser squadron and a destroyer flotilla were dispatched to the Baltic 'to help strengthen the populations of that part of the world against Bolshevism and to assist British interests in the Baltic'.

Even at this early stage it was already becoming evident that Lloyd George's position in the Cabinet was equivocal. Both on 18 October, when the War Cabinet had attempted to formulate its policy, and on 14 November, his hostility to anything in the nature of an anti-Bolshevik crusade was very marked.[9]

8. Opinions on this individual vary somewhat. Churchill has described him thus: 'No one could better express the feelings of the patriotic British Labour man' (*The Aftermath*, p. 255). Mr Peter Fleming, in *The Fate of Admiral Kolchak*, gives a very different portrait.

9. This account is based very considerably upon the Minutes of the War Cabinet at the Public Record Office. To avoid an excess of footnotes, it should be assumed that all references to proceedings of the War Cabinet are taken from this source.

Nevertheless, he approved the decisions taken. Balfour expressed the dilemma well when he wrote in a memorandum (29 November) that 'it is for the Russians to choose their own form of government', but went on to point out that 'recent events have created obligations which last beyond the occasions which gave them birth'. This memorandum was a forecast of the attitude that was to be taken by the Foreign Office throughout 1919, and which can best be described as negative.

On 10 December Lloyd George initiated a discussion in the War Cabinet, in which he made his views very plain. For the War Office, Milner and Sir Henry Wilson strongly opposed any proposal to withdraw from Murmansk; Curzon said that the British were in honour bound to remain until the anti-Bolshevik forces that they had encouraged and supported could organize themselves properly. The Foreign Office attitude – expressed in Balfour's memorandum – was to the effect that the country was opposed to any major military intervention in Russia but that any governments set up under British protection must be maintained and supported. This was the general conclusion adopted by the Cabinet. Thus, at the end of 1918, no clear decisions had been reached beyond maintaining the *status quo*. Yet, by that very fact, the Government had gone far to convert an anti-German policy into one designed against the Bolsheviks. In October, the British commander at Murmansk had been ordered to secure bases that could only be of use against the Bolsheviks. And, in addition to the commitments of men and equipment, the British had incurred a substantial moral commitment to those forces opposed to the Bolshevik Government.

All this was done before Churchill went to the War Office in January 1919, and technically – as he subsequently pointed out on several occasions – he had no responsibility for the gradual slither into intervention that had already taken place. He had, however, been opposed to the Bolsheviks from the outset, and had been among the first to see the potentiality of the Czech troops. Furthermore, as early as 1 April 1918, when he had written to Beneš on the subject, he had seen the Czechs as being of value in an anti-Bolshevik rather than an anti-

German campaign.[10] Churchill was not one to conceal his feelings. In *The World Crisis* he has drawn a warmly over-sympathetic portrait of Nicholas II, and portrayed Russia at the beginning of 1917 as being on the verge of victory when 'Despair and Treachery usurped command at the very moment when the task was done . . . With victory in her grasp she fell upon the earth, devoured alive, like Herod of old, by worms.' The account of the dispatch of Lenin to Russia 'like a plague bacillus' is perhaps one of the most famous of his images. He loathed 'the foul baboonery' of Bolshevism, described Lenin as 'the monster crawling down from his pyramid of skulls', and was eager to assist as Minister of Munitions in the rapid supply of surplus military equipment to the anti-Bolshevik forces. 'Winston all against Bolshevism,' Henry Wilson noted approvingly on 20 January 1919, 'and therefore, in this, against Lloyd George.'[11]

This divergence of attitude had already become plain. Churchill had made his first intervention in the discussion on 23 December, when he had attended a meeting of the War Cabinet. He had described the alternatives as either to allow the Russians 'to murder each other without let or hindrance', or for the Allies to intervene 'thoroughly, with large forces, abundantly supplied with mechanical appliances'. It was made plain that he favoured the latter course, and was opposed with some vigour by Lloyd George. On 31 December the division between the two was demonstrated again, when Churchill argued strongly for collective intervention 'to restore the situation and set up a democratic government'; he was convinced that Bolshevism 'represented a mere fraction of the population, and would be exposed and swept away by a General Election held under Allied auspices' – Lloyd George retorted that he was 'definitely opposed to military intervention in any shape'. On 10 January Churchill made his personal position clear at a meeting of the War Cabinet, and strongly opposed any suggestion of a withdrawal of support from Omsk. On the 16th, in Paris, Lloyd George spoke out vigorously against

10. See F. S. Northedge: *The Troubled Giant*, pp. 72–3.
11. Callwell, op. cit., Vol. II, p. 165.

intervention at a meeting of the Council of Ten, saying that 'it is hardly the business of the Great Powers to intervene either in lending financial support to one side or the other, or in sending munitions to either side'. He proposed a truce, and the invitation to Paris of the representatives of all factions in Russia. This was opposed by the French and Italian representatives, but led to the proposal on the 21st by President Wilson that the parties should end fighting and meet with representatives of the Powers on Princes' Island (Prinkipo) in the Sea of Marmara. The Council approved the invitation, whose Preamble contained the significant words: 'The Powers . . . recognize the absolute right of the Russian people to direct their own affairs without dictation or direction of any kind from outside.'

The Prinkipo Plan swiftly evaporated, the conditions of the White Russians being incompatible with both the spirit and the letter of President Wilson's proposal. Churchill subsequently wrote that 'the whole idea of entering into negotiations with the Bolsheviks was abhorrent to the dominant elements of public opinion, both in Great Britain and in France'.[12] This is a very doubtful contention, but there were substantial elements on the Conservative benches who shared Churchill's views. On 12 February the Prinkipo Plan came under heavy attack in the Commons, and Lloyd George put the case for non-intervention with vigour. 'There is no sane man in Britain who would advise us, after nearly five years of war, to undertake that enterprise.' Nevertheless, this was in effect the policy that Churchill was now advocating, without Lloyd George's opposition. Meanwhile, Bolshevik attacks on the advanced Allied forces on the Archangel front required reinforcement from Murmansk, and plans for naval reinforcements were approved by the Cabinet at the beginning of February, on the assumption that only 'an active defence' was intended.[13]

When Churchill had taken over the War Office on 14 January

12. *The Aftermath*, p. 172.
13. An excellent account of the naval side of the intervention is to be found in S. Roskill: *Naval Policy between the Wars*, Vol. I, pp. 131–69.

one of his first actions had been to circulate a memorandum to all commanders asking, among other things, whether their men would 'parade for draft to overseas, especially to Russia'. This 'Secret and Urgent' circular also requested information on the attitude of the men to orders to help preserve the public peace and for assistance in strike breaking, and of the influence of trade unionism on them. A copy was obtained and published by the *Daily Herald*, and the episode did nothing to improve Churchill's relations with the trade union movement. The uniform reply was that the men would parade for service overseas with the exception of Russia. This meant that British 'intervention' against the Bolsheviks would have to be material assistance in the form of equipment and money, and the best use of what troops were already on the spot, fortified with volunteers. This was the policy that Churchill now urged upon the War Cabinet.

On 13 February the War Cabinet had a lengthy discussion of the position, initiated by Lloyd George on the basis of a paper prepared by the General Staff. Lloyd George did not conceal his reluctance to perpetrate intervention. Churchill's contribution was lengthy, and is of sufficient importance to be quoted at some length:

Mr Churchill said that there was no doubt that the only chance of making headway against the Bolsheviks was by the use of Russian armies. If Russian armies were not available, there was no remedy. Large British and French Armies were not to be thought of . . . Unless the Russian forces could be made into an effective army, the whole undertaking was impossible . . . he felt that if we did not decide upon a policy we should have a succession of disasters, followed by wholesale massacres and the extermination in one way or another of the whole of the people who had been supporting us. If we were unable to support the Russians effectively, it would be far better to take a decision now to quit and face the consequences, and tell these people to make the best terms they could with the Bolsheviks, than to leave our troops there and continue without a policy. Prinkipo, whatever was thought of it, was a plan. He did not agree with it, but if it had succeeded it would have led to something. Assuming that Prinkipo was at an end something must take its place. He hoped it would be possible, before President Wilson left for America, to arrive at a decision.

Lloyd George criticized the General Staff's paper on the grounds that it dealt not with military facts but with political hypotheses. Churchill replied that

We were not dealing with facts which were at all certain. We were endeavouring to animate the wavering minds of the Russian forces, which were all that we could rely on. The Russian *moral* depended upon the Allies having a decided policy and carrying it out energetically . . . he would have a Paper prepared on the lines the Cabinet required. He would ask the General Staff to say what was the maximum to be attained, within the limits described, upon the basis that we declared war on the Bolsheviks by a united declaration in Paris. Unless we assumed a wholehearted effort within the limits described, none of the Russian forces could be counted on as effective forces in the scheme . . .

He drew particular attention to the condition of Omsk, and referred to the 5,000 miles of the Trans-Siberian Railway, which had been opened with extraordinary swiftness last summer by the Czechs. That Railway was at present held in a very loose condition by the ill-organized forces of Admiral Kolchak, a handful of British troops and Czechs. In view of these facts he was of opinion that it was possible to ward off the Bolsheviks with comparatively small forces in that area better than anywhere else in the world. He would make a plain proposition to the United States, that if they were not prepared to come in and do their share they should have no right to stop the Omsk Government from coming to terms with the Japanese. If the Russians could come to terms with the Japanese to send a few effective divisions to strike at the Bolsheviks, he could not see that British interests were affected. He suggested that we should send a few thousand British volunteers so that we were properly represented, and let the Japanese carry on . . .

Edwin Montagu (Secretary of State for India) asked what were the limits to be placed on British intervention, particularly if their allies were defeated by the Reds, and the British forces placed in jeopardy.

Mr Churchill remarked that he would tell the Russians plainly the limits within which they should expect assistance, and if they did

not like our terms they could reject them. It was necessary to have
a policy to place boldly before the nation, and it was imperative to
declare that no man should be sent by compulsion to Russia.

Shortly afterwards, in reply to a question by Austen
Chamberlain, Churchill said that 'there would be no difficulty
in finding the necessary volunteers'. He went on to put his
argument plainly enough:

> Mr Churchill said that if the Allies would send out a message of
> defiance to the Bolsheviks and would state in terms what material
> support they were prepared to give to the anti-Bolsheviks, he thought
> that on that basis the General Staff would be prepared to say
> whether there was reasonable hope of success. It seemed to him to be
> a choice between a forlorn hope in that case, and a certain disaster,
> if no such steps were taken.

This was followed by an account by General Poole of his
impressions of the situation in the southern Russian sector,
which he had left on 24 January. 'In his opinion General
Denikin was not a great soldier nor a good administrator, but
he was thoroughly patriotic and enjoyed the respect of everybody.' He went on to say that 'the Bolsheviks had never been
very serious fighters. The element of surprise was everything
in a campaign against them. The impression the Bolsheviks
gave him was that he was a man who wanted to live a long
time.' He gave it as his opinion that 'if we supplied the guns
we had promised, that would be quite enough'.

This disturbing evidence of the kind of information the
Secretary of State was receiving from the front did not impress
Lloyd George, who remarked that 'the Russian Generals upon
whom we were relying had no really popular movement behind
them'.

Churchill then changed his argument, and, in a rather startling direction, spoke of the probability that within five or six
years

> Germany would be at least twice as big and powerful as France in
> landpower . . . He did not expect an immediate appeal to arms by
> the Germans, but the future was full of menace . . . If no proper
> Government in Russia were brought into existence, Russia would

automatically fall a prey to Germany. . . . The Russian situation must be judged as a part of the great quarrel with Germany, and unless we were able to go to the support of the Russians there was a possibility of a great combination from Yokohama to Cologne in hostility to France, Britain and America. He regarded a friendly Government in Russia and a strong Poland as the two essentials . . .[14]

Following this meeting, Churchill secured Lloyd George's consent[15] to an immediate approach to President Wilson – about to leave Paris to return to America – in order to investigate the possibility of Allied action. The meeting took place on the evening of 14 February. Balfour at once introduced Churchill to the President, and left the account of the British position to the Secretary of State for War.

The accounts that we have of this meeting are unambiguous. In response to Churchill's questions, President Wilson made it plain that in his view all Allied forces should leave Russia. When Churchill pointed out that this would result in 'the destruction of all non-Bolshevist armies in Russia' and 'an interminable vista of violence and misery', Wilson retorted, unanswerably, that the existing Allied forces could not stop the Bolsheviks and that none of the Allies was prepared to augment its existing armies. This was, from Churchill's point of view, a highly unsatisfactory meeting.

On the following day (15 February) the Council of Ten met, without Wilson, Clemenceau or Milner being present. Churchill adopted a considerably more militant approach than on the

14. At a Cabinet on 28 February he urged humane treatment to Germany, and her restoration as a European entity. He went on to say that: 'Germany would get to work quietly producing munitions and completing her plans, but she would only come into the open when we and our present Allies or associates began to quarrel, as might unfortunately be the case in future. . . . He thought that there was a serious danger that, unless Peace came soon, Russia and Germany might make common cause. They were both in the pit of misery, which men in each country attributed to the folly shown in fighting each other. If they joined together it might have grave consequences in the future.'

15. Lloyd George is inaccurate in his account in *The Truth about the Peace Treaties*, Vol. I, p. 368, that Churchill 'adroitly seized the opportunity presented by the absence of President Wilson and myself to go over to Paris and urge his plans with regard to Russia'.

previous evening. He proposed that 'it was essential either to carry Prinkipo through to a definite result or to get it out of the way'; he proposed a telegram to the Bolsheviks offering ten days more for a cessation of fighting, after which the proposal would lapse. At the same time, he proposed the establishment of an Allied Council for Russian Affairs, with political, economic and military sections, possessing executive powers. Churchill particularly emphasized the importance of the formation of the military section at once 'to draw up a plan for concerted action against the Bolsheviks'. This would give the Allies 'a definite war scheme, together with an appreciation of the situation' on which the Supreme War Council could make a decision.

'Churchill's eloquence, enthusiasm and personality produced an electrical effect,' Hankey has recorded.[16] It was agreed to adjourn the meeting while members consulted their Governments.

Alerted by Philip Kerr,[17] Lloyd George reacted swiftly. It was clear to him that Churchill had carried the Council far along in the direction of setting up machinery for armed intervention in Russia. This, he stated emphatically in what Hankey has described as 'a very hot telegram',[18] was going far beyond what the Cabinet had authorized and would approve. Lloyd George's attitudes were sympathetic to those of the American President, and this combination was more than sufficient to destroy what chances there had ever been of a genuinely 'Allied' intervention in the Russian imbroglio.

*

Thus, even at this early stage, the main outlines of the dispute had been drawn. Despite his reservations, Lloyd George had not attempted to urge complete abandonment of the anti-

16. Hankey: *The Supreme Control at the Paris Peace Conference*, p. 70; see also *The Foreign Relations of the United States: The Paris Peace Conference, 1919*, Vol. III, 1041–2 and Vol. IV, pp. 13–17.

17. The future Lord Lothian, at that time a member of Lloyd George's Secretariat, who had been keeping a close inspection on Churchill's actions in Paris.

18. The text is given in Ullman, op. cit., Vol. II, pp. 125–6.

Bolshevist forces, but it had been possible to confine assistance to material help, and his influence in Paris had helped to quash what chances there may have been for Churchill's venture of an Allied military operation. For his part, Churchill had secured Cabinet approval to continue assistance to the anti-Bolshevist forces, and this was a victory of some substance. The Government as a whole was unenthusiastic about sanctioning any British military intervention in Russia, but it was hostile to Bolshevism and most ministers did not at this stage go so far as Lloyd George in wishing to opt out of the Russian entanglement completely. Indeed, as Curzon in particular constantly argued, such abandonment would be an act of political immorality. If Lloyd George had been attending all Cabinet and ministerial meetings it is possible – although this is questionable – that he might have pressed his own policy more successfully. The downfall of Bolshevism was universally desired in the Cabinet. Ministers hoped that this could be achieved with British material assistance but without the need to intervene militarily. It was rather reminiscent of the prelude to the Dardanelles Campaign; a leaderless Cabinet desiring a substantial victory without too much danger attached, and Churchill assuring them that this could be accomplished. Thus, taking a line between the two extremes of Churchill and Lloyd George, the Government drifted onwards in its policy of half-hearted intervention in the affairs of Russia. Even at this early stage Churchill was making the same error as he had over the Dardanelles. Without any real power, and in a subordinate position, he was attempting to assist a difficult and controversial military campaign with a sceptical Prime Minister and half-hearted support from the majority of his colleagues. The lack of enthusiasm in the Government for the Russian intervention was reflected in significant matters such as the provision of shipping to convey materials and provisions to Russia. The shipping was available, but Churchill, in spite of strenuous efforts, could not obtain any more than the basic minimum.[19]

19. Lord Salter, at that time Secretary of the Allied Maritime Transport Council and Chairman of the Allied Maritime Transport Executive, has

The issue was bedevilled by the persistent failure of the Cabinet to reach any firm decisions. Throughout the year Churchill was seeking the views of the Cabinet on the central issues of policy without success. In these conditions of drift and irresolution, with the Prime Minister frequently absent and biding his time, there was a good opportunity for a single-minded man to carry his views considerably further than would have been the case in more normal conditions.

A good example of this occurred in May. On the 14th the Cabinet expressly turned down a proposal put forward by Churchill to form additional units of the Slavo-British Legion. Churchill, after consulting Balfour but not Lloyd George, decided that it was a matter entirely within the discretion of the War Office; the Cabinet was informed on 11 June that Churchill had taken the steps to increase the Legion that the Cabinet had rejected on 14 May. The Cabinet merely 'took note' of this remarkable *fait accompli*.

Criticism of the Government's policy was already beginning to develop, and in the Commons on 3 March Churchill had neatly covered himself from both flanks: 'In this theatre we have no special British interests of any sort to serve. . . . We are simply discharging a duty to the League of Nations . . . and endeavouring to prevent new areas of the world from degenerating into the welter of Bolshevik anarchy.'

On the following day (4 March) Churchill had 'inquired whether the Cabinet were prepared to inform him more definitely as to the policy they intended to pursue with regard to Russia'. He then set out to the Cabinet the situation as he understood it:

The general intention of His Majesty's Government was to withdraw the armies from every part of Russia as soon as practicable, and then to supply Russian commanders who were friendly to the Allied cause with guns, aeroplanes and munitions and everything that might be of use, except troops and money.

---

confirmed that the shipping was available, and that if there had been a positive Government policy with regard to Russia no serious problems would have arisen.

The Secretary of State for War said that as regards Murmansk and Archangel, it would be impossible for climatic reasons for us to evacuate the Forces there until June. In the meantime, however, we must take steps to see that our Forces in both places receive proper reinforcements. Further, we should have to supplement our detachments at those ports in order that the withdrawal, when carried out, should be properly conducted. It was most important that everything should be done to ensure a safe and orderly evacuation when the time came. With a view to his being in a position to make adequate arrangements he pressed for a decision on two points:

(a) Were we to withdraw as soon as the weather permitted, and
(b) If we were to evacuate were we also to undertake the removal of the inhabitants who were friendly to us?

As regards the Caucasus, how long were our troops to remain there? Was it to be until the League of Nations had decided the fate of Georgia? Further, in respect of the Caspian, what did the First Lord intend to do with the Fleet he was at present maintaining there? If we cleared out of the Caucasus how should we 'make it up' to General Denikin?

Lloyd George then pointed out the alarming financial aspects of the British involvement in Russia, which were running at £73 millions 'for our Military Forces only, including transport' for a period of six months; 'If the cost of naval requirements were added, the total cost would be 150 million sterling per annum, for what were after all very insignificant operations.' Figures were never Lloyd George's strong suit, but this estimate of the cost of British operations in Russia was not challenged. Certainly it was an argument that appealed greatly to the new Chancellor of the Exchequer, Austen Chamberlain, who was gradually becoming more critical of the whole venture, and now wanted to withdraw from the Caucasus and Caspian as well as from Murmansk and Archangel.

The Secretary of State for War said that he himself was not responsible for the present situation, and he was still uncertain as to what the Cabinet wished done. He understood that authority had been given to take whatever naval measures might be necessary for the protection of our naval forces in Northern Russia. He claimed that he equally should be authorized to take adequate military measures to support and reinforce the men we had in North Russia until they could be withdrawn. The sooner he was informed of the Government's policy the sooner he could start on the preliminary arrangements. Unless he was given the authority he required from the Cabinet, he was deeply apprehensive that the consequences might be absolutely disastrous. His own wishes were:

(a) To evacuate North Russia in such a way that a catastrophe would be avoided.

(b) To evacuate the Caucasus, subject to a date agreed upon in Paris.

(c) 'To make it up' to General Denikin, and for this purpose he proposed to send a Military Mission for the General's assistance. This would mean withdrawing about 30,000 men, and sending instead 1,800 N.C.O.s and others who would act as instructors.

(d) To send a similar Mission to Admiral Kolchak and to recall the battalions now in Siberia under Colonel John Ward.

He regarded all these as reasonable propositions, and if our friends in Russia failed to maintain themselves with such assistance as he suggested, he did not think we could be blamed . . . .

The decision of the Cabinet was, however, solely concerned with the position in North Russia.

The War Cabinet decided:

(a) That their policy should be to press for the early evacuation of Murmansk and Archangel and to authorize the Secretary of State for War to make the necessary preliminary arrangements.

(b) To ask the Prime Minister to communicate the policy of H.M. Government as set out in the above discussion to the other British Delegates in Paris.

(c) To ask the Secretary of State for War to circulate to the War Cabinet the paper he had prepared showing the cost of maintaining our forces in the various centres in Russia.

On 11 March all naval and military commanders were informed of the decision to withdraw completely from North Russia.

On 17 March – with Law presiding – the War Cabinet again grappled with the Russian question. Curzon opened with a blunt summary of the situation:

Lord Curzon said that it was useless for the War Cabinet to take piecemeal decisions with regard to military, naval, and financial assistance to Russia until there was a definite Russian policy. At present there was no policy. A policy could not be evolved in London: it must be framed in Paris. . . . The Secretary of State for War now came forward with a scheme to organize Russian officers and prisoners, but such a scheme was useless until we defined our general policy, and that policy could only be defined in Paris by the Peace Conference.

(*At this stage Mr Churchill entered.*)

Mr Churchill stated that he had circulated the two Memoranda in response to the desire of the General Staff, but had not put them forward as his policy. He felt that the War Cabinet decision with regard to Murmansk and Archangel, when known, would deal a considerable blow to the Russian cause generally. At the same time the Murmansk–Archangel line was so unpromising in a strategic sense that he did not think it wise to press the Russians to make special efforts to defend it, as efforts there would lead to nothing . . .

Mr Churchill, continuing, said that the War Cabinet must face the fact that the North of Russia would be over-run by the Bolsheviks, and many people would be murdered. He was increasingly distressed with the way the situation had developed since the Armistice. Everything was going wrong. The continued disheartening of the Russian forces friendly to us had led to a great falling off in their *moral* . . .

Four months had passed in a policy of drift, and great potential resources which might have helped us were being dissipated. It was idle to think we should escape by sitting still and doing nothing. Bolshevism was not sitting still. It was advancing, and unless the tide were resisted it would roll over Siberia until it reached the Japanese, and perhaps drive Denikin into the mountains, while the border Baltic States would be attacked and submerged. No doubt, when all the resources friendly to us had been scattered, and when India was threatened, the Western Powers would bestir themselves and would be prepared to put forth ten times the effort that at an earlier stage would have sufficed to save the situation. He could only express the profound apprehension with which he awaited what was coming. He had been backwards and forwards to Paris in vain. He had discussed the situation with Marshal Foch, who had a definite plan for action without the use of British and French forces, or money, but only by guaranteeing loans to the smaller States. Both

the Prime Minister and President Wilson were against intervention . . .

This was Churchill's strongest personal declaration yet before
the War Cabinet. Chamberlain, once again, proved to be the
most decisive of his critics, basing his argument entirely upon
the impossibility of Britain bearing the financial burden of
resisting Russian Bolshevism alone. 'Mr Churchill said that . . .
he wished again to impress the War Cabinet with the danger
that was growing every moment and spreading with extraordinary rapidity.' On this unsatisfactory note the discussion
ended, with the War Cabinet no closer to a comprehensible
Russian policy. 'There was no British policy,' as Robert Bruce
Lockhart has written, 'unless seven different policies at once
could be called a policy.'[20]

The divisions within the Government circle were becoming
apparent to outside observers. On 9 April the Foreign Office
published a White Paper entitled *A Collection of Reports on
Bolshevism in Russia*[21] which contained only reports of Red
atrocities, some of which at least seemed based on doubtful
evidence ('The Bolsheviks are now employing gangs of Chinese
for the purpose of killing officers and deserters' may be cited
as one example). On 16 April, in the House of Commons,
Lloyd George's equivocal position was clearly demonstrated,
but he did say: 'There is a fundamental principle in the conduct of all foreign policy in this country . . . that you should
never interfere with the internal affairs of another country.'
From the Labour benches Josiah Wedgwood asked for a
guarantee that the Archangel force would not be used in an
offensive action.

This was a remarkable question, for such an operation was in
fact being considered by the Cabinet. A War Office memorandum circulated on 15 April proposed increases in the Slavo-
British Legion and an advance from Archangel to Kotlas, to
link up with Kolchak's northern wing. On the understanding
that such an operation was essential to the eventual successful

20. Robert Bruce Lockhart: *Memoirs of a British Agent*, p. 253.
21. Cmd 8 (1919).

evacuation, ministers – although divided and in some cases troubled – were disposed to argue. On 4 May the War Office telegraphed to Ironside to authorize him 'to make all preparations with the resources at your disposal to strike a heavy blow against the Bolshevists in the direction of Kotlas, if a favourable opportunity should occur for effecting a junction with [General] Gaida about that point. Before such a move is carried out, however, Cabinet approval will have to be obtained.'

On 14 May, however – as has been related – the Cabinet refused to authorize the expansion in the Slavo-British Legion, a decision that Churchill proceeded to ignore. On 26 May the British Volunteer Relief Force reached Archangel, replacing the American and French troops. Kolchak's forces advanced to within four hundred miles of Moscow, and, after receiving assurances of Kolchak's democratic *bona fides*, the Allies granted him *de facto* diplomatic recognition. Denikin placed himself under the authority of Omsk. The British fleet in the Baltic was adopting a more aggressive posture.

On the evening of 11 June, with Curzon presiding, the Cabinet considered Churchill's proposal to authorize what he claimed were Ironside's plans. Henry Wilson explained that

If once he could establish connection, we would hand over control of the operation to Admiral Kolchak, and proceed ourselves to withdraw from North Russia. The whole intention of these operations was to facilitate that withdrawal. If, however, we attempted to clear out without striking a blow first and establishing touch with the troops in the South, we would have the whole pack of Bolsheviks at our heels and would be risking a possible disaster.

On this understanding, although Montagu and Curzon were clearly uneasy, the operations were sanctioned.

But disaster had caught up with Kolchak. On the same day (11 June) he had suffered another of a series of defeats that was to fling his forces back across Siberia in less than eight months. This severe reverse necessarily made the Kotlas operation questionable in at least one respect, and on 18 June the Cabinet reviewed the situation. Churchill agreed that the situation had deteriorated, but went on:

The military experts believed that the real trouble on the Kolchak front was now coming to an end, as the distances the enemy had moved from their base would begin to operate against them. He must confess, however, that the position was not quite a happy one. On the other hand, the success of General Denikin in the South was remarkable . . .

Basing his case firmly on the views of 'the military authorities', Churchill said that it was thought that Denikin must draw Red forces from Kolchak's front, and that a case could be made for Ironside's advance 'even though the plan of joining hands with Admiral Kolchak was no longer feasible'. Curzon and Chamberlain again expressed anxieties, and Churchill gave an assurance that the War Cabinet could review the operation before it was initiated. It was accordingly decided to postpone a final decision until 27 June.

The War Cabinet, on 27 June, was again urged by Wilson and Churchill to approve the operation. Wilson, while admitting that the chances of a link with Kolchak were 'very remote', said that 'with the Russian temperament, however, anything was possible, and he did not, therefore, give up all hope of being able to effect a junction'. After Kotlas had been taken, he went on, it would be garrisoned with Russian troops, and the British force withdrawn; the force would consist of 13,000 British and 22,000 Russian troops, which were likely to be opposed by 33,700 Bolshevist troops whose 'fighting value was questionable'. Churchill spoke in approving terms of Ironside's Russian troops, and urged the Cabinet to approve the operation:

> He did not think that we could possibly slink out of the country and leave nothing between the [Archangel] Government and the Bolshevist forces but a few mines in the river. Our credit, which today stood very high throughout Russia, was at stake. All the civilized forces in that country realized that we alone (with the doubtful exception of the Japanese) had really befriended and assisted them; and if we turned round now and cleared off our reputation would suffer irretrievably . . .

Chamberlain was again gloomy and pessimistic, but admitted that he had been impressed by Wilson's argument that the offensive was essential for an eventual successful withdrawal. Sir David Shackleton, the Permanent Secretary at the Ministry of Labour – a former Labour MP, member of the Parliamentary Committee of the TUC and President of the TUC – then intervened to remind the War Cabinet of the strong feeling in Labour circles about the intervention, and went on:

He himself had been surprised at the extent to which men of all classes were now coming round to supporting the Labour view that the Soviet Government ought to be given a fair chance. A further point was that we had never attempted to interfere when the Czar was in power. There was no doubt that this feeling was spreading, and he was afraid that the agitation might assume formidable proportions . . .

Wilson suggested that 'what was necessary was careful and well-conducted propaganda to state the true facts and explain the Government policy to the working man or the country'. Churchill said that no serious resistance to Ironside was expected: 'All experience went to show that the Bolsheviks had never been able to screw up enough courage to offer any prolonged resistance. General Denikin again and again had defeated them with odds against him of 10 to 1. His own feeling was that the Bolsheviks in the present instance would not put up much of a fight.' Eventually, after discussing propaganda and the best tactics in public debate, the Cabinet agreed 'to sanction General Ironside's proposed operations, on the conditions laid down'.

The position of the British warships and troops in Russian waters and on the Russian mainland was now becoming extremely difficult, and Service resentment was growing. At a Cabinet meeting on 4 July – with, for once, Lloyd George present – the Deputy Chief of the Naval Staff, Rear-Admiral J. A. Ferguson, raised an inconveniently pertinent question: 'Both the Admiralty and the Naval Officers on the spot were really in ignorance as to the exact position: were we, or were we not, at war with the Bolsheviks?' The subsequent discussion did not carry the matter much further. 'The Prime Minister said that actually we were at war with the Bolsheviks, but we had decided not to make war. In other words, we did not intend to put great armies into Russia to fight the Bolshevist forces.' Curzon said that the Government 'must proceed with caution, as there was a strong element in the House of Commons which was opposed to intervention'. Matters then proceeded to a decision, of sorts:

The War Cabinet decided that –
(a) In fact, a state of war did exist as between Great Britain and the Bolshevist Government of Russia;
(b) In consequence of (a) our Naval forces in Russian waters should be authorized to engage enemy forces by land and sea, when necessary.
[After considering the state of operations elsewhere, however]
. . . The Prime Minister said that, whatever happened, the Government must strictly fulfil their pledge to Parliament and the country that our troops in North Russia would be withdrawn before the ice set in. He hoped the Secretary of State for War fully realized the importance of our troops not getting inextricably involved. The Secretary of State for War said that our plans included every possible precaution to avoid this . . .

On 7 July all plans were disrupted again when a mutiny occurred in Ironside's force, in which three British officers were killed and two others wounded. Ironside accordingly decided to abandon the Kotlas offensive, and Churchill and Wilson had the difficult task of explaining to the Cabinet that this offensive, hitherto described as being essential to a successful eventual withdrawal, could now be dispensed with.

On 16 July Churchill tried to spell out the larger implications – as he saw them – of a Bolshevik victory:

He hoped the Cabinet would realize that practically the whole strength of the Bolsheviks was directed against Denikin and Kolchak, and if the forces of these two men were put out of action the Bolsheviks would have available some 600,000 men with which to spread their doctrines and ravages amongst smaller States, such as the Baltic Provinces, Czecho-Slovakia, and Roumania, with whose interests we were identified.

On the 23rd, however, faced with Ironside's reports, Churchill agreed that the Kotlas offensive would have to be abandoned and the position itself evacuated before the winter. This did not mean, however, that he had abandoned hope of success elsewhere:

The Secretary of State for War said that the British troops had been in Archangel before he took over his present appointment. . . . The last chance of saving the Archangel Government had gone. He did not think, however, that the general strategic situation in Russia had undergone any great change.

On 25 July he returned to this argument: 'He regretted profoundly that it had not been possible to give the Bolsheviks a severe blow, and that now it was not possible to go on unless we embarked upon big operations; but, if we were going to do this, there were other theatres more suitable than North Russia.'

Lloyd George – who had now definitely turned against the involvement – then strongly criticized Denikin and his supporters, and the Cabinet agreed that the Archangel–Murmansk force should be withdrawn and that British troops in Siberia and in the Caucasus should be evacuated.

Churchill viewed these decisions with dismay. On 29 July he informed the Cabinet that

He was very sorry to be associated with such an operation. It would be repugnant to everyone to feel that we were leaving a small Government to fall to pieces, some of whom had stood by us and some of whom had not, and to be at the mercy of the Bolsheviks . . . The whole episode was a very painful one, and, to go back into history, reminded him of our operations at Toulon and our desertion of the Catalans.

He urged that Denikin receive assurances that he would be supported by the British Government for a fixed time, and suggested six months: 'What he specially wished to avoid was a decision to evacuate North Russia without any definite policy as regards South Russia.' In the subsequent discussion Churchill defended Denikin's supporters from the charge that they were reactionaries:

The Secretary of State for War could not agree to the term 're-actionary' being applied to a man who defended the lives of his wife and children.

The Prime Minister said it was a mistake to treat the present military operations in Russia as though they were a campaign against Bolshevism. If the Allies had decided to defeat Bolshevism, great armies would have been required. The small British force in Russia had not been sent there for this purpose. It was true that one member of the Cabinet had always urged this policy, but he himself had always protested against it. The War Cabinet had accepted the views that it was not our business to interfere in the internal affairs of Russia.

Relations between Churchill and Lloyd George were now becoming strained. Churchill submitted a memorandum to the Prime Minister in March 1920 in which he wrote that 'Since the Armistice my policy would have been "Peace with the German people, war on the Bolshevik tyranny". Willingly or unavoidably, you have followed something very near the reverse.'[22] This was an over-simplification of the position of each man, but the accusation reflects Churchill's profound concern at the failure to create a strong, independent, non-Bolshevik Germany. 'As a part of such a policy,' Churchill wrote, 'I should be prepared to make peace with Soviet Russia on the best terms available to appease the general situation, while safeguarding us from being poisoned by them. I do not, of course, believe that any real harmony is possible between Bolshevism and present civilization. But in view of the existing facts a cessation of arms and a promotion of material prosperity are indispensable: and we must trust for better or for worse to peaceful influences to bring about the disappearance of this awful tyranny and peril.'

Lloyd George might have remarked that this estimate may have been realistic, but was somewhat belated. Throughout 1919 Churchill had been the principal advocate in the Government of a policy designed to compass the defeat and downfall of the Bolshevik regime. Lloyd George subsequently wrote that 'The most formidable and irresponsible protagonist of an anti-

22. The full text is set out in *The Aftermath*, p. 337.

Bolshevik war was Mr Winston Churchill. He had no doubt a
genuine distaste for Communism . . . His ducal blood revolted
against the wholesale elimination of Grand Dukes in Russia.'[23]
This thrust was unfair; Churchill's detestation of Bolshevism
rested on deeper feelings.

*

Sir David Shackleton's warning to the War Cabinet of the rising
hostility to the Government's policies in the Labour movement had been very much to the point. By the early summer of
1919 there was sharp criticism of the British assistance to the
anti-Bolshevik cause in the Labour Party, increasingly echoed
by the Asquithian Liberals. In June the Labour Party Conference passed a resolution condemning the action of the
Government as 'war in the interests of financial capitalism'
and demanding 'the unreserved use . . . of political and industrial power' to end it.[24]

In fact, by this stage the War Cabinet had decided to cut its
losses in North Russia. Churchill managed to secure approval
for a final grant of aid to Denikin on 15 August, but the last
British troops were withdrawn from Archangel and Murmansk
at the end of October. Nevertheless, as the proceedings of the
Annual Conference of the Trade Union Congress in September
demonstrated, Labour suspicions that Churchill was advocating
a policy of intervention elsewhere were strong. One speaker
described Churchill as an 'insistent, persistent, and consistent
liar', and a resolution recommending agitation to reverse the
Government's policy was carried. The result was the establishment of the National Hands Off Russia Committee, which at
once launched verbal assaults on the Secretary of State for
War that were characterized by extreme virulence. A notable
embarrassment was the publication by the *Daily Herald* of the
account of an interview between Churchill and one of Kolchak's
leading officers on 15 May that had been captured by the Red
Army. In this interview Churchill was alleged to have said

23. *The Truth about the Peace Treaties*, Vol. I, pp. 324–5.
24. See S. R. Graubard: *British Labour and the Russian Revolution*, pp. 73–
75, for the text of the resolution and its implications.

that he hoped to send a further ten thousand volunteers to
North Russia and 2,500 to Denikin, while £24 million would be
allocated at once to the White cause. Denials of the authenticity
of this document did not carry ultimate conviction.[25]

Churchill responded to the violent attacks made upon him
with vigour, and his onslaughts upon Bolshevik philosophers
and their exponents became even more outspoken. 'The theories
of Lenin and Trotsky,' he declared in January 1920, '. . . have
driven man from the civilization of the twentieth century into
a condition of barbarism worse than the Stone Age, and left
him the most awful and pitiable spectacle in human experience,
devoured by vermin, racked by pestilence, and deprived of
hope.' In the same speech he said that Labour was 'quite
unfitted for the responsibility of Government'. He expounded
these themes on frequent occasion and with much vehemence.

But the suspicions in the Labour movement that Churchill
had merely shifted the balance of intervention from Kolchak
to Denikin were fully merited. On 25 September Churchill
called at a Cabinet meeting for 'war upon the Bolshevists with
every means in our power (except troops) . . . with a coherent
plan on all fronts at once'. By the middle of October it appeared
as though Denikin was indeed on the verge of an overwhelming
victory, and Churchill issued a public letter on 21 October that
stated:

There are now good reasons for believing that the tyranny of
Bolshevism will soon be overthrown by the Russian nation. We have
steadfastly adhered to our principles that Russia must be saved by
Russian manhood, and all our fighting troops have been safely and
skilfully withdrawn from that country.

On the other hand, we have continued to help, with arms, supplies
and organizers, those Russian National forces and leaders who were
true to us in the war against the Germans, and who are now advancing with good hopes of victory to the liberation of their native land.

Ramsay MacDonald retorted in the *Socialist Review*:

Churchill pursues his mad adventure as though he were Emperor of
these Isles, pacifying us with a pledge, and delighting his militarists

25. See R. Page Arnot: *The Impact of the Russian Revolution in Britain*.

and capitalists with a campaign. Again, we have been told one day that we are withdrawing our troops from Russia, and the next we read of new offensives, new bogus governments, new military captains as allies.

Denikin's successes were illusory. The Bolshevik forces that had defeated Kolchak now pressed hard on Denikin; by the end of March 1920 only the Crimea remained in his hands. Long before then, however, the British had abandoned him to his fate. On 8 November Lloyd George, in a speech at the Guildhall, had formally delivered the epitaph to the policy of intervention. On 20 November the Cabinet decided not to renew the naval blockade in the Baltic in the following spring. On 27 January 1920 the Cabinet was faced with a request to approve a new anti-Bolshevik combination. It resolved that 'we have neither the men, the money, nor the credit, and public opinion is altogether opposed to such a course'. On 11 November the Cabinet decided not to assist in the evacuation of refugees from the Crimea other than those of British nationality. Churchill argued against this decision, and formally disassociated himself from an act 'which, in his view, might probably result in a massacre of the civilians in the Crimea'. Throughout the saga of British intervention in Russia, Churchill's policies and attitudes may be fairly criticized. But he at least had never averted his eyes from the human implications of supporting one side in a civil war, and the censure of history may indeed fall most heavily on those ministers – particularly Lloyd George – who had permitted that participation and then withdrew without remorse for the consequences that would fall upon those whom they had supported and encouraged.

*

The episode of the Russian Intervention provides us with some revealing insights into the haphazard manner in which the Lloyd George Coalition operated. The indecision and lack of effective leadership that had been so evident in this instance was fully characteristic of its operations in other fields. As Churchill wrote in another context in October 1921, Lloyd

George's thinking 'stopped short of reaching any conclusion of a definite character on which a policy, or even a provisional policy, could be based'.[26] But the episode had also demonstrated the fact that the features of Churchill's personality that his critics found so disagreeable in the past had not really changed. In his quests for a policy agreement in the Cabinet he had underestimated the seriousness of the situation within Russia, had wholly failed to discern the very considerable political dangers at home of that policy, and, once again he had rushed into a highly complex situation with only a general and superficial understanding of its difficulties. He had committed very substantial sums of money and much political capital to a venture that aroused his most fierce emotional feelings and which he had not considered in advance with coolness. The episode had brought him little credit either outside or inside the Government, and had effectively revived the apprehensions of 1915 about his judgement and capacity. By his bold public declarations he had identified himself strongly with those who wished to see Bolshevism crushed, but by the end he could only claim an efficient withdrawal. His critics could claim with justice that their forecasts had been abundantly justified. The episode opened a schism between Churchill and Lloyd George that was never really healed; confirmed Bonar Law in his hostile view of Churchill's reliability and common sense;[27] and had alienated Labour yet again.

When, at the end of March 1920, the news reached London of the withdrawal of Denikin's hapless remnants into the Crimea, Henry Wilson noted: 'So ends in practical disaster another of Winston's military attempts – Antwerp, Dardanelles, Denikin.'

If this was an unfair judgement – and particularly so from that source – it was not an uncommon one. Nothing had been

26. Beaverbrook: *Men And Power*, Appendix IV, p. 406.

27. Beaverbrook has recorded one episode in 1919 when Law in effect invited Churchill to resign (K. Young: *Churchill and Beaverbrook*, p. 58). Lord Davidson recollects another incident when relations between the two men became heated.

gained; a great deal had been lost, in addition to the £100 million or so spent on aid and assistance to the anti-Bolshevist forces. For a politician, no less than for a commander, association with failure can perhaps be survived once; it is progressively more difficult thereafter.

Churchill's hostility to the Soviet Government did not abate after the Intervention. In May 1920 a trade delegation under Leonid Krassin visited Britain, and lengthy negotiations continued throughout the rest of the year, and culminated in the Anglo-Russian Trade Agreement of March 1921. Churchill was not the only minister who was hostile to this initiative of Lloyd George, but the discussions again brought him into opposition to the Prime Minister and Bonar Law. On 18 November 1920, when the draft agreement was under discussion, Churchill strongly opposed it. At one point he remarked that 'Signing this agreement in no way alters the general position we have taken up as to the Bolsheviks, namely, that Ministers shall be free to point out the odious character of their regime. It seems to me you are on the high road to embracing Bolshevism. I am going to keep off that and denounce them on all possible occasions.'

The most ferocious denunciations are to be found in *The Aftermath*, in which we read of 'a poisoned Russia, an infected Russia, a plague-bearing Russia; a Russia of armed hordes not only smiting with bayonet and with cannon, but accompanied and preceded by swarms of typhus-bearing vermin which slew the bodies of men, and political doctrines which destroyed the health and even the soul of nations'.[28] And, in assessing the Russian Intervention, he emphasized the value of Bolshevik concentration on internal affairs while Finland, Estonia, Latvia, Lithuania and Poland were enabled 'to establish the structure of civilized states and to organize the strength of patriotic armies. By the end of 1920 the "Sanitary Cordon" which protected Europe from the Bolshevik infection was formed by living national organisms vigorous in themselves, hostile to the disease and immune through experience against its ravages.' Those words were published in 1929, and

28. *The Aftermath*, p. 263.

they give the clearest picture of the motives which had impelled Churchill in the Intervention. His revulsion against Bolshevism was understandable; but there were other evil forces in Russia between 1910 and 1921, and the failure of *The Aftermath* as history lies essentially in these omissions. 'Russia,' Churchill was writing in 1929, 'has been frozen in an indefinite winter of sub-human doctrine and superhuman tyranny.'[29]

*

Churchill's advocacy of a vigorous policy in Russia was not accompanied by attention to the future of the two Services over which he ruled between January 1919 and January 1921. To the dismay of so many young officers he neglected the opportunity of reconstructing the Army on a modern basis, and the principal result of his period at the Air Ministry was to preserve the separate identity of the Royal Air Force while cutting its equipment and size almost to the bone. At the end of the war Britain was the leading air power. In 1919 the Air Estimates were reduced to £15 million, and the RAF was cut to eighteen squadrons abroad and four at home; the first of the latter, furthermore, was not formed until the summer of 1921. By November 1921 the Committee of Imperial Defence was informed that whereas the French had forty-seven independent air squadrons at home, the British possessed only three.[30] When expansion was envisaged in 1923, it was discovered that the RAF would be obliged to have officers from the other Services seconded to it. There was a certain justification in the bleak comment of *The Times* that: 'He leaves the body of British flying well nigh at that last gasp when a military funeral would be all that would be left for it.'

Churchill's efforts to reduce military and naval expenditure when he became Chancellor of the Exchequer in 1924 will be examined later. It must be emphasized that the dismemberment of the armed forces in 1919 was firm Government policy, and was based primarily upon economic and political factors. It was on Churchill's initiative that the Cabinet agreed that

29. *The Aftermath*, p. 276.
30. CID (145th Meeting, November 1921).

The Lloyd George Coalition, 1919–1922   161

the Service Estimates should be framed on the assumption that 'the British Empire will not be engaged in any great war during the next ten years and that no Expeditionary Force will be required'.[31] The decision was, of course, collective, but the fact of Churchill's initiative in the matter should be emphasized. The first establishment of the 'Ten-Year Rule' must be regarded as a significant moment in the history of inter-war Defence policy.

It can be argued – and with justice – that any immediate post-war Government would have reached a decision that would have been very similar, if not identical, to that of the Coalition. What was perhaps even more unfortunate was the failure to devote sufficient attention to the qualitative aspects of the RAF and the Army, and to investigate their future functions and equipment. Neither the Army nor the RAF had any reason to consider that their long-term interests had been improved by Churchill's period in office. His rejection of a proposal for Government assistance for civil aviation must also be noted. By such decisions, taken essentially for political reasons, many of the hard-won gains of the war were needlessly thrown away. The comment of Liddell Hart is severe, but just: 'He was eager to make a fresh mark in current political affairs, and the best chance lay in the post-war retrenchment of expenditure.'[32]

*

Meanwhile, as the hapless British intervention in Russia drew towards its dismal and inevitable conclusion, another crisis nearer home was increasingly occupying the attention of ministers. The Irish Question had returned. As on Russia, the reactions of ministers were characterized by vacillation, lack of leadership and grievous miscalculations.

On 21 January 1919, the victorious seventy-three Sinn Fein MPs, meeting in Dublin as the Irish Parliament (Dail Eireann), had issued a declaration of independence and ratified the existence of the Irish Republic that had been publicly proclaimed

31. PRO CAB 23/15 (War Cabinet Minutes, 8 and 15 August 1919).
32. 'The Military Strategist' (*Churchill: Four Faces and the Man*, p. 180).

outside the General Post Office in Dublin on Easter Monday, 1916. Throughout 1919 the self-styled Irish Government proceeded to usurp the functions of Dublin Castle. More ominously, under the organizing genius of Michael Collins, the famed Volunteers became the Army of the Republic – the Irish Republican Army. In retrospect, 1919 was a quiet year; it saw eighteen murders and seventy-seven armed attacks, which included an attempt to ambush the Viceroy, Lord French. The weapon of the boycott was revived, directed specifically against the Royal Irish Constabulary, and with considerable success. By the beginning of 1920 Ireland was sliding into anarchy.

In this situation it should be stressed that Churchill's miscalculations were no greater than those of the majority of his colleagues. On 5 August 1919 he gave it as his opinion at a Cabinet meeting that the present was not a good time to look for an Irish solution. In a few months the position would probably be easier. It had already improved and the people were not only very prosperous, but they were beginning to lose faith in the protagonists of Sinn Fein, who had carried out none of their promises . . . His own opinion was that if we allowed matters to remain as they were for the next few months, the Irish people would be more ready to accept a settlement than they had ever been. Walter Long (First Lord of the Admiralty) and Addison (Minister of Health) expressed agreement, and Lloyd George remarked that the Government had as much as it could handle with regard to profiteering, finance and the housing and coal crises. Churchill added that nothing would annoy the Irish more than the conviction that they were not absorbing the minds of the people of Great Britain. Throughout 1920 he was a persistent advocate of a strong policy towards Sinn Fein and the IRA. In his own account in *The Aftermath* Churchill does not conceal his bias, and has put it on record that a policy of terror in Ireland 'might have been a remedy at once sombre and efficacious'. He does not, however, give a fair portrait of his own contributions.

The policy of inaction could not be long sustained, and Churchill's expectations were wholly unfulfilled. The Government 'proclaimed' Sinn Fein in August 1919, and the Dail

was declared an illegal organization. The authority of Dublin
Castle continued to disintegrate. The Government moved into
the realm of action. In March 1920 Sir Nevil Macready, Commissioner of the Metropolitan Police, was appointed commander
of all British forces in Ireland.

The most pressing requirement was for reinforcements for
the harassed and demoralized RIC, and on 11 May 1920
Churchill undertook to raise what he called the 'Special
Emergency Gendarmerie' to be a special branch of the RIC.
This plan was approved by the Cabinet on 21 May; the force
was to be 'raised and paid by the War Office . . . The force,
when raised, should be administered by the War Office.'
Recruits were sought in England, mainly among ex-soldiers.
Churchill subsequently claimed that they 'were selected from
a great press of applicants on account of their intelligence, their
characters, and their record in the War'.[33] All other estimates
– British, Irish and American – have been considerably less
complimentary. Soon they were arriving in Ireland, equipped
with surplus khaki uniforms, with the black belts and dark-
green caps of the RIC. They were swiftly dubbed the 'Black
and Tans'. They were followed by a further group of a thousand
ex-officers, called the Auxiliary Division of the RIC and
generally known as the 'Auxis'. The Black and Tans were paid
ten shillings a day. The Auxis received a pound.

The Government had decided – or, rather, had drifted into a
decision – to meet force with force, or, to be more exact, to
meet terror with terror. The Black and Tans soon had much to
be revengeful about, and no doubt their record has been
excessively besmirched. But, after every allowance has been
made, theirs is a record of squalor that was, unhappily, not
without precedent, but which increasingly nauseated civilized
opinion in Britain and abroad. The Government of Ireland
Act, 1920, was a legislative attempt to give something to everybody, and succeeded in placating nobody.[34] As the activities
of the Dail Government and the IRA grew more daring,

33. *The Aftermath*, p. 287.

34. It provided two Irish Parliaments – at Dublin and Belfast – with Irish
representation at Westminster and a joint Council of Ireland.

extensive and violent, the Government reacted. On 2 June,
when the possibility of a settlement was discussed, the Cabinet
decided that 'before embarking on the consideration of any
such step, it was necessary for the Government first to secure
the upper hand in their policy of establishing law and order in
Ireland'. The accomplishment of this was to prove extremely
difficult. On 1 October the Chief Secretary – Hamar Greenwood
– submitted a report to the Cabinet that glowed with confidence. It was Greenwood's most consistent failing that he
was always seeing blue sky. As the skies grew even more black,
Greenwood's optimism rose in almost exact proportion. Other
reports were less encouraging. The Black and Tans had begun
the reprisals that had produced the first wave of revulsion in
Ireland and even in Britain. The destruction of a large area of
Cork on 11 December 1920 was the most flagrant act of outrage. Greenwood denied in public that the fires were started
by the British forces; the Cabinet appointed an inquiry into
the episode, and hurriedly suppressed the Report on the
justifiable grounds that 'the effects of publishing the Report if Parliament was sitting would be disastrous to the
Government's whole policy in Ireland' (29 December). The
degree of control enjoyed by Dublin Castle was smaller than
ever.

Churchill's reaction to this manifestly deteriorating situation
was fully in character. Here was an armed insurrection that
required suppression. In public he defended the Black and Tans
who, as he pointed out on one celebrated occasion, enjoyed the
same freedom as the Chicago or New York police in dealing
with armed gangs.[35] On 3 November he circulated a Cabinet
memorandum on the subject of organized reprisals:

. . . I do not consider that the present Government attitude on
reprisals can be maintained much longer. It is not fair on the troops,
it is not fair on the officers who command them. Although the spirit
of the Army is absolutely loyal and hostile to the Irish rebels, there
is no doubt that service in Ireland is intensely unpopular . . .

It is for consideration whether a policy of reprisals within strict limits
and under strict control in certain districts, in which it should be

35. 23 February 1920.

declared that conditions approximating to war exist, would not be right at the present time.[36]

On 10 November there was a conference of ministers, attended by Lloyd George, Law, Chamberlain, Greenwood, Churchill, Shortt and Fisher, at which it was decided that 'the moment was not opportune to come to a decision with regard to the question of organized reprisals'. Indeed, Greenwood was instructed to endeavour to limit reprisals being carried out by the Black and Tans. The situation continued to worsen, in spite of Greenwood's assurance (17 November) that there was 'a noticeable improvement' in the situation in Ireland. On 9 December the Cabinet decided to declare Martial Law in Cork, Tipperary, Kerry and Limerick. On 24 December it was again decided not to take the opportunity of making approaches for an armistice: 'Stress was laid on the importance of doing nothing to check the surrender of arms at a time when the forces of the Crown had at last definitely established the upper hand.' Thus, once again, the Government placed its faith in a military victory. Encouraged by the optimistic reports from his military advisers, Lloyd George had claimed on a notorious occasion in November that 'We have murder by the throat . . . we had to reorganize the police, and when the Government was ready we struck the terrorists and now the terrorists are complaining of terror.' This speech was delivered on 9 November at the Guildhall in London; on 25 October the Lord Mayor of Cork, Terence McSwiney, had died after a hunger strike that had lasted for seventy-four days. A meeting of ministers had taken place on 20 August to consider McSwiney's case, which had resolved to seek Macready's view on the effects in Ireland of his release, which was being urgently pressed by the King. Lloyd George was not present at this meeting, and when the meeting ended it was discovered that he had published a reply to an appeal from McSwiney's sister to the effect that her brother could not be released. It is worthy of mention that the 25 August meeting was in general in favour of releasing McSwiney on parole to enable him to recuperate, and that

36. Author's italics.

Balfour and Churchill were the leading ministers present. On 2 September a meeting of ministers agreed that the Prime Minister's action had made it 'impracticable' to recommend a change.[37]

The Irish situation deteriorated rapidly. The military advisers assured ministers that matters were improving;[38] in fact, matters got steadily worse. On 12 May 1921, 'after an exhausting review of the closely-balanced political and military considerations involved, during which powerful reasons were adduced both for and against the proposal, the Cabinet reached the conclusion, by a majority – "That it would be a mistake for the Government to take the initiative in any suspension of military activities in Ireland, and that the present policy in that country should be pursued"'.

On 24 May the Cabinet resolved to send more reinforcements to Ireland 'for their use in the event of it becoming necessary to set up Crown Colony Government and to extend the martial law area'. Early in June even tougher measures were agreed. But a substantial and articulate section of British public opinion had swung round in favour of a negotiated settlement.

37. PRO CAB 23/22 (Meetings of Ministers 25 August and 2 September 1920). Also Davidson Papers and Royal Archives (Davidson to Stamfordham).

38. There are many examples in the Cabinet Papers. On 29 December 1920 the military advisers spoke against a suggestion that a truce be offered. General Strickland, commanding the Cork area, 'said that, generally speaking, the situation, from a military point of view, was improving. The internment camps were going on satisfactorily, although there was rather a shortage of accommodation. He was convinced that everything was satisfactory in the Cork area . . . General Tudor said that from the Police point of view the position had improved . . . The *moral* of the Police during the last six months had made a marked advance.' Macready 'said that he thought the terror would be broken if martial law was spread all over the country'; General Boyd said that 'Our policy has been very effective, and if there was a truce now the time would be used by the murder party to re-organise themselves, and they would certainly regard a truce as a sign of weakness'; Wilson described the suggestion as 'absolutely fatal . . . He thought that perhaps in six months' time, if military law was applied to the whole of Ireland, 80 per cent or 90 per cent of the people would be on the side of the Government' (PRO CAB 23/23).

The Liberal and Northcliffe newspapers were strongly critical, and the report of the Labour Party's Commission on Ireland had included the stinging phrase that 'Things are being done in the name of Britain which must make her name stink in the nostrils of the whole world.'

By this stage a change of outlook had become evident within the Cabinet. In particular, Lloyd George had moved towards a form of settlement.[39] Churchill – who in February had become Colonial Secretary – was becoming increasingly uneasy, and advocated the offer of a generous measure of self-government that would safeguard essential British interests, in which movement he was joined by Birkenhead and Austen Chamberlain. His belief that negotiation could only be undertaken from a position of strength remained, but there were indications that a settlement was becoming possible. 'I was,' as he has written, '. . . on the side of those who wished to couple a tremendous onslaught with the fairest offer.'[40] Relations between Churchill and Lloyd George were cold in the summer of 1921 as a result of the elevation of Sir Robert Horne to the Treasury – the post which Churchill had coveted and which he had expected to receive – and it was the view of many observers that a very perceptible rift was opening between the two men. Lloyd George, in Jones's account, once 'gave Winston a dressing down about Russia. Winston had been complaining that we had no policy. This the PM described as ridiculous. Our policy was to try to escape the results of the evil policy which Winston had persuaded the Cabinet to adopt.' At a Cabinet in November 1921 Churchill flared up angrily when Lloyd George taunted him about Gallipoli, a subject on which Churchill was notori-

---

39. Nonetheless, a marked contempt for Irish capacities at Government can be seen in Lloyd George's speeches at this time. On one occasion in 1921 he declared that 'The Irish temperament is too uncertain a factor for us to risk the whole life of Britain upon the chance that they would always act rationally.' This may be compared with a comment in the *Spectator* at the same time: 'There is a natural and traditional inability among the Celtic Irish to manage affairs coolly or reasonably or to conduct any kind of political dispute without violence, or indeed the meanest form of savagery.'

40. *The Aftermath*, p. 291.

ously sensitive.[41] Politically and personally, the two were
moving in different directions.

By May 1921 Churchill's attitude had definitely changed,
and he was urging a truce as a preliminary to negotiations.
The public initiative of the King on 22 June, who appealed in
Belfast for conciliation, provided the opportunity for negotiations to open. On the previous day Birkenhead in the Lords
had repeated the standard Government intonations about the
resolution of the Government not to bow to force. Nevertheless, discussions had been proceeding for some months behind
the scenes; the King's Belfast speech had great emotional
impact, but much of the preparatory work had taken place.
The truce took place as from noon on Monday, 11 July. Both
sides now prepared themselves for the sequel.

*

The accounts of the negotiations that preceded the Irish Treaty
of December 1921 are many and detailed.[42] Churchill was a
central participant in the negotiations, as his own account in
The Aftermath emphasizes. He was fascinated by Michael
Collins, and the compliment was returned. 'Will sacrifice all
for political gain,' Collins noted of Churchill. 'Studies, I
imagine, the detail carefully – thinks about his constituents,
effect of so and so on them. Inclined to be bombastic. Full
of ex-officer jingo or similar outlook. Don't actually trust
him.'[43] These suspicions were largely removed; the two men
had much in common with each other and much with Birkenhead, whose finest hour these negotiations were. Nevertheless,
formal agreement was only reached by the naked use of force
by the British ministers. Churchill threatened 'a real war – not
mere bushranging' if the Irish delegates refused to sign; Lloyd
George put the choice with equal brutality. The delegates
signed. The Irish Treaty negotiations have been described as

41. Keith Middlemas (ed.): *Thomas Jones; Whitehall Diary*, Vol. I, pp.
105 and 179.

42. That of F. Pakenham (Lord Longford): *Peace By Ordeal* is still – in
spite of subsequent new information – incomparably the best.

43. R. Taylor: *Michael Collins*, p. 155.

Lloyd George's 'masterpiece, the triumph of his dangerous dexterity as a negotiator'.[44] Certainly the solution of the Irish Question was a notable achievement, but ministers who negotiate only when they have failed to secure military victory and then secure agreement by the threat of force can hardly claim excessive praise or gratitude.

Certainly they received neither. If the Treaty had been ratified by the Dail by a large majority at once the Government might have emerged with greater credit. The defenders and opponents of the Treaty in Ireland split bitterly; the Treaty was ratified by 64 votes to 57. De Valera resigned the presidency of the Dail, was denied re-election, and formed the Republican Party in hostility to Griffith's Provisional Government. Southern Ireland had barely time to rejoice at her deliverance from war to be plunged into the far greater agonies of civil war. On 14 April the Four Courts in Dublin was seized, and fighting broke out. An uneasy truce was arranged for the elections of the new Dail – held on 16 June – after which the conflict was renewed with far greater intensity.

Churchill, as Secretary of State for the Colonies, was closely involved in Irish affairs after the Treaty, and the burden fell upon him of placating Conservative hostility in the House of Commons, which steadily increased in the spring and early summer of 1922. On 31 May he was obliged to state that if the Treaty were wrecked, Ireland would be reoccupied: 'In the event of the setting up of a Republic it would be the intention of the Government to hold Dublin as one of the preliminary and essential steps in military operations.' This was fortunately not necessary. He told the sub-committee of the Committee of Imperial Defence, which was handling the military aspects of the Irish situation, on 1 June:

. . . his object was to prepare a plan which should provide that at the zero hour immediate action should be taken. It was essential that all our means of exercising pressure on Southern Ireland should be applied at once. We should not allow opposition to be worked up by slow and gradual measures as we have done in the past. When we begin to act we must act like a sledge-hammer so as to cause bewilder-

44. Mowat: *Britain between the Wars*, p. 91.

ment and consternation among the people in Southern Ireland . . .
It was essential that these things should be done simultaneously with
all the force that we had available . . .

MR CHURCHILL explained that . . we should not proclaim war
against Southern Ireland, but should make it clear to them that we
intended to bring such pressure upon them as might be necessary to
compel them to hold to the Treaty which they had signed.[45]

After the assassination in London of Sir Henry Wilson on 22
June, the Government's position became highly precarious,
and Macready was ordered to drive the Irregulars out of the
Four Courts. Macready wisely did nothing, and the order was
rescinded. It was imperative that the position of the new
Republic be established by the Irish Government, and Collins
resolved to act. Churchill has been criticized in some accounts
for a virtual ultimatum to the Irish leaders to end the 'gross
breach and defiance of the Treaty'.[46] This criticism seems to
have been misplaced. He had told the sub-committee of the
Committee of Imperial Defence on 2 June:

. . . It was essential that we should give the Free State Government
all the support that we could or that they would accept, as they were
fighting for the establishment of a civilized government in Ireland.

It might be that the Free State Government would prefer to be
defeated rather [than] to ask for help. In that event we must act
upon our own initiative. We could not stand by with our military
forces on the spot and see Collins and the Treaty policy for which he
stood defeated. . . . He considered that if things went badly with the
Free State troops we should support them by opening fire upon the
Four Courts with 6″ howitzers in Phoenix Park without making any
previous announcement of our intentions . . .[47]

Although Churchill's order to Macready had its dangers, the
alternative policy of leaving the matter entirely to Collins
could have destroyed the hopes – small though they were – of
the supporters of the Treaty in Ireland. It was a very difficult
decision; it is probable that it was the only possible one. In the

45. PRO CAB 16/42/1.
46. See, for example, Mowat, op. cit., p. 103.
47. PRO CAB 16/42/2.

event the Provisional Governments took the initiative with
assistance from Macready, the Four Courts were assaulted on
28 June, and the civil war entered a new and terrible phase.
De Valera accused Churchill of directly instigating the attack
on the Four Courts, and the leaders of the Provisional Government were further tainted with the charge of collaboration with
the British first raised in the bitter aftermath to the signature
to the Treaty.

In this struggle the Coalition could not stand aloof, and the
fledgling nation received arms and equipment from Britain. In
effect this decision was inescapable, and it was considerably
preferable to intervention. The civil war raged long after the
Coalition Government had fallen.[48] It was ironical that the one
achievement of that Government should have been one of the
factors which, by the autumn of 1922, imperilled its existence.

*

Churchill's period at the Colonial Office was not confined to the
Irish Question, although it was a dominating preoccupation.
His energy and self-confidence, which had faltered between
May 1915 and the end of the war, had been fully restored. He
wanted to have Egypt, which lay in the domain of the Foreign
Office, transferred to his Department; he also sought Mesopo-
tamia and the Palestine Mandate. These expansionist concepts

48. Collins was killed on 22 August in an ambush. His last message was
'Tell Winston we could never have done without him.' Erskine Childers was
executed in November; one of the noblest of all these Englishmen who took
Ireland's cause as their own, he deserved better than Churchill's brutal
description of him as a 'mischief-making, murderous renegade' (*The Times*,
13 November 1922). Churchill's views on nationalism and national loyalty
were very intense; it was beyond his comprehension why Erskine Childers,
who fought for Britain in the Great War, should fight against her afterwards,
or that he should write on the morning of his execution that 'I die loving
England, and praying that she may change completely and finally towards
Ireland.' Frank Pakenham relates of the scene at Downing Street after the
Irish Delegates had signed the Treaty: 'To Erskine Childers the abiding
image of these last few wretched hours was Churchill, striding up and down
the lobby lowering and triumphant, all heavy jowl and huge cigar projecting
like the bowsprit of a ship. The very type of overbearing British militarism'
op. cit., p. 311).

brought him into conflict with the Foreign Secretary, Curzon, who wrote to his wife at one point that Churchill 'wants to grab everything . . . and to be a sort of Asiatic Foreign Secretary'.

Churchill apparently had no qualms in moving into a complex field of political activity of which he had had no experience and on which his personal knowledge was extremely limited. He at once set up a Middle East Department attached to the Colonial Office, and in March 1921 he convened a conference in Cairo of senior British officials of the area. In his attitudes to Middle East matters he was strongly under the influence of T. E. Lawrence; he was also determined to reduce the number of British forces in the area, and to replace them by the use of aircraft and the establishment of rulers congenial to British interests. The appointment of Feisal as ruler of Iraq and the acknowledgement of Abdullah as ruler of Transjordan emphasized the second part of his policy; the complete withdrawal of British forces from Iraq between 1921 and 1928 showed the effects of the former. Henry Wilson's scathing description of Churchill's Middle East policies as 'hot air, aeroplanes and Arabs' was perhaps too severe, but it contained a strong element of the truth.[49]

When he turned to the contentious problem of Palestine, Churchill was on even less secure ground. The Cairo conference was eventually followed by a White Paper published in the summer of 1922 which attempted to give something to each side and which succeeded in infuriating both. Thus, although the principle of the establishment of the Jewish National Home in Palestine was affirmed, the White Paper went on to say that this would not involve 'the imposition of a Jewish nationality upon the inhabitants of Palestine as a whole'. The dismay of many leading Zionists – notably Dr Weizmann – at the explicit recognition of Arab rights in Palestine was only surpassed by the fury of the Arabs at the confirmation of Jewish rights in the area. Perhaps Churchill could have done little other than he did, and the fact that he failed to produce a workable settlement in the area cannot be held against him. It was a

49. Callwell, op. cit., Vol. II, p. 316.

task beyond his capacities, but it is probably true to say that it was beyond the capacities of any individual to accomplish.[50] At the time it seemed as though he had skilfully reconciled the conflicting war-time assurances made by the British to the Arabs and the Jews, and he certainly looked upon this episode with considerable satisfaction.

One does not gain the impression that Churchill's bold venture in the labyrinthine entanglements of the Middle East was based upon a full appreciation of its perils and complexities. He inherited a problem. He divined a solution. He then moved on. It was only much later that the full implications of what he had done could be properly assessed.

*

Although there were many indications of how far the Coalition had declined in popular esteem and how restive the Conservative Party was at its policies, by the late summer of 1922 Churchill was in a confident and satisfied mood. His reputation as a parliamentarian had definitely been raised as a result of his skilful handling of the House of Commons on Irish matters, and his Middle East ventures were not severely criticized. He himself has described the Session of 1921–2 as one of the most personally successful in his career up to that time, and we may accept the verdict.

Looking back over the history of the Coalition, however, a more critical judgement cannot be avoided. As has been stressed, Churchill was considerably involved in the most lamentable of the actions of the Government – the Russian Intervention and the wretched handling of the Irish Question. His period at the War Office and the Air Ministry was destined to be unfortunate for those Services in the long run, and emphasized Churchill's obsession with the immediate and his detestation of administration. Even within ·the severe limits of financial stringency, it would have been quite possible for a wise and far-sighted minister to have laid the foundations for an effective modern Air Force and Army. The opportunity was

50. For a fair assessment, see Christopher Sykes: *Cross-Roads to Israel*, p. 67.

allowed to pass, while at the same time the two Services were given tasks beyond their own, or the national, capability.

The handling of the Irish Treaty and the aftermath may be regarded in a more favourable light – and particularly the support given to Collins. But even here we may note the strong importance of the factor of personality in Churchill's motives and methods. We should also recall the limited view of Irish independence which he held, and which was not destined to be forgotten. Nevertheless, when Churchill's views of Irish affairs in 1919–20 are contrasted with those of the second half of 1921, the reality of the advance can be appreciated.

This was perhaps not sufficiently recognized outside a narrow circle. Churchill's achievements, in practical political terms, had not been very considerable in the Coalition. But a politician who has one disaster to his name – Gallipoli – and then adds a major humiliation – the Russian Intervention – and still survives is no ordinary man, and Churchill's satisfaction in the summer of 1922 was not unmerited.

Part Four ECLIPSE AND
REVIVAL
1922–1929

Although justice in politics usually has a somewhat rough-and-ready aspect, it tends to be fair justice none the less. The Lloyd George Coalition did not bestow lustre or high achievement either upon British affairs or the standards of British public life. A Government that had blundered into the Russian Intervention, consistently evaded or falsified important issues at home, had manifestly failed to build a land fit for heroes, had poisoned Ireland with the Black and Tans and had let McSwiney die, could have few claims upon affectionate or even respectful memory. At this distance of time, in our comfortable remoteness, it is possible to deliver a less stern judgement on the Coalition, and to appreciate more adequately the magnitude of the burdens that ministers had to endure than many contemporaries were prepared to concede. But the expectations of the qualifications of posterity are of little comfort to a beleaguered and reviled Administration. It is small satisfaction to the politician to brood upon the possible generosity to be bestowed in the future when he is surrounded with hostility and contempt, and when the foundations of his political house are being brutally and inexorably destroyed.

Yet, after making every allowance, it must be stated that of all modern ministries, that of 1918–22 can command the least sympathy. It is not difficult, nearly half a century later, to comprehend the bitter disillusion that fell upon the Coalition, nor why, by the summer of 1922, its repute and authority had fallen so far from the glittering eminence of November 1918.

In their photographs the Coalition leaders stand arrogant and assured, in manner domineering and in pose authoritarian, apparently epitomizing Birkenhead's celebrated faith in the 'glittering prizes' to be won by those 'with stout hearts and sharp swords'. But behind the confident appearance there lay indecision, disunity, a rootless searching for policies and programmes, and a deadly remoteness from a nation that was fast learning that the black aftermath of war is so often even more

terrible and dispiriting than the conflict itself. The character of
the Coalition, even more than its measures, was responsible for
the subtle but crucial shift in popular attitudes that was
manifest by the beginning of 1922 and that gathered momentum
through the year. As one commentator has justly remarked,
'the war fought for democracy had produced at the centre an
atmosphere more like an oriental court at which favourites
struggled unceasingly for position than anything seen in Britain
for a century or more'.[1] The justice of politics, crude, severe
and unfeeling though it may be, was about to descend upon the
Coalition and its outwardly confident leaders.

*

When Parliament adjourned for the summer recess at the
beginning of August, the Conservative Party was in a state of
simmering revolt. Whichever way men looked there was misfortune and disillusion. Unemployment, particularly in the
North, Scotland and Wales, had reached unprecedented
heights. The glitter of Lloyd George's personal attraction had
faded. The grandiloquently heralded Genoa Conference in April
had been a fiasco. The ruthlessness of the Geddes economies,[2]
the sulphurous aftermath of the Irish Treaty, and the revelation
of the squalid trafficking in Honours,[3] combined to alienate and
alarm a substantial element in the country.

It was less the policies of the Coalition than the character
that it presented which was its undoing. Its dominant features
were opportunism, cynicism and an almost obsessive desire to
live excitingly. Arnold Bennett noted after a weekend at
Cherkley at which Austen Chamberlain, Lloyd George and
Birkenhead had been present, that 'I never heard principles or
the welfare of the country mentioned'. Edward Grey wrote that
the Coalition moved him 'to indignation and despair such as I

1. Francis Williams: *A Pattern of Rulers*, p. 19.

2. The so-called 'Geddes Axe' had fallen principally upon the armed
services, education, health and war pensions. It was a typical rich man's
economy drive, and may help to explain why the British people have a
profound distaste for businessmen in politics.

3. See G. Macmillan: *Honours for Sale*, and the present author's biography
of Lord Davidson, *Memoirs of a Conservative*, pp. 278-88.

have never felt about any other British Government'. 'As a result of their inconsistencies,' *The Times* declared in bitter censure, 'the word of England lost currency throughout the greater part of the world as the word of an upright land.' In 1919 Harold Laski had written of Lloyd George that 'he seems determined to sacrifice upon the altar of his private ambition the whole spirit of our public life';[4] by 1922 this emotion was widespread. In the Conservative ranks there was apprehension and despair. As Amery has written: 'Unionists felt that they no longer had any policy of their own, but were being dragged along in the wake of an erratic Prime Minister whom they once again profoundly distrusted, by a little group of their own leaders who had lost, not only their principles, but their heads.'[5]

Not surprisingly, there was no desire on the part of any of the leaders of the Coalition to end its existence. In February 1920 the prospects of complete fusion between the Lloyd George Liberals and the Conservatives had been seriously discussed, but the project had withered, principally as a result of the coolness of the respective rank and files. The retirement of Bonar Law in March 1921 on grounds of ill-health had removed the one Conservative in the Coalition in whom the party had full confidence; Austen Chamberlain, for all his qualities, was remote and unrepresentative. His confidence in Lloyd George remained; that of the party did not. When, early in 1922, the possibility of an early election had been seriously canvassed, Sir George Younger had expressed his vehement opposition. Lord Derby, the monarch of Lancashire Conservatism, and, for all his deficiencies, a significant political weathercock, refused office in the early summer of 1922. The Coalition struggled along, its leaders increasingly divorced from the realities of the political situation and with a substantial element of its nominal followers seething with discontent.

The difficulties confronting those who desire to overturn governments and depose leaders are very considerable. Birkenhead's position in the Conservative Party was not high, but he expressed the realities of the situation when he demanded

4. *The Nation*, October–November 1919.
5. Amery: *My Political Life*, Vol. II, p. 233.

of Winterton, 'Who is going to lead you to victory if you smash the Coalition? Someone like Bonar or Baldwin?'[6]

*

It was a curious chance that made the town of Chanak, on the eastern shore of the Dardanelles, the indirect cause of political disaster for Churchill for the second time within eight years. He had consistently opposed Lloyd George's pro-Greek policies, and had viewed with deep concern the open support given for Greek ambitions in Asia Minor. In a memorandum of 11 December 1920 he had put forward his opinion that 'we should make a definite change in our policy in the direction of procuring a real peace with the Moslem world and so relieving ourselves of the disastrous reaction both military and financial to which our anti-Turk policy has exposed us in the Middle East and in India . . . I am convinced that the restoration of Turkish sovereignty or suzerainty over the Smyrna Province is an indispensable step to the pacification of the Middle East.'[7] Churchill's warnings were unheeded; on 11 June 1921 he warned Lloyd George that 'If the Greeks go off on another half-cock offensive, the last card will have been played and lost and we shall neither have a Turkish peace nor a Greek army.'[8] The eventuality did not belie this prognostication. By the summer of 1922 the condition of the Greek forces in Turkey-in-Asia had become desperate. The nationalist forces of Mustapha Kemal (perhaps the most able of the Gallipoli commanders) swept down upon the Greeks, and thrust them relentlessly towards the sea. The Greeks reached the port of Smyrna in chaos and rout, hotly pursued. The victorious Kemalist army turned north, and advanced upon the neutral zone at the Dardanelles created by the Treaty of Sèvres in 1920.

Churchill, who had been consistently critical of Lloyd George's policies, now became the vigorous and ardent advocate of a policy of firmness. 'In the Cabinet discussion of these events,' Curzon subsequently wrote, 'Ll.G., Churchill and

6. Winterton: *Orders of the Day*, p. 115.
7. PRO CAB 23/23.
8. *The Aftermath*, pp. 395–6.

The Chanak Crisis, 1922

Present frontiers of
Greece and Bulgaria
Main railway lines
Limit of Greek advance
10 Sept. 1922
Boundary of neutral zone
Boundary of international
zone by Treaty of Sevres
British defensive positions
30 Sept. 1922

BLACK SEA

BULGARIA

WESTERN THRACE

EASTERN THRACE

AEGEAN SEA

SEA OF MARMARA

T U R K E Y

Maritza R.

Adrianople
(Edirne)

The Bosphorus

Beykoz
Uskudar
(Scutari)
Istanbul
(Constantinople)

Izmit

Bolu

Cerkes

Cide

Ankara

Sakarya R.

Eskisehir

Afyonkarahisar

Bursa

Mudanya

Karabiga

Biga
Chanak
Erenkoy
Ezine
Kumkale

Gonen

Bayramic
Edremit

Smyrna
(Izmir)

Usak

The Dardanelles

scale

0   20   40
miles

GALLIPOLI
PENINSULA

Kilia

Nagara
Point

The Narrows

Chanak (Canakkale)

Koja R.

Birkenhead excelled themselves in jingo extravagance and fury.'
Churchill's account in *The Aftermath* describes his position in
somewhat more heroic terms, in which the note of virtuous
martyrdom is not absent:

> I found myself in this business with a small group of resolute
> men: the Prime Minister, Lord Balfour, Mr Austen Chamberlain,
> Lord Birkenhead, Sir Laming Worthington-Evans, with the technical
> assistance, willingly proffered, of the three Chiefs of Staff, Beatty
> Cavan, and Trenchard. We made common cause. The Government
> might break up and we might be relieved of our burden. The nation
> might not support us: they could find others to advise them. The
> Press might howl, the Allies might bolt. We intended to force the
> Turk to a negotiated peace before he should set foot in Europe.[8]

The situation presented by the arrival of the Kemalist forces
at Chanak was undoubtedly a difficult one. The Cabinet was
already committed to concede many of Kemal's requirements
for a peaceful settlement, but several ministers – of whom
Churchill and Birkenhead were the most prominent – reacted
strongly against being forced to enter negotiations under duress.
The Chiefs of Staff were justifiably concerned for the safety of
the small British force at Chanak. And, behind all the actions of
ministers there lay the strong psychological factor of the price
that had been paid for the Treaty of Sèvres, and a consequent
intense repugnance against accepting its reversal in this manner.
There were other factors as well, demonstrated by the opinion
of ministers that 'Chanak had now become a point of great
moral significance to the prestige of the Empire', and by Lloyd
George's statement that 'It would be a great triumph if we
could defeat a heavy Turkish attack alone . . . and demonstrate
to the world that even from a military standpoint we are not
as helpless as our enemies of every description might imagine.'[9]
These attitudes were well expressed in a Cabinet meeting on 7
September, during which Churchill deprecated any proposal
to bargain with the Kemalists over the safety of the Greek
Army which would 'in any way compromise our European

9. This message was communicated to a meeting of ministers by Lloyd
George on 22 September which he did not attend.

policy. The Asiatic arrangements should be kept separate. The line of deep water separating Asia from Europe was a line of great significance, and we must make that line secure by every means within our power. If the Turks take the Gallipoli Peninsula and Constantinople, we shall have lost the whole fruits of our victory, and another Balkan War would be inevitable.' Lloyd George, who was doubtful of the truth of the reports of Turkish successes, agreed with Churchill: 'In no circumstances could we allow the Gallipoli Peninsula to be held by the Turks. It was the most important strategic position in the world, and the closing of the Straits had prolonged the war by two years. It was inconceivable that we should allow the Turks to gain possession of the Gallipoli Peninsula and we should fight to prevent their doing so.' The Cabinet decided to continue the attempts to end the fighting in Asia, and also resolved that 'any attempt by the Kemalists to occupy the Gallipoli Peninsula shall be resisted by force'.[10]

It is evident that these latter factors influenced Churchill very strongly. Beaverbrook relates that 'Churchill talked of the might and honour and prestige of Britain, which he said I, as a foreigner or invader, did not understand, and of how it would be ruined for ever if we did not immediately push a bayonet into the stomach of anyone in arms who contested it. He was always ready to fight England's foes.'[11] Birkenhead gave another explanation for Churchill's change of attitude: 'Winston seems to have become almost pro-Greek having always hated them. I suspect the explanation is that the Kemalists are being helped by the Bolsheviks & W. will support anyone who attacks them.'[12]

It is evident that Churchill's role in the events of 14–29 September was a major one. The 'small group of resolute men' looks somewhat less resolute upon examination. Austen Chamberlain was characteristically irresolute. Balfour's voice

10. This account, like that of the Russian Intervention crisis, is principally based upon the Cabinet Papers.
11. *The Decline and Fall of Lloyd George*, p. 166.
12. Birkenhead to Bonar Law, 9 June 1921 (quoted in Beaverbrook, op. cit., p. 267). .

was not a strong one. Worthington-Evans could hardly be described as a minister of the front rank.[13] Lloyd George did not give as firm or as clear a lead as most accounts claim. The role of the Service advisers was certainly very important, but even more important were the decisions that ministers made on the basis of their military advice.

In any crisis of this nature the historian, however well equipped with information, is at a disadvantage. Any crisis generates its own momentum and its own personality. The stress of events; fragmentary information; the characters of individual ministers; physical tiredness; sheer chance: all these play their part, and contribute to the character and development of the crisis to an extent of which even the participants are often unaware. And thus it is that follies are committed and a sense of proportion lost for reasons which are impossible to specify with any exactness. Thus, however complete the documentation may be, the true causes are usually absent.

The Chanak Crisis was an excellent demonstration of the irrationality that so frequently comes to dominate such episodes. The necessity of concerting action with the French and the Italians – who also were guarantors of the Treaty of Sèvres – was ignored; the arguments of the Foreign Secretary (Curzon) went largely unheeded; and, by the end, the advice of the senior British officer, General Sir Charles Harington, was being misinterpreted and to a large extent overlooked. All the essential elements for a rational solution of the crisis were at hand, and all were set aside.

On Friday, 15 September, the Cabinet discussed the situation at length. Churchill, in a long intervention, said that it was vital to have real forces to meet the Turkish challenge; he was 'wholly opposed to any attempt to carry out a bluff without force', and declared that: 'However fatigued it might be, he thought that the Empire would put up some force to preserve Gallipoli, with the graves of so many of its soldiers, and they might even be willing to do this without the co-operation of

13. One colleague has described him as 'the sort of man a third-rate company would employ to draw up a dubious contract'.

France.' The Cabinet decided to arrange for an early Conference; that Curzon should contact the Serbian and Rumanian Governments to get 'their active and immediate military support in dealing with the present menace to the freedom of the Straits', should ask the Greeks for help and should inform the French Government that the British would send a Division to Constantinople if the French did the same. At the suggestion of Austen Chamberlain, Churchill was deputed to draft a telegram to the Dominion Prime Ministers asking for their support, which he was to submit to Lloyd George before dispatch.[14] On the following morning a group of ministers met – with Curzon a conspicuous absentee – which decided that Churchill should issue a communiqué for the Press. It was a very lengthy document and, although it stressed the desire of the Government for a peaceful solution, its dominant tone was bellicose. As a result of a crass error in timing, many of the Dominion ministers read of the appeal to them in the newspapers before they received it officially. It was not surprising that their reactions were cold, and that only New Zealand and Newfoundland responded favourably. Even more serious was the indignation of the French Government at the strong implication in the communiqué that they and the Italians supported the defiant British stand. The Government had already totally isolated itself from its allies.

There were also indications that it was not likely to enjoy support at home. There had been virtually no prior indications that a war situation was imminent, and after the Press had recovered from its astonishment it was evident that an influential element was strongly critical of the Government's stand. Baldwin – holidaying at Aix – came hastening home after a startled reading of the British newspapers, and Beaverbrook was already alerting Bonar Law to the potentialities of the Government's attitude.

Perhaps these indications made ministers even more determined not to climb down. On 18 September they decided that any Soviet submarines, submarine chasers and minelayers arriving in the Straits should be attacked, that 'any such craft

14. PRO CAB 23/31.

approaching the Straits on the surface from the Black Sea under the Russian flag should be warned off; and that, in the event of risk to any Allied ship from the approach of any such craft encountered in the Black Sea or Straits, it should be sunk. It was not deemed expedient to warn the Soviet Government at present of these intentions.'[15] On the 23rd, 'Considerable stress was laid by the Cabinet on the importance of further publicity to the Government's policy in regard to the situation in the Near East', and a decision to refer the matter to the League of Nations in the event of deadlock in Paris was overruled by Lloyd George after Churchill and Chamberlain had subsequently pointed out to him the possibility that the League might well insist upon British withdrawal from Chanak.[16] Curzon, conducting extremely difficult discussions with the French, was alone in wanting to cease sending troops to Chanak, or at least not to give their departure any publicity. On the same day (25 September) the Secretary of the Cabinet was authorized to make arrangements for a committee consisting of representatives of the Service Departments, the Foreign Office, the Board of Trade and the Colonial and India Offices, to examine the War Book and report back on what parts should be put into operation. The hopeful implications of a note received from Kemal on 26 September were not appreciated. Harington had Cabinet approval to take any measures he deemed essential to the safety of the Chanak position, yet on 29 September a conference of ministers resolved that he should be ordered to notify the Turkish commander of the forces at Chanak that 'if his forces are not withdrawn by an hour to be settled by you, at which our combined forces will be in place, all the forces at our disposal – naval, military, and air – will open fire . . . The time limit should be short and it should not be overlooked that we have received warning regarding the date September 30th (for Turkish operations against the neutral zone) from our Intelligence.'[17] On the evening of 29 September Curzon argued in

15. The Conference agreed that these should be the instructions from the Admiralty to the 'Naval Commander-in-Chief in the Mediterranean'.
16. ibid.
17. Telegram No. 91255.

vain for an extension of the time limit and, preferably, for suspension of the orders to Harington.

The orders to Harington had left some initiative in his hands, of which he made full use. The Cabinet was in almost constant session on the evening of the 29th and throughout the 30th, awaiting his reply. Late in the evening of the 29th Austen Chamberlain told the ministers that Harington had ordered the officer commanding at Chanak not to deliver the ultimatum; Birkenhead said that 'he was shocked to hear it . . . He was deeply desirous of averting war, and would go to great lengths for this purpose, but he did not think that war would be avoided by weakness of this kind.' Cavan pointed out that Harington had been given 'a definite, straightforward order', and strongly opposed Curzon's proposal for a delay. Churchill and Chamberlain agreed with Cavan; Curzon remarked that 'he hoped that the decision would prove a right one', and ministers agreed that his proposal was 'not commensurate with the military risks involved'.

The ultimatum was never delivered, and on 1 October Harington reported that the immediate crisis appeared to be over and that he was to meet Kemal. The Cabinet accepted Harington's inaction and the prospect of the conference. The comment of *The Times* (2 October) was very much to the point; 'An immediate conflict between British and Kemalist troops has been averted mainly by the tact and wisdom of Sir Charles Harington.' Lloyd George had commented at the conference of ministers on 30 September that 'General Harington was so much concerned with the political situation – which was not rightly his – that he did not devote sufficient attention to the military situation.' It was well that he had done so.

*

Although the details of the Chanak Crisis belong to diplomatic rather than political history, the political consequences were substantial. Much of the crisis had been played out in public, and the national newspapers were surprisingly well informed of many of the processes of the Cabinet itself. For Curzon and Baldwin the episode was decisive (if such a word may be used in connection with Curzon). Even more important was the dismay of Bonar Law, of which the first public indication was a condemnatory letter published in *The Times* and the *Daily Express* on 7 October. In expressing his concern at the unilateral action of the Government Law probably reflected a majority opinion within the Conservative Party. The fact that it appeared that Churchill's part had been an important one in propelling the Cabinet to the brink of a totally unexpected and unnecessary war was not likely to make most Conservatives view it with approval.

By itself, the Chanak Crisis would not have been a decisive event in the history of the Coalition. It is possible that it might have survived the initial stand of 15 September, and that Kemal's conciliatory message of the 26th would have been ascribed to that stand. But the ultimatum of the 29th was the decisive factor, regarded by Law and others as an act of gratuitous and irresponsible peril, from whose dire consequences ministers were rescued by good fortune and General Harington. In the context of the disillusion and dislike that the Coalition had acquired, Chanak may fairly be regarded as the event that finally drew together those Conservatives whose political activities were now centred upon securing its downfall, and who regarded Lloyd George and Churchill as the principal villains in a drama that had endured for four years and which had in their eyes brought ruin and disaster upon the Government and the Conservative Party. The emergence of Bonar Law from his retirement provided the possibility of the alternative leadership whose absence hitherto had fatally compromised any chance of a successful revolt against the Conservative Coalitionists.

As the revolt against Lloyd George gathered momentum, the leaders of the Coalition determined on a bold counter-stroke. It was evident that the Conservatives' annual conference in November was going to be a difficult occasion for the Coalition. The proposal was accordingly made to hold the election before then. The Conservative organization men – Younger, Sir Malcolm Fraser and the Chief Whip, Leslie Wilson – strongly opposed it; in the Cabinet, Baldwin's was a dissentient voice. Curzon's doubts and anxieties were rapidly developing to the verge of rupture from his colleagues. On Friday, 13 October, Lloyd George delivered a rasping, alarmist speech in Birmingham, which seemed intended – and no doubt was – to perpetuate the existence of the Anglo-Turkish crisis, to rally support behind the Government. Curzon stayed away from a dinner party given at Churchill's house on Sunday, 15 October, when it was resolved that Chamberlain should call a party meeting at the Carlton Club on the following Thursday (19 October) to determine whether the Conservatives fought the election with the Coalition or as a separate party.

This was a bold stroke indeed. The purpose was, as Chamberlain put it, 'to tell them bluntly that they must either follow our advice or do without us, in which case they must find their own Chief, and form a Government *at once*. They would be in a d—d fix.'[18] Only Members of Parliament would be permitted to attend and vote. Just to ram the point home, the meeting was deliberately timed to take place immediately after the result of a by-election at Newport was declared, at which it was confidently expected that an independent Conservative candidate would be at the bottom of the poll.

The plan misfired dramatically. After three days of frantic activity on both sides, Bonar Law was persuaded to emerge as the alternative leader and to speak against the Coalition at the Carlton Club. Baldwin, at the meeting, gave the first indication that this hitherto obscure politician had discovered, in the words of G. M. Young, 'a new eloquence; direct, conversational, monosyllabic: rising and falling without strain or effort between the homeliest humour and the most moving appeal'.[19] Wilson and Younger gave their support to the dissidents, as did Derby. The Newport result arrived just as Members were going into the meeting; the independent Conservative had won easily, with the Coalition candidate a bad third. The meeting voted against remaining in the Coalition by 185 votes to 88. Lloyd George resigned that afternoon, and the King sent for Bonar Law. Chamberlain, Birkenhead, Balfour and Horne issued a public statement with reproach and resentment declaring their

18. Blake: *The Unknown Prime Minister*, p. 451.
19. G. M. Young: *Stanley Baldwin*, p. 40.

continued adherence to Lloyd George. The Coalition, to the amazed delight of the rebels, had collapsed. The task of replacing it now pressed urgently upon them.

*

At the moment of disaster, Churchill had been prostrated by an emergency appendicitis operation, 'and in the morning when I recovered consciousness I learned that the Lloyd George Government had resigned, and that I had lost not only my appendix but my office as Secretary of State for the Dominions and Colonies'. And this was only the beginning.

Bonar Law formed a Government of sorts, and promptly called a General Election, which may be fairly described as one of the most confused in British political history. The position of the Lloyd George Liberals was peculiarly difficult, a fact that was emphasized by the low key of Lloyd George's speeches and his failure even to issue a manifesto. His only hope was to placate the Conservatives while fighting off the assaults of Labour and, in some cases, Asquithian Liberals. To a point this tactic succeeded. Law could not prevent local Conservative Associations from running candidates against Lloyd George Liberals, but he did nothing to encourage them; in this he was supported by the party managers, who hoped to attract Coalition Liberal votes for their candidates who were contesting Asquithian Liberals. These genial arrangements were undermined and in some cases destroyed by the actions of some local associations, in many instances spurred on and assisted financially by Beaverbrook, who did not approve of giving any Lloyd George Liberal a straight run against Labour.

As the campaign developed its tone became notably sharper. The *Daily Express* accused the Lloyd George Liberals of being warmongers. Churchill was still prostrated by his illness, but issued vigorous statements, describing the Law Ministry as 'the Government of the Second Eleven', and declaring that he would 'never stifle myself in such a moral and intellectual sepulchre'.

The downfall of the Coalition had been principally a Conservative reaction against Lloyd George, and in his election programme Law emphasized the differences, promising 'the minimum of interference at home and of disturbance abroad', stern economies and the reduction of the personal power of the Prime Minister. The electors confirmed the decision made at the Carlton Club. When the dust cleared it was seen that the Conservatives had won 345 seats; Labour 142; Asquithian Liberals 60, with 57 Lloyd George Liberals.[20] The sardonic comment of Philip Guedalla may be recorded:

Mr Bonar Law . . . became Prime Minister of England for the simple and satisfying reason that he was not Mr Lloyd George. At an open competition in the somewhat negative exercise of not being Mr Lloyd George that was held in November 1922, Mr Law was found to be more indubitably not Mr Lloyd George than any of the other competitors; and, in consequence, by the mysterious operation of the British Constitution, he reigned in his stead.

Of the defeated supporters of Lloyd George, Churchill was among the most conspicuous. He had represented Dundee for fourteen years, but now found himself opposed by two Labour candidates, E. D. Morel and (a Prohibitionist with Labour support) a Mr Scrymgeour, who, 'a quaint and hen dim figure' in Churchill's words, had contested the seat since 1908; there was also a Communist, Willie Gallacher. Churchill declared that 'Mr Gallacher is only Mr Morel with the courage of his convictions, and Trotsky is only Mr Gallacher with the power to murder those whom he cannot convince.' Not surprisingly such comments invited a vigorous response.

Churchill did not arrive in Dundee until two days before polling, and was still pale and weak from his operation. On the first night, before a crowd of some four thousand in Caird Hall, he defended the Chanak policy and the record of the Coalition. His second meeting, at the Drill Hall on the following evening, was a tumultuous, bitter affair. 'As I was carried through the yelling crowd of Socialists at the Drill Hall to the platform,' he recorded, 'I was struck by the looks of passionate hatred on the

20. The exact Liberal tally is a matter for some controversy. See A. J. P. Taylor, *English History, 1914–45*, op. cit., p. 198.

faces of some of the younger men and women. Indeed, but for my helpless condition I am sure they would have attacked me.' [21] He was virtually denied a hearing. During one relative lull he shouted out 'if about a hundred young men and women in the audience choose to spoil the meeting – if about a hundred of these young reptiles . . .' Abandoning his prepared speech he tried to answer questions, without success. Finally, after shouting that 'we will not submit to the bullying tyranny of the feather-heads, we will not be ruled by the mob', he was escorted by police from the meeting.

The campaign – if such it can be called – was also enlivened by a violent attack by Churchill on the proprietor of the two main Dundee newspapers, who had subjected him to 'two years of ceaseless detraction, spiteful, malicious detraction' and who was depicted as 'narrow, bitter, unreasonable, eaten up with his own conceit, consumed with his own petty arrogance'. [22]

Churchill went down to overwhelming defeat. His majority in 1918 had been over fifteen thousand; now he was rejected by over ten thousand. It was a severe personal humiliation, and one that Churchill felt deeply. The vagaries of political fortune had been dramatically demonstrated. 'In the twinkling of an eye,' as he has recorded, 'I found myself without an office, without a seat, without a party, and even without an appendix.' Many would have added, 'and without a future'.

*

Writing on 5 October 1924, Churchill commented on the two years that followed the downfall of the Coalition:

When the Coalition Government was destroyed at the Carlton Club only two years ago, it was already perfectly clear to many of us that a period of political chaos would ensue. To the best of my ability, I warned the public of what was in store. But nobody would listen. Everyone was delighted to get back to party politics. Dear to the hearts of all the small politicians were the party flags, the party platforms, the party catchwords. How gleefully they clapped their

21. *Thoughts and Adventures*, p. 212.

22. A lively account of the Dundee meeting is to be found in D. Bardens: *Churchill in Parliament*, pp. 153–4.

hands and sang aloud for joy that the good old pre-war days of faction had returned!

They have had their wish . We have had two years of insensate faction.[23]

In fact, the period of political turmoil that followed the collapse of the Coalition was extremely fortunate for Churchill. The Bonar Law Government had a brief life. In the middle of May 1923 it was discovered that Law had cancer, he resigned and was succeeded by Baldwin, whose preferment over Curzon was a serious and wholly unexpected reverse to the former Coalition Conservatives.[24] The first Baldwin Government lasted no longer than that of Law. To the general astonishment Baldwin dissolved Parliament in November 1923 and went to the country on the issue of Protection. The Asquithian and Lloyd George Liberals were flung into an uncomfortable embrace, and emerged with 158 seats, holding the balance between the Conservatives (258) and Labour (191). Asquith had virtually no choice but to support Labour, and Ramsay MacDonald kissed hands as the first Labour Prime Minister on 22 January 1924, after the Government had been defeated in the House of Commons on a motion of no confidence. The Labour–Liberal alliance (if such it can be called) was uneasy, and collapsed at the end of September. The nation proceeded to its third General Election within two years.

It was evident that, on the morrow of his defeat at Dundee, Churchill's career had reached a grievous crisis. He was offered a dozen Liberal constituencies, but declined. He was now moving to the right. It was a process which had been apparent for some time. A commentator in *The Times* (15 November 1920) noted: 'He has latterly become more Conservative, less from conviction than from the hardening of his political arteries. His early Liberal velleities have dried up, the generous impulses of youth throb more slowly, and apart from some intellectual gristle his only connections with Liberalism are personal.' Beaverbrook wrote to Lloyd George in March 1922: 'His tendency is all to the Right, and his principles are becom-

23. *Weekly Dispatch*, 5 October 1924.
24. See the author's biography of Lord Davidson, Chapter Four.

ing more Tory. I am sure he would not fancy being shut in a coop with you even for a short time.'[25] In this movement disenchantment with Lloyd George was clearly one factor. But his attitudes had always been, in essentials, conservative, and the spectres of Bolshevism abroad and Socialism at home – each of which he regarded with alarm and aversion – emphasized what Masterman had described in 1910 as 'the aboriginal and unchangeable Tory in him'. In October 1922 Churchill told Lord Derby that 'if it had not been for the break [the fall in the Coalition] he had been on the point of joining the Conservative Party as he was more in accord with their general views than he was with those of the Liberals'.[26]

Nevertheless, at the 1923 General Election Churchill stood as a Liberal Free Trader at West Leicester, and delivered a series of violent attacks on the Labour Party; it was another rough fight, and he was often howled down with cries of 'What about Antwerp?' and 'What about the Dardanelles?' At one meeting at Walthamstow he had to be protected by mounted and foot police. A brick was thrown at his car. He described the crowd in an interview with the *Evening News* as 'more like Russian wolves than British workmen'. In spite of the relative success of the briefly reunited Liberal Party in the country Churchill was defeated by F. W. Pethick-Lawrence by four thousand votes.

This was a lucky escape. It was the last occasion on which Churchill fought an election as a Liberal. Asquith's decision to put in Labour was the final and decisive event. 'The enthronement in office of a Socialist Government,' Churchill wrote warningly in a public letter on 17 January, 'will be a national misfortune such as has usually befallen great states only on the morrow of defeat in war. It will delay the return of prosperity, it will open a period of increasing political confusion and disturbance, it will place both the Liberal and Labour parties in a thoroughly false position . . . Strife and tumults, deepening and darkening, will be the only consequence of minority

25. Alan Wood: *The True History of Lord Beaverbrook*, p. 147.

26. Randolph S. Churchill: *Lord Derby*, p. 458. 'I wonder whether that is really true,' Derby commented.

Socialist rule.'[27] Poor Labour Party! Unexpectedly in office, sadly deficient in ministerial experience, earnestly anxious to achieve respectability, vigilant defenders of Free Trade!

Churchill's rightward march was quickly demonstrated. In February he supported the Conservative candidate in a by-election at Burnley, and early in March he appeared as an 'Independent and Anti-Socialist' candidate at a by-election in the Abbey Division of Westminster, with substantial Conservative support. A wealthy friend – Mr James Rankin, Conservative MP for Toxteth (Liverpool) – lent his house as Churchill's headquarters. A somewhat variegated assemblage of allies, which included Sir Philip Sassoon, Lord Darling (recently retired from the High Court), Rothermere's son, the Duke of Marlborough and Sir Eric Geddes, campaigned for him. There was a Conservative MP in charge of each of Churchill's committee rooms. The Beaverbrook and Rothermere newspapers championed his cause.

At one stage it appeared that he would be in effect the official Conservative candidate, but the local party association nominated the nephew of the former Member. Against the advice of – among others – Austen Chamberlain, Churchill resolved to go on, declaring that 'my candidature is in no way hostile to the Conservative Party or its leaders. On the contrary, I recognize that the party must now become the main rallying ground for the opponents of the Socialist Party.'

Churchill's candidature – and the strength of his support in the Parliamentary Party – put Baldwin into an embarrassing situation from the moment that the Abbey Constituency Association decided to put forward their own candidate. Churchill urgently wrote to Baldwin on 7 March:

Private

My dear Baldwin,

   You will receive today authoritative evidence of the irregularities

27. In a letter to *The Times* Churchill proposed that the House of Commons should send an Address to the King, incorporating Labour's motion of censure on the Government and a motion that repudiated Socialism; thus, he argued, the King could refuse to 'enthrone' a Labour Government on the recommendation of Parliament.

wh initiated the Selection meeting of the Abbey Const^y Ass^n. This presents the opportunity for securing a gt advantage for the cause we have at heart. Mr Nicholson's withdrawal or even the non-interference of the Central Office in the fight, will result in a resounding victory for Conservative and Imperial interests & for anti-Socialism. It will also lead directly to the creation of a Liberal wing working with Cons. party in the coming struggle.

I am sure you do not wish to be compelled by technicalities to fire upon the reinforcements I am bringing to your aid. Act now with decision, & we shall be able to work together in the national interest. I have no other thought but to unite & rally the strongest combination of forces against the oncoming attack.

Do not let this opportunity slip away, & all of us be weakened thereby.

I can come to see you if you wish at any time today.

Yours sin.ly
Winston S. Churchill

On the same day Baldwin received a letter in a very different sense from H. A. Gwynne, the editor of the *Morning Post*, urging him to forbid ex-ministers to speak for Churchill, to be 'strong and ruthless, if necessary', as it was likely to be Churchill's Jena or Austerlitz. Baldwin endeavoured to limit the area of conflict,[28] and it was agreed that no ex-ministers would take part. Baldwin could not overrule the local Association, and he persuaded Balfour not to send a public letter of support for Churchill. This was on 14 March. On the following morning, just as he was about to leave for Cannes, Balfour was startled to read in the papers that Leo Amery had made a public appeal to the Conservatives of the Abbey Division to vote against Churchill. 'This hardly seems to me to be fair play,' Balfour wrote, 'and I leave it to you to consider whether, in the circumstances, you think any change of policy is, as regards my letter, in the public interest either possible or desirable. If you do think so, you might send on the letter to Winston, who has not yet seen it.' Baldwin did think that the Amery letter had changed the situation and, on his own initiative, promptly released Balfour's letter to the press. It is

28. He refused to follow Gwynne's advice, and he also refused a virtual demand from Oliver Locker-Lampson to disown Nicholson.

perhaps worth emphasizing that Balfour left the choice of action to Baldwin, whose action was significant. Balfour's letter was probably not a decisive factor in the Abbey result, but it can hardly have failed to have an important effect. Baldwin had accordingly managed a neat balancing act. The local Association had not been interfered with; he had kept aloof from the contest; and he had seen that the balance was fairly kept.[29]

The campaign was conducted with verve and enthusiasm. Churchill toured the constituency in a coach and four, making rousing and on some occasions extremely alarmist speeches on the Socialist Peril. The official candidate produced posters that declared that 'Dundee didn't. West Leicester laughed. Westminster won't!' Churchill has described the contest as 'incomparably the most exciting, stirring, sensational election I have ever fought'. Fenner Brockway, the Labour candidate, canvassed the staff of Buckingham Palace, and issued an election address that declared that:

Mr Churchill has previously charged Labour with setting class against class. It is he who is now the chief exponent of a class war. He raised the bogy of Socialism, and seeks to combine all the selfish and vested interests who fear the onward march of Labour . . .

Of all the politicians Mr Churchill has shown himself most unfit for the responsibility of government. His forte is to be a disturber of peace, whether at home or abroad. He is a political adventurer, with a genius for acts of mischievous irresponsibility. He is militant to his finger-tips . . .

Mr Churchill's record shows him to be a public danger and a menace to the peace of the world . . .[30]

Churchill's electioneering manner was, perhaps, an acquired taste. An observer wrote after one of his meetings:

He really and truly points an accusatory finger at the crowd, and cries in sepulchral tones, 'I say, that if another war is fought, civiliza-

29. The entire correspondence relating to this episode is to be found in the Baldwin Papers at Cambridge. I am grateful to the Syndics of the University Library for their permission to see, and quote from, papers in this collection.

30. Quoted in Martin Gilbert: *Plough My Own Furrow*, p. 176.

tion will perish.' (Laughter. A sweeping gesture.) 'A man laughs,'
(out goes the finger). 'That man dares to laugh. He dares to think the
destruction of civilization a matter for humour!' Indeed, he is such
a preposterous little fellow, with his folded arms and tufted forelock
and his Lyceum Theatre voice, that if one did not detest him one
might love him from sheer perversity.[31]

In the event Churchill went down by forty-three votes.[32] 'It
is no new thing, after all, to discover that judgement is not
the most conspicuous of Mr Churchill's remarkable gifts,' *The
Times* with characteristic hostility declared on the morrow of
the declaration. In fact the result was almost perfect for
Churchill's future career. The Conservatives would have found
it difficult to forgive him for defeating their candidate, yet the
closeness of the result emphasized the power and attraction
of his personality. The long search for political sanctuary was
over.

In 1893 Archibald Salvidge had organized his first major
political meeting in Liverpool for Lord Randolph Churchill,
then in melancholy decline.[33] Since then he had become the
dominating Tory figure in the city, and a power in the party
throughout the land. He had supported the Coalition, and had a
warm personal regard for Churchill. He now achieved for
Churchill what he had tried to do for his father – to rehabilitate
him with the Conservative Party. It was a bold step; as the
Morning Post commented sourly, 'the idea of scrapping the
Conservative Party in order to make a home for lost Liberals
and returning prodigals does not appear to us to promise success'.

On 7 May 1924 Churchill stepped on a Conservative platform
for the first time in twenty years at a meeting arranged by

31. Winifred Holtby: *Letters to a Friend*, p. 246.
32. The figures were: O. W. Nicholson (Conservative)   8,187
                       W. S. Churchill (Independent)   8,144
                       A. Fenner Brockway (Labour)   6,156
                       J. S. Duckers (Liberal)   291
33. For an account of this episode, see S. Salvidge: *Salvidge of Liverpool*,
p. 273.

Salvidge in Liverpool, to speak on 'The Present Dangers of the Socialist Movement'. It was a triumph. The Socialist Government, as he said, was 'driven forward by obscure, sinister, and in part extraneous forces'. On the next day he achieved what Salvidge described as 'an impressive and complete success' when he spoke at the Liverpool Conservative Club.[34] He was then invited to address a representative gathering of Scottish Unionists in Edinburgh, presided over by Arthur Balfour. Shortly afterwards the chairman of the Epping Conservative Association, Sir James Hawkey, successfully sponsored him as candidate for the constituency. He stood as a 'Constitutionalist' again, but his attitudes were emphatically Conservative – and right-wing Conservative at that. In the General Election held in the autumn of 1924 when the minority Labour Government fell at last, he was returned by over ten thousand votes. In his campaign, as in the Abbey by-election, he laid great emphasis on the 'Bolshevik' menace of Socialism, and was quick to make use of the Zinoviev Letter. He reminded the electors of Epping of 'the story of Kerensky, how he stood there, like Mr Mac-Donald, pretending that he meant to do the best he could for his country, and all the time apologizing behind the scenes to the wild, dark, deadly forces which had him in their grip'.[35] This was followed up with an inflammatory article in the *Weekly Dispatch* (2 November) on 'The Red Plot – and After':

From the earliest moment of its birth the Russian Bolshevist Government has declared its intention of using all the power of the Russian Empire to promote a world revolution. Their agents have penetrated into every country. Everywhere they have endeavoured to bring into being the 'germ cells' from which the cancer of Communism should grow. Great assemblies have been held in Russia of conspirators and revolutionaries of every race under the sun, for the purpose of concerting world revolution. From the beginning Britain, the British Empire, and, above all, India, have been openly proclaimed as the first and chief objectives . . . There was, therefore, nothing new and nothing particularly violent in the letter of Zinoviev, alias Apfelbaum, to the British Communists.

34. Salvidge, op. cit., pp. 272–5.
35. Richard W. Lyman: *The First Labour Government*, p. 259.

Even if the letter turned out to be a forgery, he prudently added, 'not the slightest change would have occurred in our view of the character and intentions of the Soviet Government'. A year later he formally rejoined the Conservative Party, and signified his complete repentance by becoming a member of the Carlton Club once more.

The prodigal son returned to an unexpectedly rich reward. Baldwin had been anxious to include Churchill in any future Conservative Government for at least a year.[36] As he told Neville Chamberlain, 'he would be more under control inside than out',[37] but after the 1924 victory there was some problem where to put him.

There was strong opposition to the idea of giving him either a Service or an external Department, and it was Neville Chamberlain who actually made the tentative suggestion of the Treasury. Baldwin acted upon it at once. Churchill was startled, the Conservative Party was dumbfounded, and even Neville Chamberlain seems to have been somewhat surprised. The strong Protectionist element in the Party was the most amazed of all at the inclusion of this notorious Free Trader. Austen Chamberlain (Foreign Office) and Birkenhead (India) also returned to the fold. As Churchill remarked at a celebratory dinner organized by Salvidge, 'I realize the truth of the remark of Disraeli that "the vicissitudes of politics are inexhaustible".'

*

Churchill's unexpected elevation to the Treasury occurred at a particularly complex and important period of economic history in the post-war years.

The dominant feature in the British domestic economy was the persistent unemployment level of over one million, concentrated in the former industrial giants – coal, cotton, shipbuilding and steel and iron. The coal industry, employing over

---

36. Boothby: *I Fight to Live*, p. 36. At that time (1923) Boothby had been a member of Baldwin's staff, and records that Baldwin had said to him on a journey to Edinburgh, 'If and when I get back to power, there is one man I am going to have at my side – Churchill.'

37. Feiling: *Neville Chamberlain*, p. 110.

a million people, was still the largest in the country, with textiles – about half a million – second in size and importance. Both were now in dire straits. In 1913, Britain had exported 73 million tons of coal; this figure had shrunk to 25 million in 1921, and, although it subsequently rose, it was never more than 50 million tons in any one year throughout the 1920s. Rising costs of production and the movement to oil, gas and electricity played their part in this shrinkage of the market; the war had lost valuable markets, but, more significantly, it had created formidable new competitors who could undercut British prices. In the textile industry, exports had fallen by about one half on the 1913 figure, and Japan – who had not been a competitor at all in 1913 – was moving rapidly towards the twenty per cent of the world market that she had gained by 1929.

The drastic slump in the fortunes of the great pre-war exporting industries had grievous social and political consequences. By 1924 it was clear that the level of employment in the British Isles was extraordinarily varied. It was the unparalleled concentration of prolonged unemployment, with its concomitants of malnutrition, poverty, despair and human degradation, that was the novel aspect. Whole communities – indeed, almost entire cities – in the North, in Wales, Scotland and Northern Ireland, were in a condition of depression, with a high level of total unemployment and a substantial amount of part-time working. This was in sharp contrast to the relative prosperity of the South and South-East of England. A national average of ten per cent unemployment was serious enough; its concentration in formerly prosperous and confident communities meant that the extent of the slump was felt with particular feeling in these areas.

Mass unemployment tended to be explained by the dislocation caused by the war to the international trading arrangements. By this reasoning the only hope for the dying former export industries lay in the restoration of the system, which involved currency stabilization by means of a return to the gold standard and the elimination of tariffs. A consistent deflationary policy was accordingly practised by the Treasury.

On these matters there was a surprising accord. The Labour

and Liberal Parties were firmly committed to Free Trade philosophies, and the General Election of 1923 had demonstrated that they still enjoyed substantial popular support. In 1924 Snowden had removed almost the last fig-leaf of Protection possessed by British industry when, with general approval, he rescinded the McKenna Duties of 1915. It was the accepted policy of all governments since the end of the war to work towards a return to the gold standard and to the consequent restoration of Britain's position as a leading world financial centre. During the immediate post-war inflation the pound had fallen to 3·20 dollars; by 1 January 1922 it had recovered to 4·20, and rose to 4·73½ in February 1923. There had been a subsequent fall, but by the beginning of 1925 it was estimated by many authorities that the pound had reached within 2½ per cent of the pre-war figure of 4·86 dollars.

Behind the calculations there lay other, perhaps even more important, convictions. The messianic quality of Free Trade still survived. The belief that Free Trade encouraged and developed international harmony and good feeling was deeply embedded. In the early 1920s, at a series of international conferences, the British had sponsored motions deploring tariff barriers between nations, many of which had been enthusiastically approved. The fact remained that, as a result of the assistance given to a few 'safeguarded' industries, importers into Britain had to surmount a tariff level of some five per cent, whereas the tariff barriers to British exports were steadily, if stealthily, rising.

At the same time as there was this determination to move in the direction of the restoration of the pre-war trading and monetary system, there was a general refusal to accept the permanence of the decline of the former staple export industries. It was evident that the cost of production was crucial. The long-term method of surmounting this was heavy investment in new plant and methods of production; the short-term one was the reduction of wages. The necessity of the latter was widely accepted, and was even put forward by Baldwin, who said (30 July 1925) that 'All the workers of this country have got to take reductions in wages in order to help put industry on its feet.' In no industry was this believed more firmly than in the coal industry – but only by the employers.

Meanwhile, Governments since the war had been exultantly stripping themselves of the powers by which the economy could be controlled, or even substantially influenced. The function of the Treasury was generally considered to be to regulate – and cut down – Government expenditure. Monetary policy was the field of the Bank of England. Industrial matters were in the realm of the Board of Trade and the Ministry of Labour, which were very much subordinate to the Treasury.

The doctrine that the Budget must be balanced was still an article of faith. Each Chancellor of the Exchequer was expected to give the nation a healthy example by providing for a surplus and achieving it. It was another article of faith that income tax – at five shillings in the pound when Churchill became Chancellor – was too high. Furthermore, it was also regarded as essential that every Budget contained provision for the Sinking Fund, which meant in effect that every Budget in the 1920s had a sum of approximately £60 million set aside for this purpose, which had to be met by taxation and reduction in Government expenditure.

It was true that the Government did more to assist the economy than had been dreamed of in 1914. It gave financial incentives to exporters; it sometimes financed public works on a modest scale; it provided unemployment relief. But none of these were regarded as anything more than temporary measures to meet exceptional circumstances. In financial circles – and particularly in the City of London – the yearning for 'normalcy' was acute, and was pressed with enthusiasm upon all Chancellors.

This is necessarily only a very brief outline of what was a complex situation. But the economic historian of the period cannot fail to be struck by the virtual unanimity of academic economists, merchant bankers, industrialists and politicians on what were considered to be essentials. With some exceptions – notably Hubert Henderson and Keynes – the serious weakness and incompatibilities in these assumptions were hardly noticed. Any Chancellor would have been under formidable pressure to reduce taxation, to balance his Budget, to give an example of frugality and caution to the nation, and to work towards a more free international industrial situation. In this process, it was argued, the restoration of the gold standard was essential. Hardly any commentator pointed out that to maintain the pound at an unreal level would diminish even further the sums available for the investment in the ailing industrial giants, and that a 'dear money' policy had already had disastrous consequences.

*

Churchill came to the Treasury with no record of experience in, or even excessive interest in, high finance. The language of economists itself baffled him,[38] and there were occasions on which the long shadow of his economic mentor, Sir Francis Mowat, Permanent Secretary to Lord Randolph in 1886, appeared to lie very heavily upon him. But he applied himself to his unexpected task with characteristic zeal and determination. His Parliamentary Private Secretary, Robert Boothby, has written with fairness:

> The essence of genius is vitality, fecundity and versatility. These were the most impressive things about him. His output was colossal. He was basically uninterested in the problems of high finance. But his Budgets were skilfully contrived and superbly presented. And, given the conditions under which he was obliged to work . . . he could hardly have done better, or other, than he did.[39]

A vivid and interesting portrait of the new Chancellor is given by his official private secretary P. J. (later Sir James) Grigg, which may be inserted at this point:

> Winston walked into the Treasury in November 1924 carrying the Seals of Office which he had just received and which he showed the greatest reluctance to entrust to anyone less than the Permanent Secretary . . .
> It would perhaps be fitting here to describe Winston's methods

38. 'If they were soldiers or generals I would understand what they were talking about,' he once complained to Boothby. 'As it is, they all talk Persian' (Lord Boothby to the author, 8 July 1966).

39. Boothby: *I Fight to Live*, p. 44.

of work. He disliked giving snap decisions on cases stated orally. Nevertheless he did indulge in a great deal of personal discussion during which he could talk himself into a knowledge and understanding of any topic which came before him. The last duty of his Private Office at night was to fill a box with the papers and correspondence which required his direction so that it could be put at his bedside with his breakfast when he awoke in the morning. In this he would browse for, say, an hour, until a shorthand writer came to get the results of his ruminations. He would then dictate minutes on the papers in the box or on anything else which occurred to him – large or small, grave or gay. The range of his official interest was extraordinary, and it might easily happen that the minutes of a single morning covered the whole region between the draft of an important state paper or ideas for the next Budget and some desired improvement in the make-up of files or the impropriety of the Office of Works supplying Czechoslovakian matches in a British Government establishment. After he had dictated all he wanted, or if important appointments cut short the flow of minutes, he dressed and came through to the office from No. 11 more often than not looking in for a few words with the Prime Minister at No. 10 on the way . . .

I have sometimes thought that his critical faculties stopped short at his own children, and that the best service those who worked for him could provide was to ensure that he was given time to discover for himself which were the weaklings among the offspring of his own brain. This process of spartan exposure was sometimes a rough one for what he called the alguazils as well as for the ideas and many of my recollections are of heated and even violent arguments with Winston . . .

In those days, Winston, spirited and lively, tempered controversialist that he was, in the wide public sphere was absolutely free from resentment or rancour. He did, on occasion, nourish a feeling that his opponents had treated him unfairly or ungenerously, but even then he was always on the lookout for an early opportunity of reconciliation. I am not sure that his greatheartedness entirely survived his years in the wilderness from 1929–39, and the venom with which he was pursued for most of those years by Tories and Labour alike, but certainly when he was at the Treasury he was the most generous and the least vindictive of men.[40]

*

40. P. J. Grigg: *Prejudice and Judgement*, pp. 174–7.

Churchill's first Budget, presented to the House of Commons on 28 April 1925, was dominated by the announcement of the decision to return to the gold standard at the pre-war parity, and overshadowed the provision for the Widows, Orphans and Old Age Pensions Bill. To all those who had yearned for the day when 'the pound could look the dollar in the face', this was an historic moment.

The decision was neither hasty nor ill-considered. Churchill took advice from all sides, and Grigg has described 'a sort of brains trust on the subject' at a dinner given by Churchill, in which Sir Otto Niemeyer of the Treasury put forward the case for a return to gold, in which he was opposed by McKenna and Keynes. Grigg relates:

> One thing about this argument comes back to me with crystal clearness. Having listened to the gloomy prognostications of Keynes and McKenna, Winston turned to the latter and said: 'But this isn't entirely an economic matter; it is a political decision for it involves proclaiming that we cannot, for the time being at any rate, complete the undertaking which we all acclaimed was necessary in 1918, and introducing legislation accordingly. You have been a politician; indeed you have been Chancellor of the Exchequer. Given the situation as it is, what decision would you take?' McKenna's reply – and I am prepared to swear to the sense of it – was: 'There is no escape; you have got to go back; but it will be hell.'[41]

At the time the decision was generally applauded. Only a few voices were raised in criticism. Beaverbrook, Vincent Vickers – who resigned from the Board of the Bank of England – Keynes and Boothby were virtually isolated in their hostility. Even the critics were divided. There was a majority in favour of the return to the gold standard, but which criticized the restoration of the pre-war parity; Keynes was one of the few who opposed the return to gold.

The newly available Treasury and Cabinet papers confirm Grigg's account of Churchill's care in seeking expert opinions before reaching his decision. The weight of the advice – notably from Newman, Bradbury and Niemeyer – was overwhelmingly in favour of the return to gold, and Churchill eventually bowed

41. ibid., p. 184.

to it. But despite his questionings it should not be assumed that Churchill's personal inclinations were hostile to the development,[42] even though he had his serious doubts as to whether the time was appropriate and whether it would be of any value to industry. These doubts were well founded. In his speech on the Gold Standard Bill on 4 April Churchill put forward what was the core of the case in favour of the change: 'We are often told that the gold standard will shackle us to the United States. I will deal with that in a moment. I will tell you what it will shackle us to. It will shackle us to reality. For good or ill, it will shackle us to reality.'

The 'doctrine of bad advice' is always unsatisfactory in defence of any ministerial decision, but in this case it has a real justification. Former Chancellors – and notably Bonar Law – had gone against official advice from the Bank of England and the Treasury, but none had been so personally and politically vulnerable as Churchill was at the beginning of 1925. He had not the knowledge to counter the official arguments, nor the personal experience in finance or industry to buttress his instinctive suspicions. Politically, his vulnerability was acute. He was a victim – by no means the first, and to be by no means the last – of a system of economic and fiscal management which was grievously out of date and whose concentration upon Britain's monetary position acted to the serious disadvantage of industry. The 'doctrine of bad advice' may be invoked on this occasion, but it should be emphasized that the urgings of the Federation of British Industries were in a contrary direction. By acting against this advice, and taking that of the bankers, Churchill had made a decision which was fully in line with his attitudes on economic matters. It was, furthermore, a decision which both in itself and in its development restored to the Bank of England the dominance over monetary policy which had seemed to have been surrendered in 1917 when Law had

42. A new and interesting account of the gold standard crisis has been given by Dr Robert Skidelsky in *The Times*, 17 March 1969. This account's only weakness, in my opinion, lay in the fact that Churchill's feelings in favour of the return to gold were not given sufficient emphasis. See Keith Middlemas and John Barnes: *Baldwin*, p. 303.

secured the resignation of Lord Cunliffe. The decision, furthermore, demonstrated the fact that neither the Treasury nor the
Bank had really grasped the enormity of the new problems that
confronted the British economy and industry. And to this
failure of perception and analysis the Chancellor of the Exchequer was no exception.

There can be no question that the Government had taken the
wrong decision, and that the vehement attacks delivered by
Keynes in particular were, in substance, justified. Although it
benefited (at least temporarily) the merchant bankers and the
City, it did nothing whatever for industry. The maintenance of
the standard necessarily meant a high level of Bank Rate, the
hoarding of reserves and a policy of dear money. Before the
return to gold there had been little money enough available for
modernization and re-equipment. Now there was even less.
Furthermore, the primacy and independence of the Bank of
England with regard to monetary policy was restored, and what
little control the Treasury had in this area was lost. This would
have been of less consequence had the Bank been adequately
equipped to meet its responsibilities.

The decision emphasized the fact that the Government and
its principal advisers had not grasped the enormity and complexity of the problems facing the British economy, and, above
all, industry, in the 1920s. It was a step backwards into a
dream-world, in which Britannia ruled the waves and the pound
sterling commanded awe and respect throughout the world. It
was taken for granted that the restoration of parity with the
dollar would restore not merely the dominance of the London
money market but would benefit the national economy to its
1914 level. But the conditions of 1925 were not those of 1914. A
substantial amount of British assets had been sold to pay for
the war; exports could no longer produce the surplus necessary
to finance and buttress a position as a world financier.

The criticism of the decision, although the critics themselves
were in a minority, developed swiftly and was formidably
deployed. In a series of articles in the *Evening Standard* –
subsequently published under the title of *The Economic Consequences of Mr Churchill* – Keynes explained Churchill's error

thus: 'Partly, perhaps, because he has no instinctive judgment to prevent him from making mistakes; partly, because, lacking this instinctive judgment, he was deafened by the clamorous voice of conventional finance; and most of all, because he was gravely misled by his experts.'

Keynes went on to depict the future in grimly accurate colours: 'The whole object is to link *rigidly* the City and Wall Street . . . The movement of gold or of short credits either way between London and New York, which is only a ripple for them, will be an Atlantic roller for us.'

And there were other critics. Hubert Henderson wrote on 4 April: 'We make bold to say that a return to gold this year cannot be achieved without terrible risk of renewed trade depression and a serious aggravation of unemployment.'

Dominating everything else was this apprehension of the effects of the decision, on which Henderson and Keynes had no doubts. As Keynes commented, Churchill 'was just asking for trouble. For he was committing himself to force down money-wages and all money values, without any idea of how it was to be done', and the result 'must be war, until those who are economically weakest are beaten to the ground'.

An equally valid point of criticism was a substantial gulf of policy between Churchill's Budget and the decision to return to gold. The main features of the Budget were the announcement of Neville Chamberlain's measures for widows' pensions; relief to surtax payers and the reduction of income tax by sixpence; and, most astonishing of all, the imposition of duties on artificial silk and lace. Baldwin approvingly commented that the Budget followed 'the soundest lines of prudence and Conservative finance'. Others were not equally enamoured. In one of his best essays, Hubert Henderson set out the inadequacies and incon-sistencies of Churchill's approach:

The more Mr Churchill's Budget policy is studied, the more incredible does the folly of it seem. When its various aspects have been fully digested, certainly when its consequences have become apparent, it will surely rank, both from the financial and political standpoints, as an ineptitude without parallel in our recent history . . .

But more extraordinary than any of the items (if indeed anything could be more extraordinary than the silk duties) is the tenor of the Budget as a whole. British industry is labouring under great and growing difficulties. In comparison the salaried and rentier classes of the community are reasonably prosperous. Mr Churchill pays rhetorical recognition to this contrast, and he has £26,000,000 to play with. Yet he adds materially to the difficulties of industry and concentrates his favours upon the rentier and salaried man . . .

In short, it was Mr Churchill's duty, if he decided to take the plunge back to gold, to insist that expensive social measures must be ruled out meantime. Nor is that all. Relief to the income-tax payer should no less have been ruled out. The sacrifices of the return to gold fall entirely upon business and do not touch the salaried man. Mr Churchill should accordingly have used his Budget surplus . . . exclusively to help industry through the transition . . . if he had postponed the new insurance scheme and abstained from the folly of the silk duties, he would at least have done something to help industry to adapt itself to the return to gold . . .

We are driven to the conclusion that Mr Churchill's great but peculiar abilities are not well suited to the realms of finance. He has filled a large variety of public offices with (in the main) conspicuous success. His general reputation deserves, indeed, to rank far higher than it does, for his administration of the Admiralty has been most ungenerously judged. It is with regret that we are disposed to write him down as one of the worst Chancellors of the Exchequer of modern times.[43]

*

Since the end of the war, the gaunt problem of the coal industry had become remorselessly more grievous. 1925 was the worst year on record. The end of the French occupation of the Ruhr had plunged the industry back into depression, and unemployment had risen by ten per cent. The return to dollar parity caused an increase in cost estimated by some at $2\frac{1}{2}$, and by others as high as ten per cent, which sharply reduced orders. A crisis in the industry was probably inevitable; the combination of events in 1924–5 accelerated it. The owners reacted by declaring their intention of ending existing agreements, reducing wages and increasing the working day. The miners were

43. Hubert Henderson: *The Interwar Years and other papers* (Clarendon Press).

obdurate, and were backed by the General Council of the TUC in their 'resistance to the degradation of the standard of life of their members'. Further decisions were taken to support the miners in their confrontation with the owners. By the end of July 1925 the nation was moving inexorably towards what was in effect a General Strike.

It was clearly greatly in the national interest that such a calamity should be averted. A Court of Inquiry under Mr H. P. Macmillan was established to examine the industry and its problems, and reported very largely in the miners' favour on 28 July. Attached to the Report was a lengthy memorandum by Sir Josiah Stamp, that argued to the effect that the difficulties in the industry could be entirely explained 'by the immediate and necessary effects of the return to gold'. This was a very questionable allegation; it could more reasonably be charged that Government actions had done nothing to help the industry nor to resolve its deep-rooted and intractable problems.

On 29 and 30 July discussions continued, without result. In a speech made before the Court of Inquiry had reported, Baldwin had mentioned the possibility of a Government subsidy to the industry; now, under pressure from the Cabinet, he backed away from the proposal. On Friday, 31 July, with the strike imminent, the Government agreed to a subsidy for a period during which a Royal Commission would investigate the industry at length, with cooperation from both sides. The subsidy was estimated to be about £10 million; in the event it was over £23 million. This decision of course involved Churchill personally, as his agreement was essential. He became one of the leading protagonists of the subsidy in the Cabinet, although perturbed by the implications of a 'surrender' to the unions. The Government recognized that it was not prepared to meet the crisis of a national strike. This was the decisive argument. The trade union movement rejoiced at the victory of 'Red Friday', and the apparent capitulation of the Government. The Royal Commission, presided over by Herbert Samuel, began its work. The Government set about its preparations for combating a General Strike. Nine months' peace had been purchased.

*

It is necessary, at this point, to examine another aspect of Churchill's work as Chancellor that was to be of crucial significance in the future. Churchill's intense concentration on the matter in hand was one of his highest qualities. Nevertheless, there were dangers in this attitude.

In his first Budget Churchill had unwisely announced his intention of achieving economies of £10 million a year in the Service Estimates. He was constantly under attack from both sides of the House of Commons for failing to carry out his undertaking. When he introduced an Economy Bill in March 1926 he was vehemently assailed by Labour for attempting to avenge himself for his defeat at the hands of the Admiralty by cutting the social services. Churchill's reply was a valid defence of his policies, but the passage of the Bill emphasized the unwisdom of the 1925 commitment. Lloyd George, in his happiest vein, described the Bill as 'a gipsy stew-pot. What does a gipsy put in his stew-pot? A rabbit snared in a spinney, a hare trapped in a field. A chicken or two purloined from somebody's farm; and probably one or two hedgehogs.' With the necessity for reducing government expenditure, and with Europe at last apparently quiescent, the case for further economies in the armed services seemed overwhelming. Churchill had not been in office for a month before he sought from the Foreign Office a declaration which ruled out the possibility of war with Japan for the next ten, fifteen or twenty years. Austen Chamberlain was reluctant to give this undertaking, but it was eventually secured. It will be recalled that Churchill had initiated the decision of the War Cabinet in August 1919 to frame the Service Estimates on the assumption that the Empire would not be engaged 'in any great war in the next decade'.[44] Churchill now sought to have this principle formally established, and succeeded in July 1928, with the provision that 'the assumption should be reviewed each year by the Committee of Imperial Defence.'

It is always easy to be wise after the event. There was no Hitler in sight in 1928, and the possible perils of Italian and Japanese ambitions were difficult to anticipate. Nevertheless, there was substantial truth in the comment of Beatty, the First

44. See pp. 160–61 above.

Sea Lord: 'The politician says there are no external dangers. That may be true, but if so, it is due to the fact that we are strong; directly we become weak, external dangers will grow up like mushrooms.'[45] And it may be noted that Churchill himself had written in a newspaper article in 1924 that 'the enormous contingents of German youth growing to military manhood year by year are inspired by the fiercest sentiments, and the soul of Germany smoulders with dreams of a War of Liberation or revenge'.

Throughout the 1920s expenditure on the Services declined every year. If Churchill had had his way completely, the drop would have been even more sharp. When he attempted to lay strong arms on the Admiralty's cruiser programme in 1925 there was a fierce controversy. The Admiralty's Estimate for 1925–6 was some £10 million over that for the previous year, and Churchill at once questioned the justification for this increase. He proposed that there should be no new construction programme in 1925–6, with the possible exception of submarines, and no increase of personnel; the question of new cruiser construction authorized by the Labour Government should, he argued, be referred to a sub-committee of the Committee of Imperial Defence. In tone and content, as Captain Roskill has justly commented, the memorandum bore a strong resemblance to that written by Lloyd George in criticism of Churchill's 1914–15 Estimates.[46]

The reaction of the Admiralty was vigorous; as Bridgeman pointed out, the programme was to maintain the efficiency of the Fleet, not to increase the size of the Navy. Churchill's argument that the Japanese threat was virtually non-existent and that no war was possible before 1940 was, as Bridgeman expressed it, 'too comfortable an attitude'. Baldwin set up a Naval Programme Committee, chaired by Birkenhead, to examine the issue; Churchill proposed the abandonment of the policy to establish a naval base at Singapore, and emphasized the fact that the Admiralty was measuring its strength against

45. Chalmers: *Beatty*, p. 411.
46. Roskill: *Naval Policy between the Wars*, p. 446. See also Middlemas and Barnes, op. cit., pp. 326–39.

that of Japan. Was this a reasonable possibility? Austen Chamberlain considered that, within the next ten years, it was not. At one stage it appeared that the whole Board, headed by the First Lord (W. C. Bridgeman),[47] the Financial Secretary (Davidson) and Beatty, would resign. In the Cabinet they were supported by Amery, while Birkenhead and Chamberlain supported Churchill. Eventually, on 22 July, Baldwin intervened with a compromise which was in effect a victory for the Admiralty, and the Admiralty's programme – although somewhat mangled – survived.[48] In other fields of Service expenditure, however, the Chancellor was more successful.

The long-term effects of the continued run-down of the Services were considerable. When the ten-year rule was cancelled in 1932 the armament and ordnance factories had switched to other activities, or were so under-staffed that virtually the entire armament industry had to be rebuilt from scratch. The comment of Sir Warren Fisher, Permanent Secretary of the Treasury, may be quoted:

We converted ourselves to military impotence. To have disarmed so drastically in the two or three years after the war was not unnatural though possibly not wise. But the Government of 1924 to 1929 had no excuse for further reducing our armed forces to a skeleton, as by then it was known that the Weimar Republic (so called) was in process of reconstructing a disguised army on a truly formidable scale. This British Government's tragic action formed unfortunately a model for subsequent Governments.[49]

47. Bridgeman described Churchill as 'the most indescribable and amazing character of all my colleagues . . . with all his peculiarities and irritating methods, one cannot help liking him – and his ability and vitality are marvellous' (quoted from Bridgeman's unpublished 'Political Notes' in Roskill, op. cit., p. 37).

48. A detailed account of the Cruiser Crisis is given in the author's biography of Lord Davidson. The compromise was that four cruisers would be laid down in 1925–6, and three in 1926–7; most of the rest of the building programme was to be postponed. A destroyer flotilla and six submarines would be laid down in 1927–8, and 1929–30. (See Cmd 2476, 27 July 1925.)

49. Sir Warren Fisher: 'The Beginnings of Civil Defence' (*Public Administration*, Vol. XXVI).

Fisher's views have been echoed by Hankey, who wrote in July 1936:

The long continuance of this rule had created a state of mind in Government Departments from which recovery was slow. Even when the situation had become menacing it took some time before Departments as a whole realized that serious expenditure on armaments was to be undertaken. Meanwhile, contractors, kept short of orders for years and years, had perforce been compelled to close shops, leave their machinery to become obsolete, and dismiss skilled labour.[50]

It may be noted that Churchill received support from Austen Chamberlain and that his only serious opponent was Balfour, whose wise warning was not heeded.

LORD BALFOUR was of the opinion that nobody could say that from any one moment war was an impossibility for the next ten years and that we could not rest in a state of unpreparedness on such an assumption by anybody. To suggest that we could be $9\frac{1}{2}$ years away from preparedness would be a most dangerous suggestion.[51]

The Committee of Imperial Defence accepted Churchill's proposal on 5 July 1928, and it was subsequently ratified by the Cabinet. Churchill was quite justified in pointing out that the responsibility for this lamentable decision was collective, but a considerable burden must rest upon the man who initiates such a proposal, particularly if he has at his command the resources of a large and powerful Department. It may be appropriate to quote the words that Churchill used to support his proposal:

I propose that the Committee of Imperial Defence should be asked to advise the Cabinet upon the general assumption which should now govern our preparations for war, with particular reference to the Estimates of the Fighting Services. I suggest that it should now be laid down as a standing assumption that at any given date there will be no major war for ten years from that date; and that this should be the rule unless or until, on the initiative of the Foreign Office or one of the Fighting Services, or otherwise, it is decided to alter it.[52]

50. Hankey to Baldwin, 24 July 1936 (PRO Premier 1/193).

51. PRO Premier 1–193 quoting from Minutes of 236th Meeting of the CID.

52. CID Paper No. 891-B.

It should be emphasized that there were, at the time, several percipient observers who tried to divert the Government from its fatal course. As Basil Liddell Hart pointed out in an article in the *Daily Telegraph* in 1929 'every important foreign Power has made startling, indeed ominous, increases of expenditure on its army . . . Our Government, which has to keep watch for storm signals, would be false to its duty to this nation if it reduced our slender military strength more drastically until other nations imitate the lead which we have so repeatedly given.'

The mood of the 1920s in all parties was hostile to armaments, in the Conservative Party principally as a result of their cost, a fact that gave Churchill considerable back-bench support in the Cruiser Crisis. For a Conservative Government to have maintained even the existing level of expenditure would have been politically perilous. But it can be seen how Churchill was the victim of his conception of the role of the Treasury. If new schemes of social reform were to be paid for, and a policy of tax reduction was accepted, the only source of funds was reduction in Service expenditure.

In his moves, Churchill enjoyed substantial support and approval. He was fortified by the Cabinet in a deliberate policy of reductions in military expenditure, and the responsibility was collective. Nevertheless, as always happened when he was deeply engaged, he injected into the matter an intensity that prompted the exasperated Beatty to write at one point that 'that extraordinary fellow Winston has gone mad. Economically mad, and no sacrifice is too great to achieve what in his short-sightedness is the panacea for all evils – to take 1 shilling off the income tax.'[53] In the Admiralty crisis he had persistently poured scorn on the proposition that Japanese naval strength posed a serious threat to British naval supremacy, and commented that any increases in British naval strength in the East would be 'distinctly provocative'. On one occasion he said that 'if he had foreseen that the decision to develop a base at Singapore would be used as a gigantic excuse for building up armaments' he would never have agreed to the original plan in

53. Chalmers, op. cit., pp. 403–4.

1921. He objected to 'our measuring our naval strength against this fancied danger' from Japan, and considered that the Admiralty was 'unduly stressing the Japanese danger'.[54] Defeated in the 1925 Cruiser Crisis, Churchill followed a policy of persistently attacking the Admiralty's proposals in large or in detail, and managed to postpone important decisions on the Singapore defence system. It is significant that the assurance of the Foreign Office on the subject of Japanese ambition was far from complete, in which qualifications the Chiefs of Staff fully concurred.

Churchill's insistence on re-evaluation of Service expenditure and requirements was entirely proper. Nonetheless, the reader of his memoranda on this year must be impressed by the violence with which he discounted warnings from the Service Departments that were, unhappily, only too well founded on justifiable concern for the maintenance of British strength. It is not difficult to conceive the emotions of the Admiralty when they read of Churchill's assault on the London Naval Treaty in May 1930, and his charge that 'never since the reign of Charles II has this country been so defenceless as this Treaty will make it, and never in the reign of Charles II was it so vulnerable'. The 1930 Treaty certainly imposed new restrictions on future British naval development, but it hardly lay in the mouth of the Chancellor of the Exchequer of 1924–9 to excoriate an agreed international policy of warship building restriction within twelve months of leaving office.

*

Despite extensive efforts by the Government, by the end of April 1926 the gulf between the miners and the mine-owners had not been narrowed.

Since 'Red Friday', opinion had been hardening in the Conservative Party against another capitulation to the trade unions, to the point that it was quite impracticable for the Government to consider a continuation of the subsidy even if it had wished to. Within the Cabinet there was a feeling that was becoming dominant by the end of April to the effect that a

54. Minutes of the Committee of Imperial Defence, 22 July 1926.

confrontation with the unions was inevitable if they persisted in their course. Furthermore, unlike in the previous July, the Government now had its machinery for handling the strike in working condition. Baldwin remained the advocate of conciliation, but the intractability of the leaders of both sides in the coal dispute and the manifest threat of the General Strike weapon on an elected Government propelled him reluctantly towards those members of the Cabinet – notably Neville Chamberlain, Birkenhead and Churchill – who advocated a policy of firmness. It was significant that before the trade union executives had publicly called the strike the Government had set the machinery in motion to combat it, including the proclamation of a State of Emergency because of 'the present immediate threat of cessation of work in Coal Mines'. It was a clear indication that there was to be no repetition of 'Red Friday', and that the Government was prepared to meet the threat of the General Strike.

Between Saturday, 1 May – when the proclamation was published and the trade union executives resolved to support the miners – and midnight on 3 May – when the strike began – there were two days of confused negotiations and discussions. At one stage – early in the morning of 2 May – it appeared that a formula for withdrawing the strike notices had been reached. The miners' representatives had left London and, after they had been recalled, negotiations were renewed at the Treasury at 9 p.m. on the evening of 2 May. The discussions were in progress when the Cabinet was informed that operatives of the National Society of Operative Printers and Assistants had refused to print the Monday issue of the *Daily Mail* unless a provocative leading article by the editor, Thomas Marlowe, was deleted.

There was now a clear majority of ministers who were convinced that to negotiate under the threat of a General Strike was an intolerable situation for a British Government to endure; it is probable that some had been searching for a *casus belli*, and the *Daily Mail* incident seemed to provide it. Churchill, Neville Chamberlain, Amery and Joynson-Hicks were the most vocal of this group, and the feeling of the rest of the Cabinet –

fortified by reports of back-bench opinion – was sympathetic. In the circumstances, Baldwin had no realistic choice but to break off negotiations forthwith.[55] Then when the union representatives, after withdrawing for consultations with the General Council and the miners, returned to the Treasury they found the room in darkness and the ministers departed. At 1 a.m. on the morning of 3 May there was a brief announcement from Downing Street that negotiations had been broken off.

Throughout 3 May negotiations were attempted, without success. The attitude of the Government now became adaman-tine-hard. Churchill's attitude in particular was truculent, and gave greater currency to the opinion among the union leaders that he was the principal advocate of an uncompromising hostility.[56]

The conviction that Churchill had played a crucial part in the breakdown of negotiations was to assume important propor-tions in the minds of the trade union leaders, and it became customary to pick him out for particular censure. Churchill was far from being alone in his attitudes, and it was quite un-reasonable to select him specifically for condemnation; his approach before the strike-notices were issued was close to Baldwin's; after the *Daily Mail* incident he accepted that battle had to be joined. So did Baldwin. The fact was that the T U C leaders had got into a very false position by 2–3 May. The threat of the General Strike weapon was one thing; its employ-ment was entirely another. As the events of 3–12 May were to show, they had made no plans to meet with the situation that would arise if their challenge was accepted. On the 'consti-tutional' issue it was bound to arouse hostility in the middle classes and even in the Parliamentary Labour Party. The Government had all the advantages, and some ministers – of whom Churchill was among the most prominent – knew it. The T U C leaders had forced the issue upon themselves. Attempting to extricate themselves subsequently from the

55. See J. H. Thomas: *My Story*, pp. 125–6, and Citrine: *Man and Work*, for two vivid accounts.

56. W. H. Crook: *The General Strike*, p. 425.

consequences of their actions, they endeavoured to cast the responsibility upon others.

*

If Churchill's actions preceding the Strike were misrepresented and exaggerated one cause lay in reactions to his actions during its brief but exciting course.

Baldwin subsequently described the dispatch of Churchill to be editor-in-chief of the *British Gazette* as 'the cleverest thing I ever did' – a statement which admirers (and critics) of Baldwin might question. It certainly removed Churchill from any major part in the administration of the Strike – which was just as well if it were to be handled calmly and with the minimum of provocation – and the fact that the *British Gazette* was subject to the supervision of Davidson [57] further restricted Churchill's activities. Nevertheless, it is difficult to contemplate the strange, brief history of the *British Gazette* without feeling that it was one of the less attractive episodes of his career.

There was much to be said for having a Government newspaper. 'The field of battle,' Churchill wrote, 'is no longer transport but news.' [58] With their printing staffs on strike, the London daily newspapers were reduced to small news-sheets, and as the first issue of the *British Gazette* pointed out in a style that was to become very familiar:

. . . This great nation, on the whole the strongest community which civilisation can show, is for the moment reduced in this respect to the level of African natives dependent only on the rumours which are carried from place to place. In a few days if this were allowed to continue, rumours would poison the air, raise panics and disorders, inflame fears and passions together, and carry us all to depths which no sane man of any party or class would care even to contemplate.

57. Davidson was Deputy Chief Commissioner in charge of Government publicity. He was obliged on occasion during the Strike to appeal to the Prime Minister and the Cabinet for support in censoring some of Churchill's more inflammatory leading articles. His collection of the latter was unhappily destroyed by fire during the war.

58. Quoted in Liddell Hart: *Memoirs*, Vol. II, p. 144.

The offence of the *British Gazette* was its pretence to impartiality. As it resoundingly declared (11 May), under the headline 'FALSE NEWS': 'Many false rumours are current. Believe nothing until you see it in an authoritative journal like the *British Gazette*.' It was, in fact, an inflammatory, one-sided, highly provocative propaganda broadsheet – 'a first-class indiscretion, clothed in the tawdry garb of third-rate journalism' as Lloyd George not unjustly described it. Churchill retorted that 'the duty of the *British Gazette* was not to publish a lot of defeatist trash'. It was not a charge often brought against it.

The full flavour of the *British Gazette* can only be gained by a complete reading. It must be stated that this is one of the more enjoyable episodes of historical research; for all its manifold faults, no one could accuse the *British Gazette* of providing dull reading. The strikers were portrayed as 'the enemy'; wild allegations of a Bolshevik plot behind the strike were published from a French newspaper; the strike was described as 'a direct challenge to ordered government'; in its first issue (5 May) it was alleged in a headline that the strike was 'Not So Complete As Hoped By Its Promoters', when the strike was in fact virtually total; the use of patriotic poetry was much favoured (Kipling on 8, 10, 11 May, Tennyson's 'The Soul of England' on the 12th); and the use of dark innuendo was not neglected. Thus, on 12 May:

FOR WHOSE BENEFIT?

A Question for Trade Unionists

The Council of the TUC make a great virtue of returning the Soviet's cheque for thousands.

So money to subsidise the strike in this country *was* offered from this source!

Why?
Was it to serve a *British* Interest?

The distortions for which the *British Gazette* was responsible
were more serious than these examples. In the second issue it
stated that 'there can be no question of compromise of any
kind', and declared that the nation (by which phrase readers
of the *British Gazette* will recognize the non-strikers) was 'calm
and confident'. It declared that 'No man who does his duty
loyally to the country in the present crisis will be left unpro-
tected by the State from subsequent reprisals', and announced
in its fourth issue that any action that had to be taken by the
Armed Forces of the Crown in defence of the Civil Power would
receive full Government support – a statement which the King,
among many others, regarded as highly provocative and
irresponsible. Substantial prominence was given to the dramatic
speech of Sir John Simon on 6 May in which he alleged that the
strike was illegal and that every union leader was liable in
damages to 'the uttermost farthing of his personal possessions'.
This statement was doubtful law [59] but excellent politics, and
first-rate copy for the *British Gazette*. The charge – for which
there was only slight justification – by J. H. Thomas that the
main matters outstanding had been virtually settled on the
evening of 1 May was denied in an article by 'a Cabinet
Minister'. The debates in Parliament were described in
highly-coloured terms; George Lansbury, for example,
was portrayed as 'a wild Socialist, passionate and shouting'.

The *British Gazette* was run with energy and zest like an
operation of war. Beaverbrook provided the night superintendent of the *Daily Express*. A submarine crew came up from
Devonport to help with the machines. An excellent distribu-
tion system was established. London University students
studying printing were brought in to help out on the linotypes.
Much of the organization and administration was borne by the
staff collected by Davidson, but Churchill directed all operations with enthusiasm and urgency; his personal interference
was constant, and, although it nearly caused a crisis on one
occasion among the technical staff, his spirit and energy were

59. See Professor A. L. Goodhart's article in the *Yale Law Journal*,
February 1927.

spread everywhere. It was the environment of excitement, colour and drama that he loved; it was like, as he subsequently declared with relish, 'the combination of a first-class battleship and a first-class general election'. Newsprint was ruthlessly commandeered, and there were fierce disputes with Beaverbrook and Geoffrey Dawson of *The Times*, that prompted Beaverbrook to write that 'If any man living had used such outrageous language to me as he did on that occasion I should never have forgiven him. Churchill on top of the wave has in him the stuff of which tyrants are made.' [60] When a truculent crowd gathered outside the *Morning Post* offices police reinforcements, followed by a detachment of the Irish Guards, were summoned. When a machine was damaged and parts were sent to the Royal Dockyard at Chatham for repair, armed policemen escorted the convoy through a hooting mob. A characteristic touch was the appointment of Admiral 'Blinker' Hall, the famed former Director of Naval Intelligence and subsequently a Conservative MP, to the post of superintendent of personnel and security. Purple passes were issued, and elaborate checks of staff instituted.

Behind the spirit and fun there was a serious purpose. Baldwin adopted a policy of masterly inactivity. His appeals for conciliation did not deviate from the firm position that withdrawal of the strike notices must precede negotiations, but his speeches in the Commons and his wireless broadcast were characterized by a tone of moderation and sympathy. The tone of the *British Gazette* was very different. Unconditional surrender must precede any talks. The Constitution must be preserved. The enemy must be crushed. It is not surprising that the impression Churchill made was that his objective was to keep the temperature up. There were several significant incidents. On one occasion when the story was received that Plymouth strikers had played a football match against the local police, Churchill at first refused to print it; Davidson, no doubt accurately, saw in this tiny episode a serious indication of Churchill's attitudes, and insisted on the story being publicized

60. *Politics and the War*, p. 284. To be fair, the same description could, on occasion, have been applied to Beaverbrook.

in the *British Gazette*.[61] It has remained firmly in the folk-lore of the strike.

In the short run, the *British Gazette* was unquestionably a success. Its circulation rose from 232,000 on 5 May to 2,209,000 by 12 May. The other national dailies managed to keep publishing throughout the strike, and the Continental edition of the *Daily Mail* was selling over a quarter of a million copies daily by the end.[62] The counter-attack took the form of the *British Worker*, which was a somewhat lack-lustre attempt to combat the blaring propaganda of the *British Gazette*. Its greatest circulation (12 May) was 713,000, and its principal target was Churchill. Thus, on 10 May:

> The idea of representing a strike which arose entirely out of industrial conditions and had entirely industrial aims, as a revolutionary movement, was mainly Mr Churchill's. It is a melodramatic 'stunt' on Sydney Street lines . . . The nation has kept its head in spite of the alarming tricks played upon it. Mr Churchill has failed again, and everyone knows it.

There was also a reference to 'that "revolution" which exists nowhere save in Mr Churchill's heated and disorderly imagination'. Churchill rejected these and other assaults with vigour: 'I decline utterly to be impartial as between the fire brigade and the fire' was the best, and certainly the best-remembered, of his retorts.

Meanwhile, a silent – and virtually unknown – struggle had been taking place over the future of the British Broadcasting Company, which Churchill wanted the Government to commandeer. The Managing Director, John (later Lord) Reith appealed to Davidson, who supported him. Baldwin agreed, and secured the support of Joynson-Hicks. The 'independence' of the BBC now looks very questionable. In fact Reith had to

61. This episode, and the details of the origins and administration of the *British Gazette*, is substantially based upon papers and letters in the possession of Lord Davidson. The subject will be dealt with at greater length. *Memoirs of a Conservative*, pp. 236–46.

62. The approach of the *Daily Mail* was even more bellicose and alarmist than that of the *British Gazette*. But it was not a Government organ, and its attitudes towards Labour were notorious long before the Strike.

enter into a substantial degree of cooperation with, and even subordination to, Davidson in order to avert a concerted move in the Cabinet, led by Churchill, to commandeer the BBC. In the event, the influence exerted by the BBC was strong precisely where that of the *British Gazette* was weak; if not entirely impartial, its partiality was well concealed, and its responsible handling of news stories was in sharp contrast to the sensational approach of the *British Gazette*.

It is always impossible to gauge the exact effects of any newspaper or broadcasting service upon a nation. What was significant about the *British Gazette* was its indication of Churchill's views and attitudes. These were not lightly forgotten. If Churchill quickly forgot the episode, others did not. To all who wanted 'to teach the Unions a lesson' he was a hero; to the embittered and defeated strikers he appeared in a very different light. It was not surprising that during these years Churchill was – in Emmanuel Shinwell's words – Labour's 'most valuable propaganda asset'. 'Throughout the 1930s,' George Isaacs has written, 'suspicion of Churchill was one factor in preventing any attempt by the trade unions to make a closer alliance with him in opposition to the foreign policy of the Baldwin and Chamberlain governments.'[63]

It tends to be forgotten that, by the time the Strike ended on 12 May, as a result of the thankful acceptance by the TUC of a formula proposed by Samuel, the genial mood of the first day had passed. There were 1,760 prosecutions for seditious speeches and 1,389 for actual violence; some potentially serious incidents were averted by the restraint and common sense of the police, the military authorities and the strikers themselves. The myth of the Strike being a good-humoured affair throughout the country dies hard, but most observers and historians agree that it was just as well it ended when it did. In this degeneration of mood, the part played by the *British Gazette* is incalculable; but no one has ever suggested that its influence was beneficial.

*

63. Isaacs: 'Churchill and the Trade Unions' (*Churchill By His Contemporaries*), p. 383.

After the Strike was ended, Churchill's standard reaction asserted itself. During its course a vigorous advocate of defeating the unions, the victory secured, he was now anxious for a settlement of the miners' grievances. He toiled hard during the summer and early autumn, taking the initiative when Baldwin went to Aix in August. His efforts, and those of Baldwin, Steel-Maitland and Birkenhead, were unavailing. The owners were obdurate; by October the miners had started to drift back to work, deserted by the TUC, their fellow-workers, and having received no practical assistance from the Government, whose endeavours were largely unknown at the time, and are still inadequately appreciated. As Amery has written, 'the miners struggled back to the pits on the owners' terms, including longer hours, a beaten and resentful army.'

Over the whole of this tragic episode hung the grim prognostication of Keynes: 'The plight of the coal-miners is the first, but not – unless we are very lucky – the last, of the Economic Consequences of Mr Churchill.' In the context of Churchill's actions after the Strike this was unfair; but in a wider perspective it was not, unhappily, devoid of justice.

*

Churchill's period at the Treasury from 1924 to 1929 has been described in critical terms by even his warmest admirers. He has had very little to say about this period of his career in *The Gathering Storm*. Leo Amery has commented with severity that:

> The combination of deflation and free imports which he stubbornly maintained bore its immediate fruit in wage reductions, long-drawn industrial conflict and continuous heavy unemployment; its long-term results in the conviction of the working class that Socialism alone could provide a remedy for unemployment. The chief author of a great Prime Minister's defeat in 1945 was the Chancellor of the Exchequer of twenty years before.[64]

Amery was an ardent supporter of Protection, and a consistent critic of Churchill's policies in the Cabinet between 1924

64. Amery, op. cit., Vol. II. See also Middlemas and Barnes, op. cit., pp. 310–16.

and 1929, so this judgement may be deemed prejudiced. Nevertheless there is substantial truth in it.

Churchill was certainly a dramatic Chancellor, and his Budget speeches were memorable for their style, vigour and unfailing sense of occasion. He wore Lord Randolph's robes – carefully preserved by his mother since the catastrophe of December 1886 – with panache. Nevertheless, for once Churchill can be criticized for lack of imagination rather than for excess. Much of what he did was sensible in the context of the economic thinking (if such it may be called) of his time, but it is difficult to avoid the conclusion that he was badly miscast in this role. His measures bear the ineradicable impression of a man living from year to year, without any coherent strategy and without any deep appreciation of what was required of the Government. It is very difficult, with the best will in the world, to regard his record as anything more than economic and fiscal opportunism.

The 1926 Budget was introduced before the coal subsidy expired, and it was difficult to forecast the future with assurance. He curtailed the period of credit allowed to brewers for the payment of beer duty, and thus secured a windfall of £5 million for the year. He then raided the Road Fund for £7 million, while lowering the duties on motor lorries and buses as partial compensation. The main feature was a tax on betting, which he confidently expected would bring in a minimum income of some £6 million. It did nothing of the sort, and in 1929 was virtually abandoned.

In 1927, faced with a deficit of £36½ million – largely caused by the severe industrial dislocation of 1926 – Churchill met the problem with the device of non-recurring taxes. He took another month off the brewers' credit, took the remaining £12 million of Road Fund balances and made income tax under Schedule A (property) payable in one instalment instead of two, thus securing a once and for all gain of £15 million. Slight increases were made in the taxes on matches, heavy wines and tobacco. Although this Budget had very serious deficiencies, it was described as 'over two and a half hours of extraordinarily brilliant entertainment' by Lloyd George, who described

Churchill as 'the merriest tax collector since the days of Robin Hood'.

In 1928 Churchill produced a much more substantial project, to relieve industrial premises from three-quarters of the burden of local rates, and agricultural land from the whole burden. The Exchequer was to compensate local authorities for the loss in revenue. The De-Rating of Industry Bill was vigorously opposed, and it is probable that it lost the Government considerable support. It was not a very happily conceived measure. The relief to industry was not sufficient to assist the principal exporting firms to any important degree, and the exemptions caused considerable disappointment and criticism. In some areas the proposed grants did not meet the loss of income from rates, which put the new increased rate bill on small businesses and individuals. The only other matter of note was the imposition of new duties on British wines and mechanical lighters, to protect the match industry.

This is hardly a very inspiring record. A more successful aspect of his work as Chancellor was his cooperation with Neville Chamberlain. It was not a completely harmonious relationship, and Chamberlain threatened to resign in March 1928 over the proposal of block grants to local authorities put forward by Churchill, and which ran counter to Chamberlain's plans for local government reform. As a social reformer of a somewhat austere type, Chamberlain made the pace, but Churchill was closely involved. In an uncharacteristically ungenerous comment in 1937, Churchill reversed the balance of effort. Writing of Chamberlain, Churchill said that in the 1924–9 Government:

> We worked together for nearly five years in offices which were frequently in relation. I, from the Treasury, proposed and financed large measures like the Widows' Pension Scheme and the De-Rating Scheme, which he, as Minister of Health, shaped and carried through Parliament. He discharged his task in good will and good faith, even though it was not the task which he himself would have desired.[65]

It was natural – and justifiable – for Churchill to claim a share of Chamberlain's achievement; it was less justifiable to

65. *Collier's Magazine*, 16 October 1937.

claim all of it. On 19 November 1924 Chamberlain had presented a programme of twenty-five major measures, which he substantially achieved by 1929.

Grigg's comment on Churchill's tenure of the Treasury must be approached with some caution, because Grigg was also a prisoner of the very limited view of Treasury activity and Treasury authority that was its principal weakness in the 1920s. Nevertheless, his estimate seems to this commentator to be a fair one:

> Mr Churchill's five Budgets disclose a fairly consistent pattern. In spite of all the Keynesian jibes, his main object was always the reduction of unemployment. He showed himself much under the influence of the twenty years he had spent in the Liberal party, for it was he who impelled Mr Baldwin's Tory Government into the great advances in the scheme of contributory pensions, and he certainly exercised all his skill and might to oppose any serious departure from our fundamentally free trade system . . .
>
> I think I would say that, in keeping with his temperament, Winston eschewed the simple in favour of the complicated and ingenious, that he tended to overestimate revenue and underestimate expenditure, and that, as in the case of the Dardanelles, he was apt to spoil a brilliant project by not assuring himself in advance of sufficient resources to carry it through to the end. He was therefore reduced to all sorts of shifts and expedients in order to avoid having to go back on the policies on which he had perhaps too confidently embarked. Nevertheless, his financial administration as a whole disclosed a great hankering to be considered orthodox – no doubt partly because he wished to counter the readiness of the Tories and the City of London to consider him unreliable and unorthodox, but also, I think, because he had convinced himself that there was a good deal to be said at that time for respectability and realism in economic affairs.[66]

In certain terms, Churchill had been an adroit Chancellor. Certainly he had been 'respectable'; whether he had been realistic was more open to question. It was true that the general level of prosperity had risen. In the main, sacred canons of Free Trade had been vigilantly defended and preserved. But, over the North of England, Scotland and Wales, the heavy pall of

66. Grigg, op. cit., pp. 194–5.

unemployment hung still. It can be justifiably argued that the failure was the responsibility of a system which had proved inadequate to changed conditions rather than that of one man. But popular identification of Churchill as one of the authors of the Government's failure was not without foundation.

Part Five

THE INDIA
QUESTION
1929–1935

The defeat of the second Baldwin Government in tne General Election held in May 1929 evoked neither surprise nor high emotion, save, no doubt, in the breasts of those rejected by the electors. This Government had several achievements to its credit at home. Bathed in the warm glow of Locarno, the international prospects seemed benign. The Baldwin Government had been, in Churchill's words, 'a capable, sedate Government'. Perhaps this had been its undoing.

It had evidently outstayed its welcome, as Governments are wont to do. The nation's material strength had improved, but there remained a profound feeling of malaise in the country. 'A ruling class living on dividends, masses of the people on the dole, and a Government trying to maintain an uneasy *status quo*, is a picture which fills thinking people with despair,' wrote John Boyd-Orr. When Colonel Moore-Brabazon resigned from the Government in 1927 he declared that 'the snores of the Treasury Bench resound throughout the country'. Faced with problems that required urgent action, the Government had consistently procrastinated or had taken refuge in ineffectual compromise. What they had done had won them no great popularity or esteem; what they had not done with their overwhelming majority exasperated all who chafed at the failure of the nation to emerge from a prolonged period of stagnation. It was not a greatly hated Government; nor was it greatly loved, Without fuss or unseemly turmoil, the second Baldwin Government drifted placidly into retirement.

The Government had accordingly succeeded in irritating almost every substantial segment of national opinion, from organized Labour – particularly the miners – who remembered with deep bitterness the events of 1926–7, to the farmers, whose impatience at their situation had now reached a high level of disillusion. Even the motorists, a growing element, were chagrined.[1] A request to Churchill in March 1929 to reduce motor

1. By 1929 there were over a million private cars in the United Kingdom.

vehicle taxation had been rejected with contumely. The Chancellor, not content with letting it be known that he considered the request to be 'selfish' and 'made for the purpose of enriching still further an industry which was already highly prosperous', informed a delegation that he would not countenance the raising of large sums of money for the purpose of road improvement; he rubbed in the point with the gratuitous observation in his Budget speech that he considered the roads to be good enough already, and that any rapid development of them would injuriously affect the railways. When the farmers complained bitterly about the dumping of German wheat, the Government proffered its sympathy; and sympathy was not enough. The National Farmers' Union threatened to advise its members to vote against Conservative candidates in the coming election. On 19 February there was a disturbing scene in the House of Commons when Conservative back-bench wrath at the parsimony of the compensation to Irish Loyalists forced Churchill to withdraw a Supplementary Estimate.

The Chancellor's last Budget, presented in April 1929, was a sad disappointment to the Tory Party. It was, as always, a superb performance. 'None of us had ever heard anything of the kind,' Harold Macmillan has related: 'such mastery of language, such careful deployment of the arguments, such dexterous covering of any weak point.'[2] But the good impression did not last long. The Chancellor had had little to offer.

The political sky was growing dark. No less than nine by-elections had occurred in the past two months in safe Tory seats. Labour had won three, the Liberals two, and in the remaining four the Government majority had been slashed. The back-benchers looked despairingly to the Chancellor for salvation from the political doom creeping over them, and they looked in vain. Churchill dwelt with satisfaction on the improved condition of the people, manifested by the increased demand for tea and sugar; he accordingly abolished the tax on tea. That was about all the Budget did do. The Chancellor roundly attacked the principle, then exciting considerable public interest and attention, that additional employment

2. Macmillan, *Winds of Change*, p. 176.

be created by State expenditure. This, Churchill categorized as 'camouflaged inflation'. Keynes had declared that the objective of such policies was 'the transition from economic anarchy to a regime which deliberately aims at controlling and directing economic forces in the interests of social justice and social stability'. Churchill's firm rejection of these philosophies seemed to imply a declaration of faith in economic anarchy, 'the laws of supply and demand', and the ancient phantasmagoria of British economic thinking. Everyone, on right, left and centre, had much to complain of in Churchill's last Budget. His ingenious methods of treating the National Debt were condemned by *The Times* as 'concealed burglary and open robbery'. Adverse betting in the City on the Conservative chances of a further spell of office showed further evidence of the Administration's ebbing fortunes.

Churchill having failed to grant deliverance, only Baldwin remained. His performance was comparably uninspired. A grave reference to the improvement of the export of broccoli to the Continent excited popular derision; the election cry of 'Safety First' made no impact. The Labour bogey was no longer alarming. As if to emphasize the fact, the Labour manifesto was studiously moderate in tone and content. The Liberals, with a vigorous and revolutionary economic programme, forced ministers on to the defensive. Lord Robert Cecil declared in a public letter that voters should support candidates who could be trusted to support 'a vigorous and progressive peace policy', and made it clear enough that he considered that these were unlikely to be Conservative candidates. A party political broadcast by Churchill (30 April) contained a truly formidable quantity of political clichés, including the passage: 'We have to march forward steadily and steadfastly, along the highway. It may be dusty, it may be stony, it may be dull; it is certainly uphill all the way, but to leave it is only to flounder in the quagmires of delusion and have your coat torn off your back by the brambles of waste.'

When Sir John Simon, returning from his chairmanship of the special commission on India, hurled himself into the political fray, Churchill accused him of 'firing from under the white flag', as the Conservatives had agreed not to oppose Simon in Spen Valley as a condition of his accepting the chairmanship; Birkenhead supported Simon against the charges brought by his friend and ex-colleague. It was all rather unsatisfactory.

*

In spite of everything, the Conservatives did surprisingly well in the election, although it was evident that a majority of the nation eschewed Churchill's dusty, stony and dull uphill highway and preferred the quagmires of delusion. The final figures were:

Labour: 570 candidates; 8,360,883 votes; 287 seats won.
Conservative: 590 candidates; 8,664,243 votes; 261 seats won.
Liberal: 512 candidates; 5,300,947 votes; 59 seats won.

The Minister of Labour and the Solicitor-General were in the rank of the defeated; as were several junior ministers. Austen Chamberlain survived by a mere forty-three votes. Baldwin, rejecting advice to repeat the precedent of 1923 and put the onus on the Liberals for voting in a Labour Government, resigned on 4 June without facing the new Parliament. Ramsay MacDonald formed his second Administration. The *Annual Register* commented:

The fall of the Baldwin Ministry, while hailed with exultation by the progressive parties, was not deeply regretted by the bulk of its own supporters, who found much to criticise in its leading personages. Mr Baldwin had been more amiable than forcible, and had shown himself too much inclined to wait on events instead of trying to direct them. Mr Churchill had proved himself the most able debater in the party, if not in the House, but as a financier his success had been questionable; he had not fulfilled his promises of reducing expenditure, and he left to his successor a formidable task in the financing of the de-rating [of industry] scheme.[3]

Thus, not greatly lamented, Mr Baldwin's ministers gathered their political belongings and reluctantly moved from the balmy warmth of office into the cool shades of Opposition. 'We

3. *Annual Register* for 1929, p. 47.

all parted very happily,' Amery records, 'voting ourselves the
best government there has ever been, and full of genuine
affection for S.B.'[4]

*

Thus, at the age of fifty-four, Winston Churchill found himself
out of office once again. He was still the object of many estimates and evaluations, some laudatory, a few non-committal,
many condemnatory. 'He is an Ishmael in public life,' Gardiner
wrote in 1926, 'loathed by the Tories whom he left and has now
returned to; distrusted by the Liberals, on whose backs he first
mounted to power; hated by Labour, whom he scorns and
insults, and who see in him the potential Mussolini of a wave of
reaction.'[5] Derby expressed a common view when he wrote that
'I believe in Winston's capability if only he were a bit more
steady. But you never know what kite he is going to fly next.'[6]
This was a kindly attitude. Sharper criticisms were to be heard.
He was a man with a turbulent and perplexing record, and the
object of much comment. His name was surrounded with many
deep and disquieting controversies. He was accused of being
impetuous and egotistical, and of having poor judgement;
many would agree with Bonar Law's assessment of him in 1917
that 'I think he has very unusual intellectual ability, but at the
same time he seems to have an entirely unbalanced mind.'
Some of the charges against him were vague, others more precise. There was, first and foremost, the charge of inconsistency.
A man who changes his Party allegiance once is suspect; a man
who does so twice must expect to be the object of double
mistrust. And he had fought for each of the political confederations – Conservative, Liberal and Conservative again – with
great vehemence. Churchill was so self-absorbed, and threw
himself with such exclusive zest into the matter of the hour,
that the revelations of his unpopularity genuinely astonished
and dismayed him. 'I have never joined in an intrigue; everything I have got I have fought for,' he had once remarked: 'And

4. Amery: *My Political Life*, Vol. II, p. 501.

5. A. G. Gardiner: *Portraits and Portents*, p. 59.

6. S. Salvidge: *Salvidge of Liverpool*, p. 234.

yet I have been more hated than anybody.' 'Hated' was perhaps too strong a description in 1929; 'mistrusted' would be
more apposite. And he, like others, endeavoured to analyse the
causes.

Churchill still lacked any solid base of political support, either
territorially or nationally. A London politician, he had consistently failed to establish an intimate connection with any
constituency or area. Epping, in spite of many strains, was to
remain loyal, and Churchill was always a conscientious Member, but his political bailiwick did not extend further. His
relationship with the Conservatives was something less than a
love-match. 'He failed in 1915,' Beaverbrook has written of
Churchill's downfall over the Dardanelles, 'because he showed
himself too confident to be prudent. He neither tied the
Liberals to him nor conciliated the Tories.' It was at that time
that the *Morning Post* had said of him that 'Mr Churchill is still
his own Party, and the chief of the partisans. He still sees
himself as the only digit in the sum of things, all other men as
mere cyphers, whose function it is to follow after and multiply
his personal value a million-fold.' These comments could also be
applied in 1929. 'If he changes his Party with the facility of
partners at a dance,' the persistent A. G. Gardiner wrote of him
in 1926, 'he has always been true to the only Party he really
believes in – that which is assembled under the hat of Mr
Winston Churchill.' [7] If the Conservatives still viewed him with
censure, the Labour Party regarded him as a formidable
enemy. The Liberals considered him to be a renegade.

But one detects in the estimates of Churchill by the close of
the 1920s an absence of the venom that had formerly been
directed against him. Even the memories of the *British Gazette*
were not as harsh as had been those of 'Tonypandy', Antwerp,
the Dardanelles and the Russian Intervention. Between 1923
and 1929 he had published the three volumes of *The World
Crisis*. Churchill's account had been vigorously criticized, but
this formidable, brilliant masterpiece had played an important
part in the revaluation of his actions. Lord D'Abernon wrote of
him in 1930 that 'As a speaker and debater he is in the front

7. A. G. Gardiner: *Certain People of Importance* (1926).

rank; as a coiner of phrases unequalled among contemporaries; as a writer he is the rival if not the superior of the best professionals – in courage undaunted – in openness of mind an example to all.' Beaverbrook's *Politicians and the War* had much criticism of Churchill's actions, but the portrait was suffused with warm admiration and affection. The revelation of Churchill's part in the origin of the tank, and the narrowness of the margin between triumph and disaster at the Dardanelles evoked some new evaluations. If, as some thought at the time, Churchill had become more mellow with age, success and experience, so, perhaps, had his more formidable critics.

This does not mean that these critics were silent, nor that Churchill's turbulent career had moved into a calmer and more sympathetic period. To many, he now seemed old-fashioned in his attitudes, a 'mid-Victorian' as Leo Amery described him in August 1929, 'steeped in the politics of his father's period, and unable ever to get the modern point of view'. [8] Mistrust of his alleged wildness of judgement and eagerness for contrived excitement and sensationalism still aroused fundamental apprehensions. 'Winston Churchill is the most interesting man in England,' Harold Nicolson wrote in 1931. 'He is more than interesting; he is a phenomenon, an enigma. How can a man so versatile and so brilliant avoid being considered volatile and unsound? . . . His dominant qualities are imagination, courage and loyalty; his dominant defect, impatience.' Arthur Ponsonby – formerly a Liberal, and now a member of the Labour Party – wrote to Eddie Marsh in March 1930:

He is so far and away the most talented man in political life besides being charming and a 'gentleman' (a rarish bird these days). But this does not prevent me from feeling politically that he is a great danger, largely because of his love of crisis and faulty judgment. He once said to me years ago, 'I like things to happen, and if they don't happen I like to make them happen.' [9]

What may be particularly noted of Churchill's position in 1929 was the fact that he, alone of all the pre-war major political

8. Amery, op. cit., Vol. II, p. 510.
9. C. Hassall: *Edward Marsh*, p. 565.

figures, had survived. The mere fact that he was still the subject of comment and criticism was in itself of considerable significance. His persistence and skill at political survival had been remarkable in the political circumstances after the fall of the Coalition. This was the result of something more than mere ambition or dogged determination. The brashness and ebullience of his early years had not been wholly tempered by age and experience. He had demonstrated one of the most rare of political qualities, that of 'bounce'; or, as Gardiner expressed it better: 'Like the camomile, the more he is trodden on, the more he flourishes.'[10]

Thus, in May 1929, despite the controversies that still surrounded him, there seemed no reason why Churchill should not be a leading and influential member of a future Conservative Government. Had the Conservatives won the election, Baldwin had intended to move him from the Exchequer to the India Office. This position was now to be hazarded and then destroyed.

*

In 1929 and 1930 Churchill experienced much the same kind of frustration that had afflicted his father in the autumn of 1886 when confronted by the calm, massive obstruction of Lord Salisbury. Writing of that family disaster in 1930, Churchill commented:

> I can see my father now in a somewhat different light from the days when I wrote his biography . . . It is never possible for a man to recover his lost position. He may recover another position in the fifties or sixties, but not the one he lost in the thirties or forties. To hold the leadership of a party or nation with dignity and authority requires that the leader's qualities and message shall meet not only the need but the mood of both.[11]

Churchill had been a loyal colleague to Baldwin in the 1924–9 Government, but his restiveness with his leadership became quickly apparent after the election. Old apprehensions were quickly awakened by Churchill's undisguised sympathy to-

10. Gardiner: *Portraits and Portents*, p. 56.
11. *My Early Life*, pp. 46–7.

wards an alliance with the Liberals against Labour. 'It is quite evident that he has been colloquing vigorously with Lloyd George since the election,' Amery wrote on 11 July after a meeting of the Conservative front bench members, 'and is heading straight for a coalition in which no doubt everything I have ever worked for is definitely to be thrown over.' Amery's alarm was shared by others. Duff Cooper reported to Baldwin in June that Churchill was talking of allying himself with the revived Rothermere–Beaverbrook opposition to Baldwin's leadership,[12] and there were many other indications not calculated to calm the anxieties of the Conservative leaders. Churchill himself had expressed his feelings towards Baldwin in a revealing passage in *The Gathering Storm*.

My idea was that the Conservative Opposition should strongly confront the Labour Government on all great Imperial and national issues, should identify itself with the majesty of Britain as under Lord Beaconsfield and Lord Salisbury, and should not hesitate to face controversy, even though that might not immediately evoke a response from the nation. So far as I could see, Mr Baldwin felt that the times were too far gone for any robust assertion of British Imperial greatness, and that the hopes of the Conservative Party lay in accommodation with Liberal and Labour forces and in adroit, well-timed manoeuvres to detach powerful moods of public opinion and large blocks of votes from them. He certainly was very successful. He was the greatest party manager the Conservatives had ever had.[13]

The final thrust was particularly unfair to Baldwin in the context of 1929–31, but the delineation of the difference of

12. Baldwin Papers.

13. *The Gathering Storm*, Vol. XX, p. 26. It is of interest to note that Churchill used a quotation from a speech by Salisbury on the title page of *The History of the Malakand Field Force* ('They [Frontier Wars] are but the surf that marks the edge and the advance of the wave of civilisation.') On the title page of his published speeches on India there is a quotation from Beaconsfield: 'The key to India is London, the majesty of sovereignty, the spirit and vigour of your Parliament, the inexhaustible resources, the ingenuity and determination of your people – *these are the keys of India*.' (I am grateful to Mr David Jex, of Stanford University, California, for drawing my attention to this point.)

attitude between the two men was accurate enough. After the
defeat of 1929, Churchill was digging out the Imperial flag;
Baldwin had no interest in such heroic and, as he saw it, such
irrelevant stances. Already Baldwin was under fire from the
right for losing the election, and some disturbing things were
happening at by-elections, where, under the banner of Empire
Free Trade, the revivified Rothermere–Beaverbrook compact
was beginning to emerge as a very real embarrassment to the
leader.

*

That Churchill, then and subsequently, seriously underrated
Baldwin cannot be doubted. His portrait of Baldwin in *The
Gathering Storm* now has no currency among serious historians
of the period, but it has made such a substantial impact upon a
very considerable wider readership that a new evaluation must
be attempted.

Baldwin's political career had started late. Although he had
been active politically since 1898, and had been greatly under
the influence of his formidable father – a staunch admirer of
Joseph Chamberlain – he did not enter the House of Commons
until 1908, when he was forty. He made few speeches and little
mark before the war, and it was not until 1915 that he achieved
his first political advancement, when he became Parliamentary
Private Secretary to Bonar Law. When Law became Chancellor
of the Exchequer in December 1916, Baldwin went with him to
the Treasury as Financial Secretary. Beaverbrook, whose tributes to Baldwin's acumen appear to have been consistently –
and probably deliberately – exaggerated, wrote of Baldwin that
from this point 'ambition gripped him'. There is little evidence
for this statement. Baldwin was a serious, hard-working, conscientious junior minister. Very few people knew that it was he
who gave, at the end of the war, twenty per cent of his personal
fortune 'as a thank-offering in the firm conviction that never
again shall we have such a chance of giving our country that
form of help which is so vital at the present time'. He deplored
the hedonism and selfishness of the post-war mood, and had
hoped that his example would have been followed by other

wealthy men. It was not. 'He felt things deeply,' Dr Thomas
Jones has written of him, 'and his conscience was more active
than his intellect.'

When Bonar Law left the Coalition Government in March
1921, Baldwin was promoted to the Cabinet as President of the
Board of Trade. He was, as one of his colleagues subsequently
wrote, 'exceedingly capable and businesslike. . . . He was the
most silent member of the Coalition Cabinet.' His disenchantment with the character of the Coalition steadily increased. The
Chanak Incident stirred him so deeply that he seriously contemplated leaving public life. Instead, as has been related, he
was one of the most important factors in engineering the downfall of the Coalition, both in the preparations and in his speech
at the decisive Carlton Club meeting. Within eight months he
was Prime Minister. It was an astonishingly rapid rise from
relative obscurity to the premiership. His contemporaries were
baffled, and many did not believe that he was anything more
than a *locum tenens*, an impression reinforced by the disastrous
dissolution and defeat of November 1923. He withstood the
attempts to supplant him in December 1923, and, within a year
was Prime Minister again. The Coalitionists who had despised
him were now grateful to receive office at his hands.

A commentator wrote of Baldwin in 1930 that he 'cultivates
the character of an amateur in politics to a point which is
maddening to ardent politicians'.[14] His tenacity and adroitness
made some of his vanquished critics subsequently endow him
with serpentine attributes. Lloyd George described him as 'the
most formidable antagonist whom I ever encountered', and
Beaverbrook has portrayed him as a politician of infinite guile.[15]
Churchill depicted him in *The Gathering Storm* in the character
of the complete party man, wily, resourceful, ingenious, patient
and preoccupied with factional considerations. This subsequent
bitterness against such a mild and genial personality is of
considerable significance. In each case – Lloyd George, Churchill, Beaverbrook – the unprepossessing Baldwin had stood in
the way of their ambitions and expectations, and had defeated

14. *The Times*, 17 October 1930.
15. *The Abdication of King Edward VIII*, pp. 24–6.

them soundly. Given their high estimate of their respective qualities, it was natural that their own conqueror should be endowed with political capacities somewhat greater than in fact they were.

But these estimates did emphasize a recognition of the fact that Baldwin was a considerably more complex figure than he himself made out. Lloyd George once remarked, 'Baldwin is one of us; he is a Celt at heart and that is why many of you find him difficult to understand.' His son has related how 'Before an important speech the colour would leave his face, the sweat would sometimes roll off his brow and he has confessed time and time again he felt he might be sick.' He was subject to severe collapses of nervous energy after any great exertion and he husbanded himself carefully. As one observer noted, 'It is one of Mr Baldwin's most unfailing characteristics that he never rises to the heights of which he is capable till the causes for which he stands seem almost desperate. His spiritual home is always the last ditch' (*The Times*, 13 March 1931). Amery has commented on

the strong Celtic MacDonald strain – emotional, impulsive, secretive, and intensely personal in its likes, dislikes and moral judgements. Intellectually a similar lack of cohesion often showed itself between his political beliefs and his actions. He was, in any case, profoundly illogical and intuitive, browsing over a problem till the vague cloud of his thoughts condensed into some conclusions which might, as often as not, disperse again into nebulous inactivity, but might also lead to some sudden decision.[16]

Although Baldwin was a formidable polemicist when occasion required, his principal strength lay in his warm and attractive personality. Amery, who disagreed with him on so much, has written that 'Baldwin was a personality, with a breadth of outlook, a tolerance and a warm humanity which commanded the admiration, as well as the affection, of those who chafed most under the weaknesses of his leadership.'[17] Harold Macmillan has testified:

16. Amery, op. cit., Vol. II, p. 505.
17. Amery, op. cit., Vol. III, p. 398.

Baldwin had a unique hold on all sections of his party and the House as a whole. He was rarely attacked with any vigour, and if the House was excited or unruly he could usually and without difficulty reduce the temperature. His fairness in debate, the width and generosity of his approach to life, the charm of his manner, and even the skilful way in which he could avoid a difficult argument or awkward situation by a few minutes of reminiscence or philosophising; all these qualities made him a supreme Parliamentarian.[18]

Although apparently agreeable and easy-going, Baldwin had a real political philosophy and a genuine conception of the kind of Britain he wished to see. Perhaps these attitudes were best expressed in a speech he made in February 1923, when he said:

Four words of one syllable each are words which contain salvation for this country and for the whole world. They are 'Faith', 'Hope', 'Love', and 'Work'. No Government in this country today which has not faith in the people, hope in the future, love for its fellow men, and which will not work and work and work, will ever bring this country through into better days and better times.

In a real sense Baldwin's views were reactionary, in that he constantly harked back to times of gentler industrial and human relations. If his conviction that Britain needed time and calm in which to restore herself after the turbulent two decades of the twentieth century was undramatic and unheroic, it was probably the wisest analysis. It did not take account of Hitler, but no one's calculations could have conceivably foreseen that appalling phenomenon. Baldwin's model, as he said in 1936, was Sir Robert Walpole. 'There is only one thing which I feel is worth giving one's strength to,' he had declared on 1 January 1925 at Stourport, 'and that is the binding together of all classes of our people in an effort to make life in this country better in every sense of the word. That is the main end and object of my life in politics.' His sympathy with the aspirations of Labour was manifest. As Attlee has testified, 'he always seemed more at home with our people, particularly the older trade union people, than with his own lot'.[19] 'In all essentials,' MacDonald had said in 1923, 'his outlook is very close to ours.'

18. Macmillan: *Winds of Change*, p. 313.
19. F. Williams: *A Pattern of Rulers*, p. 31.

Such attitudes did not endear him to all sections of the Conservative Party. He was a moderate man in a period when moderation tended to be ill-esteemed. To an extent which is often inadequately appreciated, Baldwin was never really at home in the Conservative Party, and his leadership was almost constantly subjected to criticism from within it at quiet times and strong attack at times of crisis. There always existed a solid bloc of opinion in the Conservative Party that resented him, and yearned for a leader more congenial to their prejudices. 'The young and progressive wing of his party had a special regard for him,' Macmillan has written. 'His speeches, particularly on industrial problems, struck just the note which we thought appropriate and illuminating. The fact that the Right Wing and especially the so-called "industrials" had little love for him, confirmed our feelings.' [20]

There were substantial differences in background and outlook between Baldwin and Churchill. Churchill was combative on those issues – particularly domestic and industrial – on which Baldwin believed that pacification was essential. Baldwin did not believe that there was, as Churchill declared (4 May 1923) 'a great, vehement, deliberate attack upon the foundations of society'; he did believe that there was a threat unless there was a substantial change in the moral atmosphere, and his assault on the Coalition had been essentially prompted by moral considerations of a kind far remote from Churchill's comprehension. Baldwin's detachment from current politics could be considerable, yet his feeling for the varying moods of the House of Commons was acute. Churchill was passionately involved in the political maelstrom, yet he never matched Baldwin's sensitive skill in parliamentary debate. Baldwin was quiet, canny and interested in the world. Churchill was excitable and flamboyant, and totally self-absorbed. Baldwin liked to keep the political temperature down. Churchill was happiest when the lightning and thunder were at their height. Although Baldwin had profound feelings of national pride and a deep identity with England he did not share Churchill's romanticized concept of Britain's world role. Baldwin was a Celtic dreamer with a strong

20. Macmillan, op, cit., p. 170.

streak of good-humoured scepticism. Churchill was an English romantic. Their differences in attitude were very considerable, yet there was a large element of respect and at times affection in their relationship, a fact that made Churchill's severe condemnation of Baldwin in *The Gathering Storm* so surprising to Baldwin's family and associates.

It would be unwise, in reaction to the unfairness with which Baldwin has been treated, to carry his defence to unreasonable length. Baldwin's political philosophy and approach were essentially those of character and attitude rather than of action. Caution and scepticism can be carried too far. It may be true, as he once remarked, that 'the man who says he can see far ahead is a charlatan', but foresight is desirable. He worked only in fits and starts, and took the doctrine of waiting upon events to extreme limits. His humanitarian attitudes were often devoid of practical political consequences. He was sound, sincere, he was on most matters enlightened. But he was not energetic, either politically or intellectually. Major crises drew heavily upon his emotional resources and left him limp and exhausted. He seldom consolidated his victories. Although his interventions were usually decisive they were also often delayed too long. All the major issues of the post-war years, with the doubtful exception of those of employer–employee relations, were carefully avoided or postponed between 1924 and 1929. 'Tranquillity' is a perfectly responsible and respectable political policy, but it was Baldwin's failure that he never fully appreciated the fact that tranquillity must be worked for positively, and not merely awaited passively. And, if this attitude of passivity had been a source of weakness in the 1920s, afterwards it was to pose new perils. 'If at any time after 1929 you had asked him where he was going,' Boothby has written, 'he would, I think, have found some difficulty in answering the question.'[21]

But Baldwin remained the most formidable, the most shrewd and the most attractive of all the personages who, in 1929, stood in the front rank of British politics.

*

21. Boothby: *I Fight to Live*, p. 38.

Discontent within the Conservative Party smouldered surlily on the morrow of its defeat. It is a confederation that does not flourish and is not seen to best advantage in Opposition. Deprived of office, it becomes fractious and querulous, and casts around for an explanation of the calamity. The burden of censure naturally falls upon its leader. 1929 was no exception to this markedly consistent pattern of behaviour.

The first blow fell almost at once. Beaverbrook, who had been politically quiescent for a considerable time, dramatically launched the 'crusade' for Empire Free Trade, with the strident support of the Rothermere Press. A Conservative candidate at a by-election at Twickenham – caused by the elevation of Joynson-Hicks to the House of Lords – announced his conversion to the new cause. The Central Office withdrew its endorsement. Several Conservatives announced their intention of campaigning for the errant candidate. A compromise was patched up, but when the Conservatives lost the seat each side loudly laid the responsibility for this débâcle on the other. This was an ominous beginning.

As the Empire Free Trade campaign began to develop a surprising impetus, an even more serious crisis of leadership developed over the future government of India.

*

In the late 1960s it is becoming somewhat difficult to believe that the British Empire ever existed, and the heated arguments over its future in the late 1920s and 1930s have a peculiarly distant flavour, not unlike the effect produced by a study of the interminable Irish Question. If the story of the acquisition of the Empire is remarkable enough, that of its abandonment and disposal may be adjudged as being even more striking. In 1945 an English schoolboy could ponder on the fact that he was part-ruler of India, Burma and Malaya, large sections of the Levant and vast tracts of the African Continent, while the large and prosperous self-governing Dominions gave their fealty to the British Crown and sent their sons to fight Britain's wars. And now – nothing!

The Indian sub-continent and its teeming millions, ruled by a tiny minority of British officials and soldiers,[22] was the rock on which the Asian Empire rested. The advance towards Indian self-determination since the beginning of the century had been slow and cautious. The Morley–Minto Reforms of 1908–9 had improved Indian representation without reducing the completeness of British rule. In 1917 the British Government had accepted the principle that the progressive realization of responsible government was the purpose of British rule in India. In practical terms, what did this mean? The Government of India Act, 1919, that put into effect the Montagu–Chelmsford Reforms of 1917, was evidence of the fact that 'gradualness' was likely to be a long process. But the good effects of even this modest advance were gravely compromised by the Amritsar massacre in April 1919, and, perhaps even more compromised by the strong support – official and unofficial – that General Dyer received in British India and Britain for his indefensible actions.[23]

Although the Congress Party had voted for Swaraj (Home Rule) in 1906, India had remained quiescent until the end of the war. Now, ugly flames began to burn. Indians had had cause enough for disaffection in the past. Among the factors that gave this recrudescence of Indian nationalism a new vitality and seriousness was the emergence of the diminutive Mahatma Gandhi, whose first campaign of non-violence began in August 1920, and developed into civil disobedience in the following year. In the strange personality of this frail, determined, saintly and politically acute man many of the streams of Indian disaffection merged and met. Gandhi brought entirely new weapons into the struggle. 'An Englishman never respects you till you stand up to him,' he once wrote. 'Then he begins to like you. He is afraid of nothing physical; but he is very mortally afraid of his own conscience if ever you appeal to it, and show

22. 'Of people who made their living from India, there cannot at the maximum ever have been as many as 20,000' (Maurice and Taya Zinkin: *Requiem for Empire*, p. 66). The 1921 census revealed that the total number of Europeans (including Armenians) in India was 156,637, of whom 97,813 were adult males; the native population was over 320 million (238 H.C. Deb. 5s. Col. 2214).

23. See R. Furneaux: *Massacre at Amritsar*.

him to be in the wrong.'[24] Gandhi's appeal was, accordingly, both a national and an international one.

The crucial figure on the British side between 1924 and 1928 was Birkenhead, the new Secretary of State for India, and the only member of the Cabinet in 1919 who had opposed the implementation of the Montagu–Chelmsford Reforms. Birkenhead, as has been well expressed, accepted the principle of 'gradualness' only in the sense that 'rendered the final attainment so remote as to be incalculable'.[25] In public he said that 'I am not able, in any foreseeable future, to discern a moment when we may safely, either to ourselves or to India, abandon our trust.' In private he was even more explicit: 'To me it is frankly inconceivable,' he wrote to the then Viceroy, Lord Reading, in December 1924, 'that India will ever be fit for Dominion self-government.'[26] He had a profound intellectual contempt for the Congress leaders, and he was served by men who shared his prejudice to the full. Lord Winterton, Under-Secretary in 1922 and 1924–9, wrote subsequently of Gandhi that

his behaviour can only be explained on one of three suppositions:
   (1) That he was a conscious hypocrite;
   (2) That he was an unconscious hypocrite;
   (3) That he was mentally deranged.
Being charitable, I prefer the second theory.[27]

Under the 1919 Act a Commission to examine the working of the new Constitution had to be appointed; alarmed at the prospect of this body being set up by a Labour Government, Birkenhead hastened its establishment.[28] It was composed exclusively of undistinguished back-bench MPs and Peers, and was under the chairmanship of Sir John Simon; there was no Indian representation. The Simon Commission included the obscure Major C. R. Attlee, who proved to be a docile, conven-

24. C. F. Andrews: *Mahatma Gandhi's Letters*, p. 249.
25. S. Gopal: *The Viceroyalty of Lord Irwin*, p. 3.
26. Birkenhead: *Halifax*, p. 206.
27. Winterton: *Orders of the Day*, p. 112.
28. Birkenhead: *'F.E.'*, p. 511.

tional and relatively silent member. It fulfilled Birkenhead's expectations, and its enormously long Report when published in 1930 turned out to be wholly irrelevant to the central issue, which was that of Dominion Status.

If the Simon Commission had fulfilled Birkenhead's expectations, his strategy was completely overturned by the independent attitudes of the new Viceroy, Lord Irwin. Recommending his appointment in 1926, Birkenhead wrote somewhat condescendingly, 'how much better in life and how much more paying it is to be blameless rather than brilliant'. Irwin, in spite of the fact that he had won a Prize Fellowship at All Souls, had given few indications of exceptional ability in a somewhat nondescript political career. But now it became slowly apparent that he had been severely underestimated.

Irwin's Viceroyalty is now seen to have been a masterpiece of character and comprehension. He pursued a humane, enlightened and, above all, a realistic policy. The demand for Dominion Status was now being overtaken by the campaign for complete independence; while maintaining law and order and acting firmly in the face of civil disobedience, Irwin realized that negotiation would have to come.

When the Conservatives fell in 1929, Irwin had no difficulty in persuading Wedgwood Benn, the new Secretary of State, that there should be a conference attended by representatives from Britain, the Indian States and British India. This was announced in the *Indian Gazette* on 31 October. In a separate letter in the same issue, Irwin stated that the granting of Dominion Status was implicit in the 1917 Declaration.

It was the second statement that occasioned the storm that now broke. Birkenhead and Reading launched violent attacks on Irwin and the Government in the House of Lords. Churchill published a fierce article in the *Daily Mail* on 16 November, which was an ominous foretaste of his style and attitude:

The rescue of India from ages of barbarism, intestine war, and tyranny, and its slow but ceaseless forward march to civilisation constitutes upon the whole the finest achievement of our history . . .

No limits have been assigned within the broad constitution of the British Empire to the assumption by Indians and by India of full responsible government, except those limits – hard, physical, obvious and moral – arising from Time and Facts . . .

It is therefore the duty of public men and of political parties to make it plain without delay that the extension of Dominion Status to India is not practicable at the present time and that any attempt to secure it will encounter the earnest resistance of the British nation. There is no need, indeed we have no right, to close the long avenues of the future; but the idea that Home Rule for India or Dominion Status or full responsible government for India can emerge from anything that is now being done or inquired into is not only fantastic in itself but criminally mischievous in its effects . . . It is necessary without delay to marshal the sober and resolute forces of the British Empire and thus preserve the life and welfare of all the peoples of Hindustan.

Baldwin did not initially show up well. Under the impression that the Irwin Declaration had the approval of the Simon Commission, he had endorsed it but now had to withdraw. Nevertheless, it was quickly apparent that his sympathies lay with the Government and the Viceroy.

Churchill's disaffection with Baldwin was now very manifest. When Lloyd George attacked the Conservative leader in the Commons in November he was loudly cheered by Churchill, 'to the concern of some of us', as Winterton has written.[29] When Cunliffe-Lister – President of the Board of Trade in the 1924–9 Government – brought forward a proposal for a general tariff at the Conservative Business Committee – the equivalent of the modern 'shadow cabinet' – Churchill's Free Trade instincts were fiercely aroused, and it was with some difficulty that he was persuaded not to resign.[30] The dismissal of Lord Lloyd, British High Commissioner in Egypt, provoked a fierce speech in the Commons on 23 December, in the course of which he said:

There is a sombre philosophy nowadays which I hear in some quarters about Egypt and India. It is said:

'Give them all they ask for! Clear out and let things go to smash, and then there will be a case for us to come back again.'

The action of His Majesty's Government would bear that construc-

29. Winterton, op. cit., pp. 160–61.
30. Swinton: *Sixty Years of Power*, p. 128.

tion. . . . Such a doctrine is no foundation for the continuance of
British fame and power. Once we lose confidence in our mission in
the East, once we repudiate our responsibilities to foreigners and to
minorities, once we feel ourselves unable calmly and fearlessly to
discharge our duties to vast helpless populations, then our presence
in these countries will be stripped of every moral sanction, and,
resting only upon selfish interests or military requirements, it will
be a presence which cannot long endure.

*

The rupture between Churchill and Baldwin developed throughout 1930. Baldwin's position was in serious danger from the
Beaverbrook–Rothermere combination and back-bench disaffection, and the fact that he had to summon votes of confidence in his leadership in June and October emphasized his
declining authority. Baldwin wisely directed his counter-attacks
upon Beaverbrook and Rothermere, describing them as 'an
insolent plutocracy'. Beaverbrook responded with vigour by
declaring of the Conservative leader that: 'his successive
attempts to find a policy remind me of the chorus of a third-rate
revue. His evasions reappear in different scenes and in new
dresses, and every time they dance with renewed and despairing
vigour. But it is the same old jig.' The Empire Free Trade
crusade developed into the United Empire Party. 1930 ended
with Baldwin's leadership in a precarious position.

Birkenhead's death left Churchill as the leader of those elements in the Conservative Party who were becoming increasingly hostile towards the Indian policy of the Government. Birkenhead's influence on Churchill – on this issue if on no other – was
regrettable. Birkenhead was a man of many qualities and much
attractiveness. He was never dazzled by Churchill, who was
hardly his intellectual equal, and Churchill stood in some awe of
his often rancid epithets.[31] For Birkenhead's intellect and
judgement Churchill had a high regard. As he has written: 'For

31. Lord Boothby recollects one occasion when Birkenhead brusquely
silenced Churchill in a discussion at which several younger men were
present. 'It isn't,' Birkenhead continued, mercilessly, in the embarrassed
silence, 'as if you had a *pretty* voice' (Lord Boothby to the author, July
1966).

all the purposes of discussion, argument, exposition, appeal or altercation F.E. had a complete armoury. The bludgeon for the platform; the rapier for a personal dispute; the entangling net and unexpected trident for the Courts of Law; and a jug of clear spring water for anxious perplexed conclave.'[32]

Churchill closely followed Birkenhead's attitudes of contempt and aversion for the Congress leaders, employing language about them that still has the capacity to startle. His recollections of India were based upon his impressions as a young officer in the 1890s and his attitudes had not changed greatly from those of the young author who had described the function of Sir Bindon Blood's troops on the Indian frontier as that of holding 'the dykes of social progress against a rising deluge of barbarism, which threatens every moment to overflow the banks and drown them all'. The personal qualities, political capacity and national cause of Gandhi were incomprehensible to Churchill. The Indian leader was accordingly described as 'a fanatic and an ascetic of the fakir type well known in the East' (30 January 1931), or 'this malignant and subversive fanatic' (23 February 1931). His associates were merely 'Brahmins who mouth and patter principles of Western Liberalism and pose as philosophic and democratic politicians' (18 March 1931). And there was, as will be seen, a great deal more in the same vein.

Churchill, although still a member of the Conservative Business Committee, became the leading spirit of a body called the India Defence League, and he addressed violent speeches to other hitherto mild enough institutions, including the Indian Empire Society. On 12 December 1930 he told this body that 'Gandhi-ism and all it stands for will, sooner or later, have to be grappled with and finally crushed. It is no use trying to satisfy a tiger by feeding it on cat's meat.' He painted a dark picture of India if Congress took over, 'when the British will be no more to them than any other European nation, when white people will be in India only upon sufferance, when debts and obligations of all kinds will be repudiated, and when an army of white janissaries, officered if necessary from Germany, will be hired to

32. *Great Contemporaries*, p. 150.

secure the armed ascendancy of the Hindu'. The Congress Party, he urged, should be broken up forthwith and its leaders deported.

In January 1931 – with Baldwin's approval – the Government called for further consultations with Indian representatives. On 25 January Irwin released Gandhi and his chief colleagues unconditionally from detention and removed the proscription upon the Congress Working Committee. It was this event, Churchill states, on which 'I reached my breaking-point in my relations with Mr Baldwin.'[33] In the debate on the Viceroy's action on 26 January Churchill declared that the second Round Table Conference was premature, and that it was 'a frightful prospect to have opened up so wantonly, so recklessly, so incontinently and in so short a time ... Appetite and demand in India have been raised to the highest pitch by sweeping concessions of principle, while facts have been kept in the shade by clouds of ceremonious and benevolent generalities.' Baldwin made it plain that he supported the Government, and Churchill was strongly criticized by other Conservatives. Wedgwood Benn, winding up for the Government, asked Churchill what he wanted in the way of India reform. Churchill said that he would accept the development of 'effective and real organisms of local and provincial government in the provinces'. The ensuing exchange exposed the fundamental weakness of Churchill's position.

MR BENN . . . The Right Hon. Gentleman talks about evolving organisms. What is to be the strength of the organisms? On what will they rely for strength? Indian opinion?
MR CHURCHILL: Partly British decisions, and Indian loyalty and goodwill.
MR BENN: British decisions and Indian loyalty and goodwill! What does that mean? The lathi, the stick, and after the lathi the rifle, and after the rifle the machine gun. You must either base government on the assent of the people or govern by force. The logical consequence of the Right Hon. Gentleman's policy, if put into operation, is government by force without the assent of the people. . . . The Right Hon. Gentleman's policy, in fact, is condemned on

33. *The Gathering Storm*, p. 27.

four grounds. In the first place, it is blankly defiant of the pledges
that have been made to India; secondly, you cannot practically
base government upon it; thirdly, you cannot morally base government upon it because it lacks the assent of the governed; and
fourthly, it means government by force which public opinion in this
country could not stand . . .[34]

Two days later Churchill resigned from the Opposition
Business Committee and left the front bench to establish
himself on the corner seat below the gangway; in March
Baldwin removed him from the post of Chairman of the Conservative Finance Group and appointed Neville Chamberlain
in his place.

*

Churchill's Imperialism was a combination of romanticism and
national self-interest. For him, as Amery wrote, 'England is still
the starting-point and the ultimate object of policy.' In his view
the Empire was a possession that gave to Britain a world
position and prestige that she would not otherwise have enjoyed, and whose absolute retention was essential. In 1909
Wilfrid Blunt, after a long conversation with Churchill, concluded that he was 'championing an optimistic Liberal Imperialism whereby the British Empire was to be maintained, in
part by concession, in part by force'.[35] The phrase 'an optimistic Liberal Imperialism' describes Churchill's attitudes well,
particularly in his part in the events leading up to the granting
of self-government to the Transvaal and the Orange Free State
in 1907–8 and in the immediate prelude to the Irish Treaty.
Churchill's approach to the South African question is most
clearly seen in his memorandum of 2 January 1906 entitled
'A Note upon the Transvaal Constitution as established by
Letters Patent', and which has been rightly described by Mr
Hyam as 'a classic statement of the primary principle of political conduct of the Victorian and Edwardian ruling élite, the
principle of timely concession to retain an ultimate control'.[36]

34. 247 H.C. Deb. 5s. cols. 755–6 (26 January 1931).
35. W. S. Blunt: *My Diaries*, Vol. II, p. 283.
36. R. Hyam: *Elgin and Churchill at the Colonial Office, 1905–8*, p. 116.

Churchill's interest in Imperial matters had never been one of the major themes of his political career. He accepted the British Empire; he believed deeply in its continuance and in its civilizing mission: any diminution of its power and authority dismayed him. The concept of the Commonwealth as a world entity, which was the goal of an articulate and intelligent school most impressively represented by Amery, Lionel Curtis, Robert Brand and John Buchan, did not attract Churchill. He had opposed Imperial Preference in 1903, he disliked the Statute of Westminster and had no zest for Empire Free Trade. He drew, furthermore, a sharp line between the potentialities of the 'white' colonies and India, whose abandonment he regarded as 'a hideous act of self-mutilation'. The arguments that he put forward about racial disunion in India and the perils of massive communal strife were only too well justified, but the principal – indeed the only – theme in his argument was the absolute necessity of retaining India, not in a semi-autonomous Dominion Status concept, but as a vassal state. On 8 July 1920, in the debate over Amritsar, he had spoken of 'that spirit of comradeship, that sense of unity and of progress in cooperation, which must ever ally and bind together the British and Indian peoples', but, as the events of 1929–35 made abundantly plain, Churchill's definition of comradeship was that of master and servant.

So far as India was concerned, Churchill had not demonstrated any great interest in the future of that vast continent throughout his career. He had strongly supported the dismissal of Dyer after Amritsar, and in his speech in defence of the Government's action had stated firmly that 'our reign in India or anywhere else has never stood on the basis of physical force alone'. But his acceptance of the permanence of British rule over India was complete. While prepared to support policies that would calm nationalist ambitions, he was not prepared to contemplate recognition of equality in government between British and Indians, and was outraged by the suggestion of any diminution of British supremacy. His view of India had not changed greatly – indeed it had hardly changed at all – since the time when he had been a young subaltern in the 1890s, a fact to which much emphasis was given by passages in *My Early Life*, published in 1930, and which in part read like excerpts from Churchill's speeches on India in the years 1929–35.

Churchill's attitudes towards Empire were essentially those of enlightened late nineteenth-century liberalism. J. R. Seeley had declared in *The Expansion of England* in 1883 that withdrawal from India would be 'the most inexcusable of all conceivable crimes and might possibly cause the most stupendous of all conceivable calamities'. Lord Randolph had said that 'our rule in India is, as it were, a sheet of oil spread out over and keeping free from storms a vast and profound ocean of humanity'. Morley, the author of the Morley–Minto reforms of 1908–9, had said that 'there is a school of thought who say that we might wisely walk out of India and that the Indians could manage their own affairs better than we can. Anybody who pictures to himself the anarchy, the bloody chaos that would follow from any such deplorable step might shrink from that sinister decision.' These passages figured prominently in Churchill's speeches in the India controversy. The problem was that late nineteenth-century enlightened imperialism was no longer adequate to the new situation in India; the basic definition of enlightenment in imperial matters, in short, had changed.

Churchill accordingly set out on his campaign with a depressing lack of practical knowledge of the complexities of the India question, fortified with romanticized recollections of the 1890s, and determined that Britain's imperial sway in the Indian subcontinent must be firmly retained. He had no alternative proposals of any substance to offer. He was the advocate of the *status quo*.

*

Churchill's break with Baldwin came at a critical moment in the fortunes of the Conservative leader. The Empire Free Trade movement had badly rattled a party discouraged by defeat and divided over the India issue, and the movement against Baldwin reached its culmination in the by-election at St George's, Westminster, in March, in which an anti-Baldwin candidate – strongly backed by Beaverbrook and Rothermere – contested the seat against Duff Cooper. Baldwin resolved to resign, but was persuaded to stake everything on St George's.

Meanwhile Churchill had embarked upon a series of major speeches on the India question. At the Free Trade Hall, Manchester, on 30 January, he attacked Gandhi fiercely, urged a declaration of British determination to stay in India indefinitely and drew a dark picture of the consequences of India's secession from the Empire:

We have 45 million in this island, a very large proportion of whom are in existence because of our world position – economic, political, imperial. If, guided by counsels of madness and cowardice disguised as false benevolence, you troop home from India, you will leave behind you what John Morley called 'a bloody chaos'; and you will find Famine to greet you on the horizon on your return.

This was to become a frequent theme. In the *Daily Mail* on 27 May 1934 he wrote:

Here we are on this 24th day of May, 1934, with the population of a first-class Power, forty-five millions of us esconced in this small island and dependent for our daily bread on our trade and Imperial connections. Cut these away and at least one-third of our population must vanish speedily from the face of the earth. It is too late for us to be a Holland or a Little Belgium. We must hold our own or lose our all . . .

'Two million bread-winners in this country would be tramping the streets and queuing up at the Labour Exchanges' in the event of Indian Home Rule, he declared in a broadcast on 'The Great Betrayal' in February 1935. One-third of the population of the United Kingdom, he warned on the same occasion, 'would have to go down, out, or under, if we ceased to be a great Empire'.

On 12 February 1931 he alleged that the Montagu–Chelmsford Reforms had failed, and that 'every service that has been handed over to Indian administration has been a failure'. 'Our right and our power to restrict Indian constitutional liberties are unchallengeable,' he continued. '. . . We are free to call a halt . . . to retrace our steps, to retire in order to advance again.'

On 23 February he told the Council of the West Essex

Unionist Association – which had been specially convened to receive his explanation of the attitude he had taken over India – that it was 'alarming and also nauseating to see Mr Gandhi, a seditious Middle Temple lawyer, now posing as a fakir of a type well known in the East, striding half-naked up the steps of the Viceregal Palace, while he is still organizing and conducting a defiant campaign of civil disobedience, to parley on equal terms with the representative of the King-Emperor'. Irwin's policy, he declared, 'ought to be preserved as a patent prescription for building up the reputation of a revolutionary leader'; he made it plain that he proposed to persevere with his campaign, and that 'it follows therefore of course that I should not be able to serve in any Administration about whose Indian policy I was not reassured'. And there followed an oblique attack on Baldwin: 'Too long have the Conservative Party been exploiting and carried on from point to point. Too long have they been made responsible for events in the shaping of which they have no control.' He received a unanimous vote of confidence and support, but it would be a long time before the wicked images of 'the seditious Middle Temple lawyer' and 'the half-naked fakir' would be forgotten in India.

On 5 March he told a large audience at the Philharmonic Hall, Liverpool, that the Irwin proposals were symptomatic of national decline: 'The British lion, so fierce and valiant in bygone days, so dauntless and unconquerable through all the agony of Armageddon, can now be chased by rabbits from the fields and forests of his former glory. It is not that our strength is seriously impaired. We are suffering from a disease of the will. We are the victims of a nervous collapse, of a morbid state of mind.'

Baldwin was now literally beset left and right. At this desperate moment *The Times*, edited by his friend Geoffrey Dawson, came down emphatically on his side, talking of 'mischief-making' in the Party, and referring harshly to a 'hubbub' dominated by motives 'compounded manifestly of personal animosities, disappointed ambitions, and reckless ignorance'.

Early in March Baldwin's critics on India achieved a remark-

able coup when they packed a meeting of the back-bench Indian
Committee and passed a resolution that was a courteously
offensive expression of support for Baldwin. It was now that
Baldwin showed his mettle. In a debate in the Commons on
13 March – which, as the *Annual Register* commented, 'resolved itself into a meeting of the Parliamentary Conservative
Party, with the other two parties present as interested auditors'
– Baldwin turned on his critics with a masterly speech, quoting
the Amritsar speech made by Churchill in 1920 without naming
the speaker, and challenging his critics to depose him as leader
if they wished. It was a dramatic scene, recorded by an eye-
witness:

> The late Premier and his Chancellor, both evidently moved by
> strong emotion, were within a few yards of one another. Churchill,
> seated, with flushed features and twitching hands, looked as though
> about to spring; Baldwin, on his feet, gave that impression of a
> passion frozen with obedience which is his trump card.[37]

The assault collapsed. A few days later, with only a few
dissentient voices, the Parliamentary Party approved Baldwin's line. This was a most notable victory for Baldwin, but
Churchill battled on. On 26 March, in his most sombre mood, he
told the Constitutional Club that 'I am told that I am alone
among men who have held high office in this country in the view
I take about Indian policy . . . If I am alone I am going to
receive shortly an ally – a very powerful ally – an ally whom
I dread – an ally with a sombre title. His title is the March of
Events.'

Having checked the assault on his parliamentary position,
Baldwin now turned on the Press Lords. The St George's by-
election was, as the *Annual Register* remarked, 'a campaign of
unusual scurrility, instigated not by Communists or Socialists,
but by titled Conservatives'. Baldwin, as he had the year before,
concentrated his fire entirely upon Beaverbrook and Rothermere, and, on 18 March, destroyed their challenge with a
passage that must take its place in the annals of political
invective:

37. Hugh Martin: *Battle*, p. 229.

They are engines of propaganda for the constantly changing policies, desires, personal wishes, personal likes and dislikes of two men. What are their methods? Their methods are direct falsehood, misrepresentation, half-truths, the alteration of the speaker's meaning by publishing a sentence apart from the context, such as you see in these leaflets handed out inside the doors of this hall; suppression and editorial criticism of speeches which are not reported in the paper. These are methods hated alike by the public and by the whole of the rest of the Press . . . What the proprietorship of these papers is aiming at is power, and power without responsibility – the prerogative of the harlot throughout the ages.

'I saw the blasé reporters, scribbling semi-consciously, jump out of their skins to a man,' Lady Diana Cooper has recorded of this dramatic moment.[38]

The India Defence League took pains not to be obviously deeply embroiled in the battle; but *Daily Mail* placards in Westminster declared that 'Gandhi is watching Westminster', and there was a monster meeting in the Albert Hall on the eve of the poll, addressed by Churchill. It is now clear that this was a grievous misfortune. When the meeting was arranged the organizers had had no idea that it would coincide with the eve of the poll in St George's.[39] (But it might have been cancelled or at least postponed when the coincidence was realized.) By thus appearing to involve himself with Rothermere and Beaverbrook in their vendetta against Baldwin, Churchill compromised his personal position, and gave his campaign on the India question the appearance of a well-calculated campaign to depose the Leader of the Party. In his speech, Churchill again accused Baldwin of making the Party toe the Socialists' line on India, of having sprung this policy on the Party without consultation and of having given commitments in its name which he had no right to do. This speech, on the eve of the poll in a crucial by-election, at a meeting held on the very edge of the constituency, when the leader's position hung on the result, was bold indeed.

On the following evening, amid scenes of wild excitement,

38. Lady Diana Cooper: *The Light of Common Day*, p. 101.
39. For this information I am indebted to Mr Randolph Churchill.

Duff Cooper was declared an easy winner. Beaverbrook came to terms with the party leaders. All talk of Baldwin's resignation faded. Events in India took a more hopeful turn when the civil disobedience campaign was called off.

*

By the summer of 1931 the second Labour Government was beset with misfortunes. Although it had contributed greatly to its own difficulties, it is impossible to withhold sympathy from the second MacDonald Government. A fickle political godparent seems to have been present at the birth of the Labour movement. Having given to it so much, she withheld from it one priceless benediction – good fortune in the timing of its arrival into office. In 1929 – and again in 1945 and 1964 – the Conservatives were removed from the scene a fraction before the tempests began to rage; leaving Labour to turn dismayed and haggard into the unexpected storm.

It is possible that the Conservatives might have been able to survive the economic disasters of 1929–31. In such a situation, when international confidence in the British Government was of such importance, it is probable that the Conservatives might have had the advantage in this respect at least. It is unlikely, however, that the weapons used by Snowden would have been substantially different from those which the Conservatives would have employed, except in the raising of unemployment benefits and the complete public abandonment of the hallowed principle of contributory insurance, for which ministers were violently assailed by the Conservatives for their extravagance and by their own supporters for their niggardliness. But it is probable that any Conservative Chancellor of that time would have been more flexible than Snowden. As Boothby has commented: 'To every outworn shibboleth of nineteenth-century economics he clung with fanatic tenacity. Economy, Free Trade, Gold – these were the keynotes of his political philosophy; and deflation the path he trod with almost ghoulish enthusiasm.'[40]

As unemployment rose inexorably and the value of British

40. Boothby, op. cit., p. 90.

exports plummeted, ministers looked helplessly around them. Rejecting the sweeping proposals put forward by Sir Oswald Mosley,[41] they followed conventional, orthodox economics and appointed imposing advisory bodies. The last contributed substantially to their undoing. Under the Chairmanship of Sir George May, a Committee of National Expenditure was set up in February 1931; while it was considering the situation, the Government marked time, while the disintegration of the European monetary system and the British position as international trader and financier proceeded inexorably.

By the time that the Report of the May Committee was published at the end of July, on the day after Parliament had adjourned for the Summer Recess, withdrawals from London were running at nearly £2½ million a day, and unemployment had passed the figure of three million.

Ministers did not react with urgency to the crisis. Calmness was for once politically misplaced. The May Committee advised immediate economies of £96 million, of which over £66 million were to be achieved by the reduction of unemployment relief. On 11 August MacDonald returned hurriedly from his retreat at Lossiemouth at the urgent request of the Bank of England to be informed that the crisis was one of confidence in the Government that could only be resolved by decisive action. The Cabinet grappled with the issue in an atmosphere of alarm and crisis. Recrimination, deadlock and division within the

41. Mosley was Chancellor of the Duchy. Together with George Lansbury and Thomas Johnston, he was responsible – under J. H. Thomas – for advising on unemployment issues. In February 1930 he produced a substantial programme including tariff protection, bulk purchase agreements, extensive use of public money to finance industrial development, the rationalization of industry under central control, the granting of incentives to encourage modernization and a more thorough use of the monetary system; this was in essence the programme he and John Strachey had advocated in *Revolution By Reason* (1925). The 'Mosley Memorandum' was rejected by the Cabinet in May 1930; Mosley resigned – to be replaced by Attlee – and took his case first to the Parliamentary Party and then to the party conference. He published his manifesto in December 1930, and in February announced the formation of the New Party to put it into effect. He was expelled from the Labour Party. This was perhaps the most tragic personal and political event of these years.

Cabinet and the labour movement were brought to a startling conclusion on 24 August.[42] MacDonald formed a National Government, with Liberal and Conservative support. Snowden, Thomas and Lord Sankey remained; other ministers were Baldwin, Neville Chamberlain, Hoare, Cunliffe-Lister for the Conservatives and Samuel and Lord Reading for the Liberals. Conspicuously absent were Lloyd George – recovering from a serious operation – and Churchill.

The destruction of the Labour Government and the accession of the new administration did not stem the economic crisis; Britain went off the gold standard in September, and angry cuts caused hasty revaluation. But the storm passed, and the National Government agreed to perpetuate its existence. The result was, as one historian has commented, 'the coupon election all over again, though, let it be granted, without the coupons'.[43] It was a confused and strident election. When it was over, the transformation was remarkable. The Conservatives won 210 seats, and returned 472 strong; together with National Labour and Liberal support, the National Government following was 556. Labour went down to unimaginable ruin, only a stunned fragment of 51 crawling back to Westminster.

Not since 1886 had there been such a comprehensive political change. The spectre of Socialism vanished. MacDonald and Snowden had vied with each other in excoriations of their late colleagues and followers, and their invective had been returned with unavailing fierceness. The Liberal followers of Samuel and Simon supported the Government; Lloyd George obstinately retained his independence. Suddenly, there was no Parliamentary Opposition. The only Front Bench survivors of the Labour holocaust[44] were the popular but woolly Lansbury, the obscure and conventional Attlee and the brilliant but erratic Stafford Cripps. 'The government,' as Professor Mowat has commented, 'had nothing to fear behind it or in front.'

*

42. For detailed accounts see R. Bassett: *1931*, and R. Skidelsky: *Politicians and the Slump*.

43. Mowat: *Britain between the Wars*, p. 409.

44. As an example of the remarkable shift of votes, the Labour 1929 majority of 16,700 at Gateshead was converted to a deficit of 12,938.

Churchill had played little part in these extraordinary political
events. He supported the National Government, although the
niceties of coalition were somewhat strained when Samuel urged
the voters of Epping to reject him. Churchill's approach may
best be seen from an article written in his most blood-curdling
manner in the *Daily Mail* on 2 October, when he called for
Lloyd George's inclusion in the Government:

> An anxious and bewildered nation is waiting for Guidance, and
> not only for guidance, but for Action. The loyal forces in every street
> and village do not know what to do. The subversive forces are gaining
> in confidence and audacity.
>
> No one can doubt the malignity of the appeal to class-hatred and
> revolutionary promptings for which the Socialist Party is now
> apparently prepared to be responsible. The disturbances in the Fleet
> and the signs of disorder in great cities are symptoms which none
> should ignore. Business is at a standstill; prices are rising; the pres-
> sure of life upon all classes must inevitably grow greater. Faction is
> rampant, and winter is at hand . . .
>
> It would indeed be a shame if the whole process of national revival
> and Imperial concentration should be lost in a squalid dog-fight; and
> that the strains, so dear to British hearts, of 'Land of Hope and
> Glory' should sink amid the caterwaul cries of Tory and Liberal
> recrimination.

When the new Parliament met it was evident that the
National Government intended to press forward with negotia-
tions on the India question. Churchill also made it plain that he
proposed to persist with his opposition to them. He had warned
the readers of the *Daily Mail* (7 September) that 'the agitator
Gandhi is approaching our shores in order to exploit the Round
Table Conference, from which nothing but further surrenders of
British authority can emerge'. On 20 November he opposed the
Statute of Westminster in a detailed speech, and on 2 December
made a speech of more than one and a half hours in criticism of
the Government's policy on India which was described by
Amery as 'elephantine', and by MacDonald as 'a mischievous
speech, expressive of nothing except an antiquated relationship
between Imperial authority and the people who come under its
sway'. He predicted – alas, only too accurately – that racial

bitterness would hold sway if the British withdrew from India, and pictured 'mobs of neighbours ... who, when held and dominated by these passions, will tear each other to pieces, men, women, and children, with their fingers'. A motion that he proposed to ensure that the Government would not dispense with constitutional safeguards or take the ultimate decision out of the hands of Parliament was defeated by 369 to 43. Shortly after this speech Churchill went to America on a lecture tour and narrowly escaped serious injury when he was knocked down by a taxi in New York; but he was fully embarked upon his struggle against the Government's India policies in 1932.

*

The Government of India Act, 1935, evoked more discussion than any measure since the Irish Home Rule Bills. In Parliament it occasioned 1,951 speeches, containing 15½ million words, filling over four thousand pages of *Hansard*. A daunting quantity of Reports, White Papers and Blue Books was created. A barrage of leading and feature articles was laid down in the newspapers. India was the principal preoccupation of most politicians in these years, and it seemed at times, to adapt Henry Lucy's celebrated comment on 1892 with relation to Ireland, that 'all Parliamentary roads lead to India'.

Churchill stood in the forefront of the opposition to the Bill, inside and outside Parliament. As a sustained performance of skill and eloquence, it was one of his most remarkable efforts, but rarely can so much resource and ability have been squandered by a major political personality for a cause that was so sadly ill-favoured by the facts of the case and the pace of events. It is often difficult, in reading the speeches of Churchill and his allies, to recognize in the modest Act of 1935 the total abdication of British power and influence that they alleged. The eventual Bill – which became the Government of India Act, 1935 – provided for all India federation and greater autonomy in the provinces. The reality of power still lay with the British Government.

It must be emphasized that the opponents of the Govern-

ment's policy enjoyed a substantial measure of support in the
party, although not in the Parliamentary Party. Throughout
1932 and 1933 there was a prolonged campaign to repudiate the
official policy. In February 1933, a motion to this effect at the
National Union of Conservative Associations was narrowly
defeated by 189 to 165. In June the attack was renewed in the
General Council, where it was defeated by 838 to 316 at a
meeting held, inappropriately enough, at the Friends' House in
the Euston Road. In October the voting at the annual party
conference was 737 to 344. These figures emphasize the schisms
within the party, and the unhappiness of the rank and file at the
India policy of their leaders.

But in the House of Commons, however, the balance of
numbers (to say nothing of the balance of the case) lay more
substantially with the Government. As the debates ground
endlessly on, the acrimony grew. When Churchill was invited to
serve on the Select Committee of both Houses considering the
proposals, he refused in sharp terms. He had originally welcomed the proposal if its composition were to be 'representative
of both sides of the question',[45] but this condition did not
appear to have been adequately met. 'I see no advantage,' he
wrote to Hoare, 'in my joining your committee merely to be
voted down by an overwhelming majority of the eminent
persons you have selected . . . I will have neither part nor lot in
the deed you seek to do.' Tactically, this refusal was perhaps
unwise, and it certainly fostered the impression that Churchill
was uninterested in *any* reforms in Indian administration and
that his only purpose was a blank rejection of all change.

Churchill did, however, give evidence before the Joint
Committee, in the course of which his lack of detailed knowledge of the subject was most painfully exposed.[46] Baldwin
openly charged Churchill and Lloyd with attempting to split
the party, and the First Commissioner of Works, Ormsby-Gore,
declared of Baldwin's foes that 'no occasion or subject is too
various for them to refrain from malevolent hostility and every

45. *Daily Mail*, 30 June 1932.

46. *Joint Committee on Indian Constitutional Reform*, Minutes of Evidence,
IIc, pp. 1779–80.

form of calumny and misrepresentation against Mr Baldwin'.
Churchill protested, and Ormsby-Gore withdrew the word
'calumny'. To Baldwin's charge, Churchill replied with a defiant statement: 'Surely the whole burden rests upon a leader
who forces upon his party a policy on which it has never been
consulted and which runs directly counter to its deepest instincts and traditions. History has always assigned the responsibility for splitting a party to the leader who proposes the
departure.'

The battle continued throughout 1932 and 1933 without
respite. Churchill delivered speeches and published articles
assailing 'Irwinism' and the party's leaders under dramatic
titles ('India May Still Be Saved From Disaster'; 'India – The
Coming Clash'). An officially blessed counter-movement called
the Union of Britain and India, whose chairman was Lord
Goschen, was founded to support the Government. This development did not improve matters, and provoked a denunciation by Churchill of 'the propaganda which has been officiously
set on foot under the patronage of the Central Office by the
notorious UBI and by the Government Press'.[47] Irritation with
Churchill in the Conservative Party was developing into something considerably more serious. When, one evening in May
1932, Lansbury delivered an uncharacteristically fierce attack
on Churchill, he was cheered on by the delighted Conservatives.
Samuel declared of him that 'if indeed the truest patriot is a
man who breathes hatred, who lays the seeds of war, and stirs
up the greatest number of enemies against his country, then
Mr Churchill is a great patriot'. For his part, Churchill did not
reduce the vehemence of his opinions on Indian affairs. The
Lothian Report[48] was categorized (26 June 1932) as 'nothing
but the cheapest, chop-logic, crude, raw, semi-obsolete, half-
distrusted principles of mid-Victorian Radicalism, dished up to
serve the ends of India'.

But it was perhaps the attempt to indict Hoare and Derby on
a charge of breach of Parliamentary Privilege in April 1934 that
drew the greatest scorn and obloquy upon Churchill, and as such

47. *Daily Mail,* 14 October 1933.
48. On Indian Franchise.

episodes have considerable influence upon a man's reputation in the House of Commons, some reference must be made to it.

*

On 16 April 1934 Churchill raised in the House an allegation of Breach of Privilege against Hoare and Derby for having put pressure upon the Manchester Chamber of Commerce to withdraw its written evidence to the Joint Select Committee and to substitute different evidence. This, Churchill alleged, had occurred in the June of the previous year. Churchill also added the detail that Derby had given a dinner to bring together the Manchester witnesses, Hoare and Runciman (President of the Board of Trade). The Speaker ruled that there was sufficient *prima facie* evidence to warrant an inquiry, and on 18 April Churchill formally moved that Hoare's conduct should be referred to the Committee of Privileges.

The foundations for these grave allegations were discovered to be somewhat weak. The précis of evidence had been withdrawn by the Chamber of Commerce itself at the personal request of the Lancashire mill-owners; the famous dinner at Derby House had been for the purpose of a general discussion on the future of the Fiscal Autonomy Convention, under which the British Government undertook to accept tariff arrangements agreed between the Viceroy and the Legislative Assembly.

Churchill attempted to be allowed to cross-examine witnesses before the Committee, as he had done before the Dardanelles Commission in 1916, and he wrote to MacDonald that 'I gather we shall both be permitted to bring witnesses and marshal and present the case and counter-case, with facilities for examination and cross-examination.'[49] This is not the usual procedure for Select Committees of the House of Commons, and the Committee decided to keep to its normal practice of taking evidence individually. Churchill's evidence involved him in some sharp exchanges with the Committee. The Attorney-General (Sir Thomas Inskip) at one stage invited him to 'try to answer my questions if you can without rhetoric' (Q.233), and Austen Chamberlain remarked of Churchill that 'he is using his

49. PRO Premier 1/162. Churchill to MacDonald, 20 April 1935.

position, as a distinguished Member of this House, to address a Committee of the House in a way that Committees are not accustomed to be addressed by those who are invited to give them assistance of such evidence and information as they have' (Q.143); Churchill protested strongly at 'a most uncalled-for attack to be made by one who is sitting here with an open mind'. Churchill clearly had doubts on the impartiality of the Committee: 'I appeal to the Committee to exclude the merits of the Indian policy entirely from their minds. I recognise that almost everyone here has already shown himself in favour of the White Paper policy' (Q.150). The evidence which Churchill advanced in support of his charge against Hoare and Derby was, however, meagre, and did not fortify his bold claim in the Commons that 'I will deal with the House with complete candour. I am in possession of documentary evidence which cannot, I think, be challenged, to prove all the facts I have set out, and a good deal more.'

The inquiry resulted in a unanimous verdict that no Breach of Privilege had occurred. On 13 June it was debated in the House. Churchill was totally isolated. Simon and Amery [50] were the most trenchant of his critics. The debate collapsed without a Division being taken. It was a most serious humiliation. Churchill was seen to have made grave accusations against two leading public men on the basis of no serious evidence at all; to have had his charges contemptuously dismissed by the Committee of Privileges; and to have secured the support of not a single Member of the House of Commons. He left the

50. Amery's assault was particularly effective. 'My Right Hon. Friend had no illusions as to the gravity of the charge he brought forward or as to the consequences which would be involved if the charge had been proved, even with extenuating circumstances. What would have followed? Inevitably it would have meant the resignation of the Secretary of State [for India]. It would have meant the dislocation for months of the work of the select Committee. It would have meant a crisis which would have shattered the Conservative party, and might even have brought down His Majesty's Government. ... At all costs he had to be faithful to his chosen motto: "Fiat justitia, ruat caelum."

'MR CHURCHILL: Translate it.

'MR AMERY: I will translate it into the vernacular: "If I can trip up Sam, the Government's bust." '

debate just before it came to an ignominious end. When, today, people wonder why Churchill was not regarded seriously by so many politicians and journalists at this time, performances of this nature should be remembered. What may be forgiven in a young politician seeking to make his name and attract attention – however irresponsible – is not easily forgiven in a senior ex-Cabinet Minister on a matter of such considerable importance.

This was not the only episode that worsened Churchill's relations with the Conservative Party. Ten days before polling day at the Wavertree (Liverpool) by-election in January 1935, Mr Randolph Churchill, aged twenty-four, presented himself as an Independent Conservative candidate. His father came down to address his eve-of-poll rally, declaring that 'this is not an election, it is a national uprising'. Randolph Churchill, after a whirlwind campaign of great spirit and energy, got over ten thousand votes; Labour won the seat, and the dismay and rage of the party faithful was intense. In the Commons a few days later a Conservative asked Leslie Hore-Belisha, the Minister of Transport and originator of pedestrian crossings, if there had been 'any double-crossings at Epping'. The laughter from the Conservative benches emphasized the fact that whenever politicians laugh at their major misfortunes their feelings are exceptionally bitter.

As it so happened, Churchill had no prior knowledge of his son's intentions. Randolph Churchill, who was impatient to get into Parliament, had thought it all up for himself, and had secured Rothermere's support. Churchill was startled by this madcap venture – with the exception of two friends, his son had no supporters and no organization, and had not been waited upon by delegations of notables earnestly soliciting his candidature – but he gave it his blessing and agreed to speak. At the time it was believed that this was yet another deliberate and planned attempt to shake the prestige of the party leaders. Coming so shortly after the Derby–Hoare 'Privilege' accusations the charge was understandable.[51]

*

51. I am grateful to Randolph Churchill for information about the Wavertree by-election and his father's involvement.

The long struggle over India ended in 1935. The Conservative Party approved the policy at the beginning of December 1934, and the Bill had its Third Reading in the House of Commons in June 1935. Churchill's final speech – the ending of what Hoare has described as 'Winston's Seven Years' War' – was darkly gloomy and funereal in tone, and he described the Bill as 'a gigantic quilt of jumbled crochet work, a monstrous monument of shame built by pygmies'. He was followed by Amery, who opened his speech with the words 'Here endeth the last chapter of the Book of Jeremiah', and commented that 'the speech in more than one respect was not only a speech without a ray of hope; it was a speech from beginning to end, like all his speeches on the subject, utterly and entirely negative and devoid of constructive thought'. The censure was justified.

The obvious losses from Churchill's lengthy campaign on the India issue can be swiftly assessed. By breaking with Baldwin in January 1931 he had forfeited a very substantial expectation of becoming a leading member of the National Government appointed in August. By his violent attacks on the Government for the following four years on this issue he had cut himself off from any consideration for inclusion while the struggle continued, and certainly did not assist his claim for office when it was ended. Thomas Jones records that in May 1935 Baldwin was 'very hostile'[52] to a suggestion that Churchill should be included in the Government and he told Dawson at the same time that 'contrary to some statements that had been made, he felt no personal objection, but Winston would be a disruptive force especially since foreign affairs and defence would be uppermost. Moreover there was great feeling in the party about some of his recent activities against the Government's Indian policy.'[53] This reluctance to re-admit Churchill to the fold was not very surprising. As late as February 1935 he declared in a public broadcast that 'future ages will regard it as incomprehensible that a handful of men, less than half a dozen, but with their hands upon the party machine, could have twisted the whole mentality of the Conservative Party into its present

52. Jones: *A Diary with Letters*, p. 145.
53. E. Wrench: *Geoffrey Dawson and His Times*, p. 322.

abject mood'. Baldwin was not a vindictive nor an unreasonable man, but the vehemence and persistence of Churchill's invective on the issue of India over a period of nearly six years could not be lightly or quickly forgiven by its principal victim. What is more curious – if Churchill's egocentricity and obsession with the matter in hand is forgotten – is the fact that Churchill was genuinely surprised by the rejection of his overtures after the passage of the Act.

It can also be seen that, by identifying himself with the more obviously reactionary elements in the Conservative Party, Churchill had cut himself off not merely from its leaders but also from the younger progressive members. Future supporters – Eden, Macmillan, Duff Cooper – were strongly opposed to him on the India issue, and the revelation of his attitudes alienated potential allies. His frequent warnings on the futility of creating any kind of democratically elective system in such a backward nation jarred not only on Indian susceptibilities.[54] A fair example is a statement issued by Churchill in October 1932 in the form of a public letter to Sir James Hawkey:

Elections, even in the most educated democracies, are regarded as a misfortune and as a disturbance of social, moral and economic progress, even as a danger to international peace. Why at this moment should we force upon the untutored races of India that very system, the inconveniences of which are now felt even in the most highly developed nations, the United States, Germany, France, and in England itself?[55]

This was the development of an argument to which Churchill repeatedly referred. On 27 June 1932, in the Commons, he said: 'You are trying to build the kind of organisation which Europe struggles after, and will for generations struggle in vain, upon those humble primitives who are unable in 450,000 villages even

54. Churchill's acceptance of Anglo-Saxon racial superiority had been evident in his period at the Colonial Office in 1906–8, and can be seen in *My African Journey*. As Mr Hyam has commented: 'Churchill's attitudes towards Africans remind one strongly of the characteristics of the mid-Victorian gospel of improvement, its paternalism, and its optimism. He was patronising and condescending' (Hyam, op. cit., p. 358).

55. See also pp. 302–3.

to produce the simple organisation of four or five people sitting in a hut in order to discuss their common affairs' – a statement not likely to impress anyone with personal experience of Indian village life. In contrast, he had not secured the allegiance of the majority of his colleagues in the India controversy, who supported him on this issue alone, and who were on other matters hostile to him.

Most serious of all were the less easily catalogued losses. His parliamentary position had been in no way enhanced, despite the quality of his speeches. Samuel commented (27 March 1933) that Churchill 'makes many brilliant speeches on all subjects, but that is no reason why we should necessarily accept his political judgement. On the contrary, the brilliance of his speeches only makes the errors in his judgement the more conspicuous . . . I feel inclined to say of him what Bagehot wrote of another very distinguished Parliamentarian [Disraeli]: "His chaff is excellent, but his wheat is poor stuff." ' By the violence of his speeches and the exaggerations of his images he had grievously debased the coinage of alarmism. Many of Churchill's phrases used in the India controversy were to be subsequently repeated in another context, with inevitably a lesser impact. Thus, in July 1931, we find him warning that 'on we go, moving slowly, in a leisurely manner, jerkily onwards, towards an unworkable conclusion, crawling methodically towards the abyss which we shall reach in due course'. The description of the Indian nationalist leaders as 'evil and malignant Brahmins' with their 'itching fingers stretching and scratching at the vast pillage of a derelict Empire' was striking, but was not likely to make comparable descriptions of genuinely evil men credible. The rhetorician could still supply the rhetoric, but the audience was bored, impatient and even hostile.

It is doubtful whether the modest provisions of the Government of India Act would have met the demands of Indian nationalism. It is probable that a swift and generous granting of Dominion Status and acceptance of the principle of joint responsibility would have greatly strengthened the position of the moderate elements in India. Certainly, the Act was a cautious step forward rather than a gigantic leap. But, by their relentless opposition and harsh language, the opponents of the Act had delayed its passage, had considerably reduced the generosity and trust inherent in the original proposals, and, by their contemptuous depiction of Indian motives and Indian capacities, had grievously poisoned Anglo-Indian relations. A considerable effort by enlightened men on both sides towards a civilized, workable and enduring cooperative relationship had been endangered by the language and tactics of their critics. It could be argued that subsequent events, culminating in the partition of India and the terrible bloodshed that accompanied independence, had justified the opposition to the Act in Britain. This would be a most superficial conclusion. The Act, for all its deficiencies, was of crucial importance in the restoration of relations in India; it gave the proponents of moderation in the Congress Party a vital supremacy; and its most effective justification is an examination of the part played by India in the Second World War. The *Oxford History of Modern India* puts the matter fairly:

> The Act proved to be adequate not only for the strains of political transition but for the additional stresses of war and a world crisis . . . the Act formed a monument to the sincerity of declared British intentions.[56]

It is impossible to extract anything of advantage in this lamentable struggle. Certainly the price that was exacted has been a bitter and an enduring one. Duff Cooper did not exaggerate when he described Churchill's resolve to fight the granting of Dominion Status to India as 'the most unfortunate event that occurred between the two wars'.[57]

For, by 1935, Hitler had come, and the uneasy fabric of European peace was crumbling ominously.

56. Percival Spear: *Oxford History of Modern India, 1740–1947*, pp. 369–70.

57. *Old Men Forget*, p. 171.

Part Six THE DEFENCE
OF THE REALM
1933–1937

Even before the economic crisis of 1929–31 sharply distorted the course of European affairs, almost all of the confident expectations of 1919 had been unfulfilled. Old ailments had not been cured, and new ones had arisen. Democracy had not been the victor of the Great War. The tendency towards autocratic government, which was to be so greatly increased in the 1930s, was already apparent. The League of Nations was in existence, but the promised New World Order had not arrived. International politics were still conducted on a national, or, at best, a regional basis, and the old concept of local alliances still held. Free Trade between nations, one of the original objectives of the League, had not materialized. Despite the war, Europe had not lost its dominant position in world affairs. America had withdrawn into herself;[1] Russia remained solitary and outcast. Only in the Far East, where Japan was growing with alarming speed and menacing ambitions, was there an indication of the overwhelming challenge that was to come.

But few discerned these disquieting shadows, and the general prospects appeared benign. There seemed to be sound justification for Austen Chamberlain's claim that Locarno represented 'the real dividing line between the years of war and the years of peace'. In the second half of the 1920s, although an isolated breeze might disturb the international calm, it would swiftly die away. Although problems remained, there seemed no reason why they should not be solved by quiet reasonableness. The chronic issue of German reparations was finally resolved. Allied troops at last left the Rhineland. The Preparatory Commission of the League of Nations on Disarmament and the Kellogg Pact appeared to offer hopeful new prospects. Europe, tormented by wars and fear of wars since 1906, lay contentfully in her brief and transitory respite.

1. 'The people are tired,' Walter Lippmann had written in 1920; 'tired of noise, tired of politics, tired of inconvenience, tired of greatness, and longing for a place where the world is quiet and where all trouble seems dead leaves, and spent waves riot in doubtful dreams of dreams.'

Europe did not, however, enjoy unity, and the causes of the disasters of the 1930s were present before the economic crisis of 1930–31. In an article written in February 1930, in which he advocated a 'United States of Europe' (in which, significantly, Britain would play no part) Churchill wrote:

> The Treaty of Versailles represents the apotheosis of nationalism . . . The empire of the Habsburgs has vanished. That immense, unwieldy, uneasy but nevertheless coherent entity has been Balkanized. Poland has escaped from her eighteenth-century dungeon, bristling with her wrongs and dazzled by the light. The whole zone of middle Europe, from the Baltic to the Aegean, is split into small states vaunting their independence, glorying in their newfound liberty, acutely self-conscious and exalting their particularisms. They must wall themselves in. They must have armies to defend the ramparts. They must have revenues to pay the armies. They must have foundries and factories to equip them. They must have national industries to make themselves self-contained and self-supporting. They must revive old half-forgotten national languages just to show how different they are from the fellows across the frontier. No more discipline of great empires; each for himself and a curse for the rest. What a time of jubilee![2]

In this disturbed and unstable situation the direction of British foreign policy was hesitant and unsure. Since the end of the war, successive British Governments had followed, with only relatively minor variations, policies of non-commitment in Europe, wary association with the League of Nations and the pursuit of the gleaming goal of disarmament. In the circumstances of the 1920s these indeterminate attitudes appeared to have contained a certain measure of realism and success. In the new situation that presented itself after 1932, they were fraught with peril. It is difficult to improve upon the judgement of Lord Strang:

> In the inter-war years . . . no clear policy was framed. The new problems of a changed and changing world tended to be interpreted in terms of old conceptions. Our position in the world had altered for the worse and we did not seem to recognise this in our actions. We continued too long to believe that the horrors of the war of 1914–18

2. Article in the *Saturday Evening Post*, 15 February 1930.

would have convinced all civilised powers that they must not have
another war. We behaved as though we could play an effective part
in international affairs as a kind of mediator or umpire without
providing ourselves with the necessary arms and without entering
into firm commitments, whereas the truth was that, for lack of
international solidarity in face of the common menace, we were in
mortal peril.[3]

The situation was complicated by the maintenance of faiths,
burningly and often brilliantly pressed forward, in the possibilities of the British Commonwealth.[4] The acceptance of certain
fundamental norms in British foreign policy in the second half
of the nineteenth century had been undermined by the events
of 1906–18, but the deduction put upon those events by the
generation of men who had been deeply affected by the teaching
and example of Lord Milner was to the effect that Britain's
future did not lie in European involvements. In these circumstances, British foreign policy since 1918 had been characterized
by drift and indecision, in which the lessons of the past, the
realities of the present and the possibilities of the future were
either inadequately studied or were the subject of fierce controversy. In this, the present generation is in no position to
deliver denunciations, for almost all of the fatal defects of
British policies between the wars have been faithfully emulated
in the post-war period.

There are, of course, many dangers in hindsight over-
simplifications of what was a highly fluid and complex situation.
The opening volume of Churchill's memoirs of the Second
World War, *The Gathering Storm* (published in 1948) has
presented the issues in clear terms, and the theme that dominates the work is essentially a simple one. The Second World
War was 'the unnecessary war', whose avoidance had required
a relatively moderate degree of foresight and resolution. 'It
was,' he wrote, 'a simple policy to keep Germany disarmed and
the victors adequately armed for thirty years ... But this

3. Lord Strang: *Home and Abroad*, p. 154.
4. This subject, as that of British attitudes towards the League, is under-
explored. In particular, the contributions of Amery and Lionel Curtis await
careful examination.

modest requirement the might, civilization, learning, knowledge, science, of the victors were unable to supply.'[5] It may be
emphasized that this conclusion begs many questions. Not the
least of the requirements of such a policy was that of denying to
Germany the rights of a sovereign state after deliberately
establishing her as one, for the logic of this argument was that
Germany should be sovereign and strong – but not too sovereign
nor too strong. It was a policy that also required a willingness –
or at least a readiness – on the part of the major European
Powers to take direct action to enforce German military in-
equality. So far as Britain was concerned, such a policy also
required that the Weimar Republic be vigorously supported
and that Britain should occupy herself energetically both in
the affairs of Europe and the League of Nations. None of these
conditions applied when Hitler came to power in January 1933.

From Churchill's account, the processes of containing German
ambitions emerge with perilous clarity. Thus, we see the feeble
and lethargic Baldwin, obsessed only by considerations of Party
supremacy, failing to rearm Britain despite the insistent and
prescient warnings of Churchill and his friends. We see Germany
growing ever more powerful, ruthlessly intent upon total
European subjugation. We see the democracies, paralysed by
disunity and wishful thinking, missing chance after chance of
saving peace and lurching towards 'the unnecessary war'. We
see the League of Nations, in whose hands lay the best chance
of resisting the German expansion, discredited and destroyed.
In Britain, we see a massive governmental conspiracy to deprive
the nation of awareness of the dangers until it is too late. This
version of the complex events of the 1930s has become deeply
established. Although some historians have begun to question
parts of Churchill's account, the overall impression which *The
Gathering Storm* has had on contemporary views of the 1930s
has been scarcely affected.[6]

5. *The Gathering Storm*, pp. 14–15.
6. The comment of Professor Plumb may be noted: 'With his huge
resources [Churchill] was able to cast his work into an almost official mould,
and often it rises to a degree of objectivity rare in the memoirs of great
statesmen. Nevertheless, it is Churchill's book, in which he himself looms

This is in some respects the most personal of all Churchill's books – an intensely-felt indictment of opponents and a justification not only for his warnings in this period, but for his whole life and attitudes. The story that Churchill presents is a personal account, which closely follows the format which he used in the chapters on the Dardanelles operation in *The World Crisis*. The parallel is not confined to technique. The story is essentially about the manner in which the author attempted to warn the country of the realities abroad and the dangers it faced, but without success. And the most severe criticisms are reserved for the Conservative Party and its leaders, who ignored him and reviled him. This last point was put with particular vigour in 1939, when he was comparing the Tory Party at the end of the seventeenth century and its successors in the 1930s:

> Their action has been largely imitated in our times. No closer parallel exists in history than that presented by the Tory conduct in the years 1696–9 with their squalid conduct in the years 1932–7. In each case short-sighted opinions, agreeable to the party spirit, pernicious to national interests, banished all purpose from the State and prepared a deadly resumption of the main struggle of a Continental war. These recurring fits of squalor in the Tory record are a sad counterpoise to the many great services they have rendered the nation in their nobler and more serviceable moods.[7]

The fact that there is a substantial measure of truth in Churchill's account does not validate the whole of it and it is, accordingly, necessary to examine the circumstances under which British politicians, including Churchill, attempted to adjust themselves to a situation that was without parallel since the final defeat of Napoleon, and for which the experiences of 1906–14 did not provide an appropriate guide.

*

larger than life and his role in the drama, great as it was, magnified . . . And this will deeply influence, indeed has already deeply influenced, subsequent historians' ('Churchill the Historian', in *Churchill Revised*, p. 166).

7. *A History of the English-Speaking Peoples*, Vol. III, p. 20. The book, although substantially completed before 1939, was not published until 1954.

Churchill had been the advocate of generous terms to Germany after the Great War, but his apprehensions of a revival of German ambitions had never been stilled. He wrote in 1925 that 'from one end of Germany to the other an intense hatred of France unites the whole population. The enormous contingents of German youth growing to military manhood year by year are inspired by the fiercest sentiments, and the soul of Germany smoulders with dreams of a War of Liberation or Revenge. These ideas are restrained at the present moment only by physical impotence . . . Germany is a far stronger entity than France, and cannot be kept in permanent subjugation.'[8]

In 1932, while engaged upon his early researches on his projected biography of the first Duke of Marlborough, Churchill visited Austria. As he has written: 'I had no national prejudices against Hitler at this time. I knew little of his doctrine or record and nothing of his character. I admire men who stand up for their country in defeat, even though I am on the other side. He had a perfect right to be a patriotic German if he chose. I had always wanted England, Germany and France to be friends.'[9] His son Randolph accompanied Hitler on part of his 1932 campaign, and had sent Hitler a telegram of congratulation on the surprisingly impressive Nazi performance in the election.[10] A meeting between his father and Hitler was arranged, but never took place.[11]

8. 'Shall We All Commit Suicide?', reprinted in *Thoughts and Adventures* (1932), p. 249.

9. *The Gathering Storm*, p. 65.

10. This was subsequently a source of considerable embarrassment to Randolph. But he was only twenty-one at the time, and his record of warnings against German ambitions from 1933 onwards was as complete as his father's.

11. Churchill states (*The Gathering Storm*, p. 65) that the meeting did not take place because he had asked 'Putzi' Hanfstaengl, who had promised to arrange the meeting, about Hitler's attitude to the Jews. This version is denied by Hanfstaengl in his account (*Hitler – The Missing Years*, pp. 185–7), and he is supported by Randolph Churchill's account. Randolph had been impressed by Hitler, and had been keen that the meeting should take place, as had Hanfstaengl, and it seems that only pure chance averted it. It is, of course, fruitless to speculate upon what might have resulted from this meeting. Some British visitors to Hitler in this period were greatly im-

On his return to Britain, Churchill's concern about Germany was increased by Hitler's assumption of power at the beginning of 1933 and his claim for Germany's right to rearm. But even before this event he was speaking in serious tones of the existence of a potential threat. In May 1932 he asked those Members who favoured parity of armaments between Germany and France: 'Do you wish for war?'[12] On 11 July he said that he could not join the general applause for the end of reparations, agreed at Lausanne. He referred to a statement made by Hitler – 'who is the moving impulse behind the German Government and may be more than that soon' – to the effect that the three thousand marks payable by Germany would not be worth three marks within a few months. He went on to point out the benefits Germany had acquired under 'the Carthaginian peace'. On 23 November in a speech in the Commons Churchill, while urging that 'the removal of the just grievances of the vanquished ought to precede the disarmament of the victors', warned that to bring equality of armaments 'would be almost to appoint the day for another European war – to fix it as if it were a prize fight'. This speech marked the first major warning of the European situation that Churchill gave to the House of Commons:

Now the demand is that Germany should be allowed to rearm. Do not delude yourselves. Do not let His Majesty's Government believe, I am sure they do not believe, that all that Germany is asking for is equal status. . . . That is not what Germany is seeking. All these bands of sturdy Teutonic youths, marching through the streets and roads of Germany, with the light of desire in their eyes to suffer for

pressed; others were not. Randolph Churchill himself was subsequently very glad that the meeting did not take place, as his father might have been 'contaminated' by Hitler.

There is also the possibility that Churchill might have underestimated Hitler after meeting him. As Lord Eustace Percy has written: 'In his first year or so of power, Hitler impressed English visitors as little as he had impressed Hindenburg in 1932. Lord Lloyd, for example, experienced administrator and friend of Churchill did not think that he had the makings of a great man and to more sophisticated critics of politics he was still almost a figure of fun' (Percy: *Some Memories*, pp. 186–7).

12. House of Commons, 13 May 1932.

their Fatherland, are not looking for status. They are looking for weapons, and, when they have the weapons, believe me they will then ask for the return of lost territories and lost colonies . . .

Compare the state of Europe on the morrow of Locarno with its condition today. Fears are greater, rivalries are sharper, military plans are more closely concerted, military organisations are more carefully and efficiently developed, Britain is weaker: and Britain's hour of weakness is Europe's hour of danger.

To contemporaries such a warning must have seemed excessively despondent and alarmist, and Churchill himself went on to urge revision of the Treaty of Versailles in certain respects, 'in cold blood and in a calm atmosphere and while the victor nations still have ample superiority, [rather] than to wait and drift on, inch by inch and stage by stage, until once again vast combinations, equally matched, confront each other face to face'. Two months later Hitler came to power. 'There is no likelihood of a war in which Great Britain would be involved,' Churchill said in February 1933, in the course of a speech at Buckhurst, '. . . [and] the Government have very rightly refused to extend our obligations in Europe or elsewhere.'[13] This optimism did not last long, when the true nature of Hitler's regime began to become apparent. On 14 March he reiterated his confidence in France:

I hope and trust that the French will look after their own safety, and that we shall be permitted to live our life in our island without being again drawn into the perils of the continent of Europe. But if we wish to detach ourselves and lead a life of independence from European entanglements, we have to be strong enough to defend our neutrality . . . I am strongly of opinion that we require to strengthen our armaments in the air and upon the seas in order to make sure that we are still judges of our own fortunes, our own destinies and our own action . . . Not to have an adequate air force in the present state of the world is to compromise the foundations of national freedom.

'Nothing in life is eternal, of course,' Churchill said in the Commons on 13 April, 'but as surely as Germany acquires full military equality with her neighbours while her own grievances

13. *The Times*, 25 February 1933.

are still unredressed, and while she is in the temper which we have unhappily seen, so surely should we see ourselves within a measureable distance of the renewal of general European war.' On 12 August, in a speech in his constituency, he said that 'there is grave reason to believe that Germany is arming herself, or seeking to arm herself, contrary to the solemn treaties extracted from her in her hour of defeat'.[14]

Austen Chamberlain was one of the very few men in public life who actively shared Churchill's concern. He told the Commons on 5 July 1933:

Whether you read the story of the twenty or thirty years which preceded the war, or whether you read the story of the post-war years, you will find the same thing. While something is refused to Germany, it is vital. If you say 'Well, we will give it to you, and now our relations will, of course, be on a satisfactory footing', it loses all value from the moment that she obtains it, and it is used by her merely as a stepping-off place for a further demand.

Chamberlain was, however, by this stage a declining political figure, and his speeches on the German menace – perhaps the best speeches he delivered throughout his long career – were listened to with the respect appropriate to an Elder Statesman, without making many converts. The shock on British opinion of the news of the first excesses of the Nazis and the withdrawal of Germany from the Disarmament Conference in October 1933, to be followed by Hitler's demand that Germany should have a conscript army and types of weapons hitherto denied her, was destined to be of relatively short duration. Churchill was still deeply involved in the India question, now entering a new period of bitterness and crisis. Chamberlain was *déconsidéré*. Boothby, giving warning in his constituency on Armistice Day, 1934, was severely rebuked for his alarmism.[15] None the less, in Government circles the disturbing change in the European situation was noted. The annual report of the Chiefs of Staff made it plain that the armed forces could not be responsible for national and imperial defence under existing circumstances.

14. *The Times*, 13 August 1933.
15. Boothby, op. cit., p. 130.

The Cabinet had abandoned the Ten Year Rule in 1932; in October 1933, when the failure of the Disarmament Conference was evident, a Defence Requirements Sub-Committee of the Committee of Imperial Defence was appointed to examine 'the worst deficiencies' in the armed services. The group started its consideration with the situation in the Far East; it quickly turned its attention to dangers nearer home.[16]

*

When Hitler came to power, France's resolve was weakening and her political structure was undergoing severe stresses, while in Britain aversion to European commitments was widespread. A substantial revisionism of the background to the Great War – actively sponsored by the War Guilt section of the Wilhelm-strasse – had taken place by the end of the 1920s. But historical revisionism was not confined to the historians. It is often stated that soldiers are always preparing to fight the last war; it may also be remarked that in Britain the politicians and students of politics are always preparing to avoid the last war. The topic of why the Great War had broken out was one that not surprisingly occupied the attention and interest of politicians, writers and a wide public. Among the many 'lessons' that were being drawn from the events of 1906–14, one of the most compelling was to the effect that the arms race had, in itself, caused the war. It was argued by, among many others, Edward Grey. If this was accepted and carried to its logical conclusion, its principal assumption was that an *imbalance* of arms, even though it were to one's disadvantage, was safer than participation in an arms race. The interpretation of the pre-1914 situation may have been ill-founded, and its total acceptance preposterous; but, as an examination of the articles, books and speeches in these years show, it was accepted by a surprisingly large number of writers and politicians in Britain. In the Labour Party, at least up to the autumn of 1935, it was virtually an article of faith that for Britain to rearm in competition with another major power was a certain step towards war.

The danger of such attitudes was increased by other factors.

16. Basil Collier: *Defence of the United Kingdom*, pp. 25–6.

Keynes had inflicted serious harm on the Treaty of Versailles
by his devastating denunciation of its authors and its provisions in *The Economic Consequences of the Peace* and the work
of further demolition proceeded apace in the following decade.
To this disillusionment was added another. At the end of the
1920s there was a remarkable coincidence of books of high
literary quality that described the realities of the war. Robert
Graves's *Goodbye To All That*, Edmund Blunden's *Undertones
of War* and Siegfried Sassoon's memoirs and poems enjoyed
a very substantial popular success, while R. C. Sherriff's play
Journey's End evidently struck a receptive chord. The emotions
that had made the British fight for four years with such resolution and persistence now seemed, in retrospect, painfully unreal
and even pathetic. The war itself had destroyed many faiths
and assumptions formerly accepted with little questioning. The
new examinations of the war, and the events leading up to it,
perhaps destroyed even more.

It would be to over-simplify the matter to state that British
attitudes were pacifist in the early 1930s. There was certainly a
profound fear of another war, and a general acceptance of the
view put forward by Churchill among many others that
'another Great War would cost us our wealth, our freedom, and
our culture, and cast what we have so slowly garnered of human
enlightenment, tolerance, and dignity to different packs of
ravening wolves . . . It would be like the last war – only worse.'[17]
There were certainly pacifists in the Labour and Liberal parties,
of whom Lansbury and Sir Stafford Cripps were the best known,
the most vocal, and the most extreme. There were indications
in the first half of 1933 of hostility towards rearmament and a
new arms race.[18] But the dominant mood appears to have been

17. Article in the *Sunday Chronicle*, 28 July 1935.
18. The most famous episodes were the passing of a motion in the Oxford
Union resolving not to fight for King and Country in February 1933, and
the East Fulham by-election in June, when a Labour candidate fighting on
a largely anti-armaments campaign won the seat by a substantial majority.
It is rather doubtful whether much attention would have been given to the
Oxford resolution had not Churchill described it as 'an abject, squalid,
shameless avowal', and had not Randolph Churchill attempted to have it
rescinded. (See Christopher Hollis: *History of the Oxford Union*.)

one of wearied isolationism and an abhorrence of foreign entanglements, and described by Lord Strang as 'an almost Cobdenite non-interventionism'.[19] But it would be unwise to assume that such attitudes in British history are unknown, or are contrary to the British character. A distinguished French historian commented in 1893 on a feature of that character: 'Their history is full of alternations between indifference which makes people think them decadent, and a rage which baffles their foes. They are seen, in turn, abandoning or dominating Europe, neglecting the greatest continental matters and claiming to control even the smallest, turning from peace at any price to war to the death.'[20]

'We toss uneasily from side to side on our disordered couch,' Churchill commented in May 1934; 'neither sweet sleep nor vigorous awakening has been vouchsafed to us.' Vansittart[21] is not always a reliable commentator, but his statement that 'Right or left, everybody was for a quiet life' seems fully justified. But it would be foolish to attempt to understate the long shadow that the war had cast over Europe, not to underestimate the eager self-deception that men practised. As Churchill wrote in May 1932:

There is such a horror of war in the great nations who passed through Armaggeddon that any declaration or public speech against armaments, although it consisted only of platitudes and unrealities, has always been applauded; and any speech or assertion which set forth the blunt truth has been incontinently relegated to the category of 'War-Monger' . . . The cause of disarmament will not be obtained by Mush, Slush and Gush. It will be advanced steadily by the harassing expense of fleets and armies, and by the growth of confidence in a long peace.[22]

In November 1934, in the course of a radio broadcast, he returned to this theme:

19. Strang: *Britain in World Affairs*, p. 321.
20. Sorel: *L'Europe et la Révolution Française*, Vol. I, pp. 340–41; quoted in F. S. Northedge: *The Troubled Giant*, p. 629.
21. Permanent Under-Secretary of State for Foreign Affairs, 1930–7.
22. *Daily Mail*, 26 May 1932.

Many people think that the best way to escape war is to dwell upon its horrors, and to imprint them vividly upon the minds of the younger generation. They flaunt the grisly photographs before their eyes. They fill their ears with tales of carnage. They dilate upon the ineptitude of generals and admirals. They denounce the crime and insensate folly of human strife.

All this teaching ought to be very useful in preventing us from attacking or invading any other country, if anyone outside a mad-house wished to do so. But how would it help us if we were attacked or invaded ourselves? That is the question we have to ask.[23]

But what was to be done about Germany in the new situation? Detestation of the methods and *mores* of Nazism did not carry with it a conviction that conflict was inevitable. Lord Lothian expressed a not uncommon view when he wrote in 1933 that 'Like most Liberals, I loathe the Nazi regime, but I am sure that the first condition to reform it is that we should be willing to do justice to Germany. The second is that Liberal nations should be willing to stand together to resist any unjust pretension which she herself may later put forward.' Such views were neither unrealistic nor immoral, and they had a considerable attraction. The tasks of securing national survival and the furtherance of national interests frequently require the keeping of unsavoury company. Furthermore, revolutions of all kinds tend to be unpleasant and dictators unattractive, particularly in the immediate aftermath of their achievement of power. Was there any expectation that the Hitler regime might become more moderate, and were there any indications that its internal policies carried with them the implications of external aggressions? There were certainly many in Britain in the years 1933–7 who would have answered the first question in the affirmative and reserved judgement on the second. Churchill himself wrote of Hitler in 1935 – and republished the article in October 1937 – that 'Although no subsequent political action can condone wrong deeds or remove the guilt of blood, history is replete with examples of men who have risen to power by employing stern, grim, wicked, and even frightful methods, but who, nevertheless, when their life is revealed as a whole, have

23. *The Listener*, 21 November 1934.

been regarded as great figures whose lives have enriched the story of mankind. So it may be with Hitler.' And behind the development of the attitudes and policies later lumped together under the general description of 'Appeasement' there lay factors which have been ably summarized by Mr D. C. Watt:

> They could see a threat, but not a certainty. They could see a peril of war, but not the impossibility of evading it. It was on this point that the perpetual flow of periphrastic memoranda with which Sir Robert Vansittart bombarded them failed to carry ultimate conviction. And it was here that, troubled, perplexed and above all undecided, they listened to the voices of those within their own circles who maintained an alternative view, that a policy of judicious and controlled concessions, designed to remove the grievances and injustices on which Nazi chauvinism throve, would draw its teeth and make it tolerable as a neighbour on the European continent.[24]

British attitudes were compounded of an aversion against war, a mistrust of foreign entanglements, a sense of guilt over the Treaty of Versailles and the belief that a strong Germany was infinitely preferable to a weak, divided and vulnerable Germany. This last point was not without considerable significance. The eminent Liberal historian H. A. L. Fisher wrote in his *History of Europe* (1936) that 'the Hitler revolution is a sufficient guarantee that Russian Communism will not spread westward. The solid German bourgeois hold the central fortress of Europe'; and Lloyd George said (27 September 1933) that 'a Communist Germany would be infinitely more formidable than a Communist Russia'. Skilfully exploited by German propagandists,[25] this argument found increasing support, particularly in the Conservative Party.

The context of the times must not be forgotten. In the early 1930s the British were slowly embarking upon a long industrial and economic recovery from the misfortunes of 1930–31. Although the total figures of unemployment remained high, there was a gradual and perceptible improvement,[26] and, save in the

24. D. C. Watt: *Personalities and Policies*, pp. 118–19.

25. See Watt, ibid., for his interesting study of Nazi front organizations in Britain in 1933–5, pp. 117–35.

26. The minimum figures fell from 2,309,000 in 1932 to 1,888,000 in 1935.

intractable depressed areas, a steadily rising level of prosperity. It is a misconception common to politicians and political historians alike to believe that the mass of people are interested in politics, and, above all, in international politics, except on specific issues or at moments of great tension. Much emphasis has already been placed by historians of the 1930s upon the fatal self-deceptions concerning Germany that flourished in Britain. A few examples may suffice to underline the validity of this portrait. John Wheeler-Bennett – subsequently to become the stern historian of Munich – declared after a visit to Berlin in 1933 that Hitler 'was a man of sense . . . who did not want war', and denied that *Mein Kampf* (which he had not read) was of any significance.[27] *The Economist* (1 December 1934) declared that Germany provided no threat to Europe, and that British rearmament would seriously damage the national economy. *The Times* argued that aggressive speeches by German leaders were only for home consumption (10 July 1934), that German rearmament was only aimed at achieving equality with her neighbours (23 January 1934), that there was no reason to be concerned about the militaristic spirit in Germany (4 August 1934) and, commenting upon the brutal Roehm purge, that Hitler 'is genuinely trying to transform revolutionary fervour into moderate and constructive efforts and to inspire a high standard of public service in National Socialist officials' (2 July 1934). These examples, which could be multiplied with ease, may demonstrate something of what Churchill was fighting to combat in these years. Boothby has written that attempting to arouse apprehensions about the international situation was like 'boxing a stone wall'.[28] But even those who were perturbed by the new developments found difficulty in prescribing any solution that had any chance of success, either of solving the international problem or being acceptable to the British electorate.

In this, they were the prisoners of the attitudes on foreign policy that had obtained since 1918, and it is worth emphasiz-

27. 'The New Regime in Germany', *International Affairs*, No. 3, pp. 318–26.

28. Boothby, op. cit., p. 141.

ing that Churchill supported those attitudes. He placed little serious reliance upon the League of Nations, had been keen enough on reducing the Service Estimates while at the Treasury and did not favour close involvement in Europe. In the 1930 article to which reference has already been made, he wrote: 'We see nothing but good and hope in a richer, freer, more contented European commonalty. But we have our own dream and our own task. We are with Europe, but not of it. We are linked but not compromised. We are interested and associated, but not absorbed.'[29]

*

By the beginning of 1934, Defence questions were reasserting themselves as one of Churchill's dominant interests, although India remained the issue on which he was most active and vocal throughout that year. In a speech on the Motion for the Adjournment on 7 November 1933 he pointed out that 'The great dominant fact is that Germany has already begun to rearm', and advocated a revival of 'the Concert of Europe through the League of Nations . . . in an attempt to address Germany collectively, so that there may be some redress of the grievances of the German nations and that that may be effected before this peril of [German] armament reaches a point which may endanger the peace of the world'. The speech is of interest principally for the fact that it is the first time that Churchill advocated the use of the League and the participation of Britain in European affairs. As his son has written: 'The hope underlying the earlier speeches is that Britain will be able to steer clear of European commitments, and that France and her allies will be able to cope with any European dangers that may arise.'[30]

On 7 February 1934 he made his first major speech on air defence. He startled the House of Commons with a dramatic portrait of an aerial attack on Britain when 'the crash of bombs exploding in London and cataracts of masonry and fire and smoke will apprise us of any inadequacy which has been

29. Article in *Saturday Evening Post*, 15 February 1930.
30. Preface to *Arms and the Covenant*, p. 5.

permitted in our aerial defences. We are as vulnerable as we have never been before . . . I cannot conceive how, in the present state of Europe and of our position in Europe, we can delay in establishing the principle of having our Air Force at least as strong as that of any Power that can get at us. I think that is a perfectly reasonable thing to do . . .' On 8 March, in the debate on the Air Estimates, he said: 'All history has proved the peril of being dependent upon a foreign State for home defence instead of one's own right arm. This is not a Party question, not a question between pacifists and militarists, but one of the essential independence of character of our island life and its preservation from intrusion or distortion of any kind.' It was in this speech that he first referred to the importance of 'parity' in the air, thus introducing a word into the air debate that was to be the cause of very considerable confusion and misunderstanding over the next few years. The most significant passage ran: 'I dread the day when the means of threatening the heart of the British Empire should pass into the hands of the present rulers of Germany . . . I dread that day, but it is not, perhaps, far distant. It is, perhaps, only a year, or perhaps, eighteen months, distant . . . The turning point has been reached, and the new steps must be taken.'

In his speech, Baldwin gave assurance that the Government 'will see to it that in air strength and air power this country shall no longer be in a position inferior to any country within striking distance of our shores'.

On 21 March Churchill urged – not for the first time [31] – the creation of a Ministry of Defence. On 13 July Churchill spoke in the debate on the Foreign Office Vote, and concentrated on the value of the League: 'I could not see how better you can prevent war than by confronting an aggressor with the prospect of such a vast concentration of force – moral and material – that even the most reckless, even the most infuriated, leader would not attempt to challenge those great forces.'[32]

31. See his speech of 7 February 1934.

32. The speech is also of interest in that Churchill advocated further development of 'the reassociation of Soviet Russia with the Western European system'.

On 30 July he repeated the warning he had given in March
that Germany, now 'arming fast', would within a year or
eighteen months be strong enough in the air to threaten 'the
heart of the British Empire'. Now he returned to this theme,
despite Baldwin's reiterated assurance that the British Government would not permit such an eventuality: 'If Germany
continues this expansion and if we continue to carry out our
scheme, then some time in 1936 Germany will be definitely and
substantially stronger in the air than Great Britain.' And,
again, on 28 November: 'What is the great new fact which has
broken in upon us during the last eighteen months? Germany is
rearming. That is the great new fact, which rivets the attention
of every country in Europe – indeed, in the world – and which
throws almost all other issues into the background.'

This speech was the most formidable that Churchill had yet
made on the rearmament issue.[33] Some sections read strangely
in the light of later experience. He claimed that 'one could
hardly expect that less than 30,000 or 40,000 people would be
killed or maimed' in a week or ten days' intensive bombing
of London, which would lead to the exodus from the city of
'at least 3,000,000 or 4,000,000 people'. He said that the new
incendiary bomb would 'go through a series of floors in any
building, igniting each other practically simultaneously'.[34] He
described German munition factories 'working practically
under war conditions'. He urged a scientific approach to air
defence, and then put the case for building a bomber force
capable of deterring a possible aggressor. He stated that the
illegal German air force 'is rapidly approaching equality with
our own', and would probably be at least equal and possibly
stronger in a year; furthermore, he estimated that the German
air force would be double the size of the RAF by 1937. He
claimed that Germany already had 'between 200 and 300

33. It was made in moving an Amendment to the Address supported by
Horne, Amery, Guest, Winterton and Boothby to the effect that 'the state
of our national defences and especially of our air defences, is no longer
adequate to secure the peace, safety and freedom of Your Majesty's faithful
subjects'.

34. Churchill said that on this point 'I am assured by persons who are
acquainted with the science'. The authority was probably Lindemann.

machines of long range with great speed, 220–30 miles an hour'
easily convertible into bombers. Many of the facts and arguments in the speech were not firmly based on the known facts,
but Churchill's object was to arouse concern, and in this he
succeeded. Baldwin's reply was to the effect that the RAF still
enjoyed superiority, and would maintain it. The figures of
current ratios that he quoted were considerably more accurate
than Churchill's, but he was most unwise in giving the House of
Commons the clear impression that all would be well at least up
to the end of 1936. Indeed, 'unwise' is perhaps the wrong
adjective, in view of the fact that Baldwin had been informed
by the Air Ministry that the latest estimates gave the Germans
a superiority of between 100 and 200 aircraft by November
1936.[35]

* -

It did not require Churchill's dramatic speeches to inform
ministers of the situation. Disarmament and the running down
of the armed services had been one of the few consistent threads
in the discordant tapestry of British policies since 1918. In
1926–7, total Defence expenditure had been £116 million,
despite the swingeing economies of the then Chancellor of the
Exchequer; by 1932–3 it had fallen to just over £100 million.
The Royal Air Force was numerically sixth in the world; the
Royal Navy had a smaller complement of men than at any
time for forty years; the condition of the British Army was the
most hapless of all. Qualitatively, the situation was even more
alarming. The equipment of the RAF was obsolescent; although
the Navy was in far better condition than the other Services,
much of its vaunted strength was illusory; in the Army, after
the severe and arbitrary reductions of the 1920s and early
1930s, mechanization had almost stopped and virtually all
equipment was out of date and in poor supply. As a result of the
run-down of the Ordnance Factories and substantial conversion
of former military suppliers to civilian uses, the country did not
possess the capacity to restore the situation for a considerable
time unless the other national priorities were curtailed. This

35. PRO CAB 42/34/2 and CP 265 (34).

was the crucial point, and was commented upon by Halifax in December 1935: 'Are we in fact to judge the situation so serious that everything has to give way to military reconditioning of our Defence Forces? Such a conclusion in fact, appears to me to rest on premises not only of the inevitability but of a certain degree of certainty as to the early imminence of war, which I am not prepared to accept.'

Nevertheless it was apparent that the persistent running down of the Armed Services could not continue. When the Defence Requirements Committee reported in February 1934[36] it made it plain that Germany was 'the ultimate potential enemy, certain to become within a few years a serious menace to Britain'. The principal recommendation was that the RAF's 52-squadron scheme should be completed within ten years. This scheme, for a Home Defence Force of fifty-two squadrons, had been approved in June 1923. It had been half completed by 1925, but had been postponed until 1935–6; in 1929 the Labour Government further postponed its completion until 1938–9. Thus the recommendation of the Defence Requirements Committee was not very dramatic, and a period of five months elapsed between its first consideration by the Cabinet on 7 March and its approval on 31 July. What was even more significant than this long delay was the fact that, as a result of the vigorous opposition of Neville Chamberlain, a projected balanced programme to meet Service deficiencies of £75 million was cut to £25 million, and the new proportions greatly favoured the RAF.

The Air Ministry estimates of actual and potential German air strength had shown a startling change since the autumn of 1933, when it had been believed that no German air force of any serious size could emerge in the near future.

In July 1934 the Cabinet was informed that Germany possessed some 350 military aircraft, about 250 convertible to military uses and some 1,450 civil and training aircraft of all types. Even more alarming was the fact that the German aircraft industry, carefully maintained and developed over several years, was already producing sixty aircraft a month. At that stage the Air

36. PRO CID 1147-B

Ministry anticipated a German air force of 504 first-line aircraft by October 1935, doubled by 1939 and possibly trebled by 1942.[37] But in October it was discovered that the German plans were for 1,300 first-line aircraft with 100 per cent reserves by October 1936, and that production was up to 140 aircraft a month. A small Cabinet Committee on German Rearmament reported on 26 November that the estimate for the Luftwaffe for October 1935 was 576 first-line aircraft plus reserves, and 1,368 by October 1936, by which time the German air force would have a total of 3,264 aircraft available for military purposes.[38] Nevertheless, two days later Baldwin gave the assurance to the House of Commons in reply to Churchill's speech, to which reference has been made. The Cabinet agreed that the Home Defence Force must be substantially increased, and it is possible to trace from this decision the real turning-point in the history of British air rearmament.

The problem was not, however, simply one of numbers of aircraft. The RAF was equipped entirely with wooden biplanes with fixed undercarriages; they were highly manoeuvrable and relatively cheap to build, but even by 1934 they were obsolescent, and the British aircraft industry was not well prepared to undertake any rapid development of new and faster types then under production in Germany. The RAF was not in a condition of decay, nor was it inferior in numbers or training to the expanding Luftwaffe. But even by 1934 it was evident that its equipment was no longer adequate and that its quality must be substantially improved if the Luftwaffe continued to expand qualitatively and quantitively at its current rate. The facts were accepted by the Cabinet, and the Defence Estimates showed, for the first time since 1918, an increase. It was an inadequate increase, but one nevertheless. In the next four years the RAF was to be transformed from a front-line strength in Britain of 564 wooden biplane aircraft to 1,476 almost entirely fast metal monoplanes, while the overseas air forces was increased from 168 to 435 aircraft. Personnel of the RAF was to rise from 30,000 regulars and 11,000 reservists to 118,000

37. PRO CP 204 (3).
38. PRO CAB 42/34/2.

regulars and 68,000 reservists. By 1939 the RAF had the
Spitfire and Hurricane fighters, the chain of Radio Direction
Finder stations on the South-East and South coasts, fully
incorporated operationally into Fighter Command, while the
large long-range bombers that formed the basis of Bomber
Command were entering production. Relative to the German
advance, even this remarkable expansion was inadequate; but
it remains an achievement to which insufficient attention has
been given. The most serious charge against the 1931–8 Governments is that they neglected the Army. The debate on rearmament between 1933 and 1938 was principally on *air* rearmament,
and the rebuilding of the RAF was seen essentially as a deter-
rent. The danger was seen in terms very similar to the apprehensions concerning German naval rearmament before the
Great War, and the full implications of the part Britain would
have to play if a war-situation arose in Europe were inadequately
assessed.

Furthermore, the reality of the danger was wrongly assessed
– by Churchill as much as by any other observer. The expansion
of the German air force between 1933 and 1939 was in numerical
terms astounding; but its purpose remained that of support for
the ground forces; the German Army, with its mighty air arm,
was the real danger. Even by the outbreak of war in 1939, the
Luftwaffe did not possess the capability to inflict the damage
on Britain that Churchill and others depicted so graphically.
The eventuality that no one foresaw was the collapse of France
and the ability to use French airfields for assaults on Britain.
Only a few percipient observers – among them Basil Liddell
Hart – drew attention to the central fact of German military
thinking, the crucial role of the Wehrmacht in any offensive
operations and the gradual development of the technique of
the Blitzkrieg. As will be seen, Churchill was unimpressed by
the capability of aircraft to trouble experienced soldiers or to
present a serious danger to warships; on the land he regarded
the tank as obsolete; at sea, the submarine as an illusory
danger. In short, wholly absorbed by the one issue of the
dangers of massive air attack on Britain – in point of fact a
military feat of which Germany was incapable until the capture

of France in May 1940 – he concentrated all his energies and attentions upon this menace.

In this absorption he was not alone. The warnings of Vansittart and Warren Fisher, in particular, were concentrated upon the air problem. The fear of a pre-emptive strike by the German air force haunted these men from the advent of Hitler to the outbreak of war. Of course these fears were not groundless, but it should be noted that there was a fundamental assumption as to what the primary role of the expanding Luftwaffe would be, and it was here that the error occurred. If it is one of the purposes of history to provide lessons for the present and the future, this may be judged to be one. Defence estimates of an enemy's capability must be firmly based upon an understanding of what kind of war he is preparing to fight; estimates of the value of his equipment must be based upon qualitative as well as quantitive factors.

*

By the beginning of 1934, Churchill was assembling information about the condition of Britain's air defence and resources. On 7 July he made his first outspoken warning outside Parliament in a speech in his constituency, in which he said that 'we ought to have a large vote of credit to double our Air Force; we ought to have it now, and a larger vote of credit as soon as possible to redouble the Air Force'. It was this declaration that provoked Samuel to describe it as 'rather the language of a Malay running amok than of a responsible British Statesman. It is rather the language of blind and careless panic.'[39] Samuel did, however, make one valid point, when he said that Churchill had not given 'the smallest reasons why this colossal expenditure should immediately be undertaken'. If the campaign was to have any chance of success, speeches on German and British rearmament would have to be based on facts and figures. Up to this point, with the exception of the dramatic but unsubstantiated warning of 8 March, Churchill's speeches had lacked the kind of detailed information on the position that

39. House of Commons, 13 July 1934.

would be likely to impress the House of Commons. The
deficiency was now to be filled.

Although he was a back-bench Member of Parliament (and
one, moreover, who was openly hostile to the Government of
the day) his sources of information included official ones. One
of the most important links with these sources was Major
Desmond Morton. Churchill had first met him when he had been
on Haig's staff in 1917. 'I formed a great regard and friendship
for this brilliant and gallant officer,' Churchill has written, 'and
in 1919, when I became Secretary of State for War and Air, I
appointed him to a key position in the Intelligence, which he
held for many years.'[40] This was not strictly accurate. Morton
held other appointments between 1922 and 1929 when he was
seconded from the Army to serve under Hankey. From 1930
onwards, his principal responsibility was to form and direct a
small department to furnish the Committee of Imperial Defence
with information on the industrial and other preparation for
rearmament being made in all foreign countries. By a lucky
chance Morton was a close neighbour of the Churchills after
they moved to Chartwell in 1922, as he lived only a mile or so
away in a cottage at Crockham Hill. In 1932 Morton obtained
the permission of Ramsay MacDonald to discuss these matters
with Churchill and to pass on to him the conclusions of certain
reports compiled for the Committee of Imperial Defence by his
small department. This arrangement was subsequently endorsed by Baldwin and Neville Chamberlain. For his part
Churchill observed his side of the bargain meticulously, and
never attempted to seek additional official information from
Morton. The information that he did receive, however, was of
very considerable value to him.

There were other sources, of which perhaps the most important single one was an officer in the Air Ministry, who
considered that his public duty lay in supplying Churchill with
information about the British and German air strengths, and
who put his whole career at hazard by this action. Ralph
Wigram, the head of the Central Department of the Foreign
Office, also kept Churchill well informed, and Vansittart was

40. *The Gathering Storm*, pp. 62–3.

another informant.[41] Vansittart was obsessed by the fear of 'a knock-down blow from the air' at the beginning of a war with Germany, and it is possible that Churchill's alarming forecasts were the particular result of Vansittart's influence. There were important contacts at the War Office, the Admiralty and the Air Ministry. In 1936 the First Lord of the Admiralty (Hoare) authorized senior officers to discuss naval matters with Churchill. Contacts in Paris and Berlin were renewed, and some new ones were forged. Professor Lindemann[42] became a kind of statistical assistant and scientific adviser. Chartwell gradually developed into a representation of a Government Department, with secretaries, advisers, visitors, maps, filing-cabinets and charts. Mr Harold Macmillan has described the scene in April 1939 when the Italian seizure of Albania was announced:

It was a scene that gave me my first picture of Churchill at work. Maps were brought out; secretaries were marshalled; telephones began to ring. 'Where is the British Fleet?' That was the most urgent question . . . I shall always have a picture of that spring day and the sense of power and energy, the great flow of action, which came from Churchill, although he held no public office. He alone seemed to be in command, when everyone else was dazed and hesitating.[43]

As the evidence mounted it was clear that it pointed in only one direction. This is not to say that Churchill's information – notably on German air strength – was always accurate. Furthermore, when there was a clash of figures he selected those which were most appropriate to his case. Although Churchill was absolutely right on the central point and, above all, on the importance of time, the fact remained that throughout these years, despite his official and unofficial contacts, he was seriously out of touch with recent developments in military thinking, with the result that many of his public comments and forecasts appear, in retrospect, curious. In one article written in April 1938, entitled 'How Wars of the Future Will Be

41. See Ian Colvin: *Vansittart in Office*, pp. 135–6.
42. See pp. 307–11 below.
43. Macmillan, *Winds of Change*, p. 592.

Waged', he anticipated that the contending armies would have 'great prepared lines of fortifications which it will be very difficult indeed for the other army to break through ... The idea that enormous masses of mechanical vehicles and tanks will be able to overrun these fortifications will probably turn out to be a disappointment.' If the armies were to advance at all, 'it will very often be only as moles': 'One thing is certain about the next war, namely, that the armies will use their spades more often than they use their bayonets.'[44] In January 1938 he declared that 'the air menace against properly armed and protected ships of war will not be of a decisive character', and in an article in May he wrote that 'so far as battleships and other ships of war are concerned, especially when steaming together, it is not believed that aircraft will do much harm'. In January 1939 he wrote that 'even a single well-armed vessel will hold its own against aircraft'.[45] 'This,' he commented in March 1938, 'added to the undoubted obsolescence of the sub-marine as a decisive war weapon, should give a feeling of confidence and security so far as the seas and oceans are concerned, to the western democracies.' This was another consistent theme: 'The submarine,' he wrote (13 May 1937), 'also is not nowadays regarded as the menace it used to be.' He concluded that one of the major lessons of the Spanish Civil War was that it demonstrated 'the limitations rather than the strength of the air weapon ... so far as the fighting troops are concerned, aircraft are an additional complication rather than a decisive weapon'.

Another example may be taken from a memorandum written in March 1938 criticizing the progress of air defence: ' ... We have concentrated upon the forward-firing fixed-gun Fighter (Hurricane and Spitfire). The latest developments increasingly suggest that hostile aircraft can only be engaged with certainty on parallel or nearly parallel courses, hence that the turret type of equipment will become paramount.'[46]

44. *News of the World*, 24 April 1938.

45. *Collier's Magazine*, 14 January 1939.

46. PRO Premier 1/237. Memorandum by Churchill to the Prime Minister, 12 March 1938.

Many other forecasts, official as well as unofficial, were equally wrong. But it must be recognized that it was a serious weakness in Churchill's case that many of his arguments were based upon bad information and a serious lack of knowledge of technological developments. It was accordingly often relatively simple for ministers and officials to controvert Churchill's arguments on what were far from being points of detail, but which often overlooked the fundamental validity of many of the points Churchill was raising. Again, if we are seeking guidance from an examination of these matters, we may note the supreme importance of obtaining and maintaining a reputation for accuracy and sound judgement in dealing with ministers and their officials. Broad effects are not enough.

This raises the important question as to the quality of the advice that Churchill was receiving during this period. The fact was that many of Churchill's advisors were either individuals with grievances – often fully justified – against the existing authorities, or tended to be experts with particular obsessions. And the fact that Churchill was impressed by articulate men whose views coincided with his own excluded from his counsels some whose advice and knowledge would have been of greater value. As Boothby has written:

It must be admitted that there was some danger in all this talking, unaccompanied by sustained argument. The talk was so over-powering, the improvisations – flung out with almost reckless prodigality – so brilliant, that, as Harold Laski has pointed out, people were more anxious to commit to memory the things he said than to drive him to defend them. Few indeed were those who could 'prick him into the urgency of new thought'. Too often was he allowed to get away with dialectical murder. But they were murders no one would willingly have missed.[47]

This was a valid point, and its relevance can be seen in an account by Hankey of a long conversation with Churchill in April 1936:

. . . On the international side I found Mr Churchill's views disappointing – but he was talking rather at large, and probably without having thought the matters out.

47. Boothby: *I Fight to Live*, p. 45.

As regards Italy, for example, he proposed a plan that we ought to make up our mind to deliver an ultimatum informing the Italians that unless they agreed to come to terms with the League we should close the Suez Canal. Shortly before the presentation of the ultimatum we should notify the French of our intentions, demand their co-operation, and intimate that failing that co-operation we should ourselves come to terms with Germany. He talked in this connection of our delivering heavy bombing attacks on Italy which showed he had not thought out how it was to be done, from what bases or with what aircraft.

On the position vis-à-vis Germany he gave an admirable exposition of the dangers of the situation without his usual exaggerations as to German armaments . . .

He favours continued support of the League, and was very down on Conservative Members of Parliament whom he said were widely criticising our League policy. He himself of course has no illusions about the weakness of the League, but sees that the British people will not take rearmament seriously except as part of the League policy.

It was not this part of his remarks that disappointed me, but his positive suggestions. His general idea is to hammer away at the League for a complete encirclement of Germany (I do not think he used the word 'encirclement') . . . he had a fantastic idea of sending to the Baltic a sufficient part of the British Fleet to ensure superiority over Germany in that sea. It would stay there, permanently based on a Russian port of which we should obtain the use as part of the plan. . . . All this seemed to be very fantastic and to ignore many realities some of which I mentioned to him, though are so obvious that I need not mention them . . .[48]

Churchill's views of the development of armour are a case in point. As he himself subsequently wrote, 'I did not comprehend the violence of the revolution effected since the last war by the incursion of a mass of fast-moving armour. I knew about it, but it had not alerted my convictions as it should have done.' He wrote in 1938 that 'the tank has, no doubt, a great part to play; but I, personally, doubt very much whether it will ever see again the palmy days of 1918 . . . Nowadays the anti-tank rifle and the anti-tank gun have made such great strides that the poor tank cannot carry thick enough skin to stand up to

48. PRO CAB 21/435.

them.'[49] There was very little contact between Churchill and
Basil Liddell Hart, the often prescient Defence correspondent
of *The Times* who was the father of the 'expanding torrent'
concept of armoured warfare, which was developed to such
devastating precision by the Germans. Liddell Hart has written
that 'it was . . . very noticeable that Churchill's mind was apt
to focus on a phrase, while Ll.G. seized on the point and followed
on to the next point . . . Moreover, Churchill liked to do most of
the talking in any discussion.'[50]

It would be incorrect to create the impression that Churchill
did not listen to uncongenial advice. It would not be incorrect
to say that he had a strong tendency not to listen to uncongenial people, and, as one of his official private secretaries has
written, 'there were times when the meretricious speech of the
glib seemed to impress him more than the solid virtues of the
tongue-tied, and there were occasions when the lilt of Auld
Lang Syne was too well remembered'.[51] The central problem
of Churchill's political personality was one of containment. His
mental exuberance had survived the disappointments of his
political career and the effects of age and was, if properly
harnessed, one of his greatest assets. But it required this containment, and it was in this respect that the part played in the
Second World War of men like Ismay and Alan Brooke was so
crucial. Deprived of such advisers, the mental exuberance and
love of dealing in grand subjects at great length could lead him
into most unfortunate by-ways. In office, the problem of containment was difficult enough. Out of office the difficulties were
greatly increased.

The part played in these years by Professor Lindemann is
still difficult to evaluate fully. Few personalities of recent
political history have aroused more controversy, and it is
desirable to attempt his portrait to appreciate the factors that
occasioned these feelings.

Lindemann was a wealthy bachelor, the son of an Alsatian

49. *News of the World*, 24 April 1938.

50. Liddell Hart: *Memoirs*, Vol. I, p. 373.

51. Sir John Wheeler-Bennett (ed.): *Action This Day: Working with
Churchill*, p. 62.

father and an American mother. He was a total abstainer, a non-smoker, a philistine in most artistic matters and a vegetarian. Called 'the Prof' by Birkenhead's eldest daughter, and known generally by that title, Lindemann had studied and done research on quantum physics in Germany before the Great War, and had been secretary to the Solray Conference in 1911, which had been attended by Nerst, de Broglie, Einstein and Madame Curie. During the war he had achieved further eminence by pioneering work on spins in aircraft, and since 1919 he had been Professor of Experimental Philosophy at Oxford. His outstanding achievement had been to make the Clarendon Laboratory into the most advanced low temperature physics laboratory in the country, and probably in the world. He fought for the Clarendon and for the status of science in Oxford with absolute and concentrated ardour, and both Oxford and British science owe much to his perseverance and skill. Nevertheless, a price was paid, and it appears that after 1919 Lindemann was increasingly reluctant to undertake research himself, and imperceptibly but definitely fell back in his profession. Professor R. V. Jones has written that Lindemann 'was often unwilling to justify the exploration of a theory, and that was because he was so enamoured of theory that he was prone to ignore facts. He did not take kindly to opposition in any form, and was capable of taking a spiteful and petty revenge.' Professor Max Born has commented: 'Lindemann, though conservative in many respects, had a natural revolutionary strain which found its outlet in physical theory. He had little respect for traditional thinking and as soon as some new facts appeared not to fit in with current theory he jumped to conclusions about fundamental assumptions without the evidence in detail.' [52]

Other comments were even less favourable and the great Rutherford described him as 'a scientist manqué'. It would be wrong to state that in his profession Lindemann was regarded with universal high esteem, but this was as much the result of his personality as estimates of his professional standing.

It is difficult for someone who met him in the early 1950s,

52. Quoted in Lord Birkenhead: *The Prof in Two Worlds*, pp. 98–9.

when he was relaxed and greatly respected, to comprehend the bitter controversies that had formerly surrounded him. But, looking dispassionately at what his two biographers have written about him, and talking with those who had known him, it becomes more clear why he was so deeply disliked and distrusted. He expressed his views with a sharpness, and often a harshness, which was unattractive, and his attitudes often seemed to be based less on knowledge than on prejudice. He had a good conceit of himself, and a low opinion of the intellectual calibre of the majority of mankind. 'His experience of men was very limited,' his Christ Church colleague, Sir Roy Harrod, has written; 'One might gain the impression, and he himself perhaps believed, that he knew everyone who was anyone. But his acquaintance really only extended to a thin top crust – prominent men in politics, diplomacy and London Society . . . He was quite out of touch with the course of contemporary thought, and this considerably cramped his style.'[53] His addiction to high society did not endear him further to his colleagues, who would have been startled had they beheld him charming any of the numerous house-parties to which he was a frequent and welcome guest.

Charm alone was unlikely to create the remarkable bond that was forged between Churchill and Lindemann in the 1920s, and which developed rapidly thereafter into complete mutual confidence and respect. But Harrod has written of Lindemann with justice that 'He was a person in whom the emotions normal to mankind seemed to be raised to a higher intensity. Devoted in friendship, fierce in enmity, revengeful in thought, sensitive, angry, scornful, courageous, resolute, obstinate, abounding in humour . . . he was every inch human, palpitating with life.' The attraction to Churchill at once becomes comprehensible. Churchill always had an affinity with attractive and persuasive men who were able to present their views clearly and briefly. There is no doubt that Lindemann cultivated Churchill carefully, and his loyalty was total – the crucial test for a would-be member of Churchill's personal entourage. But Lindemann's admiration for Churchill was quite genuine. As Harrod has

53. Sir Roy Harrod: *The Prof: A Personal Memoir of Lord Cherwel*, p. 87.

written: 'The Prof was very sparing in his intellectual tributes,
especially sparing outside the world of science. From the
beginning he was quite convinced that Churchill was one of the
great intellects of our age.' [54] It is not difficult to see how his
influence grew. He was a man of astringent and controversial
views, who expressed them, particularly in writing, exceptionally briefly and succinctly. Churchill has written that 'Lindemann could decipher the signals of the experts on the far
horizons and explain to me in lucid homely terms what the
issues were.' His ideas may have been based in many instances
upon an inadequate understanding of the facts, and sometimes
even a total defiance of them, but they could be exciting, and
they certainly attracted Churchill. Lindemann was essentially
an ideas man, and one who could put them forward with great
clarity. His attitudes were not negative, and his approach was
one that was closely akin – and perhaps too closely akin – to
that of Churchill. There was in it a strong element of daring and
adventure, of impatience with practical difficulties, and of
fascination with those things not yet achieved which professional scientists usually disliked and distrusted, yet which
Churchill found refreshing and invigorating. Perhaps there is
also truth in the comment that 'Through Churchill, Lindemann
could vicariously enjoy the pleasures of life; through Lindemann, Churchill could vicariously engage in mathematical
calculations and scientific investigations.' [55]

There was another factor, and one that has tended to be
given inadequate emphasis. Lindemann was fascinated by
politics, a fact that Churchill either did not realize or take
seriously. 'Now Prof, that's politics,' he would remark with
emphasis. Lindemann was almost pathologically anti-German,
and his conservatism was of the extreme right-wing persuasion.
It would be to give an insufficient description of Lindemann's
social attitudes to say that he was a snob. His class-conscious-
ness was such that it is doubtful whether any but the most
rabid Conservative would have subscribed to it. In this, as in
Lindemann's vehement anti-Germanism, Churchill's views were

54. Harrod, op. cit., p. 12.
55. J. G. Crowther: *Statesman of Science*, p. 340.

gentler, and there are several indications that he was uneasy about this aspect of Lindemann's character. One visitor to Chartwell, who clashed with Lindemann over dinner on this matter, was later thanked by Churchill, as Randolph Churchill had been present and his father was concerned by Lindemann's influence over the young man.[56] In matters political as in others Lindemann could be a fierce hater, and he could be poisonously unpleasant. But although his influence on Churchill's political course was perhaps negligible, in matters relating to science and technology he was virtually Churchill's one-man advisory service, with consequences which were to be of considerable importance.

On the existence and peril of the German air menace Lindemann was emphatic from an early stage. The Air Exercises of 1934 demonstrated the grievous deficiencies of British air defence, making London, in Churchill's words 'the greatest target in the world, a kind of tremendous, fat, valuable cow tied up to attract beasts of prey',[57] and seeming to confirm Baldwin's sombre forecast of 1932 that 'the bomber will always get through'. Lindemann in a letter to *The Times* on 8 August 1934 attacked this 'defeatist attitude' and stated that 'bomber aeroplanes in the hands of gangster governments might jeopardize the whole future of our Western civilization'. He concluded by calling for a concerted scientific effort to meet the challenge. In the autumn Churchill and Lindemann visited Baldwin at Aix to press the matter upon him, and there was a subsequent long correspondence on the question.[58]

A committee for the scientific survey of air defence was instituted by the Secretary of State for Air (Lord Londonderry) at the end of 1934, and was immediately engrossed in the exciting possibilities opened up by Robert Watson-Watt in the detection of hostile aircraft by the reflections of radio waves. The chairman of this body was the Rector of the Imperial

56. Thomas Jones: *Whitehall Diary*, Vol. II, pp. 67–8.

57. House of Commons, 30 July 1934.

58. The following account is based primarily upon the papers concerning the Air Research Defence Committee in the Cabinet Papers, and principally upon those in PRO Premier 1/253.

College of Science and Technology, Sir Henry Tizard, and its members included the distinguished scientists Professors P. M. S. Blackett and A. V. Hill. It was a purely advisory body, without staff and with unpaid members.

Londonderry wrote to Lindemann on 20 December, informing him of the existence of the Tizard committee, and suggesting that he put himself 'in direct communication with Tizard'. Lindemann did not reply until 7 January 1935, when he wrote that 'my friends and I do not think that a departmental committee can adequately fulfil the purpose which we consider so urgent'. Two days later Churchill and Austen Chamberlain wrote jointly to Ramsay MacDonald to urge an inquiry of the kind recommended by Lindemann: 'We recall,' they wrote, 'how many problems which at first appeared insoluble were in fact solved under the dread necessity of war, and we think it premature to declare that there is no solution of the problem of defence against night bombers.' Lindemann was again invited to join the Tizard Committee on 30 January but replied on 5 February that he would defer his decision. His attitude was interpreted as being closely linked with the Churchill–Chamberlain request for an independent body which might be constituted as a sub-committee of the Committee of Imperial Defence. Hankey, for one, saw the merit in the argument, which he endorsed in a memorandum to the Prime Minister on 18 March. On the following day Baldwin announced the formation of the Air Research Defence Committee. It was not, at this stage, the type of body that Churchill and Lindemann had had in mind, but it was a significant indication of the changing attitude of the Government. The purge of Roehm and his associates in June 1934, followed by the unsuccessful attempt by the Austrian Nazis to seize power in July – in the course of which Chancellor Dolfuss had been murdered – had played their part in this changing view of the European situation. There still remained a large gulf between the concern of Churchill and Vansittart and Fisher on the one hand and the bulk of the Cabinet on the other. The Statement on Defence published on 4 March 1935 [59] was by far the clearest statement so far of the

59. *Statement Relating to Defence*, Cmd. 4827 (1935).

Government's concern at developments in Europe, and marked the important step away from deficiency programmes to real rearmament. But the actual increase in expenditure – £4 million – was somewhat less impressive.

In November 1934 Churchill had set out the dangers in a radio broadcast:

As we go to and fro in this peaceful country, with its decent ordinary people going about their business under free institutions, and with so much tolerance and fair play in their laws and customs, it is startling and fearful to realise that we are no longer safe in our island home . . . After all, only a few hours away by air there dwells a nation of nearly seventy million of the most educated, industrious, scientific, disciplined people in the world, who are being taught from childhood to think of war and conquest as a glorious exercise, and death in battle as the noblest fate for man. There is a nation which has abandoned all its liberties in order to augment its collective might. There is a nation which, with all its strength and virtues, is in the grip of a group of ruthless men preaching a gospel of intolerance and racial pride, unrestrained by law, by Parliament or by public opinion . . . From their new table of commandments they have omitted 'Thou shalt not kill.' . . . I am afraid that if you look intently at what is moving towards Great Britain, you will see that the only choice open is the old grim choice our forebears had to face, namely, whether we shall submit or whether we shall prepare . . . We must, without another hour's delay, begin to make ourselves at least the strongest air Power in the European world . . .

Anything like a balance of power in Europe will lead to war. Great wars usually come only when both sides think they have good hopes of victory. Peace must be founded upon preponderance. There is safety in numbers . . . May God protect us all.

The Statement on Defence was severely attacked by the Opposition for its excesses; it was criticized by Churchill for its inadequacies. Hitler took the opportunity of announcing the official existence of the German air force and the introduction of military conscription. When Simon and Eden went to Berlin on 25 March to discuss with Hitler the possibilities of agreements between the two countries on air and naval matters, the German leader claimed that Germany had already achieved 'parity' in the air. The claim was fraudulent, but when it was made public it immediately put Churchill's persistent warnings into an entirely new light, particularly as he had launched a formidable challenge on 19 March to Baldwin's claim of the previous November, and had been duly met with the ministerial statement (which was quite correct) that British superiority in the air remained. Hitler's claim appeared to alter the situation completely. For the first time disquiet could be detected in the Conservative ranks.

This disquiet was allayed again in a remarkable debate on 2 May, in which Churchill delivered one of his most formidable speeches to date:

> When the situation was manageable it was neglected, and now that it is thoroughly out of hand, we apply too late the remedies which then might have effected a cure. There is nothing new in the story. It is as old as the Sibylline books. It falls into that immense dismal category of the fruitlessness of experience and the confirmed unteach-ability of mankind. Want of foresight, unwillingness to act when action would be simple and effective, lack of clear thinking, confusion of counsel until the emergency comes, until self-preservation strikes its jarring gong – these are the features which constitute the endless repetition of history.

After this condemnatory opening he dwelt upon the German claim, and said that 'it cannot be disputed that both in numbers and in quality Germany has already obtained a marked superiority over our Home Defence Air Force'. Although this was not in fact correct, the circumstances of the claim made a considerable impression. Churchill went on:

> I have stated the position in general terms, and I have tried to state it not only moderately but quite frigidly. Here I pause to ask the Committee [60] to consider what these facts mean and what their consequences impose. I confess that words fail me. In the year 1708 Mr Secretary St John, by a calculated Ministerial indiscretion, revealed to the House the fact that the battle of Almanza had been lost in the previous summer because only 8,000 English troops were actually in Spain out of the 20,000 that had been voted by the House

60. The debate was on the Foreign Office Vote, in the Committee of Supply. (This is a Committee of the Whole House, presided over by the Chairman of Ways and Means, not the Speaker.)

of Commons for this service. When a month later this revelation was confirmed by the Government, it is recorded that the House sat in silence for half an hour, no Member caring to speak or wishing to make a comment upon so staggering an announcement. And yet how incomparably small that event was to what we have now to face!

On 22 May Churchill claimed that 'there is no doubt that the Germans are superior to us in the air at the present time, and it is my belief that by the end of the year, unless their rate of construction and development is arrested by some agreement they will be possibly three, or even four, times our strength'. This was even more an exaggeration than the previous statements on relative strengths, but Baldwin appeared to admit the justice of Churchill's figures. Referring to his statement of the previous November, he said that 'With regard to the figure I then gave of German aeroplanes, nothing has come to my knowledge since that makes me think that figure was wrong. I believed at that time it was right. Where I was wrong was in my estimate of the future. There I was completely wrong . . . We were completely misled on that subject.'

This apologia was unnecessarily excessive, but, coupled with the announcement of a further increase in the size of the RAF, whose home strength would now be 1,500 aircraft by 1937, it effectively removed much of the sting from Churchill's attack. He expressed his astonishment at 'the coolness with which the Committee has treated the extraordinary revelations of the German air strength relatively to our own country'. On 31 May he again spelt out the fact that 'we are entering a corridor of deepening and darkening danger', but six days later he was making his final, and somewhat melodramatic, speech on the Third Reading of the Government of India Bill, upon which Herbert Samuel commented: 'When the Rt Hon. Gentleman speaks in this Debate, or other Debates, the House always crowds in to hear him. It listens and admires. It laughs when he would have it laugh, and it trembles when he would have it tremble – which is very frequently in these days; but it remains unconvinced, and in the end it votes against him.'

*

In June Baldwin succeeded MacDonald in the premiership. Among other changes, Hoare replaced Simon at the Foreign Office and Cunliffe-Lister [61] took the place of Londonderry as Secretary of State for Air.

Up to this point, Cunliffe-Lister's career, which had begun in 1918, had not really achieved the high level of success which had been expected when he became a Cabinet Minister after only five years in politics. There was in his manner an astringency that was not always deemed agreeable, and although he did every task with great competence and was respected by his colleagues, his officials and the House of Commons, it would be incorrect to state that over the years he had succeeded in attracting warm and widespread support. But his appointment to the Air Ministry was a momentous one. It was to lead directly to the courageous decisions to order the new eight-gun metal monoplanes off the drawing board; to establish the system of 'shadow factories' [62] that could be quickly converted to the production of aircraft in an emergency; to order the development of the new long-range heavy bombers; and to press forward with the Radio Direction Finding system now being developed by Watson-Watt and the Tizard Committee. In his task of transforming the R A F, Cunliffe-Lister had the strong personal support of Baldwin. As he has written: 'All of us at the Air Ministry who set out to achieve a revolutionary programme of expansion and innovation, the ordering of thousands of aircraft off the drawing board, the Shadow Factories, the integration of leading scientists with the Air Staff which gave us radar, could not have been achieved without Baldwin's support; we knew it and were grateful.' [63]

Baldwin's techniques as Prime Minister – and it is perhaps worth emphasizing again that he was not Prime Minister between September 1931 and June 1935 – are now somewhat

61. Philip Lloyd-Greame (changed name to Cunliffe-Lister, 1924). Created Viscount Swinton, 1935.

62. The scheme, approved in May 1934 (C I D, 264th Meeting), enabled firms to receive limited military contracts on the condition that they made preparations for greatly expanded production in the event of a war situation.

63. Lord Swinton: *Sixty Years of Power*, pp. 89–90.

out of favour. It is now accepted that the Prime Minister should be peripatetic, active everywhere, and holding in his firm hands all the diverse strands of government. Baldwin's concept was more detached. He believed that ministers should run their own departments, with him always available to settle disputes or give advice. It is partly from this technique that the canard of his indolence has grown. Modern political commentators have a weakness for the Lloyd George, Neville Chamberlain and Churchill type of prime minister. The office of prime minister has no forms or rules; each premiership is unique, for it necessarily reflects the personality, attitudes and experience of each holder of the office. There was a great deal to be said for Baldwin's methods, which were emulated closely by Mr Macmillan in the first part of his premiership. It has its dangers (but so has the Lloyd George–Chamberlain–Churchill technique) and it works only if the right decisions are made about the choice of ministers. Hoare was a poor selection; Cunliffe-Lister was an excellent one.

Cunliffe-Lister was from the outset anxious to have Churchill's assistance, partly because he valued Churchill's advice and experience, but also partly because he wanted Churchill to be accurately informed of what was being done to improve the air defences. He accepted that Churchill would remain a public critic of the Government, but believed that a properly informed critic was of considerably more national value than an uninformed one. Baldwin immediately agreed to the proposal, and secured the appointment in the teeth of considerable opposition in the Cabinet, led by Neville Chamberlain.[64] The Tizard Committee was made a sub-committee of the Committee of Imperial Defence, and worked under the newly created Air Defence Research Committee, chaired by the Secretary of State. There were accordingly two bodies, a 'political' and a 'scientific' committee. Churchill agreed to join the former on the conditions that he retained full independence of action in public and that Lindemann be brought in. Hankey wrote to Baldwin on 7 June that 'it is obvious that the right place for a scientist of Professor Lindemann's attainments is on the scientific Committee and not

64. Information supplied by Lord Swinton.

on the controlling Committee'.[65] Baldwin agreed, and the
arrangement was settled on these lines. It is now possible to see
that it was here that the source of the subsequent difficulties
lay, and that Lindemann's concepts were so different from those
of the Tizard Committee that his proper place was by Churchill's
side on the main body.

From this point onwards, Churchill's position was a curious
one. On the one hand he remained a strong critic of the Government for its allegedly pusillanimous Defence programme, particularly in the air; but that same Government and Prime
Minister had permitted him to see highly confidential papers
of the Committee of Imperial Defence since 1932, and had
appointed him to serve as a member of this potentially influential body concerned with air defence. Furthermore,
Churchill's position as an opponent of the Government was no
longer as clear as it had been. The complete hostility of the
Opposition parties to any form of rearmament drew Churchill
considerably closer to his own party leaders, with whom the
difference was essentially one of degree and time rather than of
principle. Nevertheless, his public criticisms of ministers were
delivered to an audience that consisted entirely of the Conservative Party, and what support he had came from within the
party. But the vigour of those attacks was bound to have a
counter-productive effect and serve to rally support behind the
Government. Churchill did not, of course, have any executive
or ministerial responsibility for what was decided by the
Government, but he had a real quasi-official connection with
air policy, and was certainly *parti pris* to a policy that he
consistently attacked in public. One of the strongest arguments
brought by Chamberlain and others against Churchill's appointment to the ADRC had been that he would use his position
to attack the Government, and there were occasions when those
arguments seemed to have been borne out by events. A point
was reached at one stage when Swinton seriously considered
withdrawing from Churchill the privilege of seeing confidential
information.[66]

65. PRO Premier 1/253.
66. Swinton to Sir Thomas Inskip, 26 June 1936 (PRO CAB 21/426).

Two interpretations of the arrangement may be compared. The first is by Churchill, the second by Lord Swinton:

The Committee worked in secret, and no statement was ever made of my association with the Government, whom I continued to criticise and attack with increasing severity in other parts of the field. It is often possible in England for politicians to reconcile functions of this kind in the same way as the sharpest political differences are sometimes found not incompatible with personal friendship.[67]

Winston certainly believed in my expansion plans. . . . At the same time he was determined to use anything he could find to attack the Government. So he used any evidence good or bad, relevant or irrelevant, he could find about German air strength to attack the Government. The meaningless phrase of Baldwin's about 'parity' played into his hands. And the last thing he bothered about was consistency. He knew I should go on with the plans we both believed in; and at the same time he could go for the Government. He was, I am sure, genuinely horrified when the result of attacks on the Government, to which he had contributed so much, resulted in Neville sacking me.[68]

This was one aspect of the new situation, and one that has been largely ignored. The other was the presence of Lindemann on the Tizard Committee. It was soon evident that both Churchill and Lindemann misunderstood the function of this body, and their repeated arguments that it should be more influential and more political were met by Tizard's reiterated insistence that it was a purely technical body reporting to the ADRC. These arguments became heated, and a rift opened between Tizard and Lindemann that was to expand swiftly into a wide and bitter chasm.

Lindemann, furthermore, descended upon the Tizard Committee with proposals that fully confirmed the comments of Professors Jones and Born that have already been quoted. To Tizard, engrossed in the crucial technical and operational problems of RDF, which offered a really dramatic breakthrough

67. *The Gathering Storm*, p. 120.
68. Letter to the author.

if it could be perfected and incorporated into the operational plans of Fighter Command, Lindemann's schemes appeared irrelevant and even lunatic. Lindemann was obsessed by night operations, and he also put forward proposals for aerial mines (to be dropped by high-altitude aircraft in the path of bomber formations, whose pilots would presumably fly obediently into them), infra-red detection of night-flying aircraft and the placing of 'a cloud of substance in the path of an aeroplane to produce detonation'. The aerial-mine project, it has been rightly remarked, 'was a completely blind alley for research on which valuable time and money were wasted'.[69] The 'cloud of substance' proposal was based upon no practical basis whatever, and smacked more of casual reading in bad futuristic fiction than the proposal of a serious professional scientist. The proposal for research into infra-red detection was considerably more interesting, but, again, there was nothing of any serious evidence that Lindemann could produce that remotely compared with the RDF researches.

Unfortunately, Lindemann could not be easily brushed aside. He was extremely pertinacious and determined, and, most important of all, he was backed on the ADRC by Churchill. Relations between Tizard and Lindemann deteriorated badly, to the point where 'the differences of opinion on the Tizard Committee could have had a serious effect on the rapid growth of radar'.[70] In this situation neither Lindemann nor Tizard showed to best advantage. 'When Tizard was upset,' it has been written, 'he showed signs of nervous excitement, and people felt alarmed, not only for themselves, but for him. When Lindemann was upset he was preposterous.'[71] Matters proceeded towards an epic and often-described crisis.[72]

In June 1936 Churchill circulated a paper on the aerial-mine project that was in effect 'a frontal attack on Tizard's work'[73] and which had clearly been written by Lindemann. Lindemann

69. D. Wood and D. Dempster: *The Narrow Margin*, p. 131.
70. ibid., p. 131.
71. Crowther, op. cit., p. 356.
72. See Birkenhead: *The Prof in Two Worlds* and R. Clark: *Tizard*.
73. Clark, op. cit., p. 138.

then submitted a minority report to that put forward by the Tizard Committee to the ADRC, in which he objected to 'the completely novel conclusion (from which I dissent very strongly) that work on aerial mines need not be of the highest priority'. And it was at this point that Lindemann announced that he was going to contest the vacant seat for Oxford University, and would, furthermore, fight on the issue of increased air defence. For Blackett and Hill this was the last straw, and they informed Swinton of their intention of resigning from the Committee. Tizard himself had written to Swinton on 12 June about Lindemann: ' . . . His querulousness when anybody differs from him, his inability to accept the views of the committee as a whole, and his consequent insistence on talking about matters which we think are relatively unimportant, and hence preventing us getting on with more important matters, make him an impossible colleague . . .'

The letters of Blackett and Hill were even less restrained.[74] Swinton had no doubts as to whose judgement was better, and he dissolved the Tizard Committee, appointing another in its place with the same functions and members, but excluding Lindemann, who went off to fight Oxford and go down to humiliating defeat at the hands of the Independent candidate, Arthur Salter. Churchill broke all traditions in University contests by coming to Oxford to support Lindemann's candidature and to attack Salter, and this intervention probably materially contributed to Lindemann's defeat.[75]

This episode has been described at some length because it had an important bearing upon Churchill's own reputation with the Government and its leading advisers. It is also necessary to relate it in detail because many accounts – including Churchill's – miss the central points of importance. In *The Gathering Storm*,[76] Churchill claimed that the cause of the crisis was the resentment of Lindemann's colleagues on the Tizard Committee at his relationship with Churchill, and in June 1938 he wrote to

74. The letters are in PRO CAB 21/426.

75. The contest left no marks. Both were members of Churchill's wartime and post-war Governments.

76. p. 120

Swinton's successor, Sir Kingsley Wood, that 'Professor
Lindemann, who has a far greater insight in this sphere than
anyone I know, was very soon turned out of the Technical
Committee for pressing [for] more vigorous action'.[77] This was
not the case. Lindemann had had to be removed because the
proceedings of the Tizard Committee had degenerated into a
series of extremely rancorous discussions which were in danger
of wrecking its usefulness. No dispassionate observer, reading
the papers of the Committee, can seriously challenge the
correctness of Swinton's decision.

Most accounts have not been written by dispassionate
observers, however, and it is desirable to attempt a fair assessment of this episode.

The fatal flaw in the original appointment, as has been
emphasized already, was simply that Lindemann was not, and
did not regard himself as, a qualified scientist giving technical
advice to politicians. He was also obsessed, as was Churchill,
with the necessity of injecting an urgently required vitality
into the air rearmament machinery. Neither gave sufficient
attention to the point made by Lord Weir, the Director of
Aircraft Production in the Great War and who had been recalled to undertake the expansion of the RAF under Swinton,
in a letter to Baldwin: 'What I always feared has happened.
The technical structure behind our production is too weak to
carry such a load as is now to be thrust upon it.'[78] It may also
be emphasized that neither Churchill nor Lindemann appear
to have appreciated the really important part of Tizard's work,
the development of Radio Direction Finding into the operational plans of Fighter Command. Compared with this complex
and revolutionary work, Lindemann's obsessions with aerial
mines, night operations and guidance equipment for bombers
were theoretical, unproved and based on no comparable
technical or scientific foundation.

Nevertheless, the basic complaint of Churchill and Lindemann was a valid one, and it has been accepted, by implication,
by Swinton himself:

77. PRO Premier 1/253.
78. G. M. Young: *Stanley Baldwin*, p. 201.

Did we produce enough planes? It may be fair to state that we did not do enough soon enough; that the financial limits laid down were too rigid; that we should have insisted on some power in peace time to attract part of industry on to war production, a policy strenuously opposed by the Prime Minister (Chamberlain) and the Board of Trade. On these matters I shall not attempt to excuse myself; I accepted the decisions and I bear my share of the blame.[79]

It is right to emphasize that without Swinton and Tizard there would have been no victory in the Battle of Britain. It is also important to repeat that a hurried quantitative expansion of the RAF would have been quite ineffective, and that what was done between 1935 and 1939 was less the expansion of an existing Service than the creation of an entirely new one, and the necessity for this was very substantially the result of the policies pursued by Churchill in the past, and was the responsibility of the Secretary of State for Air in 1919–21 and Chancellor of the Exchequer of 1924–9. But it is equally clear that more could have been done without sacrificing quality, and it was here that the part played by Neville Chamberlain as Chancellor of the Exchequer was crucial. Swinton and Tizard can justly claim that they achieved miracles with such limited resources; it was the equally justified claim of Churchill and Lindemann that the resources should not have been so limited.

Contrary to some accounts[80] Churchill remained a member of the ADRC up to the outbreak of war. It did most useful work, but the fact that it had only sixteen meetings in a period of over two years from its formation gave some justification for Churchill's charge that

> . . . In all my experience of public offices, I have never seen anything like the slow-motion picture which the work of this Committee has presented; and I fear it is typical of a whole group of committees which have been in existence during these vital years. One could not have devised a better method of soothing this whole matter down

79. Swinton: *I Remember*, pp. 117–18. I am deeply grateful to Lord Swinton for going over these matters with me at considerable length and in much detail.

80. i.e. A. J. P. Taylor: *English History (1914–45)*, p. 392. Homer was indeed nodding when this section of his book was written.

and laying it politely in repose than the elaborate processes which have been followed . . . So far as the ADR Committee is concerned, there seems to be a complete lack of driving power. The final result is that we have nothing that will be of any effective use in the next two years, when much either in war or humiliation may be in store for us . . .[81]

The last point was not a fair one, and it was effectively countered by an Air Ministry memorandum which had some pointed comments to make of major projects which had gone awry or had been seriously delayed when Churchill had been First Lord of the Admiralty and Minister of Munitions. But although Churchill exaggerated the deficiences of the ADRC, his criticisms were valid. His charge that it lacked driving power is confirmed by one who was closely concerned in its work, and who has emphasized that, for all his technical deficiencies, Churchill was the one member urgently conscious of the shortage of time and the vital need to drive forward. It was accordingly all the more tragic that Lindemann's technical and scientific advice was not of a higher quality.[82]

In October 1938 Churchill persuaded Kingsley Wood to appoint Lindemann to the ADRC. Tizard managed to have Hill appointed as a counterweight, but it was a substantial victory for Lindemann. His final triumph, and Tizard's final defeat, came in June 1940. It would be wrong to regard the Lindemann–Tizard feud – for such it became – merely as a squalid clash of personalities, nor is it justifiable to apply the labels of 'right' and 'wrong' on either. It is right to describe it as a great tragedy, and one which, in the years 1936–9, brought little lustre to Churchill personally in his lone struggle.

*

This account of the disruptions in the ADRC and its advisory body has taken us considerably further forward in time, and it

81. PRO Premier 1/253. Churchill to Kingsley Wood, 9 June 1938.

82. This comment of one closely concerned with the episode should not, I feel, be omitted: 'You should not denigrate the lion simply because his jackal was feeding him carrion.'

is necessary to return to the situation that obtained in the midsummer of 1935.

With the long battle over India ended, Churchill, as has been related, had high hopes of returning to the Government. Although nothing happened, these high hopes still remained when the General Election was held in October. But before that event two subjects of considerable importance occurred. The Italian threat to Abyssinia loomed ever more ominously, and, on 21 June, the Anglo-German Naval Treaty, which in effect authorized Germany to build a navy up to a third of the size of the British, was announced.

On Abyssinia, as will be emphasized, Churchill's attitudes were close to those of the Government. On the Naval Treaty, his criticisms were not as strong at the time as he implies in his own version.[83] On 11 July he described the Treaty as 'a separate agreement for ourselves, of a perfectly innocent character', and supported the Government. But he also said: 'I venture to hazard the prediction that it inaugurates the arrival of Germany – not the Naval Agreement in particular – as a great naval power, and that this will inaugurate an outburst of shipbuilding in almost every country in the world, the like of which has never been seen.' On 22 July, however, he was considerably more critical, and fastened upon what was the outstanding offence of the Treaty, that it was a unilateral revision of the Treaty of Versailles. But although Churchill said that 'I regret that we have condoned this flagrant breach of the Treaty . . . I do not believe for a moment that this isolated action of Great Britain will be found to work for the cause of peace', the speech as a whole was far less condemnatory than the passage quoted in *The Gathering Storm* would suggest. Without seriously checking his pressure on the Government for increased rearmament nor reducing his warnings on the German menace, Churchill's speeches during the period preceding the General Election were considerably less fierce than they had been. Nor is this to be wondered at, or criticized. The role of independent critic is agreeable to some politicians; to a man of Churchill's capacities

83. *The Gathering Storm*, pp. 108–10.

and energy it was infinitely less agreeable and worthwhile than
the realities of office.

The General Election of October 1935 has generated more
subsequent heat than any modern election, and it still awaits a
really thorough examination. No General Election is ever fought
on a single issue, and the 1935 election was not fought on the
exclusive issue of rearmament. But it was a central issue, as an
examination of the principal speeches of the party leaders
makes plain. The Opposition parties, particularly at the constituency level,[84] treated it as the major issue, and devoted
much energy to attacking the Government's rearmament and
foreign policies. Baldwin skilfully maintained the balance
between the Government's record as a whole and the need to
rearm if safety was to be preserved.[85] In one speech, to the
Peace Society on 1 October, he gave an assurance that 'there
will be no great armaments', and this single phrase has been
fastened upon by Churchill and others to create an unsupport-
able thesis that Baldwin concealed the facts from the electorate;
it is a thesis that also depends on an equally selective and out-of-
context quotation from his speech in the House of Commons on
12 November 1936.[86]

Churchill had expected to receive office after the Conservative
victory at the election, and he was deeply disappointed by the
absence of any invitation. New overtures were made, but were
rejected. India unquestionably was a major factor, but there
are indications that Baldwin had not endured Churchill's
attacks over the previous four years with as much patience as he

84. See, for example, the author's biography of Lord Davidson, p.
408.

85. See R. K. Middlemas and J. Barnes: *Stanley Baldwin*, pp. 743–800.

86. See pp. 342–4 below. Churchill's comments on Baldwin's performance
in the 1935 Election are of significance in his careful collective portrait of
Baldwin as 'the best party manager the Conservatives have ever had': 'he
became very anxious to comfort the professional peace-loving elements in
the nation, and allay any fears in their breasts which his talk about naval
rearmament might have caused. . . . Thus the votes both of those who
sought to see the nation prepare itself against the dangers of the future and
of those who believed that peace could be preserved by praising its virtues,
were gained' (*The Gathering Storm*, p. 140).

had appeared to do.[87] Churchill later wrote: 'There was much mocking in the Press about my exclusion. But now one can see how lucky I was. Over me beat the invisible wings. And I had agreeable consolations. I set out with my paintbox for more genial climes without waiting for the meeting of Parliament.'[88] To those who saw him at the time, there was no concealment of the extent of his disappointment and chagrin. He remained abroad until the death of King George V in January 1936 brought him back to England. Much had happened in his absence.

*

The Government had scarcely entered its renewed life when it became involved in a situation that exposed the dangerous position into which it had drifted in its attitudes to world affairs. Italian designs on Abyssinia in the summer of 1935 had forced the Government, unable to employ other methods of pressure, to reliance upon the League of Nations. The sub-missions of the Chiefs of Staff presented to the Cabinet made it plain that there could be no question of the Government pursuing policies which involved even the possibility of war, a statement that coincided exactly with the views of ministers for political reasons. On 12 September Hoare pledged the Government to the collective maintenance of the Covenant of the League, and particularly to 'steady and collective resistance to all acts of unprovoked aggression'. As the historian of the League has written:

It would be difficult to exaggerate the effect of this speech. Once more, it seemed, after four years of uncertainty, timidity, opportunism, the true voice of Britain was heard. Now that the test was at hand, she was ready to take her national place as leader of the League and all it stood for – the respect for treaty obligations, the rights of small nations, the prevention, or, if need be, the defeat, of aggression, through collective security.[89]

87. See, for example, Thomas Jones: *A Diary with Letters, 1931–50*, p. 145.
88. *The Gathering Storm*, p. 141.
89. F. P. Walters: *A History of the League of Nations*, p. 648.

The barrenness of intent behind Hoare's firm pronouncement was not long concealed. On 3 October Mussolini invaded Abyssinia. Italy was pronounced an aggressor by the League, and an embargo was placed on the export to her of war materials – but excluding oil, the only effective weapon available against Mussolini. This was the first withdrawal from the firmness of the Hoare declaration. Worse was to follow. Early in December Hoare went to Paris to discuss with Laval terms under which Italy could be bought off.

Under the terms of the Pact, some two-thirds of the territory of Abyssinia would be ceded to Italy in return for recognition of the right of the Emperor to rule the remaining third and the granting of a corridor to the sea. When these terms became known, there occurred one of those occasional moral convulsions that from time to time disturb the equanimity of the normally robust British conscience, and which even succeeded in moving *The Times* from the torpidity (which was already becoming a noticeable feature of its editorial attitudes) whenever dictators were on the march. Baldwin had to bow before the storm of protest;[90] Hoare was removed and replaced by Anthony Eden; the Hoare–Laval Pact was buried; the ineffective and half-hearted application of sanctions continued until the Italians entered Addis Ababa in May 1936. It was not a glorious episode in British history, and the damage to the League was mortal.

The Abyssinian episode also emphasized a highly significant part of Churchill's attitudes to the German menace. In a speech in the Commons on 24 October he had spelt out his position clearly: 'Germany is already well on her way to become, and must become, incomparably the most heavily armed nation in the world, and the nation most completely ready for war. *There* is the dominant factor; *there* is the factor which dwarfs all others.'

90. The deliberations of the Cabinet on 18 December, from which Hoare was absent, were removed from the bound volumes of the Cabinet Minutes and Conclusions, but are now available in a separate file. Chamberlain was virtually the only minister who was prepared to put Hoare's case, and it was the overwhelming majority view that Hoare must resign.

From the moment that his attention had turned back to European affairs Churchill had been obsessed by German ambitions to the exclusion of all other perils. On virtually all the major international crises of the 1930s involving unilateral belligerence by other totalitarian regimes his position was somewhat equivocal. In effect he condoned Japanese aggression in Manchuria; his attitude to the Abyssinia question was something less than heroic; he supported the Franco regime in the Spanish Civil War. In taking such attitudes Churchill may well have been realistic, but his approach served to divorce him from those in Britain and elsewhere who were slowly beginning to see in the European and world situation a clash between fundamental ideologies. Churchill saw it in purely nationalistic terms, and when the question is posed as to why Churchill's efforts to awaken the nation to its peril so conspicuously failed, this factor requires emphasis.

Churchill's clearest statement on Japanese aggression against Manchuria was made in a speech in the House of Commons in February 1933:

> I do not think that the League of Nations would be well advised to have a quarrel with Japan . . . I hope we shall try in England to understand a little the position of Japan, an ancient State, with the highest sense of national honour and patriotism and with a teeming population and a remarkable energy. On the one side they see the dark menace of Soviet Russia. On the other, the chaos of China, four or five provinces of which are now being tortured under Communist rule.

His attitudes towards Italian Fascism were not hostile. In 1926 when he visited Italy he had expressed warm approval of Mussolini, declaring that he had been 'charmed as so many other people have been by Signor Mussolini's gentle and simple bearing and by his calm detached poise', and that 'if I had been an Italian I am sure that I should have been wholeheartedly with you from start to finish in your triumphant struggle against the bestial appetites and passions of Leninism'. It was his view that 'externally, your movement has rendered a service to the whole world', and that the new regime was 'the necessary antidote to the Russian poison'. He was hailed by

the Italian press as 'the only British statesman who under-
stands the spirit of Fascismo', and, less flatteringly, was
greeted with cheerful cries of 'Mussolini!' when he next appeared in the House of Commons. If it may be deemed unfair
to resurrect these statements from the distant past, it may be
noted that on 26 May 1935 he described the Italian leader as 'a
really great man'[91] and wrote on 10 October 1937 – after the
invasion and conquest of Abyssinia – that: 'It would be a
dangerous folly for the British people to underrate the enduring
position in world-history which Mussolini will hold; or the
amazing qualities of courage, comprehension, self-control and
perseverance which he exemplifies.'[92]

Churchill's attitude to Italian aggression in Abyssinia and the
imposition of sanctions by the League of Nations fully justified
Arthur Greenwood's complaint that he 'succeeded in boxing
the compass . . . He has been trying to have it both ways.'[93]
It was Churchill's view that the Government was 'justified in
going so far with the League of Nations against Italy as we
could carry France', but he opposed putting pressure upon
France 'because of her military convention with Italy and her
German preoccupations'. This in effect meant doing nothing at
all. Britain, he told the Commons on 11 July, must not become
'a sort of bell-wether or fugleman to lead opinion in Europe
against Italy's Abyssinian designs . . . We are not strong
enough to be the lawgiver and the spokesman of the world.' He
regarded the episode as 'a very small matter compared to the
[German] dangers I have just described', and declared (24
October) that 'no one can keep up the pretence that Abyssinia
is a fit, worthy, and equal member of a League of civilised
nations'. Nor, no doubt, was she; but she was a member of the
League, and she was in imminent danger of suffering aggression.

There was a valid logic in Churchill's attitude to the Abyssinia crisis, given the context of the central fact of his approach
to the European situation. The entire episode was a hideous

91. *Sunday Chronicle*, 26 May 1935.
92. *News of the World*, 10 October 1937.
93. House of Commons, 22 October 1935.

embarrassment at a moment when it seemed that the chances were auspicious for effecting a permanent independence of Italy from Germany. Compared with this objective, the fate of the Abyssinians was relatively a matter of little moment. In this appraisal he had general support, and not least from Vansittart, the true author of the Hoare–Laval Pact. But this logic was grievously at fault, for it wholly ignored the position and authority of the League – already gravely compromised by the Manchurian episode – and it also ignored feelings in Britain, a fact that was given dramatic emphasis by the storm over the Hoare–Laval Pact. Churchill was in Spain, and he was urged by some friends to return to London. Others urged him to stay away. Churchill accepted the latter course. He has written that he subsequently regretted his decision not to return: 'I might have brought an element of decision and combination to the anti-government gatherings which would have ended the Baldwin regime.'[94] This is a highly doubtful contention. Hoare's critics on the Conservative benches lacked neither decisiveness nor unity, and both might have been irreparably harmed by Churchill's intervention. And, if he had intervened, what could he have said? If consistent, he should have supported the Government; if intent on ending the 'Baldwin regime', he would have had to abandon his previous attitudes on the issue. It may be judged that it was a lucky chance that found him in Spain at this time.

The crisis over the Hoare–Laval Pact was of very real significance. The Italian policy itself had resulted in a new awareness in the Labour movement of the nature of Fascist aggression and had led directly to the downfall of Lansbury. The condonation of that aggression and the desertion of the League of Nations aroused an opposition that was surprisingly widespread and had no relevance to party lines. Churchill's attitude demonstrated that he saw the possibilities of the League simply in terms of containing Germany. As he was by now developing the theme of 'Arms and the Covenant' (of the League), this aspect requires some attention. Churchill's lack of practical interest in the League beforehand has been noted;

94. *The Gathering Storm*, p. 144.

his somewhat belated attention to its possibilities lacked
ultimate conviction, and was solely directed towards building
up popular feelings in favour of rearmament and hostility to
Germany.

On 13 July 1934 he said that 'the League of Nations should
be the great instrument upon which all those resolved to maintain peace should centre' – but it would appear that this was
not applicable when the victims were Chinese or Abyssinian.
By March 1936, by which time the position of the League had
been fatally undermined, Churchill was saying that 'in fostering
and fortifying the League of Nations will be found the best
means of defending our island security', and that 'if the
League of Nations were able to enforce its decree upon one of the
most powerful nations of the world found to be an aggressor,
then its authority would be set upon so high a pedestal that it
must henceforth be the accepted sovereign authority by which
all the quarrels of the people can be determined and controlled'
(House of Commons, 13 March 1936). This conversion – if it
really can be described as such – came somewhat late. No
doubt the members of the League of Nations Union were guilty
of what Churchill described in November 1932 as their 'long-
suffering and inexhaustible gullibility', but their existence was
in itself evidence of a genuine and deeply-felt attachment to the
League, which was not shared (among many others) by
Churchill, Vansittart or Duff Cooper. And it can be argued that
the real significance of the Peace Ballot organized by the
League of Nations Union in 1934–5 lay in the answers to the
question, 'Do you consider that if a nation insists on attacking
another, the other nations should combine to compel it to stop
by (a) economic and non-military measures? (b) if necessary,
military measures?' Eleven million answered (a) in the affirmative, and nearly eight million approved (b). As this is the
nearest approach to a referendum on world affairs in the 1930s
that we possess, it is perhaps right to attach some significance
to it.

Churchill's attitude to the Spanish Civil War, which is
described later,[95] was wholly consistent with his approach to

95. See pp. 406–409 below.

the Abyssinian episode. Macmillan has recorded that 'I remember Churchill talking to me with great fervour on this aspect of the Spanish question. He decided to declare himself neutral, for his eye was on the real enemy.'[96] Churchill's 'neutrality' may be questioned, as may his definition of 'the real enemy'. It is not being suggested that Italy or Spain represented a comparable threat to Britain as did Germany, but Churchill's concentration on what he deemed the central issue cut him off from a substantial potential public support, and reminds us of the essential truth of Esher's comment in 1917 to which reference has already been made.[97]

*

Churchill returned from his Spanish holiday in January 1936 upon the death of King George V. The Government had not recovered from the shock of the Hoare–Laval crisis, and as the Abyssinian war continued on its miserable course, dissatisfaction with ministers grew. Baldwin's advisers pressed upon him the necessity for strengthening the Government, and the names of Austen Chamberlain, Churchill and even – somewhat surprisingly – Hoare, were discussed. In particular, the case for a Minister of Defence, so long urged by Churchill in speeches and newspaper articles, was seriously considered.

On 7 March, shortly before the Government's decision was announced, Hitler marched troops into the Rhineland. This electrifying coup was immediately followed by proposals for settling the outstanding issues in Europe, a technique of following unilateral action with soothing assurances that was practised for the first time. Hitler had correctly gauged the reaction of Britain and France. The Government took the advice of Eden, that no military action should be contemplated unless France or Belgium were directly threatened with aggression; that the French should be strongly discouraged from taking any military action on their own; and that renewed attempts should be made to reach 'as far-reaching and enduring a settlement as possible [with Germany] while Herr

96. Macmillan, op. cit., p. 475.
97. See p. 52 above.

Hitler is still in the mood to do so'.[98] The argument that this was the moment for 'stopping' Hitler has been propounded incessantly since then, but the argument is an academic one. Lothian's comment that the Germans were only moving into 'their own back-garden' has been often cited, usually with derision, but Lothian's point was a solid one; as he wrote in September 1936, 'So far, Hitler has done little more than resume for Germany the essential rights of equality that are accorded to all sovereign states.'[99] This comment only makes sense in the context of the derogation of the Treaty of Versailles, and in the belief in a sovereign, strong, independent Germany to which reference has already been made. By his action Hitler ignored treaty obligations and, with one stroke, gravely upset the military balance in Europe. But the deed was done, and to overrun it required a decisive and united action by Britain and France whose implications must have necessarily included the threat of force. In short, the choice was between threatening a preventive war or accepting Hitler's action as a *fait accompli*.

The evidence is overwhelming that there was no realistic chance of following the former course. Harold Nicolson, who saw the full implications of what had happened, spelt out the dilemma in a letter to his wife on 12 March:

. . . if we send an ultimatum to Germany, she ought in all reason to climb down. But then she will not climb down and we shall have war. Naturally we shall win and enter Berlin. But what is the good of that? It would only mean communism in Germany and France, and that is why the French are so keen on it. Moreover, the people of this country absolutely refuse to have a war. We should be faced by a general strike if we even suggested such a thing. We shall therefore have to climb down ignominiously and Hitler will have scored . . .[100]

On 23 March he noted in his diary: 'The feeling in the House is terribly "pro-German", which means afraid of war.'[101] Eden described Hitler's offer of negotiations as being evidence of

98. PRO CAB 16 (36).
99. *Round Table*, Vol. 26, p. 664.
100. Nicolson: *Diaries and Letters 1930–39*, pp. 249–50.
101. ibid., p. 254.

Germany's 'unchangeable longing for a real pacification of Europe', and won general approval when he said that the objectives of British foreign policy were to avert war, to create the conditions for negotiation, to strengthen collective security and that 'it is the appeasement of Europe as a whole that we have constantly before us'.[102] The attitude of the Opposition parties was quite clear; Dalton stated the obvious when he said that public opinion, particularly in the Labour Party, would not tolerate military or even economic sanctions against Germany. Although few went so far as the *Spectator*, which declared that the remilitarization of the Rhineland was 'a small thing in itself', there was virtually no support, in the Government or outside it, for action against Germany that necessarily involved the implied threat of force. The attitude of the French Government, as we now know, was far less resolute than Churchill and others have described it;[103] even if Britain, the dominant partner in the alliance, had held firm, the strong probability – virtually a certainty – is that she would have had to do so alone. But it is, as has been remarked, very much an academic argument.

The event occurred at a peculiarly difficult moment for Churchill. He agreed with Austen Chamberlain that a serious, well-nigh irreparable, blow had been struck, not merely at the sanctity of treaties but at the balance of power in Europe. As he wrote at the time: 'There has rarely been a crisis in which Hope and Peril have presented themselves so vividly and so simultaneously upon the world scene.'[104] Like Austen Chamberlain – who warned the House of Commons that Austria would be the next objective, and that 'if Austria perishes, Czechoslovakia becomes indefensible' – he saw the full probable implications for Britain and Europe. But he also knew that the appointment of the Minister of Defence was hanging in the balance. His speech on 9 March was therefore careful and mild. He subsequently wrote that 'I was careful not to derogate in the slightest degree from my attitude of severe though friendly

102. House of Commons, 9 March.
103. *The Gathering Storm*, pp. 151–4.
104. *Evening Standard*, 13 March.

criticism of Government policy, and I was held to have made a successful speech.'[105] The friendliness is more evident than the severity. Neville Chamberlain recorded that Churchill had 'suppressed the attack he had intended and made a constructive and helpful speech'.[106]

On 12 March Baldwin announced the appointment of a new post, that of Minister for the Co-ordination of Defence, which was a very different thing from the expected appointment of a Minister of Defence. Furthermore, the post was to go to the Attorney General, Sir Thomas Inskip. The general astonishment at this choice was shared by Inskip himself, who said that 'I may say with all sincerity that it never occurred to me that I was likely to be asked to accept these responsibilities. Nor did it ever occur to me – I can say this in all seriousness – that I would ever be able to discharge these duties even if they were offered to me.' What chances Churchill had had of the appointment – and the available evidence suggests that they were not great, particularly in view of Neville Chamberlain's growing interest in the whole machinery of Government and in the conduct of foreign affairs – had been destroyed by the German action in the Rhineland and the Government's decision to work actively for better Anglo-German relations. As Chamberlain wrote at the time, Inskip 'would excite no enthusiasm but he would involve us in no fresh perplexities'.[107] Duff Cooper,

105. *The Gathering Storm*, p. 156.

106. Feiling: *Chamberlain*, p. 193. In a newspaper article on 13 March Churchill emphasized the dangerous implication of unilateral abrogations of treaties for the peace of Europe, and urged that the League should exercise the powers that its members possessed. 'The Constabulary of the world is at hand.' But the main theme of the article was an appeal to Hitler 'and the great disconsolate Germany he leads . . . to place themselves in the very forefront of civilisation. By a proud and voluntary submission not to any single country or group of countries, but to the sanctity of Treaties and the authority of public law, by an immediate withdrawal from the Rhineland, they may open a new era for all mankind and create conditions in which German genius may gain its highest glory.' He also wrote that 'instead of retaliating with arms, as the previous generation would have, France has taken the correct course by appealing to the League of Nations.'

107. Macleod: *Chamberlain*, p. 193.

according to one account, was among those who considered that Churchill's chance had long passed.[108] General Ellison wrote thankfully: 'As regards the Inskip appointment I have only one comment, and that is "Thank God we are preserved from Winston Churchill." '[109]

Churchill's feelings about this rejection can be easily seen from his account in *The Gathering Storm*, when he makes use of the episode to carry his portrait of Baldwin one stage further:

> Mr Baldwin certainly had good reason to use the last flickers of his power against one who had exposed his mistakes so severely and so often. Moreover, as a profoundly astute party manager, thinking in majorities and aiming at a quiet life between elections, he did not wish to have my disturbing aid. He thought, no doubt, that he had dealt me a politically fatal stroke, and I felt he might well be right. How little can we foresee the consequences either of wise or unwise action, of virtue or of malice![110]

For an ambitious man, and particularly for an ageing ambitious man, it is always unpleasant to be passed over. It is even less tolerable when it is the reward for sacrificing the pleasures of bold independent criticism at a critical moment. From October 1935 to March 1936 Churchill had not delivered one major speech of criticism of ministers comparable to his assaults of the previous four years. Now, with hope twice deferred, a harsher note was struck.

*

By the summer of 1936 the position of the Baldwin Government was manifestly weakening. Its prestige, already undermined by the Hoare–Laval Pact, was further shaken by the ignominious abandonment of sanctions in June 1936, an event also significant in that it marked the first public intervention by Neville Chamberlain in foreign affairs. Chamberlain's description of the policy of sanctions as 'the height of midsummer madness' was a deliberate rebuff for Eden. Lord Swinton has commented that

108. Liddell Hart, op. cit., pp. 319–20.
109. R. F. V. Heuston: *Lives of The Lord Chancellors*, p. 589.
110. *The Gathering Storm*, p. 157.

'a man beaten once in politics at this level can be beaten again. Chamberlain knew from that moment that he had the measure of Eden.'[111] The Government emerged from the ensuing debate intact, but without distinction. From the Opposition benches Arthur Greenwood denounced 'this trembling, vacillating, cowardly government, which is leading people backward instead of forward', while Lloyd George depicted ministers in full retreat, 'running away, brandishing their swords – still leading!' Writing of Baldwin and MacDonald on 13 July, Churchill commented that both 'excelled in the art of minimizing political issues, of frustrating large schemes of change, of depressing the national temperature, and reducing Parliament to a humdrum level . . . If the supreme need of John Bull after the war and its aftermath was a rest-cure, no two nurses were better fitted to help silence around a darkened room and protect the patient from anything in the nature of mental stress or strong emotion.'

There were several indications that Baldwin's mastery over the House of Commons was faltering. He was in fact on the verge of a nervous breakdown, and the strain of thirteen years of party leadership, most of which had been in high office, was beginning to tell. When, on 22 May, Winterton invited some friends to his Sussex house, Shillinglee Park – including Austen Chamberlain, Croft and Churchill – the incident was given much prominence. Baldwin's comment in the House of Commons that it was 'the time of year when midges come out of dirty ditches' was uncharacteristic. But there had been a sharpness in his exchanges with Churchill since the appointment of Inskip that was reminiscent of some of the India debates. On 6 May, to take one example, Churchill had intervened briefly at the end of a debate on Abyssinia to criticize Baldwin for not taking part; he was warmly cheered from the Labour benches, but the Conservatives reacted with angry shouts.[112] When Parliament

111. Swinton: *Sixty Years of Power*, p. 166.
112. See Dalton, *The Fateful Years*, p. 93, for an account of this incident. It was at this time that Baldwin remarked to Tom Jones: 'One of these days I'll make a few casual remarks about Winston. Not a speech – no oratory – just a few words in passing. I've got it all ready. I am going to

adjourned for the summer recess, ministers were more than ordinarily thankful for the respite.

Shortly before this, Churchill had succeeded in arranging for a deputation of senior Conservatives in both Houses of Parliament to discuss rearmament with Baldwin, Halifax and Inskip. Despite attempts by Churchill, the two Opposition parties declined to take part. Churchill has described it as 'a great occasion. I cannot recall anything like it in what I have seen of British public life . . . If the leaders of the Labour and Liberal Oppositions had come with us, there might have been a political situation so tense as to enforce remedial action.'[113]

This is not quite the impression that is derived from a reading of the proceedings of the meetings on 28 and 29 July, or of a subsequent one in November.[114] The exchanges were very similar to those that had already taken place in Parliament, although some points were made with a stronger emphasis. Churchill made a long statement, in the course of which he said:

. . . Germany has the power at any time henceforward to send a fleet of aeroplanes capable of discharging in a single voyage at least 500 tons of bombs upon London. We know from our war statistics what the destruction of lives and property was per ton dropped. One ton of explosive bombs killed 10 people and wounded 30, and did £50,000 worth of damage. Of course, it would be absurd to assume that the whole bombing fleet of Germany would make an endless succession of voyages to and from this country. All kinds of other considerations intervene. Still, as a practical measure of the relative power of the bombing fleets of the two countries, the weight of discharge per voyage is a very considerable measure . . .

He then repeated his figures of the existing size of the German air force, and emphasized the significance of a weapon

---

say that when Winston was born lots of fairies swooped down on his cradle bearing gifts – imagination, eloquence, industry, ability, and then came a fairy who said "No one person has a right to so many gifts," picked him up and gave him such a shake and twist that with all these gifts he was denied judgement and wisdom. And that is why, while we delight to listen to him in this House, we do not take his advice' (Jones, op. cit., p. 204).

113. *The Gathering Storm*, pp. 178–9.
114. PRO Premier 1/193.

with which he was particularly obsessed at this time, a 'therm-ite bomb', which was 'little bigger than an orange', and which had devastating penetrative effects. 'A single medium aeroplane can scatter 500. One must expect in a small raid literally tens of thousands of these bombs, which burn through from storey to storey . . . Nothing like it has ever been seen in world history.' No direct reply was made to these remarks, although the Air Ministry figures again challenged Churchill's estimates of German air strength, supplied by General Milch of the Luft-waffe.[115]

The most remarkable feature of this meeting was, however, the contribution of Baldwin in reply to the deputation's remarks:

. . . Most of you sit for safe seats. You do not represent industrial constituencies; at least, not many of you. There was a very strong, I do not know about pacifist, but pacific feeling in the country after the war . . . It was a question in 1934 whether if you tried to do much you might not have imperilled and more than imperilled, you might have lost the General Election when it came. I personally felt that very strongly, and the one thing in my mind was the necessity of winning an election as soon as you could and getting a perfectly free hand with arms. That was the first thing to do in a democracy, the first thing to do, and I think we took it at the first moment possible . . . We fought the election, and we won it and won it more handsomely than anyone in this room, I think, would have expected before the election. That was a great thing done. It was done, and you had the support of the democracy for your arma-ments . . .

I am not going to get this country into a war with anybody for the League of Nations or anybody else or for anything else . . .

115. Absolute confirmation that Milch was the source may be found in PRO 5 (37) 42. This paper was filed separately from the rest of the Cabinet Conclusions for 1937. It was opened in 1954 by the late Sir Norman Brooke, who minuted that 'the figures are no longer of such secrecy that the envelope need be re-sealed. 2-11-54.' The important point, of course, was not the figures of German air strength but the source, which was Milch, and the recipient, who was the Deputy Chief of the Air Staff. The confidence of the Air Staff in their figures of German strength, as opposed to those of Churchill and the Foreign Office, is explicable. See also Colvin: *Vansittart in Office*, pp. 133–4.

The final exchange between Churchill and Baldwin may also be noted:

MR CHURCHILL: ... I certainly do not consider war with Germany inevitable, but I am sure the way to make it much less likely is to afford concrete evidence of our determination in setting about rearmament.

PRIME MINISTER: I am with you on that.

MR CHRCHILL: I am sure that is a Bull point.

PRIME MINISTER: I am with you there whole-heartedly.

*

The Government had had a bad nine months, and in these circumstances Churchill's stock was beginning to rise again. For the first time he had the nucleus of a wider support in his campaign. The creation of the World Anti-Nazi Council in London, whose chairman was Walter Citrine, general secretary of the TUC, was one sign of the changing temper. Another was the 'Focus' group, which had held its first meeting at the Victoria Hotel in June 1935. As one of its leading members, Lady Asquith (then Lady Violet Bonham Carter) has written: 'We had at the outset no material and little moral backing. We were a small group of likeminded individuals swimming against the tide – not only of government policy but of the prevailing public attitude and mood.'[116] The sixteen persons who attended this first meeting included an émigré German, Eugen Spier, Churchill, Lady Violet, Sir Robert Mond, Wickham Steed and Sir Archibald Sinclair. Churchill spoke after the lunch, and urged that the group should issue a manifesto and attempt to recruit members, and a drafting committee for this purpose was set up, with Steed as its chairman. There then occurred an interesting episode, described by Spier:

The secretary agreed, but asked where the money to defray expenses was to come from. His bald request came like the explosion of a bomb. Expressions of embarrassment appeared on every side, and Churchill himself looked displeased, even angry. For a moment it looked as if the whole effort was about to come to grief. To avert

116. Foreword to E. Spier: *Focus* (1963), p. 9.

catastrophe I took Richards[117] aside and asked him to announce
that all our requirements had been taken care of. The tension was
immediately eased. Churchill seemed greatly relieved and the other
guests were clearly delighted.[118]

It was decided that the group should not become formalized,
but should describe itself as 'a "focus" for defence of freedom
and peace, and to have neither rules nor members'.[119] Those
connected with Focus included members of the main political
parties and distinguished outsiders such as Lord Cecil of Chel-
wood, Professor Gilbert Murray and Kingsley Martin.

Focus did not, in itself, achieve very much.[120] It was of
importance, however, in a wider context, for it brought together men and women with very different political backgrounds
and interests to discuss the one subject on which their views
converged. The fruit of this association was the 'Arms and the
Covenant' movement, which began to make some real progress
in 1936, greatly assisted by the succession of Government
humiliations and failures. Its first large meeting was arranged
for 3 December at the Albert Hall, intended to be the first of a
series, in which leading representatives of the main political
parties and the distinguished outsiders would put forward the
case for strengthening the League of Nations and British defence
(the order of priorities tended to vary in each case).[121]

Three weeks before this meeting, Churchill had one of his
greatest successes in the House of Commons. On 12 November,
in the debate on the Address, he delivered one of the most
brilliant of his philippics on the deficiencies in Britain's air
defences, that included this passage: 'The Government simply
cannot make up their minds, or they cannot get the Prime
Minister to make up his mind. So they go on in strange paradox,
decided only to be undecided, resolved to be irresolute, adamant

117. A. H. Richards, who had arranged the meeting.
118. Spier, op. cit., p. 22.
119. ibid., p. 25.
120. For a fair criticism of Focus, see D. C. Watt, op. cit. pp. 133–4.
121. Churchill (*The Gathering Storm*, pp. 195–6) gives the incorrect
impression that this was the culminating meeting of the campaign, when it
was in fact the beginning of it.

for drift, solid for fluidity, all-powerful to be impotent. So we go on preparing more months and years – precious, perhaps vital, to the greatness of Britain – for the locusts to eat.'

In reply Baldwin made a speech that has haunted his reputation to and beyond the grave. His custom of departing from his notes and speaking extempore to the House, taking it, as it were, into his personal confidence, had been one of the secrets of his great mastery over the Commons. On this occasion it betrayed him. He said that he would speak to the House 'with appalling frankness', and the fatal passage ran as follows – fatal because, if quoted out of context it was damning: 'Supposing I had gone to the country, and said that Germany was rearming and that we must rearm, does anybody think that this pacifist democracy would have rallied to that cry at that moment? I cannot think of anything that would have made the loss of the election from my point of view more certain.'

In *The Gathering Storm* Churchill pounced on this passage which, he averred, referred to the 1935 election and, he claimed, 'carried naked truth about his motives into indecency'. The index reference rubs in the message: 'Baldwin, Rt Hon. Stanley . . . confesses putting party before country.' Churchill did not continue the quotation from Baldwin's speech which made it clear that Baldwin was talking of an election in 1933, and contained the statement that the 1935 election had been fought on this issue, and 'we got from the country, with a large majority, a mandate for doing a thing that no one, twelve months before, would have believed possible.' Baldwin's supporters, and independent commentators with no personal interest involved, have pointed out time and again the inaccuracy and unfairness of Churchill's charge.[122] But it has stuck.

122. See, in particular, R. Bassett: 'Telling the truth to the people: the myth of the Baldwin "confession"', *Cambridge Journal*, November 1948, and the subsequent correspondence. But it may be noted that G. H. Gathorne-Hardy's *A Short History of International Affairs, 1920–39*, whose Fourth Edition was first printed in 1950 and which was reprinted in 1952, 1960 and 1964, states that 'a democratic electorate grew so opposed to the least hint of rearmament that when this policy became urgently necessary, a British Prime Minister was deterred from advocating it by the fear of

The important fact at the time was that the House itself was disconcerted by Baldwin's frankness. This episode, on top of the long saga of ministerial failures throughout the year, dealt the Government another blow to its sagging repute, and gave the Arms and the Covenant movement a new encouragement. Then, at this apparently hopeful moment, the situation was reversed.

*

Throughout the summer and early autumn of 1936 the American and European press had been absorbed in the relationship between King Edward VIII and Mrs Wallis Simpson. This relationship had been common knowledge in London society and the political world for several months before his accession to the throne in January 1936, but even in these circles the possibility of the King marrying Mrs Simpson had not been seriously considered. Walter Monckton, who was to become the King's principal confidant and agent for negotiations with the Government, has written that 'I did not, before November 1936, think that marriage between the King and Mrs Simpson was contemplated . . . I thought throughout, long before, as well as after there was talk of marriage, that if and when the stark choice faced them between their love and his obligations as King-Emperor, they would in the end each make the sacrifice, devastating though it may be.'[123] The British people were unaware of the situation, as the British press maintained a self-imposed silence on the matter, in increasingly marked contrast to the flaring headlines and eager speculations abroad. On 27 October Mrs Simpson was awarded a decree nisi against her husband, Mr Ernest Simpson, at Ipswich, but the British press, in response to a personal appeal from the King to Beaverbrook, reported the case without comment.

Baldwin had been told as early as February that it was the

---

losing an election', and cites the same extract as Churchill from Baldwin's speech. The similarities between the November speech and Baldwin's statement to the Conservative deputation in July, quoted on p. 266, do not require notice.

123. Lord Birkenhead: *Walter Monckton – The Life of Viscount Monckton of Branchley*, pp. 123–4.

King's intention to marry Mrs Simpson when she was free, but the sources of the information were indirect, and both he and his close friend J. C. C. Davidson had found the suggestion literally unbelievable.[124] The King concealed his intentions from the Prime Minister, his solicitor, Mr Theodore Goddard, and even from Beaverbrook and Walter Monckton.[125] It was not until 16 November that he informed Baldwin of his determination, and the crisis that followed, which has often been related, lasted for three weeks. Although Baldwin's attitude to the King was extremely sympathetic – for which he received little thanks, then or afterwards – the situation was an impossible one to resolve. There had been, on the King's part, a lack of candour in his relations with the Prime Minister; on Baldwin's side, there had been a failure of nerve to lay the matter squarely before the King in October, although the onus surely lay on the King to inform Baldwin of his intentions. But from the outset of the crisis Baldwin was convinced that the country would not take the twice-married Mrs Simpson on any terms. The attitude of the rest of the Royal Family was intensely antagonistic to the lady. The views of the official Labour and Liberal parties were emphatic in the same sense. There seems no evidence to support Beaverbrook's charge that Baldwin had long intended to get rid of the King;[126] indeed, all the available evidence is that he endeavoured to keep the King on the throne, but without Mrs Simpson. The King would not have this. The impasse, from which there was only one way out, was the result of these two incompatible requirements. By the end of November the main question was how long the news could be kept out of the British newspapers, and when the constitutional crisis would be brought out into the open. This occurred on 3 December.

*

In the weeks preceding the crisis Churchill was not personally involved to a significant extent. He knew of the rumours, and he had means of knowing how justified they were. When Walter

124. R. K. Middlemas and J. Barnes: *Stanley Baldwin*, p. 980.
125. Beaverbrook: *The Abdication of King Edward VIII*, p. 37.
126. Beaverbrook, op. cit., pp. 13–15.

Monckton spoke to him in June about the situation, he expressed his opposition to a divorce and remarked that he regarded the presence of Mrs Simpson 'as a safeguard'. He urged Monckton to impress upon the King the importance of the fact 'that his friendship [with Mrs Simpson] should not be flaunted in the eyes of the public'.[127] As Churchill quickly discovered, the advice was wholly ignored. On 17 November Lord Salisbury headed a deputation of senior politicians that consulted with Baldwin; Churchill was invited to attend, but declined. On the morning of 25 November he took part in a considerably more important meeting with Baldwin, attended by Attlee and Sinclair. Baldwin asked them if they would support the Government if the matter came to the point of resignation. Attlee and Sinclair said that they would not form an administration if they were invited; Baldwin's biographers state that 'Churchill replied that "though his attitude was a little different, he would certainly support the Government".'[128] It was not until Friday, 4 December that the King, with Baldwin's permission, discussed the situation with Churchill. By this time it was too late for his advice to have any decisive effect on the King's position, but it was not too late to damage himself.

On 3 December the Arms and the Covenant movement had its first great meeting in the Albert Hall. Citrine was in the chair. Leading members of the Conservative and Liberal Parties, the League of Nations Union and the trade union movement were present. 'We had the feeling,' Churchill has written, 'that we were on the threshold of not only gaining respect for our views but of making them dominant.'[129]

Just before he left for the Albert Hall Churchill saw the draft of a broadcast speech which the King wanted to deliver to the nation. Citrine relates that Churchill said to him just before the meeting – which was late in starting as a result of Churchill's delay – that 'people will expect a statement from me' about the King. Citrine said that the meeting had nothing to do with the King, and that 'you will certainly be challenged, and if no one

127. Birkenhead: *Walter Monckton*, pp. 129–30.
128. Middlemas and Barnes, op. cit., p. 999.
129. *The Gathering Storm*, p. 170.

else does I will.' Churchill was taken aback, and said that 'I must consider my position.'[130]

Before Churchill replied to the Vote of Thanks there was a cry of 'God Save the King' and prolonged cheering. According to his account[131] Churchill made a short speech in which he said that 'I hope and pray that no irrevocable decision will be taken in haste, but that time and public opinion will be allowed to play their part, and that a cherished and unique personality may not be incontinently severed from the people he loves so well.' Churchill claimed that he made this declaration 'on the spur of the moment', but no available contemporary record that the author has discovered refers to this section of his speech. Citrine states specifically that Churchill did not refer to the King at all,[132] and this is confirmed by the account of Lady Violet Bonham Carter:

I knew, of course, where Winston stood in this conflict and I feared that he would do grave harm to his own fortunes (which had risen so high after his last powerful House of Commons speech) and to our cause, of which he was the spearhead.

I had once or twice tried to reason with him, and had been met by black hostility. I realized that what had (as I thought) misled him were in part his noble qualities – his romantic and protective loyalty and his emotional sympathy with the human needs of his young King – and in part his inability to gauge or guess at the reaction of the ordinary man and woman. Did hostility to Baldwin play a part, as many thought and openly suggested? They may have added a cutting edge to his emotions, but the first two reasons I have given were in themselves enough.

When I set out for the Albert Hall that night my expectancy was pierced by a sharp 'needle' of apprehension. I knew that Winston could never think of two things at once. Would his eye be 'off the ball' tonight?

Huge crowds were surging round the Albert Hall when I arrived. Groups of Communists and Fascists were distributing leaflets and attempting demonstrations. I went to the Green Room where the speakers had been told to assemble, and found there Walter Citrine,

130. Citrine: *Men and Work*, p. 357.
131. *The Gathering Storm*, pp. 170–1.
132. *Men and Work*, p. 357.

who was to take the chair, Victor Lytton, Archie Sinclair and other key figures from the Focus and the League of Nations Union.

When Winston arrived I knew at a glance that our anxiety was justified. His face was sombre and overcast. He went straight up to Citrine and said that he felt that at this critical juncture in our affairs he must make some statement about the present crisis. Both Citrine and Victor Lytton expressed strong disagreement. It would be fatal to introduce this unresolved, contentious and extraneous issue, and would distract the audience from our main purpose . . .

Finally, as time was getting short, Walter Citrine declared quite firmly that if this was Mr Churchill's intention, he could not take the chair. This clinched the matter. . . . But though Winston was obliged to bow to Citrine's ultimatum, I could see how much he minded being overridden.

And so we all filed on to the crowded platform and were given a tumultuous reception. I felt throughout my own speech that I had never spoken to a more responsive and inspiring audience.

At last came Winston's turn. He got a tremendous reception, and of course he made a good speech. (He could not make a bad one.) But many of us felt that he was not at the zenith of his form, and of course we knew why. His heart and mind were engaged elsewhere. At the end of the meeting he commented to Mr Spier on the enthusiasm with which the audience had sung the National Anthem, which he interpreted as an endorsement of his attitude on the royal marriage issue.[133]

The most reasonable deduction is that Churchill came to the meeting intending to refer to the royal crisis, but never did. In any event, Churchill was carried away by what he judged to be the enthusiasm of the audience for the royalist cause and saw in it the views of the British people. In this he was fatally wrong.

After the meeting he conferred with Beaverbrook and Mr Allen, the King's Solicitor, at Stornoway House (Beaverbrook's London home) on the draft broadcast. Both Churchill and Beaverbrook doubted whether the Cabinet would give permission for it to be delivered, and, on the following day, were proved correct.

By this stage abdication had virtually been agreed upon.

133. *Daily Telegraph*, 11 March 1965.

Churchill was appalled, and when on 4 December he saw the
King, he urged him vehemently not to abdicate. He also urged –
as did Duff Cooper – the importance of reflection. Monckton
records that 'His advice was that the King should ask for time.
He said that he could not say that the King would win through
if he stood and fought, but that he ought to take time to see
what measure of support he received. 'His presence was a great
encouragement to the King, who liked him and mimicked his
mannerisms superbly without the slightest malice: 'We must
have time for the big battalions to mass. We may win; we may
not. Who can tell?' Monckton's biographer comments that
'The King was affected, but only temporarily, by Churchill's
zeal.' [134]

The King has recalled that Churchill had said that 'whatever
else might happen . . . the hereditary principle must not be left
to the mercy of politicians trimming their doctrines "to the
varying hour".' [135] Churchill seems to have come away with the
impression that he had made progress. When Beaverbrook told
him bluntly on the following day that 'our cock won't fight', he
could not convince him of the fact; 'he would not believe my
miserable news'. [136]

On 5 December Churchill issued a public statement appealing
for delay. It was a lengthy document and it contained the clear
implication that the King was being forced into a hasty decision
by the Government:

I plead for time and patience. The nation must realize the character
of the constitutional issue. There is no question of any conflict
between the King and Parliament. Parliament has not been consulted in any way, nor allowed to express any opinion.
The question is whether the King is to abdicate upon the advice
of the Ministers of the Day. No such advice has ever before been
tendered to a Sovereign in Parliamentary times . . .
In this case we are in presence of a wish expressed by the Sovereign
to perform an act which in no circumstances can be accomplished for

134. Birkenhead: *Walter Monckton*, p. 144.
135. Duke of Windsor: *A King's Story*, p. 382.
136. Beaverbrook, op. cit., p. 80.

nearly five months, and may conceivably, for various reasons, never be accomplished at all.

That, on such a hypothetical and suppositious basis, the supreme sacrifice of abdication and potential exile of the Sovereign should be demanded, finds no support whatever in the British Constitution. No Ministry has the authority to advise the abdication of the Sovereign. Only the most serious Parliamentary processes could even raise the issue in a decisive force . . . The Cabinet has no right to prejudge such a question without having previously ascertained at very least the will of Parliament.

If the King refuses to take the advice of his Ministers, they are, of course, free to resign. They have no right whatever to put pressure upon him to accept their advice by soliciting beforehand assurances from the Leader of the Opposition that he will not form an alternative administration in the event of their resignation, and thus confronting the King with an ultimatum. Again, there is cause for time and patience . . .

National and Imperial considerations alike require that before such a dread step as a demand for abdication is taken, not only should the constitutional position be newly defined by Parliament, but that every method should be exhausted, which gives the hope of a happier solution . . . if an abdication were to be hastily extorted the outrage so committed would cast its shadow forward across many chapters of the History of the British Empire . . .

Howsoever this matter may turn, it is pregnant with calamity and inseparable from inconvenience. But all the evil aspects will be aggravated beyond measure if the utmost chivalry is not shown, both by Ministers and by the British nation, toward a gifted and beloved King, torn between private and public obligations of love and duty.

The Churches stand for charity. They believe in the efficiency of prayer. Surely their influence must not oppose a period of reflection. I plead, I pray, that time and tolerance will not be denied.

The King has no means of personal access to his Parliament or his People. Between him and them stand in their office the Ministers of the Crown. If they thought it their duty to engage all their power and influence against him, still he must remain silent.

All the more must they be careful not to be the judge in their own case and show a loyal and Christian patience even at some political embarrassment to themselves . . .

The King has described this document as 'a masterly and objective exposition'.[137] In fact, it not only came too late, but by its emphasis upon what was by clear implication the unconstitutional action of ministers aroused deep resentment not merely among ministers themselves but among all those who had been involved in the abdication crisis. The King is surely wrong in stating 'under different circumstances the effect of Mr Churchill's magnificent plea on my behalf would almost certainly have been profound. It might well have reversed the situation.'[138]

It is doubtful whether this statement, delivered at any time in the crisis, would have had the slightest effect either on public opinion or on the position of the King. Matters had gone infinitely further than Churchill realized at the point that he made his ill-advised public intervention. The statement also contained at least one major inaccuracy, when he implied that the marriage of the King to Mrs Simpson 'may conceivably, for various reasons, never be accomplished at all'. If Churchill was fully cognizant of the situation, then this was a direct and deliberate misrepresentation of the facts. But it would appear that even then he was not fully aware of the extent of the King's determination to marry Mrs Simpson under whatever circumstances might be forced upon him.

Churchill was convinced that public opinion, given time, would rally round the King. This misjudgement was fatal and fundamental. 'I do not find people angry with Mrs Simpson,' Harold Nicolson recorded on 3 December; 'But I do find a deep and enraged fury against the King himself. In eight months he has destroyed the great structure of popularity which he had raised.'[139] Hugh Dalton has described the bitterness of feeling in South Wales, where the King's popularity had been supposed to be high.[140] Furthermore, when Churchill urged that 'no irrevocable decision' had been reached, he was unaware of the fact that it had already been reached by the King himself. His

137. *A King's Story*, p. 388.
138. ibid., p. 389.
139. Nicolson: *Diaries*, Vol. I, p. 282.
140. Dalton, op. cit., p. 144.

wife and friends urged him to remain silent. The Labour and
Liberal parties had made it plain that he would not give Mrs
Simpson up. There could be only one end to this unhappy
situation. Churchill subsequently wrote that Baldwin 'undoubtedly perceived and expressed the profound will of the
nations'. He proceeded on every careful step with glum
national approval until the inevitable conclusion.

In these circumstances Churchill's attempts to delay the
issue aroused intense wrath. The fact that he was supposed to
be in league with Rothermere and Beaverbrook – whose papers
consistently supported the King – did him further harm, and
the support of Oswald Mosley and his followers was even more
damaging.

On 7 December the House of Commons shouted him down
when he rose yet again to plead for delay. Amery thought that
'he was completely staggered by the unanimous hostility of the
House'. It was with some difficulty that Churchill retained
control over himself in the tumult. 'You won't be satisfied until
you've broken him, will you?' he shouted angrily at the Prime
Minister, according to one version.[141] After vainly trying to gain
a proper hearing, he lowered his head and angrily stalked out
of the Chamber; the ever-loyal Bracken left his place and
followed him. Winterton has described this episode as 'one of
the angriest manifestations I have ever heard directed against
any man in the House of Commons'.[142]

Thus were the political fortunes of Baldwin and Churchill
exactly and fatally reversed. The Premier's reputation soared
to its zenith; that of Churchill to its nadir. 'He had undone in
five minutes the patient reconstruction work of two years,'
Nicolson noted on 9 December.[143] The other members of the
Arms and the Covenant movement were dismayed or outraged
by what they, and many others, regarded as another clumsy
attempt to remove Baldwin by forming a 'King's Party'. As
Harold Macmillan has written: 'All the effect of the Albert

141. Beaverbrook, op. cit., p. 78 (footnote).
142. Winterton: *Orders of the Day*, p. 223.
143. Nicolson: *Diaries*, Vol. I, p. 284.

Hall meeting was destroyed – first by the Abdication and secondly by the catastrophic fall in Churchill's prestige. It was not possible to restore the situation.'[144] Lady Asquith, commenting on Churchill's own account of how 'all the forces I had gathered together . . . were estranged or dissolved' has written that 'it is, alas, true that many of them were. Several loyal members of the Focus expressed to me (and no doubt to others) the view that if he continued to lead us our cause would be hopelessly compromised.'[145]

There is no reason whatever to doubt that Churchill's motives were wholly honourable and disinterested. Mr A. J. P. Taylor has stated that Churchill 'had grasped at any means to overthrow the government of feeble men'.[146] All the available evidence points to the fact that although this was Beaverbrook's main motive it was not Churchill's. Of course, his dislike and distrust of the Government must have played a part. In crises of this kind personal motives are usually mixed. But it would seem that Churchill's main concern was for the King, and not to remove Baldwin. He rendered a last invaluable service to the King by assisting him with his poignant farewell broadcast to the nation.

Churchill was a romantic. He had a profound feeling for the continuity of things. He believed in the hereditary principle. He was a devout royalist. He felt deeply for the King in his tragic predicament. His mind flew back to the glittering promise of the King's youth and his immense popularity in the Empire. He reacted from the heart and not the head. He spurned the urgent advice of friends to remain silent. It was a mad thing to do. As Mr Taylor has commented, 'Churchill made every possible blunder during the crisis.' Churchill himself has written that 'I was myself smitten in public opinion that it was the almost universal view that my political life was at last ended.'[147] But, in a way, one would not have had it otherwise. Halifax

144. Macmillan, op. cit., p. 480.
145. *Daily Telegraph*, 11 March 1965.
146. A. J. P. Taylor, op. cit., p. 404.
147. *The Gathering Storm*, p. 171.

once remarked of Churchill's mind that it was 'a most curious mixture of a child's emotion and a man's reason'.[148] On this occasion the emotional side of his nature predominated.

*

The abdication was a major catastrophe. For several months 'the King's Matter' had taken up a disproportionate amount of the time and energies of ministers at a critical period. It had probably prevented Baldwin's retirement for a year. Baldwin, by his handling of the crisis, had entirely restored his fading popularity. Churchill was once again alone and reviled. It was a disastrous beginning to 1937. Many years later, Churchill and Beaverbrook were discussing the many issues on which they had been on opposite sides, and Beaverbrook reminded him of their support of the King in the abdication crisis. 'Perhaps we were both wrong that time,' Churchill replied.[149]

The feeling of dismay and bitterness among Churchill's small band of friends over his actions was in some cases intense. Boothby wrote him an angry letter of reproach which he subsequently regretted and for which he apologized. Churchill replied:[150]

Personal   12th December, 1936
My dear Bob,

Thank you so much for your letter. Even if you had not written it, our old relations would have been unchanged.

I reached the House on Monday rather prepared in my mind to be attacked for what I had written over the week-end, and addressing myself too attentively to that possibility, I did not sufficiently realise how far the Prime Minister had gone to meet the views I had expressed. I ought of course to have welcomed what he said. I cannot however think that it was wrong to repeat the request that no irrevocable decision should be taken.

I made careful enquiries yesterday at Belvedere and am absolutely satisfied that the point was put to the King most fully, Archie's name and mine being used; and that he turned it aside on the grounds that

148. Birkenhead: *Halifax*, p. 459.
149. Beaverbrook, op. cit., p. 109.
150. Boothby Papers.

it would not be honourable to play for time when his fundamental resolve was unchanged, and as he declared, unchangeable. It was certainly this very strict point of honour which cost him his Crown. Whether I could have prevailed upon him personally, I do not know. It is however certain that I should not have been allowed access to him, as the Ministers were already angry with Baldwin for having given him permission to see me on Friday, and he had been made aware of this fact. Therefore I feel you are right in saying that no human effort could have altered the course of events.

The only thing now to do is to make it easy for him to live in this country quietly as a private gentleman, as soon as possible, and to that we must bend our efforts by discouraging noisy controversy (apart from quasi-historical investigation) and refusing to take part in it. The more firmly the new King is established, the more easy it will be for the old one to come back to his house.

Yours ever,

W.

*

In this part some emphasis has been placed upon certain of Churchill's inconsistencies and failures in diagnosis of the international situation in the years 1933–6. The criticisms made of his actions and attitudes may be at least partly ascribed to a determination not to permit the version put forward in *The Gathering Storm* to remain unchallenged. But it is important to appreciate these elements to understand fully why his prolonged and vigorously conducted campaign had such relatively little effect.

These qualifications are necessary, but they must not be permitted to distort the picture. For three years he had persevered with a theme and a warning virtually without support in Parliament or in the country. He had made mistakes, but these may be accounted of lesser moment than the fact that, on the main issue, he was right. Above all else, he was right on the issue of timing. He has written that he had expected an even shorter interval between the remilitarization of the Rhineland and the seizure of Austria than two years,[151] but it was an error in the right direction. Lord Eustace Percy has written

151. *The Gathering Storm*, p. 165.

about Hitler: 'that he would succeed, in little more than five years, not only in mobilising a nation and abolishing its un-employment, but in equipping a great army and bringing the dreams of a new strategy within the bounds of reality, seemed to English observers, official and unofficial, wholly in-credible.'[152] This factor of the *pace* of Germany's expansion has tended to be under-emphasized; it was the factor that over-whelmed not merely the British, whose reaction to German rearmament was the most vigorous of all the European powers, but all countries. It was the remarkable feature of Churchill's warnings, from 1932 onwards, that he did not regard this revival as incredible and impossible. In a manner that perhaps owed as much to intuition as it did to actual knowledge, he saw the danger, and regarded the pace of British rearmament, sub-stantial though it was, as inadequate to that danger. As this account demonstrates, his estimates and forecasts, and his diagnoses for remedy were faulty in many respects. His own subsequent account of the events of these years and his own part in them must be approached with caution. But he saw and felt something that few other contemporaries did – that the world was in the presence of a terrible personal and national phenomenon for which there was no parallel since Napoleon.

The history of Churchill's campaign on Defence between 1933 and 1936 must be seen in its context – personal and political. Until June 1935 it seriously overlapped with the struggle over the Government of India Bill, with the doleful effects of that controversy on Churchill's reputation. Many of his greatest speeches on rearmament were made to an inattentive or sceptical audience. We must return to Rosebery's wise com-ment on the total importance of 'the character breathing through the sentences' in any speech. Wisdom issued into the void remains wisdom, but is without significance beyond that fact. It is the alchemy of association between speaker and audience that makes speeches relevant, and if that alchemy is absent there is no effect. For the politician does not rise to speak without bearing on his shoulders the reputation, good or ill, that he has acquired over the years. The words that he utters

152. Percy, op. cit., p. 187.

may be meticulously phrased and impressively delivered, or may be uttered ramblingly and haltingly. The important factors are the reputation that he carries, the character that breathes through the sentences and the consequent response of the audience, rather than the words themselves.

These elements are difficult for subsequent generations to comprehend. The circumstances of the speech are gone, only the words remain, and these so often provide a fickle guide to the value of the speech itself. Rosebery, in the passage in his monograph of Lord Randolph Churchill referred to before, made an exception to the rule that 'Genuine political speeches that win the instant laurels of debate soon lose their savour. All the accompaniments have disappeared – the heat, the audience, the interruptions and the applause; and what remains seems cold and flabby,' and that exception is of considerable interest: 'Of course, in the case of speeches that are treatises, like those of Burke, treatises clothed in a literary form and carefully prepared for publication as pamphlets, the remark does not apply. But then these were not speeches at all, or at any rate not successful speeches. Their triumph was literary and philosophical, not that of the arena and the moment.'[153]

Historical parallels and comparisons are dangerous to make. A comparison between Churchill and Burke could be pushed only to a certain point, yet even that limited comparison has its relevance. Burke and Churchill prepared their speeches with infinite care. Each came into the House of Commons with a speech that had been developed and burnished over a number of days, and even weeks. It was not designed to reflect the mood of the hour or have any relevant place in the debate. It was a declaration of position, attitudes and beliefs. Members did not listen to Burke because his delivery was so lamentable; they preferred to read his speeches on the morrow. Members listened to Churchill, but the effect, if any, was of short duration. But it is here that the parallel with Burke abruptly ends. For it was in contemplating his speeches, and in absorbing his arguments subsequently that Burke's influence on his contemporaries was so great. Even Churchill's greatest oratorical successes did not

153. Rosebery: *Lord Randolph Churchill*, p. 83.

leave a comparable mark. Lord Eustace Percy has commented that 'Churchill's earlier speeches [on Defence] were, perhaps, discounted because of what seemed a romantic lack of discrimination.'[154] The later ones tended to be discounted for several reasons; the reiteration of a single theme is not congenial to the House of Commons, for, as in all human assemblies, there is a weariness in being constantly exposed to frequent harangues that, in content and style, are virtually indistinguishable from one another. And then, with the fundamental ruthlessness that characterizes the House of Commons, there is interest in the rising man and the man in possession, little interest save a detached professional one in the man who is either down or on the way down.

The speeches, accordingly, remain on the record. The historian, toiling through them, learns much. Yet, in reality, he learns little, if he cannot gauge their impact and relevance. And the evidence is overwhelming to the effect that Churchill's speeches on Defence between 1933 and the end of 1936 achieved little in relation to their quality and the sound sense of much of their content. And we must address ourselves to the question, why was this so?

Some of the answers have already been given. By the end of 1933 Churchill was widely regarded as a failed politician, in whom no real trust could be reasonably placed; by June 1935 these opinions had been fortified further. His habit of exaggerating problems, and in clothing relatively minor questions in brightly coloured language, had the effect that when a really major issue did arise there was no easy way of differentiating it, either for orator or audiences. His sense of the dramatic had ceased to excite the emotions as it had once done – and was to do again in 1940. His few political friends were neither collectively nor individually impressive nor influential. Many who were coming to agree with him on fundamentals were alienated by his assertions on particulars. Others were affronted by his conception of total personal and political friendship. Some questioned whether the campaign was national or personal, and shared the view of T. E. Lawrence that 'if Winston's

154. Percy, op. cit., p. 186.

interests were not concerned in a question, he would not be interested'.[155]

Churchill's campaign for rearmament lacked the essential qualities of a crusade. It was limited; it was personal; it was far from national; and it was closely linked to the political fortunes of its leader. Great speeches in Parliament and stirring public appeals do not constitute a crusade. This was very much a politician's campaign, conducted in the main in the House of Commons, and accordingly conducted before a highly sceptical and, above all, a limited audience. Churchill did not at this time stand above party politics. He did not enjoy the privilege of being regarded as a national figure in the same sense as a Pitt, a Burke, or a Gladstone. Perhaps the real cause of his failure was that he was regarded at large as just another politician, and by the House of Commons as just another failed and disappointed politician.

These comments do not controvert Churchill's record on Defence matters in the years 1932–6. The inconstancies and errors of timing and judgement do not seriously affect the central fact that he sensed danger long before most of his contemporaries discerned it. His principal theme was unanswerably right. But the failure of his campaign was not entirely the result of the folly of others. A dispassionate assessment of why his reputation remained so low at the end of 1936, after a period in which his warnings had been proved to be abundantly justified, must return to the quotation which is the central theme of this work: 'Every man is the maker of his own fate.'

155. Liddell Hart, op. cit., Vol. I, p. 347.

Part Seven   THE RETURN
FROM EXILE
1937–1939

There is little consistency or pattern in the momentum of political events. In the words of Sorel: 'Politics are not a drama where scenes follow one another after a methodical plan ... Politics are a conflict of which chance seems to be modifying the whole course.' Periods of excitement and drama are followed by interludes of apparent tranquillity, to be succeeded in their turn by turmoil and crisis. As the tides ebb and flow, the politician finds himself at one moment in danger of being swamped and at the next of being stranded on the shore. He is the prisoner of the varying moods and climates of the environment in which he must operate, and where nothing is constant. Attitudes which hold validity in a context of crisis have no impact in a period of calm, while, conversely, policies which are deemed appropriate to quiet times appear lamentably inapposite when danger looms. The public man knows that his personal fortunes can change drastically, largely as a consequence of events beyond his control; he also knows that the art of politics lies in adaptation, in swift movements, in agility, so that he may hopefully avoid extinction.

It could be said with justice that the whole of Churchill's career up to the end of 1936 had been a struggle for political survival. Throughout this period, and particularly since 1915, he had usually been out of total sympathy with the political party with which he was cohabiting, and his attitude to Party had not greatly changed with the years. The dictum that 'an independent is a man in whom no dependence may be placed' is well established in Party thinking, but there is truth in Rosebery's words:

Independence is at once the choicest and the least serviceable of all qualities in political life. Independence in a public man is a quality as splendid as it is rare, but it is apt to produce and develop acute angles. Now a colleague with acute angles is a superfluous discomfort. And independence in a great orator on the Treasury Bench is a rocket of which one cannot predict the course.[1]

1. Rosebery: *Introduction to The Windham Papers* (1913).

As has been emphasized already, Churchill's peculiar difficulty in his campaign for increased Defence expenditure since
1933 had lain in the fact that it was a campaign directed against
a Government whose thinking was much closer to his own on the
principle of the matter than its opponents. Until the middle of
1936 at least there was no possibility of support from the
Labour or Liberal parties, and there had been few indications
that there was a mass of public feeling outside Westminster to
which Churchill could appeal and which could put pressure upon
ministers. On certain issues, of which the Abyssinia crisis and
the Spanish Civil War were the most important, such a mass of
feeling did exist, but Churchill's views on these questions were
closer to those of the Government than those of its critics.

Churchill's political character contained many facets, but the
most important one of all was now manifest beyond question.

Of all the political qualities, persistence is perhaps the most
admirable, and among the most difficult. To persist in a political
career that appears to others, and even on occasion to the politician himself, as finished, demands exceptional strength of
character in a sensitive and a proud man. 'Politicians rise by
toil and struggles,' Churchill wrote in *Great Contemporaries*.
'They expect to fall; they hope to rise.' But there are moments
when even the most hopeful begin to lose hope, and when even
the most optimistic are oppressed by depression and racked by
ugly uncertainties. Throughout his period of exclusion and
isolation Churchill had maintained his public poise. Only those
who knew him best appreciated the depths of depression into
which he descended on occasions, and the triumph of character
which his political fortunes had occasioned.

*

By 1937, Churchill was in his sixty-third year, and it was eight
years – a political eternity – since he had held public office.
Since 1929 he had conducted a lonely campaign against the
Imperial, Defence and Foreign Policies of the Government with
limited success, and what had been achieved had been very
substantially lost by the abdication crisis. He had been fighting
his campaign less against an Administration than against a

national temper. He had delivered warnings which should have
been heeded; he had advocated policies which should have been
adopted; he had argued against foolish measures, and had
proposed wise ones. He had, unquestionably, made many mistakes of strategy and tactics, but he could have justifiably
complained in the words used by his father in 1891 that 'there
has been no consideration, no indulgence, no memory or gratitude – nothing but spite, malice and abuse.'

Although he was not as solitary a man as Lord Randolph
Churchill, he had few close friendships outside the immediate
family circle. His mind and imagination – so eager and questing
when facts, issues and problems were concerned – were less
active and perceptive when people were involved. His estimate
of character was uneven, and his capacity to detect central
aspects of personality could be at fault. A man with a distinguished war record was always welcome, as was the buc-
caneer. Some were worthy companions; others less so. He had a
tendency to classify people under a few headings; once you were
assessed, you could, if you were careful, do no wrong, or, however careful you were, no good. His definition of friendship was
a severe one. 'He demanded,' as Lady Asquith has written,
'partisanship from a friend, or, at the worst, acquiescence.'[2]
'"Thou shalt have none other gods but me" has always been
the first, and the most significant, of his Commandments,'
Boothby has commented.[3] For Churchill, friendship meant total
commitment, all or nothing. This aspect of Churchill's character
must be seen in proportion, and the judgement of Sir Desmond
Morton must not be omitted: 'The full truth, I believe, is that
Winston's "friends" must be persons who were of use to him.
The idea of having a friend who was of no practical use to him,
but being a friend because he liked him, had no place ... He
certainly gave all those who knew him at least as much pleasure
as they may have given him use or interest. He owes them no
debt.'[4]

Even at the lowest point of his fortunes he always had

2. Lady Asquith: *Winston Churchill As I Knew Him*, p. 132.
3. Boothby, op. cit., p. 46.
4. Quoted in R. W. Thompson: *The Yankee Marlborough*, p. 253.

followers and admirers; in his family he was the central and beloved figure; in politics and outside it he had a wide circle of acquaintances; but his real friendships were few.

Of his political friendships, perhaps that with Birkenhead had been the closest. Birkenhead was a gay and exciting companion, in good times or bad, but his judgement, the quality that Churchill so deeply admired in him, could often be seriously at fault. It was the opinion of many observers that Churchill was always somewhat in awe of Birkenhead, and he was certainly careful to avoid his scathing invective: 'Even I, who knew him so well,' he had written, 'refrained from pushing ding-dong talk too far when others were present lest friendship should be endangered',[5] a comment that is perhaps more illuminating about Churchill than about Birkenhead. Although in many respects inferior to Churchill, Birkenhead was definitely his intellectual superior, a fact that each recognized. Furthermore, he possessed many faculties that Churchill envied, and perhaps most of all his spontaneous and magnificently delivered speeches, made without notes, and, apparently, without any noticeable effort.

But Birkenhead had died in 1930, and in the 1930s a new generation of allies were at his side. Outside this tiny group were some allies on certain issues, inside and outside the purely political field. But they were few in number, and small in influence.

In the House of Commons, Churchill's following over India had consisted of some sixty Conservatives, whose support faded away rapidly after 1935. In his struggles over Defence his parliamentary following really consisted only of Brendan Bracken, Robert Boothby and, subsequently, Duncan Sandys, who married Diana Churchill in 1935. Of the older generation, the only important Commons ally was Austen Chamberlain, but whose influence was waning long before his death early in 1937. The political importance of Lord Lloyd was even smaller than Austen Chamberlain's, and he, like Churchill, still suffered from the aftermath of the struggle over the Government of India Bill. As his biographer has sadly commented: 'Few sights are more embarrassing and distressing than that of an embittered

5. *Great Contemporaries.*

man nursing a personal grievance which perceptibly over-
powers his judgement.'[6] And the comment of T. E. Lawrence
on Lloyd may be recalled: 'He will always be the despair of his
friends and the chief target of his enemies.'

Among the younger Conservatives Churchill had very little
support. Some, like Harold Macmillan, Duff Cooper and Anthony Eden, sympathized with him on certain issues, but none
could remotely be described as belonging to his personal following. Macmillan was at that time, in Lord Kilmuir's phrase, 'a
lone independent gun barking on the left of the Conservative
Party'.[7] He was a rebel, an intellectual, and essentially solitary.
His hostility to the kind of Conservative who had supported
Churchill over India was considerable. 'A party dominated by
second-class brewers and company promoters – a Casino capitalism – is not likely to represent anybody but itself,' he had
written on one occasion. His political path and Churchill's very
rarely converged until the end of 1936, but he could never be
described as one of Churchill's adherents until much later. He
voted against the Government on the ending of sanctions on
23 June 1936, and on 29 June resigned the Whip in protest.[8]
He subsequently took his political life again in his hands when
he supported A. D. Lindsay in the Oxford by-election of 1938.[9]
In his attitudes to Defence and Foreign Affairs, as in other
matters, Macmillan made his own decisions.

Duff Cooper similarly, although he had always admired and
liked Churchill, did not act closely with him. For much of this
period, indeed, he was on the other side. He was successively
Financial Secretary to the Treasury, Secretary of State for War
under Baldwin, and First Lord of the Admiralty under Neville
Chamberlain. He had written a popular biography of Talley-
rand, and the official biography of Haig. He was small in
stature, pugnacious and notoriously hot-tempered, with a vein
in his forehead that enlarged and pulsated alarmingly when he
was angered. He was a controversial personality. His friends

6. Colin Forbes Adam: *Life of Lord Lloyd*, p. 226.
7. Lord Kilmuir: *Political Adventure*, p. 45.
8. He applied for its restoration, which was granted, in May 1937.
9. See p. 434 below.

considered him brilliant, witty and profound; his critics regarded him as indolent, opinionated and somewhat *farouche*.
His influence in the Cabinet, despite the high offices he filled,
was never very great. As Liddell Hart has written with justice:
'He had delightful qualities, but was not a dynamic man.'[10]
His resignation over Munich in September 1938 has obscured
the fact that he shared a very real responsibility for the situation with his colleagues. There is, after all, something less than
impressive about a man who, when introducing the Army
Estimates in 1934, declared his faith in 'the importance of
cavalry in modern warfare'.[11] On a more serious level, his
vehement hostility to Germany and love of France gained him
the reputation – not wholly undeservedly – of being somewhat
unbalanced in his views of international affairs. The most
charming and interesting of men when in the mood – an important qualification – he was, politically, a lightweight. It was not
until he became Ambassador to France in 1944 that he at last
found a position which was wholly suited to his tastes and
temperament. Throughout the years 1933–8 he kept his links
with Churchill, while remaining firmly in the Government, and
there are indications that he, too, shared the views on
Churchill's reliability and capacity that prevailed in ministerial
circles.[12]

Anthony Eden, Foreign Secretary from December 1935 –
when he succeeded the unfortunate Hoare – until his virtual
dismissal in February 1938 by Neville Chamberlain, was the
preux chevalier of the Tory Party, and one of the favourites of
the House of Commons. Although Eden was never a member of
the Churchill circle at this stage, nor, indeed, a member of it
before the outbreak of the war, Churchill had a good opinion of
him, and described him as 'the one fresh figure of the first
magnitude arising out of a generation which was ravaged by the

10. Liddell Hart: *Memoirs*, Vol. I, p. 379.

11. In March 1936, when announcing the mechanization of certain
cavalry units, he paid a tribute to their acceptance of this melancholy
development: 'It is like asking a great musical performer to throw away his
violin and to devote himself in future to a gramophone.'

12. See Liddell Hart, op. cit., Vol. I, p. 320.

war'. The fact that Eden – like Duff Cooper and Macmillan – had served with conspicuous gallantry in the war was an additional, and a most important, factor in Churchill's estimation.

It is, of course, too early to form a measured estimate on Eden's tenure of the Foreign office between 1935 and 1938. The recently-revealed Cabinet and Foreign Office papers disclose a less vigorous hostility to the advance of the Dictators than has usually been ascribed to him, and his relationship with Vansittart has not yet been fully explored, although the general pattern is clear enough. Vansittart was elaborately patrician, was of a passionate nature beneath a professional exterior, and although highly skilled was often unsubtle in his methods. Vansittart was, as Eden has commented, 'more like a Secretary of State in mentality than a permanent official',[13] a revealing and accurate observation in which probably lay much of the difficulty between the two men. Furthermore, the stream of minatory memoranda that Vansittart submitted on the German menace had a counter-productive effect. Eden has denied that he had lost confidence in Vansittart,[14] but it is clear that relations between the two men were not entirely harmonious, and that the vigour of Vansittart's attitudes was a source of difficulty to the Secretary of State. A potentially strong and even decisive partnership did not develop as such, and ended when Vansittart was removed to a post of honorific impotence at the close of 1937. Within two months Eden also had gone. As will be seen, his departure from the Foreign Office was not followed by close cooperation with Churchill.

In the House of Commons, Churchill's only consistent supporters were Robert Boothby and Brendan Bracken, once derided – somewhat inaccurately – by Baldwin in Kiplingesque terms as 'the faithful chelas' and also known, because of the contrasting colour of their hair, as the 'Black and Tans'.

So little is generally known about Brendan Bracken that an attempt should be made to draw his portrait, even though he has covered his tracks so well that little more than the outlines can reasonably be depicted. He had been introduced to

13. Avon: *Facing the Dictators*, p. 242.
14. See Ivan Colvin: *Vansittart in Office*, p. 170.

Churchill in 1923 by Oliver Locker-Lampson.[15] Bracken was then twenty-two, and already had about him an aura of mystery that he did nothing, then or later, to discourage. In fact he had been born in County Tipperary in 1901, and was the son of Joseph K. Bracken, who owned a small building business, and Hannah Bracken (*née* Ryan). His birth is registered in Templemore on 23 October 1901. He was the third child, and second son, of the marriage, which was his father's second. After the death of Joseph Bracken the family moved to Dublin. Bracken was educated in Dublin by the Christian Brothers, in a school known as O'Connell's, and was brought up a Roman Catholic.[16]

By all accounts he was a difficult child to manage, and in 1915 he was sent to a Jesuit boarding school in Dublin. He stayed there only a short time. Mrs Bracken married Patrick Laffan at this time and her brother-in-law – Father Thomas Laffan – agreed to take Brendan to Australia. His years in Australia are somewhat obscure; what is known is that he returned to England in 1919.[17] He was given £200 by his mother, which gave him sufficient funds to pay for a year's fees at the eminent Yorkshire school, Sedbergh. (The version that he paid his fees with a gold bar is, unhappily, apocryphal.) It is believed – and the story seems well authenticated – that he had inspected other educational establishments before deciding on Sedbergh. In the Register, under the heading 'Parent or Guardian', he wrote firmly 'Brendan Bracken'. His brief sojourn at Sedbergh, for which he developed a love that bordered on the fanatical, has spawned a myriad of legends. The brother of a subsequent Sedbergh headmaster was on firmer ground when he wrote that 'he was difficult to place in any form, for in subjects like economics, currency, and finance he should have been teaching the masters, whereas in others he was more ignorant than the greatest duffer in the school.'[18]

15. Another version is that they were introduced by J. L. Garvin.

16. This information has been supplied to me by Mrs Farren, of Blackrock, Co. Dublin, whose brother was at the same school.

17. Bracken's mother died in 1928, and her second husband remarried in 1932. I am grateful to his son, Mr Patrick Laffan of Dublin, for information concerning his family.

18. Sir Robert Bruce Lockhart: *Friends, Foes and Foreigners*, pp. 228–9.

After leaving Sedbergh he went, briefly, into schoolmastering at a boys' preparatory school near London where, according to a colleague, he spent much of his time studying *Who's Who*, *Crockford*, the *Directory of Directors*, and the professional lists of lawyers and doctors. When subsequently asked by a Sedbergh friend for the secret of his later success, Bracken airily replied 'By knowing the right people'. The true answer would have been 'by impressing the right people'. He cultivated the local Conservative Member of Parliament, Admiral Sueter, and began to appear in London political circles. He practised public speaking in the League of Nations Union. In 1923 he was introduced to Mr Eyre of Eyre and Spottiswoode, and entered the worlds of journalism and banking. If he did not enter these new careers at the top he was very close to doing so. Sir Oscar Hobson has related his astonishment when, invited to luncheon to discuss with the directors of Eyre and Spottiswoode the founding of a new banking magazine, 'there was this boy of twenty-two with his mop of red hair, sitting at the head of the table flanked by two or three elderly co-directors and another guest or two besides myself, addressing us each in turn as "my dear" and relating with great gusto the latest "inside stories" from the political world'.[19] He had very little money, but abundant confidence in his own judgement, and a considerable flair. He was instrumental in the founding of *The Banker* by Eyre and Spottiswoode in 1926, and then persuaded the Eyre Estate to acquire *The Financial News* and *The Investor's Chronicle*, and, in 1929, to take a half-share in *The Economist*. The manner in which this was done is a good example of Bracken's methods and throws some light on his character:

In 1929 he fought hard to buy control of *The Economist*, then still held by the Wilson Trust for the benefit of the descendants of the original founder of the papers. The trustees were prepared to sell if a purchaser could be found who could be relied upon to maintain the prestige and traditions of the paper. In association with Sir Henry Strakosch and others, the then editor (now Lord Layton) made a bid, but before the negotiations had proceeded far, Brendan Bracken entered the field on behalf of Financial Newspapers Proprietors Ltd,

19. *The Banker*, September 1958.

a company which he had lately formed to acquire a group of financial
and other papers. Lord Layton recalls that he represented to
Bracken that the editorial independence of *The Economist,* untied to
any party or special interest, had from its inception been its greatest
asset. Bracken entirely agreed; it had, he said, been the intention of
his group to maintain this tradition and he suggested that the two
groups should buy the paper jointly and work out a constitution to
guarantee the independence that both desired.[20]

The width of his interests was demonstrated by the acquisition of *The Practitioner* in 1926, and by the founding, in 1950, of
History Today. He became chairman and managing director of
The Financial News and *The Investor's Chronicle,* while continuing – still in his twenties – as editor to *The Banker* for a
period, and subsequently he became a director of *The Economist.* 'He seemed to have conquered London, to have got to
know everyone, and to have been able to make the most
important do his bidding before he was thirty,' one observer
has commented.[21]

Bracken's personal attraction was very considerable. He was
a big man, with flaming carrot-red hair in a tousled mop, with
gig-lamp spectacles. Wholly self-educated, the width of his
interests and knowledge was remarkable, even if his understanding sometimes lacked depth. He was one of the best talkers
in London, but he could also listen. Success improved him, and
he was among the kindest of men, always generous with time,
sympathy and understanding. He was deeply sensitive, subject
to periods of black depression. He did not lack either ambition
or shrewdness, and on his way up he could be fierce. But he was
never cold. He often used the word 'tough' with relish, and his
manner gave chance acquaintances the impression of a brash
extrovert on the make, but he was in reality compassionate,
civilized and humane. As Lord Radcliffe has written: 'He was
a romantic who liked to express himself as a cynic.'[22]

20. *The Economist,* 16 August 1958.

21. *Brendan Bracken; Portraits and Appreciations* (privately published,
1958). I am most grateful to Mr Alan Hodge for information on Bracken's
early career.

22. ibid., p. 15.

Bracken had been immediately attracted to Churchill, and had hurled himself zestfully into Churchill's election campaigns at Leicester, Westminster and Epping. At Leicester he ran a Churchill news-sheet; in Westminster he organized barrow boys for a variety of electoral tasks; at Epping he campaigned and spoke vigorously for Churchill. But there then followed a period of estrangement. Churchill considered that Bracken had been guilty of sharp practice in a journalistic matter that affected him, and for over four years there was no contact between them. Bracken won North Paddington in the 1929 election for the Conservatives entirely on his own account, the rift was healed, and henceforth he was Churchill's man totally. Indeed, so close was their relationship that the ludicrous story arose that he was Churchill's illegitimate son (by one account, by the actress Maxine Elliot). Bracken was always more than a 'faithful chela', for he was counsellor, friend, informant and critic. His contacts in the City and other high places provided Churchill with much valuable information which he might otherwise have missed.

He himself was Churchill's most vigorous propagandist. Everywhere and in every circle, he preached the Gospel of Winston. He knew everyone who mattered, and, if he was far from being omniscient, he covered the ground with immense thoroughness. Randolph Churchill has recalled one occasion on the Sunday in 1931 when Britain went off the gold standard, and Bracken arrived at Chartwell at about 10.30 a.m. in a chauffeur-driven Hispano-Suiza 'which the early writings of Mr Michael Arlen had led him to believe was the appropriate vehicle for a rising and fast-moving young man'. He had come from Mereworth, having spent the night as the guest of Esmond Harmsworth (subsequently Lord Rothermere). Before leaving London he had discussed matters with the Deputy Governor of the Bank of England (the Governor, Montagu Norman, being in Canada at the time). He declined an invitation to lunch at Chartwell as he was en route to confer with Lloyd George at Churt and then with Beaverbrook at Cherkley. On the Monday morning he moved briskly around the Bank of England and the chairmen of the Big Five Banks. By the time the House of

Commons met in the afternoon Bracken was fully conversant
with the situation. It is an excellent example of Bracken's
methods in action.[23]

But, in spite of his qualities, Bracken had very little political
influence in the thirties. He attracted attention, but it was by
no means all favourable. His curious twang – part Australian,
part Irish, part Cockney – his extravagant gestures and statements when speaking in the House and his 'Winston-mania',
all combined to make people regard him with curiosity but
without excessive admiration. It was a curious paradox that
Bracken, the most passionately sincere of men, exuded insincerity to chance observers. He seemed at times to embody
the popular image of a cynical politician, and to have stepped
out of Boston ward-politics rather than the British House of
Commons. The fact that his political position was very definitely right of centre did not endear him to the Labour Party nor
to the serious young social reformers in the Conservative
Party.[24] His brand of politics was a robust one – perhaps too
robust for the thirties. It was only much later that the House
of Commons woke up to Bracken's real qualities. Had his health
(which was always poor) lasted, there is no saying to what
heights he might have risen.

He was a man of mystery to the end. He died of cancer in
August 1958, after years of ill-health, and left explicit instructions that his papers were to be destroyed. Churchill and
Beaverbrook, then holidaying in the South of France, tried
unsuccessfully to prevent the disaster. Bracken gave strict
orders that there was not to be a funeral service, and no formal
memorial. His ashes were scattered over Romney Marsh by a
devoted member of his personal staff. Most of what remained of
his wealth – for, when he realized he was doomed, he gave much
of it away to his most cherished institutions – went to educational charities, schools and scholarships. He disappeared as
strangely and as swiftly as he had arrived, leaving only an

23. *Evening Standard*, 8 August 1958.

24. This was not confined to the twenties or thirties. Even in the late
forties and early fifties, he embodied, to many young Tories, the worst
features of the 'old gang'.

aching gap in the hearts of his many friends. He never married.

Boothby was a swashbuckling, swarthily combative and highly articulate young man, who had entered the House as Member for East Aberdeenshire in 1924 at the age of twenty-three. Boothby has always taken pleasure in swimming against the tide, and particularly against the Party tide. It would be a mistake to regard him merely as a 'chela' in the 1930s, for he was always original and independent; as a friend has commented, 'God may have intended him to be a knight-errant, but never surely a disciple.'[25]

Although he had strongly criticized the return to the gold standard in 1925, Boothby had served as Churchill's Parliamentary Secretary at the Treasury between 1926 and 1929. He had not taken part in Churchill's India campaign, but had consistently supported him on Defence and Foreign Affairs matters. He was always an excellent speaker, with a mordant wit, a splendid voice and an excellent sense of timing. His long-term judgement on major issues was remarkably acute. But however much the House of Commons relished Boothby as a performer, he rarely made any real or lasting impression. Perhaps he loved his independence too much, and excessive modesty was never one of his dominant characteristics. Men who tend to be right and do not hesitate to draw attention to the fact are never congenial in political company.

His relationship with Churchill was marked by storms, and was not destined to last long. Boothby's defiant refusal to serve as a docile henchman in the Churchill entourage was perhaps one factor. The antipathy between himself and Lindemann – and antipathy is perhaps too mild a description of the relationship – must have played some part. Boothby's divorce certainly did not help his prestige at Chartwell. Their differences over the Abdication did not help. Whatever the causes, the close friendship that had existed at one time was definitely cooling by 1937, and it ended in 1940. This sad episode may be conveniently referred to at this point.

Boothby had been active in 1939 in urging the blocking of

25. Sir Robert Bruce Lockhart, op. cit., p. 225.

Czechoslovak assets in Britain. In 1940, after the fall of Holland and Belgium, Richard Weiniger, a Czech friend of Boothby, was interned. His papers disclosed that he had given Boothby a loan in the previous year, a fact which Boothby had not disclosed to the House of Commons or the Chancellor of the Exchequer (Simon) at the time.[26] By this stage (October 1940) Boothby was a junior minister in the Ministry of Food, and the papers were sent to Churchill by the Home Office. Churchill wrote to Boothby, who in reply asked for an interview. Boothby's account of that meeting may be given:

In due course the summons came, but it was very different from the one I had expected. When the Marconi case blew up, Asquith asked Lloyd George to come and see him alone, and listened for a long time to all he had to say. Lloyd George was Chancellor of the Exchequer, but apart from this Asquith owed little to him. Asquith then decided that, although he had been foolish, he would give him his full support as Prime Minister. I was only a private Member at the time I was active in the cause of Czechoslovakia: but Churchill owed quite a lot to me in terms of faithful service for over a decade, most of it in the political wilderness. I was not summoned for a private talk, but to the Cabinet room. There I found the Attorney-General at the Prime Minister's side, and a number of secretaries. There was no discussion. Churchill simply informed me that he had decided to refer my case to a Select Committee of the House of Commons. I was in no doubt then that he had turned against me. Why, I do not know.[27]

The Select Committee investigated Boothby's affairs with great thoroughness, and produced a Report of immense length and detail, including reproductions of Boothby's bank accounts. The conclusion was that his conduct had not been of the standard expected of a Member of the House of Commons; the evidence of Simon in particular was devastating. The rights and wrongs of the matter belong more properly to a biography of Boothby than a study of Churchill, but there were many who

26. Technically, he had no need to have declared his financial interest, but it was unwise not to have done.

27. This quotation is taken from a memorandum on the episode written by Lord Boothby many years later, which he has placed at my disposal.

considered – and still consider – that the retribution was grotesquely out of all proportion to the offence.[28] What was strange was Churchill's refusal to come to Boothby's assistance. As Boothby has written: 'Churchill held out no helping hand in this time of trouble, and I began to feel that he wanted to do me in. Sometimes I woke up in the night trembling. I could not understand why this mighty Titan, then at the zenith of his power, and carrying the main burden, whom I had known so well, and served for so long to the best of my capacity, should harbour such resentment against anyone as completely un-important as myself.'[29] As Churchill's side of the story has not yet been given, no definite judgement can be given. It was a melancholy ending to a relationship that had cost Boothby much politically, and which had provided Churchill with a courageous and hard-hitting supporter when his fortunes were lowest.

Duncan Sandys, who married Diana Churchill in 1935 after meeting her during the Norwood by-election when Sandys entered the House of Commons, was the third member of Churchill's tiny band of supporters in the House of Commons. He had already given proof of his courage by resigning from the Foreign Office when a memorandum on German ambitions, prepared on his return from service in Berlin in 1933, was dismissed by Simon. Sandys was talented but somewhat slow in expression, a man of great seriousness of purpose and intolerant of anything slipshod, if a plodder rather than a meteor at least a professional almost from the beginning. His capacity for work was truly Churchillian, and his most important political facet was a dogged persistence, coupled with an absolute personal integrity. Of the men who served Churchill at this time, he was the steadiest, the most serious, the most professional, and the most underrated.

The story of the long relationship, lasting over fifty years, between Churchill and Beaverbrook, with its alternating periods

28. Sir Colin Coote (*Editorial*, p. 269) relates that Sir Kingsley Wood protested at Boothby's 'persecution' in the War Cabinet. He was not the only protestor.

29. Boothby: *My Yesterday, Your Tomorrow*, pp. 74–5.

of warm intimacy and cool estrangement, lies outside the ambit of this study.[30] It was a curious relationship, not devoid of a certain reciprocal wariness. Beaverbrook always found the facets of other men's lives, good or bad, of perennial fascination and diversion;[31] Churchill was wholly uninterested in such matters. Beaverbrook relished participation in political intrigue at all levels; Churchill disliked intrigue, and was conspicuously inept in a field in which Beaverbrook was a master. Beaverbrook's was a complex personality, in which good and bad were so intermixed that an objective judgement is exceptionally difficult to make. He could be mean and vindictive; he could be generous and magnanimous. He could harbour and nourish bitter grievances; he could forgive and forget injustices and disappointments. He could be cruel; he could be overwhelmed with remorse over a minor social peccadillo. He prided himself on his judgement of men, yet was often surrounded by the second-rate and meretricious. He loved argument, yet welcomed sycophants. He was beloved most by those who were not beholden to him. The personalities and the world of Churchill and Beaverbrook were far apart, and on most major issues, from the Dardanelles to the menace of Hitler, they were on opposite sides. It was not surprising, therefore, that their relationship was often strained, and that periods of estrangement could occur. Beaverbrook had been a critic of Churchill's performances at the War Office and the Treasury, and as he himself wrote not long after, Churchill 'resents an assault on his public policy as much as Lloyd George does an attack on his private life'. Duff Cooper attempted a reconciliation in 1920 after Churchill had remarked that 'the Press is easier squashed than squared', and Beaverbrook had taken this ill.[32] The dinner had been a success, good relations had been re-established, only to suffer further periods of strain when the Coalition fell in 1922. They had come together subsequently, but over the return to the gold standard Beaverbrook attacked Churchill vigorously. Keynes's trenchant criticisms of Churchill, subsequently pub-

30. See Kenneth Young: *Churchill and Beaverbrook* (1966).
31. See Moran, *Churchill, The Struggle for Survival*, p. 7.
32. Duff Cooper: *Old Men Forget*, p. 89.

lished under the title *The Economic Consequences of Mr Churchill*, first appeared in the *Evening Standard*.

Beaverbrook had been Bonar Law's closest confidant and most warm admirer; he had backed Bonar Law completely over the Dardanelles, and to the end of his life regarded that operation as a terrible blunder. Churchill despised Law and deeply resented any criticisms of his part in the Dardanelles operations. Their views differed very sharply over Russia in 1919–20 and Chanak in 1922, and they had had disputes over the availability of newsprint in the General Strike. Beaverbrook always regarded Churchill with reservations, even during their periods of close friendship. As he once wrote:

I remember once a terrible scene with him when he was in a position of uncontrolled power and authority in dealing with public affairs, which closely concerned me.

If any other man living had used such outrageous language to me as he did on that occasion I should never have forgiven him. Churchill on top of the wave has in him the stuff of which tyrants are made.[33]

It is to Beaverbrook that we owe some shrewd comments on Churchill's character. Beaverbrook liked Churchill best in his hours of dejection and misfortune, and did not care for what he described as 'the self-confidence, the arrogance, of his hours of power and prosperity'.[34] Like Law, he distrusted Churchill's judgement – although not to the same extent – and his capacity for self-deception: 'He is strictly honest and truthful to other people, down to the smallest details of his life ... Yet he frequently deceives himself.'

During the thirties they drifted further apart politically on almost every issue in home and foreign affairs. After 1931 Beaverbrook regarded Churchill, as he put it, 'as "a busted flush"'. Churchill was not enthusiastic about Beaverbrook's darling, the Empire Free Trade movement. Beaverbrook did not share Churchill's black estimates of Russian and German ambitions. In the abdication crisis they found themselves, briefly

33. Beaverbrook: *Politicians and the War* (1959 edition), p. 284.
34. For an example of what Beaverbrook meant see his account of Churchill's changed attitude towards him after he became Chancellor of the Exchequer in 1924, quoted i n Young, op. cit., pp. 71–3.

and disastrously for both, on the same side. They saw each other from time to time. The *Evening Standard* carried Churchill's articles for years. But, as Mr Kenneth Young has written, 'The old easy interchange of ideas died away; even the *sympathie* faded somewhat, and in the years leading up to the Second World War the two men almost lost interest in each other.'[35]

In 1938 Beaverbrook saw to it that Churchill's contract with the *Evening Standard* was not renewed; Churchill was eagerly welcomed by other newspapers, but he was angry. The Beaverbrook papers vehemently supported Munich; although they urged rearmament, they daily preached against the folly of foreign entanglements. 'Pacific Isolationism' was the theme of Beaverbrook and his papers in these years, and it was not a philosophy likely to endear itself to Churchill. As he wrote in 1935, 'There would be a great deal to be said for this policy if we could only arrange to have the United Kingdom towed out fifteen hundred miles into the Atlantic.'

This, then, was the company Churchill kept in the 1930s. There was a small inner circle of personal adherents and intimate friends – Eddie Marsh – now retired from the Civil Service and moving perceptibly out of Churchill's real life, politics – Bracken, Lindemann, Boothby and Sandys. Apart from this very small group, there were a few public figures who were with him on his Defence policy, and which included Lady Violet Bonham Carter, George Lloyd, Austen Chamberlain, Oliver Lyttelton and Leo Amery. (A qualification must be inserted about Amery. Although he had known Churchill since Harrow, when the young Churchill pushed Amery into the swimming pool, there was always a definite restraint in their relationship, a lack of warmth, a noticeable caution and reserve.) There were some other well-wishers. The subsequent eminence of many of Churchill's supporters in the 1930s should not mislead the reader into making an incorrect evaluation of their influence at that time.

*

35. Young, op. cit., p. 116.

There was a considerable irony in the fact that one of the elements in Churchill's personality which did not help him to garner greater support in the Conservative Party in the 1930s was his conservatism. As has been emphasized, even in his Liberal period Churchill was a firm believer in the social order in which he had grown up. These tendencies had developed further after the war. It is conspicuous that in the 1930s he had no solid support – indeed, virtually no support whatever – in the more progressive elements in the Conservative Party. (Boothby may be deemed an exception in some aspects; but, as has been related, Boothby was never really in the inner circle.) And it is not difficult to discern in Churchill's attitudes in the 1930s a considerable development of Conservative attitudes which went beyond his views of India and Imperial questions. Of course, in such a development, age plays its part. As William Johnson had commented some sixty years before, 'an ardent reformer is pretty sure to become Conservative when he marries into a worldly family, when he has encumbrances, when he becomes post-prandial. He will be happier at 40 or 60 if his mind can fly back to a year of generous impulse and aspiration, when he was a Canning, a Peel, a Manin, a Cavour, a Hampden.' Churchill's life had not developed exactly on these lines, and his radicalism has always assumed the preservation of the social order, but age and experience had certainly not encouraged the development of such reforming zeal as he had ever possessed. The tone of the Elder Statesman looking back on happier and better days is very apparent in his writings and speeches by the close of the 1920s, and was to become even more dominant in the 1930s. Thus, in *My Early Life* we find him describing Joseph Chamberlain addressing a meeting in Oldham in 1900 in significant terms: 'I must explain that in those days we had a real political democracy led by a hierarchy of statesmen, and not a fluid mass distracted by newspapers. There was a structure in which statesmen, electors and the Press all played their part . . . All this was before the liquefaction of the British political system had set in.'

And then, in his portrait of John Morley – published in *Great*

Contemporaries in 1937, but originally published in November 1929 – he wrote that:

> He shared my father's trust in the British people. When I, one day, reminded him of Lord Randolph's words 'I have never feared the English democracy' and 'Trust the people' and said I had been brought up on this, he said 'Ah, that is quite right. The English working man is no logician, like the French "Red", whom I also know. He is not thinking of new systems, but of having fairer treatment in this one.' I have found this true . . .
>
> Such men are not found today. Certainly they are not found in British politics. The tidal wave of democracy and the volcanic explosion of the War have swept the shores bare. . . . The leadership of the privileged has passed away; but it has not been succeeded by that of the eminent. We have entered the region of mass-effects. The pedestals which have for some years been vacant have now been demolished. Nevertheless, the world is moving on; and moving so fast that few have time to ask – whither. And to these few only a babel responds.

This nostalgia for a departed political system is natural, but it is interesting. The 'real political democracy' of 1900 involved the ownership of the vote by less than 27 per cent of the adult population; less than 60 per cent of adult males were enfranchised. With very few exceptions, the House of Commons was available only to those of independent means; certainly a full-time political career was the privilege of a small fragment of the nation. It was a nation in which, moreover, less than 2½ per cent of its population owned two-thirds of its total wealth, and in which there were less than 1¼ million tax-payers, although income tax did not commence until income exceeded £160 per annum.

Churchill's attitude towards the British working classes is one on which his admirers are extremely sensitive. Mr Martin Gilbert, in a sympathetic summary of Churchill's career,[36] has written that 'For twenty years Churchill, often in close partnership with Lloyd George, dominated the Liberal Party, driving it into bold social reform which changed the character of

---

36. Martin Gilbert: *Churchill* (Great Lives Observed Series, 1967), p. 4.

Britain . . . Churchill's record as a social reformer was remarkable, an achievement which future historians may well rank with his war leadership.' Churchill's son has devoted a substantial section of the second volume of his biography to the same theme.

The question accordingly may fairly be asked why it was that Churchill evoked such remarkably little affection and gratitude for his strivings on behalf of the working classes? The essentially paternalistic tone of the 1908–14 reforms and of Churchill's contribution has already been noted in the first part of this study; it was a tone that was acceptable in that period, but less so afterwards. But the essential cause may be more clearly seen to lie in the combination of the rasping hostility towards Labour when it did not know its place and what seemed to be a certain absence of compassion and comprehension of the circumstances in which so many of his fellow-countrymen lived but which was in fact ignorance and acceptance.

A significant indication of these attitudes may be seen in his persistent opposition to the principle that unemployment benefit was a right. He clung firmly to the Liberal principles of contributory insurance schemes, and rigidly differentiated between Insurance and Relief. In two articles entitled 'On the Abuse of the Dole' in the *Daily Telegraph* in March 1930 he put forward these arguments with characteristic vigour. He denounced 'the folly of all plans of marching off the unemployed in gangs and battalions to artificially fomented public works, and professing thereby to remedy unemployment', and declared that: 'There is, indeed, a small proportion for whom some disciplinary control in labour colonies might well be appropriate, but the vast majority must look only to re-absorption in the normal or natural industries.' And what if 'the normal or natural industries' were decaying and dying? Churchill's remedy was 'for the sheep, compassion; for the goats, discipline'. There must be firmness towards 'the ne'er-do-well, or the confirmed sturdy loafer, or the Bolshevik misfit, or other members of the tribes of Tired Tims and Weary Willies – alas! I must add manœuvring Marthas'. These arguments were reiterated in a series of withering speeches in the House of Commons and outside in the years 1929–31, while the Depression spread and the unemployment figures relentlessly rose.

These attitudes may fairly be seen in the context of his economic faiths, already described. Nevertheless, one clearly detects in them an absence of understanding that emphasizes Churchill's essential remoteness from the grim realities that were the daily burden of so many people in these years. Just as Erskine Childers in December 1921 had seen in Churchill 'the very type of overbearing British militarism' so did many unhappy people see in him in the inter-war years the personification of the remote politician who thought in grand and global terms and who listened to their protests with at best impatience, and often with hostility.

In this relationship one must emphasize the crucial importance of mood. The British working classes had, no doubt, much to be grateful for to Churchill. But the measures for which he had been responsible barely touched the real problems, and in reality he had little to offer beyond the continuance of *ad hoc* paternalistic reforms to meet the most pressing grievances. He often spoke feelingly and even with vehemence of the plight of the oppressed; whenever he was presented with suffering and distress his warm humanity revolted at the spectacle. But no Labour leader at any level regarded Churchill as a friend, or even sympathetic to his cause. If it be argued – as it has been – that the nature of Churchill's background and life took him far away from the existence of the majority of mankind, it may equally fairly be pointed out that these arguments applied with even greater force to King George V, who nevertheless succeeded to a remarkable extent in earning and retaining the trust of official Labour and the people. The roles of active politician and Monarch are, of course, very different, but it may be remarked that if the occupant of Buckingham Palace, Windsor Castle, Sandringham and Balmoral could have this comprehension, that of Chartwell might have possessed it as well.

Churchill's essentially conservative attitudes at this time can be seen in other ways.

In 1934 he was urging what was in effect a movement away from universal suffrage, and from one man, one vote. He wished to give 'extra votes to the millions of men and women, the heads of households and fathers of families who are really bearing the burden and responsibility of our fortunes upon their shoulders, and are pushing and dragging our national barrow up the hill'.[37] What did this mean? On 24 January, to the readers of the *Evening Standard*, he explained at greater length.

His diagnosis was that 'the proceedings of the House of Commons have sunk to the lowest ebb', that there was no interest in Parliament, and that popular discontent might well result in the next election in 'a majority of inexperienced and violent men' with the result that 'the responsible elements in the country will lose all control both of the House of Commons and of the executive'. 'There is,' he declared, 'a total lack of any continuity of political thought or direction. All we have is vague mass-driftings interrupted from time to time by spasmodic mob-votes.' Nor was this all: 'The old life of the House of Commons is rapidly passing away. In its place we have a timid Caesarism refreshing itself by occasional plebiscites ... It is perhaps no exaggeration to say that the next ten years may well see the end of the English parliamentary system'; the cure for this state of affairs was to retreat from universal suffrage, 'a universal suffrage electorate with a majority of women voters will have shown themselves incapable of preserving those forms of government under which our country has grown great and from which all the dignity and tolerance of our present life arise'. He proposed that every householder – 'by which I mean the man or woman who pays the rent and the rates of any dwelling in which more than two persons habitually reside'[38] – should have a second vote. 'They would all be persons who had to face the real problems of life in a manner quite different from the lodgers of all kinds of both sexes, dependent or otherwise.'

Nor did he wish to end here. If this was acceptable, 'there is no reason why it should not be further developed as time went

37. *The Listener*, 17 January 1934.
38. This would have been rather rough on property-owning bachelors and spinsters, not to mention property-owning childless couples.

on with the object of making the total vote at the poll representative of the pulling and driving power of the country, instead of its more dependent and more volatile elements'.

The basis of this attitude was – or certainly appeared to be – distrust and suspicion of a mass electorate. He attacked the 'throwing [of] an enormous mass of irresponsible voters into the scales as was done in Mr Baldwin's last administration' (of which he had been a leading member) for the reason that: 'All experience goes to show that once the vote has been given to everyone, and what is called full democracy has been achieved, the whole [political] system is very speedily broken up and swept away.' He had strenuously opposed women's suffrage before the war and the granting of the equal franchise for women in 1927. 'This decision,' Hankey wrote in a memorandum (12 April 1927) which was detached from the Cabinet Minutes and filed separately, 'was taken by a majority. The Chancellor of the Exchequer asked that his dissent might be placed on record, and the Secretary was instructed to note this on the file copy of the Minutes.'

Churchill was genuinely concerned about the decline of political life and by the possibility that unless reform was undertaken 'we shall see ourselves involved in a succession of disastrous fluctuations attended by continued constitutional decay, and that the establishment of sincere and vigorous government will be achieved through agencies very different from those which have hitherto been the peculiar glory and achievement of our island'. This concern was not unmerited in 1934, but the cure he proposed – proportional representation for 'the great cities' and plural voting for property-owners – was in effect a return to the pre-1914 electoral system. His argument that universal suffrage 'deprives the House of Commons of the respect of the nation', and that 'there are no longer eager political classes following keenly the progress of events' was, no doubt, wholly sincere. But the prescription was to return to the old privileged arrangement. And much had happened since 1914.

*

'Few are the public men in any modern state who have reached exceptional eminence without there being passed from foul lips to pricked-up ears some tale of shamefulness,' Churchill wrote in his biography of Marlborough. '"This one was corrupt"; or "that one was immoral": or "the other perverted". In the clubs, messes, and pothouses of every country such atrocious stories are the inseparable shadow of worldly success.'[39] For the whole of his political career Churchill's experience had confirmed this dismal aspect of public life. The allegation that he had behaved dishonourably on the occasion of his famous escape from the Boer prisoner-of-war camp at the age of twenty-five was whispered throughout his life, and repeated actions for libel never really succeeded in silencing the charge.[40] He was equally unsuccessful in rebutting the repeated canard about 'Tony-pandy'.

His private life afforded no material for justified criticism. There is a certain tedium in the fact that all popular heroes are claimed to have private lives of supreme nobility and purity,

39. *Marlborough*, Vol. I, p. 379.
40. Randolph Churchill has published the relevant documents in Volume I of his biography (pp. 479–84) but has not referred to the central fact that the allegation was based on the release to the Press by the Boer authorities of Churchill's letters seeking his release and offering 'any *parole* that may be required not to serve against the Republican forces'. This was an incorrect use of the word, and it is clear from reading contemporary reports that in some cases there was a genuine misunderstanding about what Churchill had offered. Another factor that prompted some British papers to take a hostile view of Churchill's actions was his reiterated claim in his letters to the Boer authorities that he had played no part in the defence of the armoured train immediately prior to his capture and that he was unarmed. Churchill was in fact armed, although he did not use his weapon, and he did not hesitate to point out after his escape that he had played a considerable part in the defence of the train. (His letter to Joseph Chamberlain of 4 May 1901 concerning 'some sort of military mention or decoration' for himself is quoted in Companion Volume I, Part 2, pp. 1069–70.) The comment of the *Westminster Gazette* to the effect that 'Mr Churchill's non-combatancy is indeed a mystery, but one thing is clear – that he cannot have the best of both worlds' was to the point. But there was of course a substantial difference between a genuine misunderstanding of Churchill's use of the word 'parole' and the deliberately malicious distortions of the facts that took place.

but Churchill was among the relatively few modern British politicians with an unshakeable reputation for absolute personal probity. He himself has written of his marriage that it was 'much the most fortunate and joyous event which happened to me in the whole of my life. For what can be more glorious than to be united with a being incapable of an ignoble thought?' The devotion of the Churchills to each other was so evident and so touching that Eddie Marsh's tribute that 'you have given your countrymen illustration of faith and happiness in marriage' is in no sense exaggerated.

Charges against Churchill's character were accordingly concentrated upon his unreliability. As Winterton has written: 'A "whispering campaign" about him sedulously encouraged by, if not originating from, Ministers started in the lobbies of the House of Commons and in the country. He was, it was hinted, another but a lesser Lloyd George, with the same brilliant gifts and power of oratory, but unstable in character; he would never be in any Government again, because he invariably tried to domineer over his colleagues and persist in wrong courses.'[41] Part of this was based on the suggestion that he was a man in decline. Liddell Hart has recorded Duff Cooper's comment in 1936 that Churchill was 'not so quick as he had been in grasping points',[42] and as early as 1931 Nicolson had written that he had 'A great round white face like a blister. Incredibly aged. Looks like pictures of Lord Holland. An elder statesman. His spirits also have declined and he sighs that he has lost his old fighting power.'[43] These comments, and others to the same effect, appear somewhat absurd in view of subsequent events, but it is striking that one of the principal characteristics of accounts of Churchill in 1940 emphasize his renewed vitality and marked improvement in appearance. A man of intense vitality and with ambition undimmed who is languishing in political impotence almost invariably bears the marks of his frustration and underemployed energies, and there is no reason to doubt the veracity of the reiterated opinions of contemporaries in the 1930s on the

41. Winterton: *Orders of the Day*, p. 185.
42. Liddell Hart, op. cit., Vol I, p. 320.
43. Nicolson, *Diaries*, p. 41.

signs of Churchill's apparent decline. He was, after all, at an age at which most men yearn for retirement.

Churchill's enjoyment of alcohol has created legends – to which he himself contributed[44] – which have assumed startling proportions. Later, at the height of his fame, the grossly exaggerated stories of his drinking habits became a subject for admiration and affection, but in the 1930s they were not always received with such emotions. 'I always found L.G. much the quicker in uptake,' Liddell Hart has written; 'L.G.'s greater abstemiousness may have helped to keep his mind clearer.'[45] As there have been hints that Churchill drank more heavily at this period of his life than at any other,[46] I am grateful to a close friend of this time for the following comment:

He never drank the sort of quantities of alcohol frequently ascribed to him at the time, though indeed he drank *somewhat* more than the average. He was basically a wine drinker – champagne at lunch sometimes and dinner always. But the idea that he drank a whole bottle or more at either meal was untrue. . . . He might or he might not have a glass of brandy as a liqueur afterwards. Infrequently he would have one glass of sherry before the meal. He did not really like sherry. He did not drink port. He would have about three really mild whiskies and sodas – sometimes brandy and soda – as a thirst quencher during the day. Not before 11 a.m. (one, sometimes), one at tea-time, and one before going to bed, perhaps one other during the evening. . . . W. was usually most careful never to absorb a lot of *mixed* drinks. . . . You are of course quite right about the wildly exaggerated stories circulated, and also W's curious humour in enjoying them and not contradicting them.

Another who saw a great deal of Churchill at this time has emphasized what he has called 'the mathematical exactness' of the amount Churchill drank daily, and the times at which he drank. He has also stressed the fact that Churchill hardly ever mixed his drinks. The statement that Churchill drank '*some-*

44. See, for example, his gay morning greeting to Lord Kilmuir: 'David, have *another* glass of port.' (Kilmuir, op. cit., p. 166.)

45. Liddell Hart, op. cit., p. 373.

46. See, for example, Anthony Storr: 'Winston Churchill; the Man', op. cit., p. 243.

what more than the average' requires some qualification. People who tried to equal his consumption often found themselves in difficulties.

During these years Churchill spent as much time as possible at Chartwell, which he had bought in 1922 when it had been long uninhabited and was, as one of his daughters has written, 'wildly overgrown and untidy, and contained all the mystery of houses that had not been lived in for many years'.[47] Although Mrs Churchill was responsible for most of the alterations and the running of the house, its personality was very much that of Churchill, and it was, as one who knew it well has remarked, 'an astonishing combination of private home, Grand Hotel, and a Government Department'. He kept a *pied-à-terre* in London at Morpeth Mansions, close to Westminster, but used it only occasionally. It was at Chartwell that his real life was spent. Here, in this surprisingly peaceful part of Kent, he built walls, created lakes, roofed cottages, painted and wrote. He devoted intense thought and applied much energy on laying out the Chartwell grounds. Every visitor – however distinguished or sedentary – was liable to summary conscription for these enter-prises, which were administered with dash and spirit. His ponds were inhabited by fat and complacent goldfish, who occupied a particularly warm place in Churchill's affections. The Chartwell swans were almost equally favoured. The swimming pool heated by two immense boilers with gargantuan appetites was another feature on which much care and attention, and no small expense, had been lavished. A friend has a vivid recollection of one Christmas Day, when the air was crisp and cold, and the frost lay on the ground. Chartwell was enveloped in a deep and mysterious fog. On arriving at the house, after groping his way up the drive, the guest discovered the entire Churchill family in bathing-suits in the drawing-room. The cause of the fog was now apparent. The bathers skipped across the frosty grass to the simmering, shrouded pool, 'now bubbling like a New Zealand hot spring'. Churchill entered first, and emerged gasping at the heat. The rest of the party entered the water shivering, and

47. Sarah Churchill: *A Thread in the Tapestry*, p. 32.

emerged very pink, very hurriedly. There was then a frenzied scamper back to the house.

Churchill, at home as elsewhere, imbued everything with a gusto and a freshness which was endearing and exhilarating. As Lady Asquith has written, 'every ploy became "a matter of pith and moment".' He still retained the ardour, gaiety and excitement of youth, and only those who knew him best also knew of the periods of deep depression, the unwelcome visitations of 'The Black Dog'. But Beaverbrook has not been alone in his preference for 'Churchill Down' to 'Churchill Up', and the emergence of the quality that Birkenhead once described as 'almost feminine in its caressing charm'. Light always kept breaking in. His happy family, his enthusiasms and activity saved him from the full effects of the Churchill melancholia. He was a devoted and indulgent father. Unlike Lord Randolph, he had consolations and activities which re-charged his emotional batteries, fortified him against misfortune and gave him revivals of hope for the future.

An account by Lady Diana Cooper of a visit to Chartwell in September 1934 deserves to be quoted as an excellent portrait of the family at this time:

Forty winks in the afternoon and then (unexpectedly) bathing at 7 in pouring rain, intensely cold with a grey half-light of approaching night, yet curiously enough very enjoyable in its oddness. Freda Ward, Winston, Duff, Clemmie, Randolph and a child, in fact the whole party, were splashing about with gleeful screams in this sad crepuscle. The secret is that the bath is heated, and it is Winston's delightful toy. Just now, again, twenty-four hours later, he called for Inches, the butler, and said: 'Tell Allen to heave a lot more coal on. I want the thing full blast.' Inches returned to say that Allen was out for the day. 'Then tell Arthur I want it full blast', but it was Arthur's day out as well, so the darling old schoolboy went surreptitiously and stoked it himself for half an hour, coming in to the verge of apoplexy. Again all had to bathe in the afternoon.

Then 'feeding the poor little birds' is a huge joy to him. They consist of five foolish geese, five furious black swans, two ruddy sheldrakes, two white swans – Mr Juno and Mrs Jupiter, so called because they got the sexes wrong to begin with, two Canadian geese ('Lord and Lady Beaverbrook') and some miscellaneous ducks. The basket of bread on Winston's arm is used first to lure and coax and then as ammunition.[48]

Thus, in spite of political misfortune, and although it would be wrong to deny the existence of strains and tensions within the family circle, life at Chartwell was suffused with gaiety and happiness. As Churchill has written of this period, 'I never had a dull or idle moment from morning till midnight, and with my happy family around me dwelt at peace within my habitation.'[49]

*

During these years Churchill lived by his pen, or, as he has put it, 'I lived in fact from mouth to hand.' He demanded a very high standard of living, and he worked for it. With the exception of his parliamentary salary and an unexpected family inheritance in the early 1920s, he was dependent upon writing for his income. The 1930s was in quantity if not in quality his most productive period, when he published *My Early Life*, *The Eastern Front*, *The Life of Marlborough*, in four volumes, and wrote most of *The History of the English-Speaking Peoples*. He also wrote well over two hundred newspaper and magazine articles, and selections from these were published in *Thoughts and Adventures* (1932), *Great Contemporaries* (1937), and *Step By Step* (1939). Selections from his India speeches and those on Defence and Foreign Affairs in the House of Commons, edited by his son and published under the title of *Arms and the Covenant* in 1938, emphasized the extent of Churchill's activity in these years.[50] This is, by any standard, a very substantial record of work. 'Writing a long and substantial book,' he once remarked, 'is like having a friend and companion at your side, to whom you can always turn for comfort and amusement, and whose society becomes more attractive as a new and widening field of interest is lighted in the mind.'

Churchill's technique did not change very much during his life, although it became more sophisticated and professional. By

48. Lady Diana Cooper: *The Light of Common Day*, pp. 155–6.

49. *The Gathering Storm*, p. 62.

50. For a comprehensive list, see F. Woods: *Bibliography of the Works of Sir Winston Churchill* (Revised edition, 1969).

this time he was able to execute his major works with some lavishness. He assembled his assistants with care, and entrusted them with particular aspects of the project in hand.[51] With the material assembled, he would dictate the narrative, frequently at inconvenient moments for his secretaries. He re-wrote copiously and extensively. The work marched on from draft to draft, until the proofs, which he regarded in much the same light as most authors have to regard the penultimate typed version; he himself has testified to his pleasure in 'playing with the proofs', which is an expensive form of literary satisfaction. Eddie Marsh was entrusted with the grammatical details.

In essentials, this had been the technique used in his biography of his father. In that case, Churchill had had his father's papers printed and numbered. When he wanted a document inserted he would give its number to the secretary, who would cut it out and paste it in the appropriate place. The long process of amendment and improvement would follow – and this process frequently involved the changing of the original documents to fit in more neatly into the narrative, to the point when it was sometimes difficult for the subsequent biographer of Lord Randolph to recognize the original.[52]

There are several aspects of Churchill's technique that require emphasis. In the first place, although he did receive assistance in his major works, he was always careful to keep the real control in his own hands. His memory was, as one assistant has recorded, 'Napoleonic'. Although he was always willing to receive advice and incorporate it, he could be obstinate on some points.[53] Then, he himself read very extensively on the subject,

51. Among the assistants during this period were Mr John Wheldon, Mr Maurice Ashley and Mr F. W. Deakin. I am most grateful to the latter for advice in this section of this study.

52. See the author's *Lord Randolph Churchill*, Introduction (1959). Sir Winston and the Duke of Marlborough kindly gave me permission to examine his drafts for Churchill's biography, in the Blenheim library.

53. One example was significant. To the dismay of his advisers, Churchill insisted upon retaining the story of King Alfred and the cakes in his *History of the English-Speaking Peoples*, making the point that legends and fables are of as great importance in a nation's history as well-authenticated facts. The advisers subsequently realized the wisdom of this argument.

and every discussion with his assistants was a fully informed one. He did not claim that his knowledge and reading were comprehensive, but he endeavoured to cover the field with great thoroughness.

It is always of interest to trace some of Churchill's most striking passages from their often crude beginnings to the final version. *Lord Randolph Churchill* opens with a magnificent description of Blenheim, which was the final version of a very long and excessively grandiose and cumbersome earlier version that is too long for quotation here. Another example may be given to demonstrate the point. He wrote to his mother on 22 May 1898: 'It is the fault of all booms of sentiment that they carry men too far and lead to reactions. Militarism degenerates [in] to brutality. Loyalty promotes tyranny and sycophancy. Humanitarianism becomes maudlin and ridiculous. Patriotism shades into cant. Imperialism sinks to Jingoism . . .' [54]

In *The River War* this theme is developed:

All great movements, every vigorous impulse that a community may feel, become perverted and distorted as time passes, and the atmosphere of the earth seems fatal to the noble aspirations of its peoples. A wide humanitarian sympathy in a nation easily degenerates into hysteria. A military spirit tends towards brutality. Liberty leads to licence, restraint to tyranny. The pride of race is distended to blustering arrogance. The fear of God produces bigotry and superstition. There appear no exceptions to the mournful rule, and the best efforts of men, however glorious their early results, have dismal ending, like plants which shoot and bud and put forth beautiful flowers, and then grow rank and coarse and are withered by the winter. [55]

In assessing Churchill's writings, the assessment of the critic is inevitably swayed by personal likes and dislikes. It is the opinion of this critic that Churchill's literary work showed a certain decline in the 1930s. The rhetorical note is increasingly more evident than before, and the contrast between the rhetoric of *The World Crisis* and *Marlborough* is very evident if

54. Randolph S. Churchill: *Winston S. Churchill*, Companion Volume I, p. 938.

55. *The River War* (1951 edition), p. 35.

they are re-read one after the other. For all its pitfalls as history, *The World Crisis* must surely stand as Churchill's masterpiece. After it, anything must appear as an anti-climax. But, even allowing for this, the weaknesses of Churchill's technique and style seem to become increasingly apparent in *Marlborough* and *The History of the English-Speaking Peoples*, and in the later articles in *Great Contemporaries*. Philip Guedalla has referred to 'the fatal lullaby of a majestic style'; but it is not so much this fact as the ponderousness and massiveness of his later work that limit its effectiveness. Churchill had written as a young man that: 'Few authors are rich men. Few human beings are insensible to the value of money ... Hurried style, exaggerated mannerisms and plagiarism replace the old careful toil. The author writes no more for fame but for wealth. Consequently his books become inferior. All this is very sad but very true.' This description could certainly not be applied in its entirety to Churchill, but his dependence upon writing for his income was certainly an element in the decline in his very high standards, and the mannerisms became undoubtedly exaggerated. As the present Lord Birkenhead had commented: 'Churchill the writer never wholly freed himself from Churchill the orator. Sometimes we feel that the rhythm is metallic and remorseless, and that the sentences spring to attention like soldiers on parade. At other moments we are conscious of his lack of historical objectivity, of the fact that he is usually justifying a policy or a cause, and that this perception of the feelings and motives of others is dim and uncertain.' [56]

Churchill's massive biography of John, Duke of Marlborough, of which the first volume was published in 1933, was his only venture into biography apart from that of his father. Like that work, it was a labour of love, of reclamation, and of family piety. The last factor was important. Churchill's sense of family loyalty was one of his most endearing traits, and he always deeply resented any slight, real or imagined, upon his family's name. It was Rosebery who had first opened the key to the biography of 'Duke John' by drawing Churchill's attention to Paget's *Examen*, and the answer to Macaulay's censures of

56. Report of the Royal Society of Literature, 1965.

Marlborough. Churchill's account of this episode is given in the Preface: 'The aged and crippled statesman arose from the luncheon table, and, with great difficulty but sure knowledge, made his way along the passages of The Durdans to the exact nook in his capacious working library where "Paget's Examen" reposed. "There," he said, taking down this unknown, out-of-print masterpiece, "is the answer to Macaulay."'

(The Rosebery family version is that Rosebery, who could only move in a wheel-chair, summoned his butler and told him exactly where the book was to be found in his vast collection; the butler found it at once.)

If anything, Churchill identified himself even more fiercely with Marlborough than he had with Lord Randolph. It is indeed this intense feeling of personal identification with his subject that is so conspicuous a feature of both of his biographies. It is unfortunate that his vaguely projected biography of Napoleon came to nothing, but it is probable that in this case as well the sense of personal identification would have been predominant. In the case of Marlborough, as soon as Paget had given him the clue, he pursued Macaulay with relentless ardour, to the point that it assumed the proportions of an obsession; he was intent, as he put it, that Truth would 'fasten the label "Liar" to his [Macaulay's] genteel tail-coats'. Having devoted some three chapters to Macaulay's treatment of the Brest Expedition – which had been the principal contribution of Paget in 1874 – he does not end there. Time and again Macaulay is summoned up – often quite irrelevantly – for further reprimands. Any historian who had accepted any part of Macaulay's thesis received similar treatment. Thus, Basil Williams, 'apparently oblivious of forty years of accepted opinion and research, inertly or docilely reproduces the crude, exploded slander that "the gallant General Talmash" fell "as victim to Marlborough's treachery in the ill-fated Brest Expedition".' Historians who have in any way accepted the Jacobite Papers as genuine are slated for 'an aberration of historical technique'. There is no historian so ferocious as the amateur who believes that he has got the professionals on the run. It is good lusty stuff – if that is the sort of thing you like. G. M. Trevelyan was justified in pointing

out that with the exception of the Brest Expedition episode,
Churchill accepted all Macaulay's facts; that Marlborough's
patron was the man who kept his sister; that he took money
from his mistress and invested it well; that he deserted James II
when in his military service; that he subsequently corresponded
with the Jacobites. As Trevelyan pointed out, 'An historian
who, before the days of our modern research, was deceived by
these phenomena into thinking Marlborough a bad man was not
necessarily dishonest.'[57]

The most marked feature of *Marlborough* apart from the
special pleading that characterizes it throughout, is the style. It
is Churchill at his most florid. I cannot improve upon Professor
J. H. Plumb's comments on this aspect of Churchill's writing:

> So long as the events or the human reactions were on a bold scale –
> dealing with courage, endurance, misery or defeat – he wrote with
> authority and with deep understanding: often his words clothed his
> feeling in majestic and memorable phrases. If the human or political
> situation became complex – a mixture of conscious or unconscious
> motives, of good and evil, of treachery and patriotism, existing side
> by side – then he tended to stumble or to evade the issues. That is
> why the overall pictures both of Marlborough and Lord Randolph
> are too simple, too direct.[58]

In *Marlborough*, the accounts of the battles – notably Blenheim and the storming of the Schellenberg – are magnificent, for
the crash and pomp of the battle are faithfully reflected in the
crash and pomp of Churchill's style. The same is true of the
political parts although the depiction of motives tends to be
somewhat crude: 'Shaftesbury was at the head of a flaming
Opposition . . . The ferocity of the Whigs knew no limit, and
their turpitude lay not far behind.'

But away from battle and the high drama of politics, it does
not work. Indeed, parts of *Marlborough* read like a parody of
Churchill's style at its worst. The portrait of Louis XIV may
be cited.

57. *Times Literary Supplement*, 19 October 1933.
58. *Spectator*, 1 July 1966.

We have no patience with the lackey pens which have sought to invest this long, hateful process with the appearances of dignity and honour. During the whole of his life Louis XIV was the curse and pest of Europe. No worse enemy of human freedom has ever appeared in the trappings of polite civilization. Insatiable appetite, cold, calculating ruthlessness, monumental conceit, presented themselves armed with fire and sword. The veneer of culture and good manners, of brilliant ceremonies and elaborate etiquette, only adds a heightening effect to the villainy of his life's story. Better the barbarian conquerors of antiquity, primordian figures of the abyss, than this high-heeled, beperiwigged dandy, strutting amid the bows and scrapes of mistresses and confessors to the torment of his age. Petty and mediocre in all except his lusts and power, the Sun King disturbed and harried mankind during more than fifty years of arrogant pomp.

So much for Louis XIV! Churchill's histories are populated with the Good and the Bad. Churchill was always greatly given to broad effects. It is not the least of the occupational hazards of politics. *Marlborough* abounds in broad effects. He writes of 'public opinion' in twentieth-century terms. We read of 'the mass of the nation' being 'stirred to its depths' by the Revocation of the Edict of Nantes, how 'in the ale-houses or upon the village greens ballads and songs expressed the popular sentiment against the French', and how 'the sense of common cause grew across the barriers of class, race, creed and interest in the hearts of millions of men'. These are exactly the kind of magnificent but wild generalizations for which the despised Macaulay received such a drubbing.

But it is the portrait of England, and England's history, that is perhaps the most intriguing and also the most revealing aspect of *Marlborough*. This portrait, to be carried forward much further in *The History of the English-Speaking Peoples*, which may accurately be described as the last of the Whig histories, reflects Churchill's idealized and over-romanticized concepts, and is of interest for that purpose: in particular, the glowing portrait of 'the small island' carrying forward 'intact and enshrined, all that peculiar structure of law and liberty, all her inheritance of learning and letters, which are today the treasure of the most powerful family in the human race'. Are there not echoes here of passages in *The Story of the Malakand Field Force*?

No examination of Churchill's political career in the 1930s can ignore the significance of the tone and style of his historical writings. His sense of history was more emotional than intellectual, but it is in this period of his life that the dominance of his faith in England's historical destiny, and his romanticized view of her past become particularly manifest. Much of his contempt for MacDonald, Baldwin and Neville Chamberlain was based upon his disgust at what he deemed to be their betrayal of England's grandeur and destiny.

In this context the contrast drawn in *Marlborough* between the embattled hero and the snarling politicians at home is particularly significant. Churchill had no professional training as a historian, and had no experience, even rudimentary experience, of the complexities of historical criticism. He was not, furthermore, a man greatly interested in matters intellectual, and would demand brief memoranda from his assistants to summarize the principal points at issue rather than involve himself in the problem. His outstanding technical quality was as a narrator. His books tended to be of enormous length – in almost every case far too long, with masses of material proudly laid out, much of which could have been eliminated, and some of which had clearly not been digested by the author – but the pace is maintained to the last page.

But if *Marlborough* fails both as biography and history, its results on Churchill himself went far beyond the writing of the book. It gave him an absorbing interest at a dark moment in his political fortunes and it also gave him a more acute realization of the problems and hazards of creating and retaining a Grand Alliance. Some of the best passages in the book deal with these complexities. In casting himself as Marlborough, grappling with the manifold problems of diplomacy, strategy, supply, terrain and tactics, he was affording himself a kind of dress rehearsal for the problems of 1940–5. Leo Amery goes even further, and has said that 'In his great ancestor, Marlborough, he discovered that fusion of political and military ideals, as well as the inspiration of family piety, for which he had all his life been groping.'[59]

*

My Early Life (1930) is in so different a vein that it is difficult to believe that it came from the same mouth. Of all his books it is the most genial and, in a very real sense, warm. Churchill's memory – like that of all autobiographers – was conveniently selective. Like F. E. Smith, who dwelt so mournfully on the allegedly grinding poverty of his youth as he grew older until he firmly believed the harrowing fictions himself, Churchill subsequently exaggerated his early backwardness at school – thus providing countless wily schoolboys and troubled parents with exaggerated comfort. The narrowness by which he avoided the fate of 'social wastrel' drawn for him by his father is described in detail by Randolph Churchill, and need not be emphasized here. The charm of the book lies in its warmth and wit; it contains, furthermore, some remarkable portraits of individuals, of which those of Mrs Everest and Colonel Brabazon, commanding the 4th Hussars, may be particularly noted.

The most well-known parts of *My Early Life* are what might be called the 'adventure' parts, particularly the accounts of action on the North-West Frontier, in Cuba and in South Africa, and other features of the book have tended to receive less consideration. The outstanding feature of the work is the development of Churchill's self-portrait, often wittily drawn. Some examples may suffice.

I had a feeling once about Mathematics, that I saw it all – Depth beyond Depth was revealed to me – the Byss and the Abyss. I saw, as one might see the transit of Venus – or even the Lord Mayor's Show, a quantity passing through infinity and changing its sign from plus to minus. I saw exactly how it happened and the tergiversation was inevitable: and how the one step involved all the others. It was like politics. But it was after dinner and I let it go!

Certainly the prolonged education indispensable to the progress of Society is not natural to mankind. It cuts against the grain. A boy would like to follow his father in pursuit of food or prey. He would like to be doing serviceable things so far as his utmost strength allowed. He would like to be earning wages however small to keep up the home. He would like to have some leisure of his own to use or misuse as he pleased. He would ask little more than the right to work or starve. And then perhaps in the evenings a real love of learning would come to those who were worthy – and why try to stuff it into those who are not? – and knowledge and thought would open the 'magic casements' of the mind . . . I am all for the Public Schools but I do not want to go there again.

Twenty to twenty-five! These are the years! Don't be content with things as they are. 'The earth is yours and the fulness thereof.' Enter upon your inheritance, accept your responsibilities. Raise the glorious flags again, advance them upon the new enemies, who constantly gather upon the front of the human army, and have only to be assaulted to be overthrown. Don't take No for an answer. Never submit to failure. Do not be fobbed off with mere personal success or acceptance. You will make all kinds of mistakes; but as long as you are generous and true, and also fierce, you cannot hurt the world or even seriously distress her. She was made to be wooed and won by youth. She has lived and thrived only by repeated subjugations.

And there is an account of a dinner with Lord Sandhurst, at Government House, Poona:

His Excellency, after the health of the Queen-Empress had been drunk and dinner was over, was good enough to ask my opinion upon several matters, and considering the magnificent character of his hospitality, I thought it would be unbecoming in me not to reply fully. I have forgotten the particular points of British and Indian affairs upon which he sought my counsel; all I can remember is that I responded generously. There were indeed moments when he seemed willing to impart his own views; but I thought it would be ungracious to put him to so much trouble; and he very readily subsided. He kindly sent his aide-de-camp with us to make sure we found our way back to camp all right. On the whole, after forty-eight hours of intensive study, I formed a highly favourable opinion about India. Sometimes, thought I, one sees these things more completely at first sight .

My Early Life is an authentic adventure story, full of night marches, cavalry charges, expeditions on the North-West

Frontier, polo-matches, pitched battles against the hordes of the Khalifa or the crack shots of the Boers, with an escape from a prisoner-of-war camp and two parliamentary elections thrown in. The touch is light, and the pace vigorous and gay. It is, deservedly, a classic of autobiography.

*

Churchill's books, no less than his many newspaper articles, provided him not only with essential income and a necessary outlet for his energies, but the means by which he could keep his name before the public. Writing, fortunately, was a pleasure to him. 'Writing a book was an adventure,' as he said many years later (2 November 1949). 'To begin with it was a toy, and amusement; then it became a mistress, and then a master, and then a tyrant.' He chose his subjects well, and he worked on them assiduously. Although he had his young men to research for him, the finished product very much bore the stamp of his personality; everyone who worked for him was impressed by the width of his knowledge and by the enormous care he took over his books. As a contributor to newspapers and magazines he was supremely professional, and not least over the fees he charged. If he was well paid by the standards of the time – as he was – he gave excellent value. And the money, after all, was put to admirable use. If the thirties are to be regarded as wasted years in Churchill's political career, this opinion must be substantially offset by the opportunities given to him to study and to write. He re-created an old and valuable link between literature and public life in England. Indeed, with the possible exception of Morley, whose best writing had been done before he entered politics, Churchill is the only British politician of the front rank in this century who has made a genuine, original and valuable contribution to the literature of his country. And it can hardly be stressed sufficiently that Churchill's sense of history was of deep importance in his outlook on life. Berlin has drawn attention to a criticism of Churchill's style written in 1928, and has commented that 'the stern critic and his audience were profoundly mistaken. What he and they denounced as so much tinsel and hollow pasteboard was in reality solid: it was this author's natural means for the expression of his heroic, highly coloured, sometimes over-simple and even naïve, but always genuine, vision of life.'[60] If his interpretations were somewhat dramatic and, in a good sense, schoolboyish, it remains a very real factor in his emotional composition, and endows his work with an excitement and an immediacy which is rarely seen in the professional historian. In his views of history as in his politics, he was a romantic, with a romantic's eye on men and events. For in this, as in all else, there was no concealment and no dissimulation.

*

When Baldwin retired in May 1937 – 'No man,' Harold Nicolson wrote, 'has ever left in such a blaze of affection'[61] – and was succeeded by Neville Chamberlain there was virtually no expectation that Churchill would receive major office in the new Administration. He himself, now somewhat in the role of elder statesman, seconded the motion to elect Chamberlain leader of the Conservative Party in Baldwin's place. The dramas and anxieties of 1936 seemed to belong to some extraordinary and remote past. After the storms and tempests, calm. Only those who knew the treachery of the political tides could appreciate that this would only be an interlude.

On 11 June Churchill wrote:

How has it all gone in Europe while we have been thinking about our own affairs? I, personally, have never been able to forget Europe. It hangs over my mind like a vulture . . .

It is curious that Parliament, which a year ago showed itself genuinely concerned with our defence, has now forgotten even that there could be such a fact as danger. Some say 'How right the Government were not to be alarmed by the scaremongers! How right they were not to have a Ministry of Supply and not to upset the ordinary business prosperity of the country! A whole year has passed and nothing has happened. How stultified are those who pride "alarm"!' But this complacent movement may soon be stirred by less comfortable reflections.

60. Isaiah Berlin: *Mr Churchill in 1940*, p. 9.
61. Nicolson, op. cit., p. 301.

Although Churchill continued his speeches on defence, and his fortnightly articles in the *Evening Standard* throughout 1937, he was conscious of the sharp fall in the atmosphere of alarm in the country, and it is apparent that he himself entertained some doubts about the future course of events in Europe. This year he republished his 1935 article on Hitler in *Great Contemporaries* which, despite its attention to 'the darker side of his work and creed', was not entirely hostile. Hitler's 'long, wearying battle for the German heart' was described with sympathy: 'The story of that struggle, cannot be read without admiration for the courage, the perseverance, and the vital force which enabled him to challenge, defy, conciliate or overcome, all the authority or resistances which barred his path.' While Churchill strongly criticized Hitler's methods and particularly his victimization of the Jews he reserved his main censure for the follies of 'the complacent, feckless and purblind victors' for giving him his opportunity. And the final portrait was not unhopeful:

What manner of man is this grim figure who has performed these superb toils and loosed these frightful evils? Does he still share the passions he evoked? Does he, in the full sunlight of worldly triumph at the head of the great nation he has raised from the dust, still feel racked by the hatreds and antagonisms of his desperate struggle: or will they be discarded like the armour and the cruel weapons of strife under the mellowing influences of success? Evidently a burning question for men of all nations! Those who have met Herr Hitler face to face in public business or on social terms have found a highly competent, cool, well-informed functionary with an agreeable manner, a disarming smile, and few have been unaffected by a subtle personal magnetism. Nor is this impression merely the dazzle of power. He exerted it on his companions at every stage in his struggle, even when his fortunes were in the lowest depths. Thus the world lives on hopes that the worst is over, and that we may yet live to see Hitler a gentler figure in a happier age.

Meanwhile, he makes speeches to the nations, which are sometimes characterised by candour and moderation. Recently he has offered many words of reassurance , eagerly lapped up by those who have been so tragically wrong about Germany in the past. Only time can show, but, meanwhile, the great wheels revolve; the rifles, the cannon, the tanks, the shot and shell, the air-bombs, the poison-gas cylinders, the aeroplanes, submarines and now the beginnings of a Fleet, flow in ever-broadening streams from the already largely war-mobilized arsenal and factories of Germany.

The virtual duplication of this article in the *News of the World* on 10 October, and other comments in articles at the same time, demonstrates that Churchill – at least in public – was still reserving final judgement on Hitler. It was in October that he made his comment on Mussolini to which reference has already been made,[62] and on 17 September he denied he was 'an enemy of Germany' and wrote of Hitler that 'if our country were defeated I hope we should find a champion as indomitable to restore our courage and lead us back to our place among the nations'. Although he continued to argue for better defences and a more positive foreign policy, the trumpet was beginning to give a less certain sound. This was to be detected in an article in the *Evening Standard* on 15 October, entitled 'War is NOT imminent.' Churchill emphasized that the Dictators must be treated firmly, and from a position of strength, and that the Anglo-French Alliance, particularly in the Mediterranean, should be strong. Churchill was not arguing that dangers had passed, or that vigilance could be relaxed, which is an impression that could be gained if passages in this article are quoted out of their context.[63] Nevertheless, this passage is of significance:

Three or four years ago I was myself a loud alarmist. I tried to bring home all the dangers that were coming upon the world, and to arouse Parliament, and the Government who were misleading Parliament, to the need of rearming. In those days the danger was distant and the time ample. Now the dangers are more clearly defined, and at the same time great exertions are being made to meet them. This, therefore, is not the time to exaggerate dangers. On the contrary, they must be faced with courage. In spite of the risks which wait on prophecy I declare my belief that a major war is not imminent, and I still believe there is a good chance of no major war taking place in our time . . .

62. See p. 330.
63. See, for example, Sir Basil Liddell Hart's article in *Encounter*, April 1966.

It cannot be taken for certain that as time passes the general balance of European armaments will become more favourable to the Parliamentary nations. Well was it written: 'Agree with thine adversary quickly whilst thou art in the way with him.'

Perhaps of greater significance was his attitude to the Spanish Civil War, which, as Mr A. J. P. Taylor has remarked, 'provided for the generation of the thirties the emotional experience of their lifetime'.[64] As has been emphasized Churchill had been strongly opposed to any British or French involvement. No avowedly Communist movement was likely to attract his sympathy. As he himself subsequently wrote: 'In this quarrel I was neutral. Naturally I was not in favour of the Communists. How could I be, when if I had been a Spaniard they would have murdered me and my family and friends?'[65] But the second reason was hardly less important: 'I was sure however that with all the rest they had on their hands the British Government were right to keep out of Spain.'[66] The dominant factor in Churchill's thinking was the crucial importance of concentrating attention upon the German threat, but it is difficult to accept the contention of his 'neutrality'. His description of the Republican Government (10 August 1936) gave an early indication of his bias:

The constitutional and would-be Liberal and democratic Republic found itself sliding steadily towards the Left. Its Ministers soothed the middle classes by the appearances of a Parliamentary system. They weakened or paralysed the resisting power of Conservatives and Monarchists: but they found themselves falling into the grip of dark, violent forces coming ever more plainly into the open, and operating by murder, pillage and industrial disturbance.

Churchill went on in the same article to declare that 'Two antagonistic modern systems are in mortal grapple. Fascism

64. Taylor: *English History* (1914–45), p. 395.

65. *The Gathering Storm*, p. 167.

66. ibid., p. 167. It may be noted that in the version of an article of 4 September 1936, published in *Step by Step*, the final words are omitted: 'Britain must arm herself against dangers from abroad. She must also discern and unmask the many false pretences under which Communism advances among her Continental friends, and even tries to rear its head at home.'

confronts Communism. The spirit and prowess of Mussolini and Hitler strive with those of Trotsky and of Bela Kun'; but he concluded that: 'revivified Fascist Spain in closest sympathy with Italy and Germany is one kind of disaster. A Communist Spain spreading its snaky tentacles through Portugal and France is another, and many will think the worse.' 'This Spanish welter,' he wrote, 'is not the business of either of us.'

It was Churchill's manifest support for the Franco-ists as the lesser of two evils that aroused such irritation among the ardent supporters of the Republicans. In article after article he emphasized this fact, notably by his habit of referring to Franco's forces as 'the Anti-Red movement'. In one article (21 August 1936) he said that the majority of the nation supported Franco, and referred to the Republicans as 'the Communist, Anarchist and Syndicalist forces which are now openly warring for absolute dominance in Spain'. And there follows a passage which demonstrates his attitude:

Around Burgos and Valladolid, around Cadiz and Seville, dwell communities as solidly Conservative as our Home Counties. In these regions the army leaders find themselves upheld by a friendly population with a wealthy middle class and a daring martial youth. In the Carlist provinces there are other reserves of strength which provide, as long ago in La Vendée, the spectacle of a countryside passionately united in support of Church and Monarchy. Here are strong foundations and bases for the rebel armies. All history shows that armies without civil populations behind them are prone to collapse. No such weakness afflicts the Anti-Red Movement.

Although he expressed repugnance at the atrocities committed by both sides, it was unfortunate that Churchill always managed to differentiate between them. Thus, the Communists indulged in 'butcheries' while Franco was only guilty of a grievous error of military judgement by not offering fair terms of surrender to beaten foes, for 'such a course would markedly help the winning side'. But the Madrid Government, he declared (2 October 1936) had committed the 'hideous series of nightly butcheries which have robbed [it] of the lineaments of a civilised power' and Largo Caballero was referred to as the 'Lenin of Spain'. It would appear, from Churchill's version of events, that the Government forces dragged 'helpless and defenceless political opponents' whose only crime was that 'they belong to the classes opposed to Communism' to slaughter whereas the Franco-ist forces never descended to this 'lowest pit of human degradation'. He averred that:

> Although it seems to be the practice of the Nationalist forces to shoot a proportion of their prisoners taken in arms, they cannot be accused of having fallen to the level of committing the atrocities which are the daily handiwork of the Communists, Anarchists, and the POUM . . . It would be a mistake alike in truth and wisdom for British public opinion to rate both sides at the same level. (9 October 1936.)

Churchill was understandably obsessed by the German menace, and both in public and in private deplored any diversion of attention from 'the real enemy'. He constantly reminded his readers of the Abyssinian fiasco; 'It is no use once again leading other nations up the garden and then running away when the dog growls' (8 January 1937). It has been argued that his point of view, which was shared by the Government, was justified. This is questionable. The Non-Intervention Committee set up in London only succeeded in further reducing all international agreements into contempt. 'I expect that the Non-Intervention Committee is full of swindles and cheats,' Churchill said on 14 April 1937; 'anyhow, it falls far short of strict interpretation and good faith, but it is a precious thing in these times that five great nations should be slanging each other round a table instead of blasting and bombing each other in horrible war.' The League of Nations was completely ignored, Germany, Italy and then Russia intervened, and the former, at least, gained excellent practical experience of using modern unproved weapons in combat conditions and training inexperienced pilots in particular.

But in another sense Churchill's position was a false one. He failed to see that in the eyes of many people Fascism was indivisible, that the same spectre that haunted Germany now stalked through Italy and brought death and devastation to Spain. As an historian of the period has written, 'More than any other issue, the Spanish war forced on the British people the

knowledge that there were things happening in Europe which
even a selfish and isolationist opinion could not safely ignore.'[67]
It is possible – indeed probable – that the most promising hope
of securing national unity lay in concerting opposition to international Fascism wherever it appeared; by concentrating on
Germany, by dealing with the crisis in purely nationalistic
terms, Churchill missed a good opportunity. More seriously, he
forfeited – indeed in many instances alienated – the kind of
crusading spirit which he was trying to arouse in the Focus
meetings he was addressing.

It was not until the summer of 1938 – after a visit to Spain by
Duncan Sandys – that he changed his attitude. He wrote in
December 1938 that 'the British Empire would run far less risk
from the victory of the Spanish Government than from that of
General Franco'. On 20 April 1939, ignoring his own previous
record of tantamount support of Franco, he was writing that
'the British Conservative Right Wing, who have given him such
passionate support, must now be the prey to many misgivings'.
The *volte face* was considerable from the day in 1936 when he
had turned angrily away from the Republican Ambassador,
rejecting his handshake, and muttering 'Blood, Blood, Blood.'
The British supporters of the Spanish Republicans may have
been misguided and naïve. But here was a cause for which many
were prepared to fight and die, and it might be recalled that
five hundred did in fact die in the International Brigade.
Churchill's attitude over Abyssinia was, as has been noted,
somewhat unheroic; that over Spain could be regarded in an
even less favourable light. It was unfortunate that it was on
these two major international incidents that his attitudes were
closest to those of the Government.

*

It should be emphasized that although some of the vigour of
Churchill's earlier assaults on the national defence situation
lessened in 1937, he stuck firmly to his principal themes in his
speeches and writings. The public meetings organized by the
Focus were moderately – and in some cases very – successful,

67. W. McElwee: *Britain's Locust Years*, p. 254.

but they were relatively few in number and received poor press
coverage. One Conservative wrote after a Churchill speech in
July 1937 that 'it was almost exactly the same speech that he
delivered fourteen months ago and again last March . . . He is
becoming a man with an *idée fixe*.'[68] This was a very real
problem. It was extremely difficult for Churchill to vary his
speeches on Defence and Foreign Affairs, for the message that
they contained was always the same. The House of Commons
has a horror of being bored, and the indications are that in 1937,
for the first time in his career, Churchill was committing this
crime. At least on one occasion he succeeded in half-emptying
the Chamber merely by the act of rising to speak.[69] Churchill's
manner of treating the House of Commons was not helpful. He
was far happier making speeches than listening to them, and the
proceedings of *Hansard* in the 1930s are bespattered with
annoyed observations about Churchill's cavalier methods. A
Labour Member referred in May 1930 to his 'habit of making
very controversial speeches in this House, of refusing to give
way to Hon. Members . . . and then disappearing . . . The Rt
Hon. Gentleman has come down here and made a flamboyant
speech and has then run away out of the House.' Lansbury
attacked him in 1932 for behaving 'as if he had a right to walk
in, make his speech, walk out and leave the whole place as if
God Almighty had spoken'.

Miss Virginia Cowles has given a particularly good description of the reactions of the House of Commons to what was in
fact one of Churchill's greatest speeches, delivered on 24 March
1938 after the fall of Austria. The House was filled. 'He stood
addressing the Speaker, his shoulders hunched, his head thrust
forward, his hands in his waistcoat pockets.'

For five years I have talked to this House on these matters – not
with very great success. I have watched this famous island descending
incontinently, fecklessly, the stairway which leads to a dark gulf.
It is a fine broad stairway at the beginning, but after a bit the carpet

68. *The Diaries of Sir Henry Channon*, 27 July 1937.
69. I am grateful to Major John North, who was present on this occasion
in 1937, for describing it to me.

ends. A little farther on there are only flagstones, and a little farther on still these break beneath your feet . . .

Look back over the last five years. It is true that great mistakes were made in the years immediately after the war. But at Locarno we laid the foundations from which a great forward movement could have been made. Look back on the last five years – since, that is to say, Germany began to rearm in earnest and openly to seek revenge . . . The victors are vanquished, and those who threw down their arms in the field and sued for an armistice are striding on to world mastery. That is the position – that is the terrible transformation that has taken place, bit by bit. I rejoice to hear from the Prime Minister that a further supreme effort is to be made to place us in a position of security. Now is the time at last to rouse the nation. Perhaps it is the last time it can be roused with a chance of preventing war, or with a chance of coming through to victory should our efforts to prevent war fail. We should lay aside every hindrance and endeavour by uniting the whole force and spirit of our people to raise again a great British nation standing up before all the world; for such a nation, rising in its ancient vigour, can even at this hour save civilisation.

Miss Cowles's account continues:

When Mr Churchill sat down there was a deep silence for a moment: then the show was over. The House broke into a hubbub of noise; Members rattled their papers and shuffled their way to the lobby. A prominent Conservative came up to the gallery to take me to tea. I was talking to a friend, and when we asked him what he thought of the speech he replied lightly: 'Oh, the usual Churchillian filibuster; he likes to rattle the sabre and does it jolly well, but you always have to take it with a grain of salt.' [70]

Events had taken a new turn with Neville Chamberlain's accession to the premiership. 'We seem to be moving, drifting, steadily, against our will – against the will of every race and every people and every class – towards some hideous catastrophe,' Churchill said in the Commons on 14 April 1937. 'Everybody wishes to stop it, but they do not know how.' It was the particular feature, and deficiency, of Chamberlain that he came to believe he did know how. Hard-working, determined and authoritarian, in public debate he was a first-class

70. Virginia Cowles: *Winston Churchill, The Era and the Man*, pp. 308–9.

destroyer of weak arguments or windy rhetoric, and did not conceal his contempt for those who contradicted him. Although he evoked great devotion among those who knew him best, the public appearance did not really belie the inner character. His contempt for his opponents was real, as was his condescension towards most of his colleagues, and this impatience with criticism becomes more marked in his letters and diaries as his career advances. His mind, although clear and well-ordered, was neither original nor profound, and once he was set on a course it was virtually impossible to deflect him.

It must be remembered that he had grown up in the heavy shadow of his dominating father, of whom Beatrice Webb (who had nearly married him) once wrote that he possessed 'energy and personal magnetism, in a word masculine force, to an almost superlative degree', and in the knowledge that it was Austen who was marked for a political career. After a disastrous failure to grow sisal in the Bahamas he had immersed himself in Birmingham business and politics. When he entered the House of Commons in 1918 he was in his fiftieth year, and had achieved – politically – virtually nothing. He was, like Baldwin, a late starter, and his rise had been no less remarkable, but success had not made him more flexible and tolerant; indeed, its principal effect had been the very reverse, so that by 1937 the authoritarian aspect of his complex character had become dominant. 'Neville's manner freezes people,' Austen Chamberlain once wrote. '. . . Everybody respects him but he makes no friends.' His competence was unquestioned, but it seemed to many to be a frigid competence, an intolerant competence, and – increasingly – a self-satisfied competence.

Lord Salter has given a contemporary portrait of this perplexing man that can hardly be improved upon.

Spare, even ascetic, in figure, dark-haired and dark-eyed; with a profile rather corvine than aquiline; he carries his seventy years well and looks and seems less than his age. His voice has a quality of harshness, with an occasional rasp, and is without music or seductive charm, but it is clear and resonant and a serviceable instrument of his purpose. In debate and exposition his speech is lucid, competent, cogent, never rising to oratory, unadorned with fancy, and rarely touched by perceptible emotion. But it gives a sense of mastery of what it attempts, well reflects the orderly mind behind and, if something is lost, it derives strength from its disregard of all that is not directly relevant to the close-knit argument of his theme.

In manner he is glacial rather than genial. He has neither the spontaneous ease of intercourse of some of his colleagues, nor the *fausse bonhomie* of others. It is unfortunate, and of some importance, that his expression often tends to something like a sneer, and his manner to something like a snub, even when there is nothing in either his intentions or his feelings to correspond . . .

His instinctive attitude to a critic, even one who intends to be helpful and constructive, is to bear down, not to resist and conciliate or to compromise. An opponent must be opposed; and a supporter who shows signs of independence must be disciplined. To a somewhat exceptional extent he regards unquestioning loyalty, obedience, pliability, as giving better claims to his favours than signs of personal initiative or judgement . . . he prefers the even running of his craft to the vigour of the individual oar.[71]

The possibility of including disturbing and independent elements such as Churchill or Amery in the Chamberlain Government was unthinkable save in dire emergency. Churchill had let it be known that he was willing to serve under Chamberlain, but the new Prime Minister was not attracted by the prospect. As he told Hore-Belisha, who had been the intermediary, 'If I take him into the Cabinet he will dominate it, he won't give others a chance of even talking.' When, at a later date, Hore-Belisha tried again, Chamberlain retorted, 'I won't have anyone who will rock the boat.'[72] 'I did not feel that he [Churchill] was much disappointed,' Macmillan has commented.[73] '. . . In his heart he believed that it was already too late; and that he was being reserved by destiny to take up the supreme burden when the time came.' Chamberlain had had considerable regard for what he called 'this brilliant, erratic creature', but had no intention of willingly incorporating him into his Government. He had written in February 1936, 'If we were now to follow Winston's advice and sacrifice our commerce to the

71. (Sir) Arthur Salter: *Security, Can We Retrieve It?* (1939) pp. 284–5.

72. R. J. Minney: *The Private Papers of Hore-Belisha*, p. 130.

73. Macmillan, op. cit., p. 520.

manufacture of arms, we should inflict a certain injury on our trade from which it would take generations to recover, we should destroy the confidence which now happily exists, and we should cripple the revenue.'[74] He agreed with *The Times* that Churchill was 'temperamentally unsuitable' for the post of Minister of Defence in March 1936, and that the remilitarization of the Rhineland had made his appointment absolutely impossible.

It was not only a matter of attitudes and policies; as Lord Salter has emphasized, Chamberlain was an authoritarian Prime Minister, and 'he acquired, or assumed, a dominance over his Cabinet which had scarcely been approached in the interval between Gladstone and Lloyd George'.[75] Anyone who showed signs of independence was disposed of; Swinton, Eden and Ormsby-Gore were the most conspicuous victims of this stern attitude. In seconding the motion for Chamberlain's election as party leader, Churchill expressed the hope that he would not resent 'honest differences' in the party on policy matters; it was, unhappily, an unfulfilled expectation.

Chamberlain's character and career cannot be delineated in swift strokes. He was, as Lord Strang has remarked, 'a man of cool, calm mind, strong will and decisive purpose, wholly devoted to the public cause and with a firm confidence in his own judgement'.[76] It was the last element that was the fatal one, for Chamberlain increasingly saw the international situation in starkly clear terms. He was not a weak man; certainly he was not lacking in courage. As has been written: 'Pliability in the modification rather than the execution of a policy he never possessed. Once his mind was made up on a course of action he pursued it to the bitter end. He was in no sense a deep or original thinker.'[77]

Under Baldwin there was some drift and indecision, but a certain air of realism which vanished under Chamberlain. 'Unhappily it is part of my nature that I cannot contemplate

74. Feiling: *Chamberlain*, p. 314.
75. Salter, op. cit., p. 282.
76. Lord Strang: *Home and Abroad*, p. 125.
77. D. C. Watt: *Personalities and Policies*, p. 163.

any problem without trying to find a solution to it,' as he wrote himself.[78] Swinton quickly discovered that rearmament was looked at in a very different manner than in Baldwin's day; 'I cannot honestly say that on rearmament I had much active support from Chamberlain,' he has written, and Chamberlain seized his first opportunity for removing Swinton from the Air Ministry. 'He gave me no warning, he just sent for me and said I must go.[79] The argument that Chamberlain inherited a hopeless military and political situation in 1937 is often advanced; his own responsibility as Chancellor of the Exchequer from 1931 to 1937 for that situation is less frequently emphasized.

Chamberlain's hostility towards full rearmament in the past had been dominated by economic factors. Thus, between 1934 and 1937, rearmament had been a vexatious nuisance; thereafter, it became an irrelevancy. In his premiership – and particularly after the end of 1937 – the search for peace became obsessional, and was, indeed, the sole end and purpose of British policy. This obsession was not, however, apparent at the beginning of his premiership. In March 1937 he responded warmly to an overture from Henry Morgenthau, Secretary to the US Treasury, writing that 'the main source of this fear of war in Europe is to be found in Germany. No other country . . . is for a moment accredited with any aggressive designs . . . The motive for this aggression on the part of German policy rises from her desire to make herself so strong that no one will venture to withstand whatever demands she may make whether for European or Colonial territory . . . The only situation which would influence her to a contrary decision would be the conviction that her efforts to secure superiority of force were doomed to failure by reason of the superior force which would meet her if she attempts aggression.' The argument could not have been put more clearly by Churchill or Vansittart.

What subsequently happened? We may note some elements. Austen Chamberlain had died; the United States, to Chamberlain's dismay, had passed the Neutrality Act which divested herself of the traditional rights of a neutral nation to trade with

78. Feiling, op. cit., p. 259.
79. Swinton, op. cit., pp. 117–19.

a belligerent; and the Commonwealth Prime Ministers' Conference in the summer of 1937 had disclosed alarming schisms in the Empire. Mackenzie King was unhelpful on Canadian assistance in rearmament, Hertzog declared flatly that South Africa would not support Britain in a war over Central Europe, and Menzies went so far as to say that Far East tensions made Australian participation in a European war impossible.[80] Other factors were the advent of a new British Ambassador in Berlin, Sir Nevile Henderson, who took a very different view of Nazi intentions from his predecessor, and the suspicions of the Foreign Office (and particularly Vansittart) felt by Chamberlain himself and his close mentor, Sir Horace Wilson, Chief Industrial Adviser to the Government.

No doubt, all these played their part, yet the true cause surely lay in Chamberlain's own character and methods of work. He was drawn to the problem; he pondered over it; and then, slowly emerging but gradually becoming more clear, the solution was seen. One is conscious of a movement of Chamberlain's mind throughout 1937 and then, by the close of the year, the sudden ending of the period of quest. British foreign policy, which had drifted purposelessly for a generation, was transformed into real policy, centrally controlled and logically conceived.

'Appeasement' has become a phrase that is usually employed imprecisely to describe British foreign policy in the late 1930s. Like most phrases of this kind, it is unsatisfactory, if only because it has been constantly employed with different meanings. The preservation of peace – and, above all, European peace – had been the main purpose of British policy for a century, and no policy that was not firmly based upon this objective could have had any support in Parliament or the country. It has been recently argued that 'Appeasement was a traditional policy, based upon concessions made from a position of strength,'[81] but this use of a particular word to describe a *tactic* of national policy – for a policy of concessions is not

---

80. See D. C. Watt: 'The Commonwealth and the Munich Crisis', in *Personalities and Policies*, pp. 159–74.

81. Martin Gilbert: *The Roots of Appeasement*, p. 179.

normally regarded as a strategic concept, particularly from a position of strength – is not appropriate. The central strategic problem is one of priorities; the tactical movements must operate within the boundaries of those priorities. The Rhineland was not regarded in March 1936 as a priority; by the end of 1937 the preservation of peace in Europe, rather than the preservation of the total European Continental *status quo*, had become the strategic priority. And it was this factor that gave the policies of 1938 their particular characteristics, and which justify the use of the word 'Appeasement' as an historical term of art.

It may be emphasized that it was not merely a policy of peace at any price, for there were certain strategic priorities – primarily the integrity of France – which lay outside the area in which concessions could be made. But it was a policy which was founded on the conviction that a European war fought on a non-priority issue (as in 1914) was the most disastrous of all possibilities, and whose avoidance was the dominant purpose of British policy. Beyond this calculation there lay moral considerations which gradually became dominant. Increasingly, as 1938 progressed on its tragic course, 'Appeasement' acquired a self-righteous and even sanctimonious character which repelled its few critics and subsequent commentators. But this has tended to obscure what was a carefully conceived and by no means illogical policy of limited concessions.

In assessing the acceptance of this policy, it must be emphasized that it was Chamberlain's increasing confidence in the rightness of his policy that gave him so strong a position. A man who has made up his mind on a central feature of policy is always well situated; if he is in such a dominating political position as was Chamberlain, that superiority is, self-evidently, enormously increased.

The critics of these policies were in a substantial difficulty from the outset. In the first place, the development of the policy was itself gradual. There was no declaration of doctrine; it was only as events unfolded, and Government reactions were seen, that the direction of British policy could be discerned. In the second, it was extremely difficult to produce an alternative that seemed viable. It is never difficult to speak grandly of a policy of 'firmness'; it is less easy to spell out where, when and how such a policy could best be applied. Furthermore, if 'firmness' is to be a real policy, it must imply the use, explicit or implicit, of force, and it was here that the advocates of 'firmness' were in their quandary. Eden wrote to Chamberlain in September 1937, pointing out that there were dangers in taking too pessimistic a view of the condition of British Defences, upon which Chamberlain noted that 'the proposition that our foreign policy must be, if not dictated, at least limited by the state of the National Defences remains true'. There was certain justification in Eden's warning, but perhaps the effect was somewhat weakened by another letter to the Prime Minister on 3 November:

I must confess to you that I am profoundly worried about the state of our rearmament in relation to the present international situation. . . . I do feel that our strength in armaments within the next twelve months may be decisive for peace and, therefore, the financial consideration appears to be secondary. If I judge the temper of our people aright, they are ready to make sacrifices and appreciate , perhaps more clearly than some of our colleagues, that we have got to meet the challenges of the dictators and that to do so we have to be strong in armaments, even at some cost in other spheres . . .[82]

The advocates of 'firmness' were accordingly operating on two fronts. They first had to state that the material conditions existed for such a policy, and then to urge further rearmament because a situation of real national danger existed. They were on much stronger ground when they pointed to the advantages of genuine collective security, which Churchill had been urging for years, but here they were necessarily involved in an acceptance of commitments on the Continent of Europe which had been sedulously avoided by all governments and parties since 1919. Inevitably, the proponents of 'firmness' had their own individual interpretations of their policy, and how it might best be accomplished. The Prime Minister's developing policy, in marked contrast, was increasingly clear and well defined.

Another important factor was Chamberlain's skill in re-

82. PRO Premier, 571/210.

moving all those who were likely to stand in his way. At the end of 1937, Vansittart was shunted into a back-water; Eden's resignation in February 1938 was more of a carefully planned dismissal than a resignation. After a debate on the Air Estimates in March in which Lord Winterton was quite unable to meet the criticisms delivered by Churchill and his supporters, the opportunity was taken to get rid of Swinton. The influence of the Foreign Office on foreign policy fell into virtual abeyance, and the most important features of Swinton's plans for the revivification of the RAF were seriously jeopardized. Chamberlain, with Horace Wilson close at hand, took virtual complete control of foreign policy, to the point when neither the new Foreign Secretary, Halifax, nor the Permanent Under-Secretary to the Foreign Office, accompanied him on his missions to Berchtesgaden, Godesberg and Munich in the autumn of 1938.

The Cabinet records for 1938, only made available at the beginning of 1969, graphically demonstrate the strength of Chamberlain's leadership in the Cabinet and the extent to which the pursuit for peace in Europe became obsessional to the point when all other considerations were increasingly lost sight of.[83] The fall of Austria on 2 March was the first blow, so swiftly delivered and successfully achieved that Europe was presented with a complete *fait accompli*. 'Europe,' Churchill said on 14 March, 'is confronted with a programme of aggression, nicely calculated and timed, unfolding stage by stage, and there is only one choice open, not only to us, but to other countries who are unfortunately concerned – either to submit, like Austria, or else to take effective measures while time remains to ward off the danger and, if it cannot be warded off, to cope with it.' Writing in the *Evening Standard* on 18 March, Churchill declared that 'The scales of illusion have fallen from many eyes, especially in high quarters. There is a new spirit stirring throughout the nation.' The expectation was, however, premature.

83. For a brief study of the military advice given to the Cabinet by the Chiefs of Staff in September 1938, and its irrelevance to the Cabinet's attitudes, see Robert Blake: *The Spectator*, 3 January 1969.

Attention now turned to Czechoslovakia. 'The overriding consideration with Chamberlain and his colleagues,' Hoare has written, 'was that the very complicated problem of Czechoslovakia ought not to lead to a world war and must at almost any price be settled by peaceful means.' [84] The view of the Prime Minister was virtually identical to that expressed in the *Observer* on 28 November 1937: 'We cannot allow the British Empire to be dragged down to disaster by the separate French Alliances with Moscow and Prague.' After some fluctuations, British policy moved rapidly towards the objective of preserving the European peace rather than the preservation of the independence of Czechoslovakia, and it was but a short step from this attitude to one of regarding the Czechs rather than the Germans as providing the real menace to European peace. As Lord Strang has commented: 'The ambivalence of our policy of trying to deter the Germans from armed action by pointing to the probability of British intervention, and to discourage the Czechs from fighting by hinting at its improbability, was not long concealed.' [85]

*

In the years 1935–7 Churchill's speeches and articles had exerted at least some influence upon the Government. But throughout 1937, and even more markedly in 1938, he was a critical spectator. His speeches and articles in the summer and early autumn of 1938 were among the best and most prescient that he had ever delivered. They were ignored by ministers, and at large he was still compromised by the suspicion with which he was regarded, and by the mistrust of even those who now found themselves in considerable agreement with his views. It was most unfortunate that two episodes – small in themselves but significant in this context – in the period between the fall of Austria and the climax of the Czechoslovak crisis should have given further examples of what many regarded at the time as serious errors of judgement.

It is necessary to refer to these episodes, for reputations in

84. Templewood: *Nine Troubled Years*, p. 289.
85. Strang, op. cit., p. 134.

politics vary rapidly. When tensions are high and matters urgent, this fact is most graphically illustrated. By some mysterious evil alchemy, Churchill had in the 1930s cast away on several occasions advantages he had laboriously gained. The absurd Derby–Hoare 'privilege' case of April–June 1935 and his involvement in the abdication crisis were two conspicuous examples. In May 1938, when the tides were again showing clear signs of moving in his favour, there was another unfortunate intervention.

The abdication of King Edward had given de Valera the opportunity, which he had swiftly seized, to withdraw Ireland further from the tentacles of the Irish Treaty. In April 1938 another feature obnoxious to Ireland was removed when the British rights to Queenstown and Berehaven and to the naval base in Lough Swilly were abandoned. Of all the parts of the original Treaty, this was the one to which Churchill had attached the greatest importance; it was also among the most disliked by the Irish. As Ireland's separation from England became more real, the continuance of these British rights appeared more odious.

In *The Gathering Storm* [86] Churchill has described the Irish ports as 'a vital feature in the naval defence of our food supply', and on 5 May he delivered a vehement attack on the Government for what he subsequently described as 'this improvident example of appeasement' when he compared the abandonment of the Irish ports to that of Gibraltar and Malta. It was not difficult then, nor is it difficult now, to point out the differences in the relative situations. What was the significance was the persistence of Churchill's attitudes towards Eire, and his failure to appreciate that the Irish Government was intent upon the achievement of the reality of independence – in which course they had the support of all parties save the Ulster Unionists. The Irish Treaty of 1938 can now be seen as enlightened and sensible. Churchill alleged that 'Mr de Valera was surprised at the readiness with which the British Government had deferred to his request. He had included it in his proposals as a bargaining counter which could be dispensed with when other points

86. Churchill's account of the episode is to be found on pp. 215–17.

were satisfactorily settled.'[87] This version is not confirmed by others. The ports were a vital part of de Valera's long-term plans, and it may be remarked that the situation would have been extremely delicate in the war if the British had had the use of ports in a country that remained firmly neutral throughout the conflict.

But we are here concerned with the immediate effects of Churchill's speech of 5 May. Churchill states that 'I was listened to with a patient air of scepticism.' To judge from a reading of the debate, the feeling was rather stronger than this, and he found himself, once again, completely isolated. Again the vehemence of his language was significant: 'You are casting away real and important means of security and survival for vain shadows and for ease.'

It was not a major episode, and it was quickly forgotten. But, at least for several days and perhaps weeks it diminished his reputation at a time when that reputation had been again on the ascendant. It confirmed many wavering Members in their suspicions about Churchill's lack of a sense of proportion, and it drew only censure from Government and Opposition alike. When matters hang in the balance with such delicacy, what Churchill called 'this lamentable and amazing episode' must not be overlooked.

This incident was almost immediately followed by what was known at the time as the 'Sandys Storm', in which Duncan Sandys was the leading participant. Perhaps significantly, it is not referred to at all in *The Gathering Storm*. In June, Sandys wrote to the Secretary of State for War, Hore-Belisha, informing him that he proposed to put down a parliamentary question, whose terms he enclosed, relating to deficiencies in anti-aircraft defences. It was the opinion of the General Staff that Sandys's information could only have come from a confidential source. Chamberlain, when consulted, suggested that the Attorney General, Sir Donald Somervell, should be informed. It was Somervell's view that 'a serious breach of the Official Secrets Act had been committed', and he informed Sandys of this fact on 23 June. On the 27th Sandys raised the matter in the House

87. *The Gathering Storm*, p. 216.

alleging that Somervell had told him that if he refused to disclose his informants, 'I might render myself liable to a term of imprisonment not exceeding two years.' The disclosure excited a considerable stir, and the matter was referred to a Select Committee of the House of Commons.

Meanwhile, a military Court of Inquiry had been ordered, and Sandys, who was a Second Lieutenant in a West London anti-aircraft battery, was summoned to attend. He immediately (29 June) raised this as a possible breach of privilege, and the new matter was referred to the Committee of Privileges. It reported quickly that a breach of privilege had indeed occurred, but that no action should be taken by the House. It was then discovered that the Committee had been under a misapprehension in criticizing the Court of Inquiry for summoning Sandys. The Court had done nothing of the sort, indeed at that time it had had no corporate existence. Sandys had been ordered by Eastern Command to attend the court. It was not perhaps a major point, but it made the Committee of Privileges look foolish, and an agitated correspondence took place in which Chamberlain, Simon and Churchill were involved. Simon wrote to Chamberlain on 14 July that 'I have the impression that Winston & Co are getting thoroughly sick of this business and would not be sorry to see it dropped, provided, of course, that they escape the discredit which may come to them . . .' [88]

As so often happens, the episode had suddenly rebounded to the disadvantage of Sandys and Churchill. The Select Committee appointed to rule on the Somervell–Sandys episode, with careful impartiality, criticized Sandys, Somervell and Hore-Belisha. Churchill proceeded to attack the Report, of which he had been a nominal signatory, [89] in one of his least successful speeches on 5 December. [90] By this stage everyone had lost

88. The correspondence is in PRO Premier 1/283.

89. It should perhaps be pointed out that all Reports of Select Committees are technically unanimous. Members may move alternative Reports or amendments to the chairman's draft, but unless these are accepted by the Committee as a whole they are not included in the Report. Minority Reports are not permitted, although the defeated drafts are included in the Minutes of Proceedings of the Committee.

90. See Nicolson, op. cit., p. 382, for an account of it.

interest, and there was general approval for a sharp rebuke delivered by A. P. Herbert:

> I cannot understand how the Rt Hon. Gentleman reconciles – I will not say with his conscience, but with considerations of taste and dignity – that he should sit on this Committee of Privileges in this matter at all. He seems to be attempting to combine the incompatible and separate functions of the centre forward and the referee. One minute he is bounding forward to the attack, shooting goals in all directions, and then next moment, with dignity but still bounding, he is blowing the whistle.

This was, of course, an even less major episode than that of the Irish ports, and one not to be compared with the great issues now looming darkly over Europe. But parliamentary reputations are as susceptible to minor incidents as to great ones, and their significance should not be ignored.

*

Churchill's hostility to the entire trend of Government thinking during this period was at least partly based upon what might appear to have been a somewhat over-optimistic view of the condition of British military strength and a belief that the moment of greatest peril had passed. In short, that a policy of 'firmness' towards Germany was now a practical possibility. He wrote after the fall of Austria: 'Many high authorities agree that the German army is not yet in a condition to undertake a major aggressive war. Neither her stores of raw material nor the state of her officer-cadres are sufficiently complete to encourage during the present year a hasty challenge to a group of well-armed States, with Great Britain and France at the core.'[91] The point was academic so far as the Government was concerned, which had no intention of pursuing a policy of firmness to the point when the peace of Europe was seriously jeopardized. Churchill's policy did not shrink from the possibility of war, although he believed that war itself might not be needed to contain Hitler. But his approach revived suspicions which had been long harboured about his attitude to war. We may

91. *Evening Standard*, 18 March.

turn to a comment written by one of his most devoted admirers (despite the speech on the Sandys case) Sir Alan Herbert, to appreciate how deep was this feeling:

> I never liked Mr Chamberlain (I hardly knew him): but I admired him. For more than twenty years I had adored (that is the right word, I fear) Mr Churchill . . . I did not think, as so many thought in those days, that he was brilliant, resourceful, brave, but nearly always wrong. I thought he was nearly always right – right for example, about the Dardanelles, right about Antwerp, in both of which affairs our Division (the Royal Naval Division) was involved. But I did think that he rather enjoyed a war: and, after three years in the infantry, in Gallipoli and France, I did not.[92]

As has already been emphasized, Churchill's absorption with war, at a time when few wanted to think of it, had aroused misgivings since 1911. As Keynes commented in 1927, 'Mr Churchill does not dissemble his own delight in the intense experiences of conducting warfare on the grand scale which those can enjoy who make the decisions.' It was true, as Keynes pointed out, that Churchill did not conceal 'its awfulness for those who provide the raw material of those delights', but Alan Herbert's feelings that Churchill 'rather enjoyed a war' was shared by many others. It should be recalled that five of his books had been devoted to the subject, and he himself once wrote that 'it is impossible to quell the inward excitement which comes from a prolonged balance of terrible things'. What jarred on many people was the element described by Keynes of 'his delight in the intense experiences of conducting warfare on the grand scale', and which was self-evident to any reader of *Marlborough*. H. G. Wells had been excessively harsh when he wrote of Churchill that 'he believes quite naïvely that he belongs to a peculiarly gifted and privileged class of beings to whom the lives and affairs of common men are given over, the raw material of brilliant ideas', but it must be conceded that there was some truth in the charge. Herbert Morrison's depiction of him in the 1935 General Election as 'a fire-eater and militarist' may be dismissed as electioneering slander, but Churchill's

92. A. P. Herbert: *Independent Member*, p. 109.

attitudes were of a kind that gave some superficial justification for the charge. Gardiner's observation that 'Churchill will write his name in history; take care he does not write it in blood' was quoted with approval by a Conservative MP in a foreign affairs debate in 1938.

The charge was not a new one, nor was it fated to be forgotten in the final period of Churchill's career. In *Men Like Gods* (1922) H. G. Wells had drawn a portrait of Churchill which included the phrases: 'he has lived most romantically. He has fought bravely in wars. He has been a prisoner and escaped wonderfully from prison. His violent imaginations have caused the deaths of thousands of people'; and it will be recalled that his Labour opponent in 1923 had described him as 'militant to the finger-tips'.[93] To describe Churchill as a war-monger is grotesque but it must be fairly admitted that Baldwin's comment that 'war is the environment in which he thrives' had substantial truth in it. To a remarkable extent, Churchill had a feeling for war at all its levels which is unique in modern British politics, and his attitude towards the subject was compounded of fascination and loathing. It was perhaps understandable that the former element was more apparent to contemporaries than the latter. And if the epithet war-monger is to be regarded as wholly absurd, no discussion of the events of 1938 can ignore the presence of memories of the Russian Intervention, nor Churchill's part in the Irish Question and Chanak. In 1919 Osbert Sitwell had put these words into his mouth:

> There are only two sorts of Englishmen,
> Those who like war –
> And therefore like me –
> And those who don't like either.
> The latter are Bolsheviks.[94]

Furthermore, in analysing Churchill's speeches and actions in 1938 it is also important to recall Churchill's concept of negotiation, which should only be conducted from strength, and preferably from a position of dictation of terms.[95] In Chamber-

93. See p. 197 above.
94. *Daily Herald*, 22 July 1919.
95. See pp. 60–61 above.

lain's policies throughout the year, culminating in the Munich agreement, Churchill saw not only a wanton abandonment of a position of relative strength but a fundamental lack of understanding of how such arrangements should be made. There was a substantial rationale in his view that the Western Nations must adopt a firm and united stand against Germany's European ambitions, but there was also a deep revulsion against Britain abandoning what seemed to him to be the only practicable basis of successful negotiation.

As events in 1938 proceeded to their logical conclusion at Munich, Churchill's warnings grew more insistent, yet, if anything, had less effect than ever before. Beaverbrook's political judgement was far from infallible, and his differences with Churchill at this time were so profound that his comment in November 1938 that 'this man of brilliant talent, splendid abilities, magnificent power of speech, and fine stylist, has ceased to influence the British public'[96] must be regarded with caution. But it was of very considerable significance that the mounting hostility towards the Government in the Conservative Party did not group itself around Churchill. In effect three distinct groups were formed, headed by Eden, Churchill and Amery, and of these the former was by far the largest. Its attitude was also far less belligerent. It worked in the belief that Government policy could be amended, and even perhaps reversed, by pressure and influence rather than by all-out attack. This group, known to the irritated Whips as 'the glamour boys', took very considerable care not to be associated with Churchill; indeed, when Duncan Sandys asked to attend one of its meetings he was left in no doubt that his presence was not required.[97] It is perhaps significant that Macmillan describes the Churchill Group as the 'Old Guard' in his memoirs.[98] Within the tiny group of Churchill supporters, their isolation now even more dramatically emphasized in the Conservative Party, this attitude caused a personal resentment against Eden personally that was to be of very long duration. (Significantly,

96. Young, op. cit., p. 128.
97. Private information.
98. Macmillan, op. cit., p. 548.

it was not shared by the ever-generous Brendan Bracken, nor
by Churchill himself.) Eden's caution at this time exasperated
those Conservatives whose confidence in Chamberlain had
fallen. His resignation speech on 21 February was so carefully
non-provocative that, as Macmillan has commented, it 'still
left Members somewhat uncertain as to what all the row was
about'[99] and Liddell Hart has related that at a meeting in the
Queen's Hall on 29 November Eden's caution was such that the
audience became restless and impatient, and Lady Violet
Bonham Carter, who proposed the vote of thanks, said, afterwards that she felt more like moving a vote of censure.[100] For
their part, the members of the Eden Group regarded Churchill
and his allies, in Nicolson's words, as 'more bitter than determined, and more out for a fight than for reform'.[101]

The absence of seriously concerted action by the three groups
opposed to the Government reflected their differences of objective. The Eden group, which consisted of Eden, J. P. L. Thomas,
Mark Patrick, Paul Emrys-Evans, Lord Cranborne, Lord
Wolmer, Sir Edward Spears, Harold Nicolson,[102] Ronald Tree,
Sydney Herbert, Derrick Gunston, Anthony Crossley, Harold
Macmillan, Ronald Cartland and Richard Law, believed that
the most effective results would stem from reasoned and careful
pressure upon the Government;[103] the Churchill group, which
in the House of Commons now only consisted of Churchill,
Bracken and Sandys, did not share this expectation. The
Amery group really only included Amery and Boothby, and
although its views were closer to Churchill's than to Eden's, its
effect was negligible.

These differences were demonstrated during the Munich
crisis and in its immediate aftermath.

99. ibid., p. 538.

100. Liddell Hart, op. cit., p. 211.

101. Nicolson, op. cit., p. 378.

102. Harold Nicolson wrote to his wife on 2 March: 'Don't be worried, my
darling. I am not going to become one of the Winston Brigade.' (Nicolson,
op. cit., p. 328.)

103. Nicolson relates after a discussion with Eden on 19 September: 'He
doesn't wish to lead a revolt or to secure any resignation from the Cabinet.'
(op. cit., p. 361.)

Lady Asquith has given a vivid portrait of Churchill's attitudes during those tense and difficult days.[104] Chamberlain returned from Godesberg on 24 September to find the Cabinet virtually unanimous in its dismay at the German demands. On the 26th Churchill saw Chamberlain and Halifax, and on that evening a declaration was issued by the Government to the effect that Britain would not fail to support France if she went to the assistance of Czechoslovakia in the event of a German attack. When Lady Asquith telephoned Churchill, she found that he was 'happier' than he had been, but with reservations. 'He rightly mistrusted Chamberlain,' Lady Asquith writes, 'who, he was convinced, was still searching desperately for a way out.' Neither knew that Chamberlain had in fact sent a private message to Hitler that set the stage for Munich. On the following day, at the end of a detailed speech to the House of Commons, Chamberlain was able to announce the receipt of an invitation from Hitler to meet himself, Mussolini and Daladier at Munich. Amidst the tumult of excitement and applause, Churchill remained seated. On 29 September Chamberlain flew to Munich.

On the same day the Focus lunched at the Pinafore Room at the Savoy. Lady Asquith's account continues:

Winston's face was dark with foreboding. I could see that he feared the worst as I did. I finally suggested that during the afternoon a few of us should draft a telegram to the Prime Minister adjuring him to make no further concessions at the expense of the Czechs and warning him that if he did so he would have to fight the House of Commons on his return. The telegram was to be signed by Winston, Lord (Robert) Cecil, Attlee, Archie Sinclair, Eden and Lord Lloyd.

The telegram was duly drafted (with the threat omitted) and at 7 o'clock that evening we met again at the Savoy Hotel, where all approved the draft. Winston then called for the signatures. Cecil Lloyd and Archie Sinclair were eager to sign.

Eden, to whom we telephoned, refused – on the ground that it would be interpreted as an act of hostility to Chamberlain. (Was he not hostile to his policies?) Attlee, with whom Noel-Baker pleaded urgently (also by telephone) refused to sign without the approval of his party . . .

104. *Daily Telegraph*, 12 March 1965.

The telegram was not dispatched and one by one our friends went out – defeated. Winston remained, sitting in his chair immobile, frozen, like a man of stone. I saw the tears in his eyes. I could feel the iron entering his soul. His last attempt to salvage what was left of honour and good faith had failed.

I spoke with bitterness of those who had refused even to put their names to principles and policies which they professed. Then he spoke: '*What are they made of ?* The day is not far off when it won't be signatures we'll have to give but lives – the lives of millions. Can we survive? Do we deserve to do so when there's no courage anywhere?'

'We sat there gloomily realising that nothing could be done,' Harold Nicolson wrote. 'Even Winston seemed to have lost his fighting spirit.'[105]

Eden has no recollection of the episode, nor of having refused to sign the telegram. Attlee's caution was characteristic. In any event, it is hard to see what effect this message could have had on Chamberlain unless the threat contained in the original draft had been a real and serious one. And the hysteria in the House of Commons on the 28th had clearly demonstrated that the threat was hollow.

That evening there was a dinner at the Other Club, also at the Savoy, when the tensions of the day culminated in a celebrated scene which went well into the night. Sir Colin Coote describes it thus:

The Munich terms were not known yet, but the Godesberg terms were, and a violent argument developed. One began to understand why, in the House of Commons, a red line on the carpet, just beyond rapier reach of the opposite bench, marks the limit beyond which the speaker must not stray. One Munichite, J. L. Garvin, was assailed with such fury that he departed in high dudgeon, never to return. Winston was snarling and clawing at the two unhappy Ministers present, Walter [Elliot] and Duff Cooper, and they were retorting in kind. Duff, in particular, was choleric not merely because that was his temperament but because, as he explains in his memoirs, he was still a member of the Government and felt honourably obliged to defend them for the last time . . . Far into the night the exchanges continued. Then, in the small hours somebody thought that the early

105. Nicolson, op. cit., p. 372.

editions of the papers must be on the streets. He went out, and there, sure enough, they were with snatches from the Munich terms in the Stop Press. He brought back a copy and read out the news. There was silence. Nobody attempted to defend them. Humiliation took almost material shape.[106]

Chamberlain triumphantly returned from Munich, to an ecstatic reception, bearing 'Peace with Honour'. 'No conqueror returning from a victory on the battlefield had come adorned with nobler laurels,' *The Times* declared. The attitude of the Dominions throughout the crisis had been strongly in favour of conciliation; the Australian, South African and Canadian High Commissioners in London had been active in urging concessions on Chamberlain. Vincent Massey was representative when he wrote in his diary on 28 September (before Chamberlain had received Hitler's invitation to go to Munich): 'Surely the world can't be plunged into the horrors of universal war over a few miles of territory or a few days one way or other in a timetable.'[107]

Churchill, although incensed by Munich, found himself almost alone in the Conservative Party on the morrow of Chamberlain's return. He had to make his way with extreme caution. In private he was emphatic. Of Chamberlain he is said to have remarked: 'In the depths of that dusty soul there is nothing but abject surrender.' To another he said: 'The Government had to choose between war and shame. They chose shame, and they will get war too.'[108]

The emotions aroused by Munich in Britain were heated. Churchill did not exaggerate when he wrote: 'Among the Conservatives, families and friends in intimate contact were divided to a degree the like of which I have never seen. Men and women, long bound by party ties, social amenities and family connections, glared upon one another in scorn and anger.'[109] In these circumstances, the best chance of attacking the Government would come only from within it. But ministers had been pre-

106. Colin Coote: *A Companion of Honour*, p. 174.
107. Vincent Massey: *What's Past is Prologue*, p. 261.
108. Dalton: *The Fateful Years*, p. 198.
109. *The Gathering Storm*, p. 253.

sented with a *fait accompli* – and one, moreover, enthusiastically backed in the country.

Several ministers were thought to be deeply unhappy about the Munich Agreement, and the Churchill group was hopeful that Duff Cooper, Walter Elliot, Oliver Stanley and Malcolm MacDonald might resign, but in the event only Duff Cooper resigned – 'the pioneer,' as Vyvyan Adams said, 'along the nation's way back from hysteria to reason'. The hysteria lasted for some time. When Churchill described the agreement in the Commons as 'a total and unmitigated defeat', an angry hubbub broke out on the Government benches, and it was some time before Churchill could resume his speech. It was perhaps his best in this period. 'All is over. Silent, mournful, abandoned, broken, Czechoslovakia recedes into the darkness.'

The feeling against him within the Party was now intense. As Macmillan has written, 'everyone knew that so great was the strength of the Government in the country that nothing could seriously shake them in Parliament. At our almost daily conferences with our friends, we had the gloomiest forebodings. The tide was, at present, too strong and it was flowing against us.'[110] Most of Churchill's allies in the India struggle were now the most devoted adherents of the Prime Minister. It was only by a vote of three to two that Churchill's constituency organization did not disown him, and the chairman of the Chigwell Unionist Association – himself a future Conservative MP – called for his removal. 'Mr Churchill's post-Munich insurrection was shocking,' Mr Colin Thornton-Kemsley declared. '. . . Loyal Conservatives in the Epping Division have been placed in an intolerable position. I feel that unless Mr Churchill is prepared to work for the National Government and the Prime Minister he ought no longer to shelter under the good will and name of such a great party.' Hawkey, who had brought Churchill to Epping in 1924 and who was, as Churchill had testified, 'my ever-faithful and tireless champion,' won the day. 'But it was,' as Churchill has written, 'a gloomy winter.'

But the tide was already turning. Halifax had startled the Prime Minister on his triumphal ride from Heston Airport to

110. Macmillan, op. cit., p. 567.

London on his return from Munich by urging him to bring back
Churchill and Eden and to attempt a National Government by
inviting Labour to join. 'He seemed surprised, but said he
would think it over,' Halifax has recorded.[111] In the post-
Munich debate thirty Conservatives abstained, although none
actually voted against the Government. The calibre of the
abstainers – which included Churchill, Eden, Duff Cooper,
Amery, Cranborne, Sir Roger Keyes, Boothby, Macmillan,
Louis Spears and J. P. L. Thomas – was of greater importance
than the size of the dissident group. The attitude of many others
was similar to that of Sir Alan Herbert.

My soul revolted at the thought of another, and, I was convinced
by many expert opinions, a much worse war. (Mr Churchill himself
had painted the possibilities in colours even blacker than we ever
saw in the event.) . . . I hated the dictators as much as Mr Churchill
did and often said so in the Press . . .

But, 'wishful thinker', 'anxious hoper', 'old soldier', or 'Christian
believer' – what you will – I wanted Mr Chamberlain to be right,
and keep the peace successfully . . . I voted sadly for Munich: and
the whole thing made me ill.[112]

The immediate reactions to Munich soon showed signs of
changing. Attlee's depiction of it as 'a victory for brute force'
and 'one of the greatest diplomatic defeats that this country
and France have ever sustained', although angrily disputed
from the Government benches, was echoed in parts of the
Conservative Party. On 18 November Churchill, Harold Macmillan and Bracken voted against the Government on a motion
to create a Ministry of Supply, while several other Conservatives abstained. This was the first occasion in which Churchill
had voted against the Government in the whole of this period.
Macmillan has pointed out the significance of abstentions in
important debates, and his argument has strong House of
Commons logic. Unfortunately, or perhaps fortunately, House
of Commons logic is often unappreciated elsewhere. Abstention
in a major division is a brave act, but the valour of the deed

111. Halifax: *Fulness of Days*, p. 200.
112. A. P. Herbert, op. cit., pp. 109 and 113.

tends to be viewed sceptically outside Westminster. The tactic of delivering hostile speeches and then failing to vote does not appear heroic to the distant observer. The moment when Churchill began to vote in the Opposition lobby must accordingly be seen as an important one.

His failure to take any part in the one major demonstration against the Government after Munich, however, has not been satisfactorily explained. Dalton has recorded how Macmillan complained to him at this time that Churchill 'was in danger of relapsing into a complacent Cassandra. He would say: "Well, I have done my best. I have made all these speeches. Nobody has paid any attention. All my prophecies have turned out to be true. I have been publicly snubbed by the Government. What more can I do?"'[113] Such views of Churchill's tactics at this time are understandable, although it can be justifiably remarked that any accusation of reluctance on Churchill's part to come forward against the Government over its defence and foreign policies was somewhat inadequately founded. In any event he took no part in the Oxford by-election of November, at which an anti-Government candidate, A. D. Lindsay, the Master of Balliol, stood against the official Conservative, Quintin Hogg. Harold Macmillan and Randolph Churchill were among those Conservatives who campaigned for Lindsay[114] in what was an exciting and vigorous election. The dominant factors in the contest were the extreme reluctance with which the Labour candidate[115] stood down, the consequent half-hearted support for Lindsay given by Labour, Lindsay's own substantial defects as a candidate, and the capacity of the young Conservative candidate. Although Hogg won with a majority cut by 3,000 votes on the 1935 figures, this was an extremely disappointing result for the opponents of the Government, and may be seen as evidence that revulsion against Munich had not yet assumed really substantial proportions. The fact that the Government

113. Dalton, op. cit., p. 202. Mr Macmillan has told the author that he considers Dalton's account gives rather too strong a view of his attitude towards Churchill's attitude at the time.

114. As did a Balliol undergraduate, Edward Heath.

115. Mr Patrick Gordon-Walker.

lost the Bridgwater seat to an Independent candidate shortly afterwards was an encouragement, but it was soon checked when the Duchess of Atholl resigned her seat in protest against the foreign policy of the Government, stood as an Independent, and was defeated. These indications of the popular feeling, although by no means overwhelming, demonstrated that the post-Munich situation was still on the balance to the Government's advantage.

It perhaps requires emphasis that the real turning-point did not come until the occupation of the rest of Czechoslovakia in March 1939. 'There is, alas, insufficient justification for the ripples of optimism which have spread across the surface of British and European opinion,' Churchill wrote on 9 February, with justification. He was perhaps less justified in claiming that 'in England there has been a reconciliation of national Union. The attitude of the Government has stiffened . . . Above all, there is a sense of gathering strength.' But the attitude of the Government and the bulk of the Press was hopeful almost to the point of euphoria until, at 2 a.m. on the morning of 15 March, Czechoslovakia ceased to exist as a separate state.

Until this moment, Appeasement had not assumed its subsequent totally pejorative meaning, but the rapidity with which ministers were forced to abandon their previous positions emphasized the enormous impact that the events of 15 March had on British opinion. The subsequently hasty British guarantee to Poland – announced on 31 March – has been assailed by Churchill in *The Gathering Storm* with withering contempt. At the time his attitude was less critical; as he wrote on 4 May: 'The preservation and integrity of Poland must be regarded as a cause commanding the regard of all the world,' but he also spelt out the essential corollary: 'There is no means of maintaining an Eastern front against Nazi aggressions without the active aid of Russia.' It was the failure to seize this basic point that doomed the new British policy. The guarantee was an act of folly in the context of the attitude of the British Government towards Russia, an attitude that became painfully more clear in the lethargic conduct of the Anglo-Soviet negotiations throughout the summer of 1939.

But after a period of feverish activity, which included the introduction of military conscription and the creation of a Ministry of Supply, so long urged by Churchill, the original and real motive force of Government attitudes reasserted itself. Churchill had seemed the obvious candidate for the Ministry of Supply, and it appears that he again expressed his willingness to serve in the Government.[116] 'The feeling that Winston is essential is gaining strength,' Nicolson wrote on 19 April, 'and we shall probably see him in the Cabinet within a short time.'[117] But, as Hoare has written: 'To the world at large, Churchill appeared to be the very embodiment of a policy of war',[118] and Chamberlain noted in his diary that 'Churchill's chances improve as war becomes more possible, and *vice versa*. If there is any possibility of easing the tension and getting back to normal relations with the dictators, I wouldn't risk it by what would certainly be regarded by them as a challenge.'[119] This was the policy that was continued until September, when the Chamberlain Government was dragged unhappily to war.

It is not possible in politics to categorize and document changes in the public temper. What may be inadequately described as 'mood' is the most difficult of all political elements to recapture and convey to a later generation. And we must be careful to differentiate between House of Commons mood – which is exceptionally sensitive and unpredictably volatile – and other manifestations. Newspaper articles, speeches, letters and even diaries are inadequate guides, although they often mark the change of political emphasis. All that can be said, and said with absolute justice, is that after the annexation of Czechoslovakia in March 1939 the possibility of averting war with Germany was entertained only by a minority in Britain. By some strange process which is inexplicable to those who were not alive then, the fear of war which had been too evident in 1938 seemed to evaporate. The British did not want war, but the spirit in the air was not pacific. There was a weariness with

116. Templewood: *Nine Troubled Years*, p. 385.
117. Nicolson, op. cit., p. 398.
118. Templewood, op. cit., p. 386.
119. Feiling, op. cit.

procrastination, an aversion from false promises and wishful thinking, and a yearning for a simple, clear solution.

For understanding how such abrupt changes occur the sociologist and even the psychologist is perhaps a better guide than the political historian. Kingsley Martin, in one of the best examinations of what he called 'the psychological mechanism of war fever', has remarked upon a very important human phenomenon, which appears to apply with particular emphasis to the British:

We all live in constant awareness of a highly coloured moving picture; we watch a three-dimensional cinerama. In our own immediate domestic surroundings we are aware of the details, and act, if not necessarily with wisdom, at least as a result of intimate and direct contact with events ... [Although] our world picture is the least distinct and precise, [it is] not for that reason incapable of arousing in us a high degree of emotional response whenever it seems to affect the security or interests of our own group. Because of our essential ignorance of other nations, we are far more easily swayed by propaganda in national than we are in domestic disputes. At any time we can be switched to the belief that a country, which we regard as friendly, has become our enemy. A few selected incidents of atrocities may create a picture which will compel us to quite irrational action ... The popular picture of the world is set and vivid and the response virtually unanimous.[120]

Perhaps the most striking manifestation of the new mood was the Press campaign advocating Churchill's return to the Government. Morrison had described him in 1935 as 'a fire-eater and a militarist'. After Prague, this was suddenly the person for whom men began to seek. The *Daily Telegraph* led the pace, after the publication of a letter urging his admission to the Government which was refused by *The Times*; it was closely followed by the *Manchester Guardian*, and on 13 July the *Daily Mirror* described Churchill as 'the most trusted statesman in Britain ... The watchdog of Britain's safety. For years he warned us of dangers which have now become terrible realities. For years he pressed for the policy of STRENGTH, which the

120. Kingsley Martin: Introduction to revised edition of *The Triumph of Lord Palmerston* (1963).

whole nation now supports.' This new development, however significant, was not likely to have substantial influence upon Chamberlain. In Hoare's words: 'He resented outside pressure. The more, therefore, the Press clamoured for Churchill's inclusion, the less likely he was to take any action . . . Sure of himself and his programme, he was convinced that he could make almost any Ministers work well in his Cabinet, and was opposed to changes that might spoil his carefully laid plans.'[121]

The call for Churchill was far from universal, and within the Conservative Party the demand for a broader-based Government was still not dominant. But the fact that the call for Churchill now existed at all was remarkable enough, and the discontent in the Conservative Party was sufficiently loud to constitute a real political fact. On 24 March Churchill, Eden and Duff Cooper placed a motion on the Commons Order Paper demanding a National Government, which attracted nearly thirty names. In the middle of April forty-six Conservatives supported another motion 'in favour of immediate acceptance of the principle of the compulsory mobilisation of the man, munition, and money power of the nation'. The handing over to the German Government of £6 million of Czechoslovak gold by the Bank of England provoked a debate in which the Government had a most uncomfortable time. These pressures could only be resisted so long as war was averted.

As the weeks and months passed, the conviction that war was inescapable became dominant. Only in the Cabinet was this assumption challenged and disputed. The emotional isolation of ministers became increasingly evident. A violent debate over whether the House of Commons should adjourn for the summer recess on 2 August demonstrated the passions that now divided the Conservatives.[122]

Ministers still had their majority support on the Government benches, but it was an ever-dwindling superiority, and the doubts and dismays that now permeated it were manifested by ill-temper and a nervousness that was almost palpable. Even within the ministerial circle, hopes were fading. At the end of

121. Templewood, op. cit., p. 378.
122. Some forty Conservatives abstained in this Division

June Halifax said at the annual dinner at Chatham House that 'the threat of military force is holding the world to ransom, and our immediate task is to resist aggression.' The general air of resignation to the inevitable, which had become so clear since Prague, was now seeping into the Cabinet Room. Chamberlain still had hopes, but the events were now moving rapidly out of the control of any Government. On 23 August the Russo-German Agreement was signed in Moscow. On 1 September Poland was invaded. There was manifestly no escape from the Guarantee, but throughout 2 September the determination of the Government remained in doubt. That day Churchill was invited to return to the Admiralty, but hours passed, and the position remained unclear throughout an evening characterized by a fierce thunderstorm that fell on London. The House of Commons, expecting the announcement of a Franco-British ultimatum, became almost ungovernable.

The Cabinet was now in a state of acute tension, which was heightened after scenes in the House of Commons when Chamberlain refused to make a definite commitment. It was at the end of his statement that Greenwood, rising for the Labour Party, was greeted with a shout of 'Speak for England!' – ascribed by some to Leo Amery and by others to Bob Boothby – from the seething Conservative benches. Ministers made their way to Downing Street, to deliver what one subsequently called 'a plain *diktat*'. —The same account states that: 'The climax came most dramatically. The PM said quietly: "Right, gentlemen, this means war." Hardly had he said it when there was the most enormous clap of thunder, and the whole Cabinet Room was lit up by a blinding flash of lightning.'[123] Thus, nearly at midnight on that wild night the die was finally and unhappily cast for war.

The House of Commons met on the following morning after the proceedings had been delayed by a false air-raid warning. Churchill has described his emotions:

As I sat in my place, listening to the speeches, a very strong sense of calm came over me, after the intense passions and excitements

123. Sir R. Dorman-Smith (Minister of Agriculture in 1939) in the *Sunday Times*, 6 September 1964 (quoted in Birkenhead: *Halifax*, p. 447).

of the past few days. I felt a security of mind and was conscious of a kind of uplifted detachment from human and personal affairs. The glory of Old England, peace-loving and ill-prepared as she was, but instant and fearless at the call of honour, thralled my being and seemed to lift our fate to those spheres far removed from earthly facts and physical sensation.[124]

In the debate he made his last speech from the back benches. His appointment to the Admiralty was announced later in the day, and the Board of Admiralty signalled to the Fleet: 'Winston is back.' In his own words: 'So it was that I came again to the room I had quitted in pain and sorrow almost exactly a quarter of a century before . . . Once again we must fight for life and honour against all the might and fury of the valiant, disciplined and ruthless German race. Once again! So be it.'[125]

*

In terms of office and achievement, Churchill's career may be said to have divided itself into three periods. From 1900 until 1915 he was a rising, highly successful, controversial politician. Between 1915 and 1939 his career entered a period of only limited achievement and, in terms both of office and influence, a substantial measure of failure. From 1939 until 1955 he was, whether in office or out of it, *the* towering personality in British politics. This study has been concerned with the first and second periods; the third will be described subsequently when the documents are available. But no appreciation of that final period can be attempted without an understanding of what had preceded it.

It is always unwise to attempt to divide a man's life into sections; the characteristics that had made Churchill successful between 1900 and 1914 also contributed materially to his downfall in 1915. The politician of the 1920s carried with him the record, good and ill, of the previous twenty years; the Secretary of State for War of 1919–21 and the Chancellor of the Exchequer of 1924–9 were not forgotten in the 1930s, nor

124. *The Gathering Storm*, p. 320.
125. ibid, p. 321.

in 1945. In Churchill's own words: 'Life is a whole and luck is a whole, and no part of them can be separated from the rest.'[126]

We may return to the central features of Churchill's political personality with which we were concerned in the study of his career between 1900 and 1915, and which remained constant throughout his life.

The first point to reiterate is that he was a career politician, for whom politics were his life, and for whom the essential goal was office. Beaverbrook's preference for 'Churchill Down' over 'Churchill Up' was shared by others, but the student of Churchill's career cannot avoid the strong impression that his talents were best demonstrated in office and his deficiencies most evident when out of it. Lord Riddell wrote in his diary of him in January 1915 that 'He is one of the most industrious men I have ever known. He is like a wonderful piece of machinery with a flywheel which occasionally makes unexpected movements.'[127] His critics were more conscious of the 'unexpected movements' than of the solid achievements, and although many of his actions as a minister can be justifiably criticized, it cannot be doubted that this was his best and most natural environment.

The dispassionate observer can hardly fail to be struck by the absence in Churchill's career, until the mid-1930s, of any great identifiable cause, and by his preoccupation with the immediate. This may appear an unfair judgement, in view of Churchill's warnings of 1912–14, 1934–9, and subsequently, 1946–8. But it should be emphasized that in all these cases he was drawing public attention to actual situations, and that his achievement – which is not to be disparaged at all – lay in diagnosis rather than in prognosis. His attitude towards Defence matters in the 1920s provides one example of an inability to envisage changed situations, and his 'settlement' of the Middle East situation in 1921–2 demonstrates his concentration upon the immediate and tangible. Foresight in politics is rare, and is usually a matter of fortune rather than genius. We need not criticize Churchill for being deficient in long-term views were it not for the fact that his admirers have claimed it as one of his principal qualities.

126. *My Early Life*, p. 100.
127. *Lord Riddell's War Diary*, p. 49.

Churchill's character was not as simple or as clear-cut as it has often been portrayed, but his views on political matters had a strong tendency to the simplistic. He was not, politically or intellectually, a sophisticated man. Certainly his mind was not profound. In many respects this was a source of great strength, for he often cut through to the heart of the matter and was impatient of the quibbling and qualifications to which many politicians of superior intellectual ability are prone. It was not for nothing that one of his favourite maxims was 'Here firm, though all be drifting.' But there are occasions in which intellectual imagination is crucial. Churchill had much imagination and he was always fertile in ideas and projects. But compared with Gladstone, Disraeli, Salisbury or even Palmerston, there is a certain absence of political depth, comprehension and wisdom. The self-made man, caught on the helter-skelter of his career, has to pay many prices for his success and survival; in Churchill's case, this was one of them. He marched magnificently on the surface of affairs; we look in vain for evidence of comprehension of deeper and more permanent things.

We also look in vain for signs of real development – political or intellectual. Isaiah Berlin has rightly commented that:

> Far from changing his opinions too often, Mr Churchill has scarcely, during a long and stormy career, altered them at all. If anyone wishes to discover his views on the large and lasting issues of our time, he need only set himself to discover what Mr Churchill has said or written on the subject at any period of his long and exceptionally articulate public life, in particular during the years before the First World War: the number of instances in which his views have in later years undergone any appreciable degree of change will be found astonishingly small . . . When biographers and historians come to describe and analyse his views . . . they will find that his opinions on all these topics are set in fixed patterns, set early in life and later only reinforced.[128]

In war, these characteristics are of supreme advantage. In quieter times they have many dangers. The dictum that peace hath her heroes is, perhaps regrettably, not really true, and the

128. Berlin, op. cit., pp. 16–17.

pursuit of objectives in normal democratic politics is hard and infinitely complex. Churchill's faith in his own star and his desire for direct action led him into hasty conclusions, unwise interventions and some serious errors. In war conditions these were serious enough in all conscience, but in these conditions the credit side – the energy, the application and the boldness – was perhaps of greater importance. In peace, his essentially superficial approach, the fixity with which he adhered to a point when he had settled upon his course, and the drama with which he invested everything he undertook, fully justified Lady Asquith's critical comment on Churchill that 'armies are just as necessary in politics as in war. And they can only be recruited by persuasion.'

We may judge that it was here that his prime deficiency lay. He had always lived on a different plane from the vast majority of mankind, in a world – often contrived and personal – of drama and colour where, as Gardiner had written, 'It is always the hour of fate and the crack of doom.' This remoteness was more mental than physical. The romantic is aloof and apart because his portrait of mankind is a reflection of his own personality, preconceptions and dreams. The essential ingredients of the romantic's world are colour, noise and excitement. When he discovers them, he accepts them as confirmation of his own attitudes. The point has been vividly made in Isaiah Berlin's memorable essay:

As much as any king conceived by a Renaissance dramatist or by a nineteenth-century historian or moralist he thinks it a brave thing to ride in triumph through Persepolis; he knows with an unshakeable certainty what he considers to be big, handsome, noble, worthy of pursuit by someone in high station and what on the contrary he abhors as being dim, grey, thin, likely to lower or destroy the play of colour and movement in the universe.[129]

The essentially romantic nature of Churchill's character was constant throughout his life. His second daughter has written that 'England had been to him rather like a mistress that could

129. Berlin, op. cit., p. 17.

tease, please, baffle and refuse him', and he clothed England's history with romance, and her national character with his own grand conceptions. England remained to the end the Laurania of his imagination, whom he courted and loved, and yet never fully comprehended. For most of mankind, life is at best a chore, in which 'dim, grey, and thin' matters are of paramount significance. The inability of most people to identify with Churchill was understandable enough, for he did not identify himself with them.

He was a highly emotional man, easily touched to tears and profoundly stirred by glamorous and ardent actions. Any period of quiescence was intolerable, and the fact that many men sought and found deep satisfaction in calm times was incomprehensible to him. He was always an activist, always restless, always eager, and always imbued with a profound sense of playing the leading part in a great drama. The romantic approach to political affairs is highly attractive to contemplate at a distance; it quickly loses its savour when the beholder is cast in a minor role which he finds ridiculous, distasteful and highly unwelcome. He was, politically, a most uncomfortable man.

Although a man's essential character may remain unaffected by the strains and burdens of public life, his political character can change very considerably. Early prejudices and assumptions are challenged and destroyed; first alliances and creeds lose their attraction; new influences land on unexpectedly fertile ground. In many cases without realizing the metamorphosis, the politician finds that, politically, he is a very different man at the end of a decade than he had been at the beginning. But in Churchill's case it is a striking fact of his political character that it altered so little. Compromises had to be effected; themes had to be amended; new situations required new counter-measures. But at the end of this process we behold essentially the same man that we glimpsed taking his seat in the House of Commons for the first time in February 1901, and it is this fact that prompted Amery's comment in 1929 that 'the key to Winston is to realise that he is mid-Victorian . . . and unable ever to get the modern point of view.' And we may judge that it was in this fact that his failure, particularly in the 1930s, truly lay.

The theme of this study may be found on its title page, and it is that 'each man is the maker of his own fate'. I have attempted to analyse and understand the causes of the dramatic successes and no less dramatic disasters of Churchill's career. The real cause lies less in a detailed study of the political circumstances of moments in that career than in a comprehension of Churchill's political character. And we may again emphasize and ponder upon the fact that, after almost forty years of total participation in politics, he enjoyed virtually no personal support of any political significance. We may view with reservation the argument that the fault lay in others, and not in himself. It has become customary to censure those who did not follow his standard; it is therefore appropriate to point out that some responsibility should be attached to the leader whom they refused to follow.

This study has been, accordingly, a study of a remarkable failure. It has been an examination of a career that had a beginning as brilliant and exciting as that of Lord Randolph Churchill; which suffered a check as severe as that which had destroyed Lord Randolph, and from which it had not really recovered by September 1939. It is one of the tragedies of England that men are seldom given a second chance. Although Churchill appeared to have had such an opportunity in 1917 and again in 1924, in reality the upward surge of his career had stopped in May 1915 and had never been resumed. In 1931 Harold Nicolson wrote of him that 'he is a man who leads forlorn hopes, and when the hopes of England become forlorn, he will once again be summoned to leadership.'[130] The comment was as significant in its contemporary importance as in its prophecy.

We may be somewhat sceptical of Amery's judgement that Churchill's exclusion from office between 1931 and 1939 was 'one of the best things that ever happened to England. For they were the years in which the strong vintage of his personality matured; the years in which he wrote the story of his great

130. *Vanity Fair*, 1931.

ancestor, Marlborough, and so trained himself for the conduct of another Grand Alliance; the years in which he earned the right to leadership by his consistent warnings of the danger ahead.'[131] The judgement may be challenged because it alleges a late development of political and personal character which is difficult to substantiate. It was Churchill's greatest deficiency in the 1930s that he was unchanged; it was to be his greatest strength in the ordeal that began on 3 September 1939.

If the story had ended in 1938 or even 1939, we should be in the presence of a great personal tragedy. We should be obliged to dwell upon the moral that great abilities and industry cannot, in themselves, secure political success. We should have pondered on the paradox that a mind so fertile and a character so many-faceted should have proved incapable of full development, and how Churchill, granted so many splendid attributes, had been denied that of sensitivity.

We should have emphasized the wisdom of Asquith's 1915 comment on Churchill that 'he will never get to the top in English politics, with all his wonderful gifts; to speak with the tongue of men and angels, and to spend laborious days and nights in administration, is no good if a man does not inspire trust.' We should have to lament a career that opened in such prominence and triumph, that suffered a grievous check, that was bravely revived, but thereafter went into melancholy decline. We should have been obliged to have used words very similar to those which Churchill had employed in the Preface to his biography of Lord Randolph:

His part in national affairs is not to be measured by long years in office . . . No tangible or enduring records exist of his labours, and the great and decisive force which he exerted might be imperfectly realised by a later generation, unless it were explained, asserted, and confirmed by the evidence of those who came in contact or collision with his imperious and vivifying personality . . . this account will, I think, be found to explain in almost mechanical detail the steps and the forces by which he rose to the exercise of great personal authority, as well as the converse process by which he declined.

131. Amery, op. cit., Vol. II, p. 511.

Select Bibliography

An excellent and indispensable *Bibliography of the Works of Winston Churchill* has been prepared and published by Mr Frederick Woods (Nicholas Vane, 1969). Although the number of books about Churchill has not yet assumed Napoleonic proportions, the trend is emphatically in that direction. In this select bibliography I have concentrated on those books and articles which seem to me to be of particular interest and value for an understanding of Churchill's career before 1940.

Adam, Colin Forbes: *Life of Lord Lloyd* (Macmillan, 1948).

Amery, Julian: *Joseph Chamberlain and the Tariff Reform Campaign*, Vols. V and VI (Macmillan, 1969).

Amery, L. S.: *My Political Life*, Vols. II and III (Hutchinson, 1955).

Aspinall-Oglander, C. E.: *Military Operations: Gallipoli* (2 Vols., Heinemann, 1929 and 1932).

Avon, Earl of: *Facing the Dictators* (Cassell, 1962).

Baldwin, A. W.: *My Father, the True Story* (Allen & Unwin, 1955).

Bardens, Dennis: *Churchill in Parliament* (Hale, 1967).

Beaverbrook, Lord: *Politicians and the War* (Oldbourne, one-volume edition, 1959)
  The Decline and Fall of Lloyd George (Collins, 1963)
  Men and Power (Revised edition, Collins, 1966)
  The Abdication of King Edward VIII (Hamish Hamilton, 1966).

Birkenhead, Earl of: '*F.E.*' (Eyre & Spottiswoode, 1960)
  The Prof in Two Worlds (Revised edition, Collins, 1964)
  Halifax (Hamish Hamilton, 1965)
  Walter Monckton (Weidenfeld & Nicolson, 1969).

Blackett, P. M. S.: *Tizard and the Science of War* (Tizard Memorial Lecture, 1960).

Blunt, Wilfred Scawen: *My Diaries* (Secker & Warburg, 1965).

Bonham Carter, Lady Violet (Lady Asquith): *Winston Churchill As I Knew Him* (Eyre & Spottiswoode, 1965)
  Articles in *Daily Telegraph*, 1965.

Boothby, Robert: *I Fight to Live* (Gollancz, 1947)

My Yesterday, Your Tomorrow (Hutchinson, 1962).

Bruce Lockhart, Sir Robert: *Memoirs of a British Agent* (Putnam, 1936)

   Friends, Foes and Foreigners (Putnam, 1957).

Bullock, Alan: *Hitler: a Study in Tyranny* (Revised edition, Odhams, 1964).

Butler, J. R. M.: *Lord Lothian* (Macmillan, 1960).

Cabinet Minutes and Memoranda 1900–1939 (Public Record Office, London).

Callwell, Sir C. E.: *Field-Marshal Sir Henry Wilson* (Vol. II, Cassell, 1927).

Churchill, Randolph S. (editor): *Arms and the Covenant* (Harrap, 1938)

   Lord Derby 'King of Lancashire' (Heinemann, 1959)

   Winston S. Churchill, Vols. I and II (Heinemann, 1966 and 1967).

Churchill, Winston S.: *The World Crisis* and *The Aftermath* (Butterworth, 1923–31)

   Speeches on India (Butterworth, 1931)

   Step by Step, 1936–1939 (Butterworth, 1939)

   The Gathering Storm (War Memoirs, Vol. I) (Cassell, 1948).

Citrine, Lord: *Men and Work* (Hutchinson, 1964).

Clark, R. W.: *Tizard* (Methuen, 1965).

Cole, Margaret (editor): *Beatrice Webb's Diaries, 1924–32* (Longmans, 1932).

Colvin, Ian: *Vansittart in Office* (Gollancz, 1965).

Coote, Colin: *A Companion of Honour: The Story of Walter Elliot* (Collins, 1965).

Cowles, Virginia: *Winston Churchill, The Era and the Man* (Hamish Hamilton, 1953).

Crowther, J. G.: *Statesmen of Science* (Cresset Press, 1965).

Dalton, Hugh: *The Fateful Years, 1931–45* (Muller, 1957).

Dardanelles Commission: Evidence and Memoranda (Public Record Office).

Dawson, R. M.: *Winston Churchill at the Admiralty* (Oxford, 1940).

Eade, Charles (editor): *Churchill by his Contemporaries* (Hutchinson, 1953).

'Ephesian' (C. E. Bechofer-Roberts): *Winston Churchill* (Mills & Boon, 1927).

Esher, Lord: *Journals and Letters of Reginald, Viscount Esher* (Nicholson & Watson, 1934–8).

Feiling, (Sir) Keith: *The Life of Neville Chamberlain* (Macmillan, 1946).

Gardiner, A. G.: *Prophets, Priests and Kings* (Dent, 1908)
   Pillars of Society (Nisbett, 1913).
Garnett, David (editor): *Letters of T. E. Lawrence* (Cape, 1938).
Gilbert, Martin: *The Roots of Appeasement* (Weidenfeld & Nicolson, 1966).
Gopal, S.: *The Viceroyalty of Lord Irwin, 1926–31* (Oxford, 1957).
Gott, R. and Gilbert, M.: *The Appeasers* (Weidenfeld & Nicolson, 1963).
Graubard, S. R.: *British Labour and the Russian Revolution* (Harvard, 1956).
Gretton, Admiral Sir Peter: *Former Naval Person: Winston Churchill and the Royal Navy* (Cassell, 1968).
Grigg, P. J.: *Prejudice and Judgement* (Cape, 1951).
Guinn, Paul: *British Strategy and Politics (1914–18)* (Oxford, Clarendon Press, 1965).
Hankey, Lord: *The Supreme Command, 1914–18* (Allen & Unwin, 1961)
   The Supreme Control at the Paris Peace Conference (1919) (Allen & Unwin, 1963).
Harrod, (Sir) Roy: *The Prof: A Personal Memoir of Lord Cherwell* (Macmillan, 1959).
Hassall, Christopher: *Edward Marsh* (Longmans, 1959).
Higgins, Turnbull: *Winston Churchill and the Dardanelles* (Heinemann, 1963).
Hyam, Ronald: *Elgin and Churchill at the Colonial Office, 1905–8* (Macmillan, 1968).
Jones, Dr Thomas: *A Diary with Letters (1931–50)* (Oxford, 1954).
Keynes, J. M.: *The Economic Consequences of the Peace* (Macmillan, 1919)
   Essays in Biography (Hart-Davis, 1951).
Liddell Hart, (Sir) Basil: *Memoirs*, Vols. I and II (Cassell, 1965 and 1966).
Lloyd George, David: *War Memoirs* (Nicholson & Watson, 1933–6).
McElwee, William: *Britain's Locust Years, 1918–40* (Faber, 1962).
Macleod, Iain: *Neville Chamberlain* (Muller, 1961).
Macmillan, Harold: *Winds of Change* (Macmillan, 1966)
   The Blast of War (Macmillan, 1967).
Marder, A. J.: *Portrait of an Admiral* (Cape, 1952)
   From the Dreadnought to Scapa Flow, Vols. I and II, (Oxford, 1961 and 1966).
Masterman, Lucy: *C. F. G. Masterman* (Nicholson & Watson, 1939).

Medlicott, W. N.: *The Coming of War in 1939* (Routledge & Kegan Paul, 1963).

Middlemas, R. K. and Barnes, J.: *Stanley Baldwin* (Weidenfeld & Nicolson, 1969).

Minney, R. J.: *The Private Papers of Hore-Belisha* (Collins, 1960).

Moon, Sir Penderel: *Divide and Quit* (Chatto & Windus, 1964).

Morley, Lord: *Memorandum on Resignation* (August 1914) (Macmillan, 1928).

Mowat, C. L.: *Britain Between the Wars* (Methuen, 1955).

Nicolson, Nigel (editor): *Harold Nicolson, Diaries and Letters (1930–39)* (Collins, 1966).

Norwich, Lord (Duff Cooper): *Old Men Forget* (Hart-Davis, 1954).

Percy, Lord Eustace: *Some Memories* (Eyre and Spottiswoode, 1958).

Petrie, Sir Charles: *Life and Letters of Sir Austen Chamberlain*, Vol. II (Cassell, 1940).

Plumb, J. H.: 'Churchill the Historian' (in *Churchill: Four Faces and the Man*, ed. A. J. P. Taylor, Allen Lane, 1969).

Powers, R. H.: 'Winston Churchill's Parliamentary Commentary on British Foreign Policy, 1935–8' (*Journal of Modern History*, June 1954, pp. 179–82).

Rhodes James, Robert: *Lord Randolph Churchill* (Weidenfeld & Nicolson, 1959)

Gallipoli (Batsford, 1965).

Memoirs of a Conservative: Memoirs and Papers of J. C. C. Davidson (Weidenfeld & Nicolson, 1969).

Rodd, Sir J. Rennell: *Social and Diplomatic Memories (1902–19)* (Edward Arnold, 1925).

Roskill, S.: *Naval Policy Between the Wars*, Vol. I (*1919–29*) (Collins, 1968).

Spier, E.: *Focus* (Wolff, 1963).

Taylor, A. J. P.: *The Origins of the Second World War* (Hamish Hamilton, 1961)

English History 1914–45 (Oxford, 1965).

Templewood, Lord (Sir Samuel Hoare): *Nine Troubled Years* (Collins, 1954).

Thomas, Hugh: *The Spanish Civil War* (Eyre & Spottiswoode, 1961).

Ullman, R. H.: *Intervention and the War* (Princetown U.P., 1961).

Vansittart, Lord: *The Mist Procession* (Hutchinson, 1958).

Walder, David: *The Chanak Affair* (Hutchinson, 1969).

Walters, F. P.: *A History of the League of Nations* (Royal Institute of International Affairs, 1952).

Watson-Watt, Sir Robert: *Three Steps to Victory* (Odhams, 1959).

Watt, D. C.: *Personalities and Policies* (Longmans, 1965)
Britain looks at Germany (Longmans, 1965).

Webb, Beatrice: *Our Partnership* (Longmans, 1948).

Young, G. M.: *Stanley Baldwin* (Hart-Davis, 1951).

Young, K.: *Churchill and Beaverbrook* (Eyre & Spottiswoode, 1966).

Index

In this index C = Churchill

in 1945. In Churchill's own words: 'Life is a whole and luck is a whole, and no part of them can be separated from the rest.'[126]

We may return to the central features of Churchill's political personality with which we were concerned in the study of his career between 1900 and 1915, and which remained constant throughout his life.

The first point to reiterate is that he was a career politician, for whom politics were his life, and for whom the essential goal was office. Beaverbrook's preference for 'Churchill Down' over 'Churchill Up' was shared by others, but the student of Churchill's career cannot avoid the strong impression that his talents were best demonstrated in office and his deficiencies most evident when out of it. Lord Riddell wrote in his diary of him in January 1915 that 'He is one of the most industrious men I have ever known. He is like a wonderful piece of machinery with a flywheel which occasionally makes unexpected movements.'[127] His critics were more conscious of the 'unexpected movements' than of the solid achievements, and although many of his actions as a minister can be justifiably criticized, it cannot be doubted that this was his best and most natural environment.

The dispassionate observer can hardly fail to be struck by the absence in Churchill's career, until the mid-1930s, of any great identifiable cause, and by his preoccupation with the immediate. This may appear an unfair judgement, in view of Churchill's warnings of 1912–14, 1934–9, and subsequently, 1946–8. But it should be emphasized that in all these cases he was drawing public attention to actual situations, and that his achievement – which is not to be disparaged at all – lay in diagnosis rather than in prognosis. His attitude towards Defence matters in the 1920s provides one example of an inability to envisage changed situations, and his 'settlement' of the Middle East situation in 1921–2 demonstrates his concentration upon the immediate and tangible. Foresight in politics is rare, and is usually a matter of fortune rather than genius. We need not criticize Churchill for being deficient in long-term views were it not for the fact that his admirers have claimed it as one of his principal qualities.

126. *My Early Life*, p. 100.
127. *Lord Riddell's War Diary*, p. 49.

pared with Gladstone, Disraeli, Salisbury or even Palmerston,
there is a certain absence of political depth, comprehension and
wisdom. The self-made man, caught on the helter-skelter of his
career, has to pay many prices for his success and survival; in
Churchill's case, this was one of them. He marched magnificently on the surface of affairs; we look in vain for evidence of
comprehension of deeper and more permanent things.

We also look in vain for signs of real development – political
or intellectual. Isaiah Berlin has rightly commented that:

Far from changing his opinions too often, Mr Churchill has scarcely,
during a long and stormy career, altered them at all. If anyone wishes
to discover his views on the large and lasting issues of our time, he
need only set himself to discover what Mr Churchill has said or
written on the subject at any period of his long and exceptionally
articulate public life, in particular during the years before the First
World War: the number of instances in which his views have in
later years undergone any appreciable degree of change will be found
astonishingly small . . . When biographers and historians come to
describe and analyse his views . . . they will find that his opinions
on all these topics are set in fixed patterns, set early in life and later
only reinforced.[128]

In war, these characteristics are of supreme advantage. In
quieter times they have many dangers. The dictum that peace
hath her heroes is, perhaps regrettably, not really true, and the

1915–16; Lord President, 1916–19; Foreign Secretary, 1919–23), 38, 105n, 110, 111, 128, 172; and anti-Bolshevik campaign, 135, 143, 146–7, 149–50, 152; and Chanak, 185, 186–8; and fall of Coalition, 188–9

Czechoslovakia, 132, 135, 139, 152, 335, 420, 438; and Munich, 429, 432; full occupation of, 435, 436

D'Abernon, Lord, 238

Dail Eireann, 127, 161, 162–3, 169

Daily Express, 188, 190

Daily Herald, 138, 155

Daily Mail, 8, 19n, 218, 224, 251–2, 266

Daily Mirror, 437

Daily News, 17, 49–50

Daily Telegraph, 216, 383, 437

Daladier, Edouard, 429

Dalton, Hugh (later Baron) (1887–1962. Labour politician. Under-Secretary Foreign Office, 1929–31; served in C's wartime Government; Chancellor of the Exchequer, 1945–7; Chancellor of the Duchy of Lancaster, 1948–50; Minister of Town and Country Planning, 1950–51), 335, 338n, 351, 431n, 434

Dardanelles, 76, 79, 81–114, 143, 181, 229, 238, 378, 425

Dardanelles Commission, 82, 83, 85, 88, 91, 111, 115

Dardanelles Committee, 102, 105–6, 108–9, 111

Darling, Lord, 195

Davidson, John Colin David, Viscount, 158n, 214, 345; and

British Gazette, 220, 222, 223–4; and BBC, 224–5

Dawson, Geoffrey, 223, 260, 273

De Robeck, Rear-Admiral Sir John, 93, 94

De Valera, Eamon, 169, 171, 421

De-Rating of Industry Bill (1928), 228

Deakin, F. W., 393n

Defence, Ministry of, 335, 336, 414; C presses for, 295, 333

Defence, Minister for Co-ordination of, 336–7

Dempster, D., 320n

Denikin, General Anton, 134, 141, 146, 147, 149, 150, 151, 152, 153, 155, 156, 157, 158

Derby, Edward Stanley, 17th Earl of, 110, 179, 194, 237; C's 'Privilege' accusation against, 270–72, 421–2

Dilke, Sir Charles, 18

Disarmament Conference (1933), Germany leaves, 287, 288

Disraeli, Benjamin, Lord Beaconsfield, 3, 49, 200; similarities with C, 17, 275; on India, 241n

Division, 29th, and Dardanelles, 89, 91, 94n, 98–100

Dollfuss, Dr Engelbert, 312

Donaldson, Frances, 68n

Dorman-Smith, Sir Reginald, 439n

Dublin, 9, 161–2, 163n, 169

Duckers, J. S., 198n

Duff Cooper, Alfred (later Lord Norwich), 60n, 241, 259, 263, 332, 349, 378, 388, 391; opposes C on India, 274, 276; considers C's chances passed, 336–7; relations with C, 367–8; opposes Munich, 430, 432,

Dardanelles, 85–7, 89, 94; resigns, 100, 101–2

Fisher, H. A. L., 165, 292

Fisher, Sir Warren, 214, 301, 312

FitzGibbon, Lord Justice, 6

Fitzroy, Sir Almeric, 10, 31, 69

Fleming, Peter, 134n

Foch, Marshal, 147

'Focus' group, 341–2, 348, 409, 429

Foreign Office, 302, 416; and intervention in Russia, 135, 148; assurance on Japan, 212, 217; Hoare at, 316; Eden at, 369; Chamberlain's control of, 419

'Fourth Party', 20

France, 417; and Great War, 81, 93, 106, 125; and Chanak, 184–6; C's confidence in, 286; and German occupation of Rhineland, 333–4, 335; and Munich, 429, 433

Franco, General, 407–8, 409

Fraser, Sir Malcolm, 188

Free Trade, 25, 26, 27n, 129, 202, 203, 229, 279

French, Sir John (later Earl of Ypres), 61, 162

Furneaux, R., 249n

Gaida, General, 149

Gallacher, Willie, 191

Gallipoli, 82, 83, 87, 90, 96–100, 105–12, 167, 183, 184

Gandhi, Mahatma, 249, 250, 254, 255, 259, 260, 266

Gardiner, A. G., 23, 40, 120, 238, 240, 443; on C's 'frankness of child', 17; on his rhetoric, 36; on C following 'politics as he would . . . hounds', 43; doubts his staying power, 45–

6; 'will write his name in history', 70, 426; on C 'always playing a part', 49–50; considers him an 'Ishmael in public life', 237

Garvin, J. L., 104, 370n, 430

Gateshead, 265n

Gathorne-Hardy, G. H., 343n

Gaulois (French ship), 93

Geddes, Sir Eric, 195

'Geddes Axe', 265n

General Elections: (1886), 9; (1900), 16; (1905), 56; (1910), 56, 127; (1918 'Coupon'), 118–20, 128, 129; (1922), 190–92; (1923), 193, 194, 202, 236, 243; (1924), 193, 199; (1929), 233, 236, 240, 373; (1935), 325, 326, 343, 426

General Strike (1926), 211, 219–25

Genoa Conference (1922), 178

George V, 104, 105, 168, 222, 327, 333

George, William, 23

German Air Force: parity with Britain, 296–7, 314–15; C's estimates of, 314–15, 339–40

German Army, 79, 300

German Navy, 74, 125

German Rearmament, Cabinet Committee on, 299

Germany: and Great War, 74, 79, 80, 125, 132, 134; C's forecast of future strength, 141, 284; reparations, 279; increasing power and ambition, 282–8, 415; rearmament, 285–6, 287, 293, 294, 296–7, 300–301, 356; C's concern over, 284–8, 294–7, 306, 328, 329, 339–42, 408–10; conscription, 287, 314; apologists for, 291–2, 334–5, 356; increasing air

interests 'interwoven with
Liberalism', 46; disillusionment with C, 48, 49, 50; and
1918 election, 119, 127; opposes Russian Intervention,
148, 151, 155–6; and 1922
election, 190, 191; first time
in office (1924), 193; C attacks,
194, 199; defeat (in autumn
1924,) 194, 199; and Free
Trade, 201–2; and General
Strike, 219; second time in
office (1929), 235–6; C suggests
Liberal and Conservative
coalition against, 240–41; and
economic crisis, 263–5; in
National Government, 265;
opposes rearmament, 288;
pacifism in, 289; awareness of
fascist danger, 331
Lamlash, 61, 62, 63
Lancaster, Duchy of, 102
Lansbury, George (1859–1940.
Labour politician. First Commissioner of Works, 1929–31;
Leader of the Labour Party,
1931–5), 222, 264n, 265, 269,
289, 331, 410
Lansdowne, Lord, 65, 105n,
110
Laski, Harold, 179, 305
Laval, Pierre, 328
Law, Andrew Bonar (1858–
1923. Conservative politician.
Leader of the Conservative
Party, 1911–21; Colonial
Secretary, 1915–16; Chancellor of the Exchequer, 1916–
18; Lord Privy Seal, 1919–21;
Prime Minister, 1922–3), 27,
64n, 101, 102, 105n, 118, 128,
146, 165, 207, 208; and Ulster,
54, 57–8, 62, 64; and Dardanelles, 105n, 108–9, 110,

379; fall of Asquith, 115, 116,
117; in Coalition, 127; conflict with C, 158, 159; retirement, 179; and Chanak, 185,
188; becomes Premier after
fall of Coalition, 189, 190, 191;
resigns, 193; on C's 'entirely
unbalanced mind', 237, 379;
Baldwin and, 242
Law, Richard (now Lord Cole-
raine), 428
Lawrence, T. E., 172, 359–60,
367
Layton, Lord, 371, 372
League of Nations, 186, 279,
280, 282, 294, 306, 342, 408;
C on value of, 295, 306, 331–2;
and sanctions on Italy, 328,
330; and occupation of Rhineland, 336n
League of Nations Union, 332,
346, 348, 371
Leicester, West, 1923 election,
153, 194, 197, 373
Lemnos, 89
Lenin, V. I., 136
Liberal Party, 244; alliance by
some members with Conser-
vatives against Home Rule
(1886), 9, 14, 25n; C's movement towards, 25–9; opening
gap between them, 42, 48, 49–
50; and Labour, 46–7; C's
declining position in, 54; support of Home Rule, 56; C's
efforts to strengthen himself
with, 58–9; and Great War,
66–7; in Asquith Coalition,
103; destroyed in 1918 election, 118, 119, 120, 127; in
Lloyd George Coalition, 127,
179; and 1922 election, 190–
91; division into Asquithian
and Lloyd George, 190–91,

Penguinews *and*
Penguins in Print

Every month we issue an illustrated magazine,
Penguinews. It's a lively guide to all latest Penguins,
Pelicans and Puffins, and always contains an article
on a major Penguin author, plus other features of
contemporary interest.

Penguinews is supplemented by *Penguins in Print*, a
complete list of all the available Penguin titles – there
are now over four thousand!

The cost is no more than the postage; so why not write
for a free copy of this month's *Penguinews*? And if you'd
like both publications sent for a year, just send us a
cheque or a postal order for 30p (if you live in the United
Kingdom) or 60p (if you live elsewhere), and we'll put
you on our mailing list

Dept EP, Penguin Books Ltd,
Harmondsworth, Middlesex

Note: *Penguinews* and *Penguins in Print*
are not available in the U.S.A. or Canada